Brown in the Windy City

HISTORICAL STUDIES IN URBAN AMERICA
Edited by Timothy J. Gilfoyle, James R. Grossman, and Becky M. Nicolaides

Also in the series:

Additional series titles follow index

Brown in the Windy City

Mexicans and Puerto Ricans in Postwar Chicago

LILIA FERNANDEZ

The University of Chicago Press
Chicago and London

The University of Chicago Press, Chicago 60637
The University of Chicago Press, Ltd., London
© 2012 by The University of Chicago
All rights reserved. Published 2012.
Paperback edition 2014
Printed in the United States of America

23 22 21 20 19 18 17 16 15 14   2 3 4 5 6

ISBN-13: 978-0-226-24425-9 (cloth)
ISBN-13: 978-0-226-21284-5 (paper)
ISBN-13: 978-0-226-24428-0 (e-book)
DOI: 10.728/chicago/9780226244280.001.0001

Portions of chapter 1 were previously published in Lilia Fernandez, "Of
Migrants and Immigrants: Mexican and Puerto Rican Labor Migration in
Comparative Perspective, 1942–1964," *Journal of American Ethnic History* 29,
no. 3 (2010): 6–39, and are reprinted here with permission of the University
of Illinois Press.

Portions of chapters 2, 3, and 6 were previously published in Lilia Fernandez,
"From the Near West Side to 18th Street: Un/Making Latina/o Barrios in Post-
war Chicago," in *Beyond el Barrio: Everyday Life in Latina/o America*, ed. Gina
Perez, Frank Guridy, and Adrian Burgos, Jr. (New York: New York University
Press, 2010), and are reprinted here with permission of NYU Press.

Library of Congress Cataloging-in-Publication Data

Fernandez, Lilia.
  Brown in the Windy City: Mexicans and Puerto Ricans in postwar Chicago /
Lilia Fernandez.
    pages ; cm — (Historical studies of urban America)
    Includes bibliographical references and index.
    ISBN 978-0-226-24425-9 (cloth : alkaline paper) — ISBN 0-226-24425-3
(cloth : alkaline paper) — ISBN 978-0-226-24428-0 (e-book) (print) —
ISBN 0-226-24428-8 (e-book) (print)   1. Mexicans—Illinois—Chicago—
History—20th century.   2. Mexican Americans—Illinois—Chicago—
History—20th century.   3. Puerto Ricans—Illinois—Chicago—History—
20th century.   4. Hispanic American neighborhoods—Illinois—Chicago—
History—20th century.   5. Near West Side (Chicago, Ill.)—History—
20th century.   6. Pilsen (Chicago, Ill.)—History—20th century.   7. Young
Lords (Organization).   8. Mujeres Latinas en Acción—History.   I. Title.
II. Series: Historical studies of urban America.
    F548.9.M5F47 2012
    305.89'6872077311—dc23
                                                          2012007979

♾ This paper meets the requirements of ANSI/NISO Z39.48-1992
(Permanence of Paper).

CONTENTS

ILLUSTRATIONS

FIGURES

TABLES

ACKNOWLEDGMENTS

In order to acknowledge those who have helped produce this book, I must go back considerably further than most scholars usually do because I am truly indebted to those who have influenced and supported my education since I can first remember. Several women in my life were my first teachers: my mother, my grandmother, and the women who taught me at Komensky Elementary School and Skinner Classical School—Sherry Sharvat, Fran Allen, and Roseanne Patterson, among others. Each of them in her own way instilled in me a love of learning and an interest in history that drew a child like me down the unlikely path to a doctoral degree and the writing of a book. As I continued to develop intellectually, the teachers at the Latin School of Chicago—including Jill Acker, Ernestine Austin, Ingrid Dorer Fitzpatrick, Lillian Mackal, and especially David Spruance—continued to develop my passion for intellectual inquiry and a love of history and writing. They gave me the foundation that took me to college and prepared me for an unexpected academic career.

I am a native-born Chicagoan, and this project emerged out of my interest in understanding the city's Mexican and Puerto Rican communities and their histories. I greatly appreciate the people who allowed me to do oral histories with them—Alicia Amador, Carlos Arango, Sijisfredo Aviles, Phil Ayala, Mathew Barcelo, Maria Cerda, the Reverend Walter L. Coleman, Linda Coronado, Joe Escamilla, Rosemary Escamilla, Hector and María Gamboa, Jesus García, Jane Garza-Mancillas, Dr. Aida Giachello, "Cha Che" Gomez, Rosa Hernandez de la Llata, José "Cha Cha" Jiménez, Professor Luis Leal, Monse Lucas-Figueroa, María Mangual, Pablo Medina, María Ovalle, Laura Paz, Sylvia Puente, Gamaliel Ramírez, Leonard Ramírez, Modesto Rivera, Myrna Rodriguez, Aida Sanchez-Romano, Steve Schensul, Gwen Stern, Carlos Valencia, Mike Vásquez, and Pat Wright. They gave generously of their time and connected me with other important community leaders. Special thanks to Phil Ayala, who welcomed me into El Centro de la Causa like an old friend and shared with me the agency's historical archives. John Harrington shared with me a copy of his dissertation. The late Alicia Amador allowed me access to her personal archives, as did Leticia Guerrero. María Pesqueira and Carmelo Rodriguez graciously gave me access to the records and private archives of Mujeres Latinas en Acción, before my visit inspired them to deposit them at DePaul University's Special Collections. The late María Mangual also shared generously of her time to tell me how she helped start Mujeres.

My mentors and advisers, Vicki L. Ruiz and Ramón Gutiérrez, provided invaluable guidance and direction when I first started this project and have been supportive throughout my academic career. Thanks also to Yen Espiritu, George Lipsitz, Matt García, Gabriela Arredondo, Anne Martínez, Mike Innis-Jiménez, Jim Barrett, Gina Pérez, Pablo Mitchell, Adrian Burgos, David Gutiérrez, and Carmen Whalen, who have all enthusiastically supported my scholarship.

This book could have not been completed without the assistance of the archivists and librarians who helped me with research at a number of places: the Chicago History Museum; the Municipal Reference Collection and the Special Collections at the Harold Washington Branch of the Chicago Public Library; the university archives at the University of Notre Dame; and the Special Collections Library at Stanford University. Special thanks go to Mary Diaz at the Special Collections Library at the University of Illinois at Chicago; Martin Tuohy at the National Archives and Records Administration, Great Lakes Region; Kathryn DeGraff and Morgen MacIntosh at Special Collections, DePaul University Library; Juan Carlos Román, Neftali Quintán, and José Charón at the Archivo General de Puerto Rico; Julio E. Quirós Alcalá and staff at the Fundación Luis Muñoz Marín; Amílcar Tirado at the University of Puerto Rico, Río Piedras; and Nélida Pérez, Pedro Juan Hernández, Félix Rivera, Jorge Matos, and their staff at El Centro de Estudios Puertorriqueños, Hunter College.

This book benefitted from generous funding from the Center for the Study of Race and Ethnicity at the University of California, San Diego; a Ford Foundation Dissertation Fellowship as well as a Ford Foundation Postdoctoral Fellowship hosted by Brown University; and a Chancellor's Postdoctoral Fellowship hosted by the Latino/a Studies Program at the University of Illinois, Urbana-Champaign. The College of Arts and Humanities and the History Department at Ohio State University also provided me critical research funds.

Numerous people have commented on my work or offered feedback at various stages. Gina Pérez, Carmen Whalen, and Merída Rua gave me suggestions and references early on in my research that proved very useful. The organizers of the Mexican American History Workshop at the University of Houston—Luis Alvarez, Monica Perales, Raul Ramos, and Guadalupe San Miguel—and their participants provided a wonderful environment for exchanging work and offering one another suggestions. I thank Gina Pérez, Shelley Lee, and Pablo Mitchell at Oberlin College and the audiences at numerous academic conferences. During my year at the University of Illinois, Urbana-Champaign, I found a supportive community among Arlene Torres, Lisa Cacho, Richard T. Rodriguez, Isabel Molina, Adrian Burgos, Larry Parker, Wanda Pillow, James D. Anderson, Aide Acosta, and Abel Correa. At Brown University, thanks go to Evelyn Hu-DeHart, Rhacel Parrenas, Matt García, Elliott Gorn, and Samuel Zipp.

Thanks to dear friends Angelica Rivera, Dalia Rodríguez, Jillian Baez, Julie Hua, and Grace Kim for their friendship, support, and encouragement since our days in graduate school. Solangel Cubas, Adey Fisseha, Lourdes Castro-Ramírez, Jorge Ramírez, Luis and Rosa Urrieta, and their families have offered their friendship and welcomed me into their homes on various occasions.

In the History Department at Ohio State University, a number of colleagues have provided a warm and welcoming community and have kindly read my work and given me important feedback. Thanks to Leslie Alexander, Judy Wu, Stephanie Smith, Hasan Jeffries, Mytheli Sreenivas, Alcira Dueñas, Ousman Kobo, Ahmad Sikainga, Derek Heng, Ying Zhang, Kevin Boyle, Lucy Murphy, James Genova, Susan Hartmann, Birgitte Soland, Ken Andrien, Donna Guy, Bill Childs, David Steigerwald, David Stebenne, Margaret Newell, Robin Judd, Chris Otter, Manse Blackford, and Steve Conn. Theodora Dragostinova and Kristina Sessa formed a wonderful writing group with me in which we shared insightful and helpful comments with one another across our vastly different fields. Wendy Smooth motivated me as a great writing partner as well. Graduate students Angela Ryan, Danielle Olden, Delia Fernandez, and Cameron Shriver offered critical research assistance, as did one of OSU's finest history undergraduates, Kyle Lincicome. The Latino/a Studies faculty and those affiliated with the Center for Latin American Studies at OSU (Pat Enciso, Guisela Latorre, Frederick Aldama, Theresa Delgadillo, Jeff Cohen, Ignacio Corona, and Laura Podalsky) have provided a supportive community, as have Debra Moddelmog, Pranav Jani, Joe Ponce, Chad Allen, Maurice Stevens, Mark Walters, and members of OSU's Latino/a community (Indra Leyva-Santiago, Inés Valdez, Francisco

Gómez-Bellengé, Yolanda Zepeda, José Cabral, Valente Alvarez, and Victor Mora). Special thanks go to Leslie Alexander, Judy Wu, Stephanie Smith, Lucy Murphy, and Debra Moddelmog for their warm friendship and unwavering support.

The staff at the University of Chicago Press did tremendous work to see this book come to press. A special thanks to Robert Devens, who took an interest in the project from the beginning and has guided it over its long journey. Thanks to the series editors and to Mary Corrado and Russell Damian. Susan Cohan did meticulous copyediting, and I thank her for all her hard work and patience. Lorrin Thomas and an anonymous reviewer provided excellent comments and suggestions and improved this manuscript significantly. All errors and omissions are of course my own.

Finally, I thank my family for their support and inspiration. Our everyday lived experiences, especially those of my late grandmother, provided the spark for my academic exploration. I did not fully understand and appreciate the historical significance of my grandmother's stories until she passed away, and while she did not see this book come to fruition, she is in these pages nonetheless. I thank my mother, brothers, sisters, their spouses, and my niece and nephews for all their love and support. They have waited very patiently to see the completion of this book, which I dedicate to them.

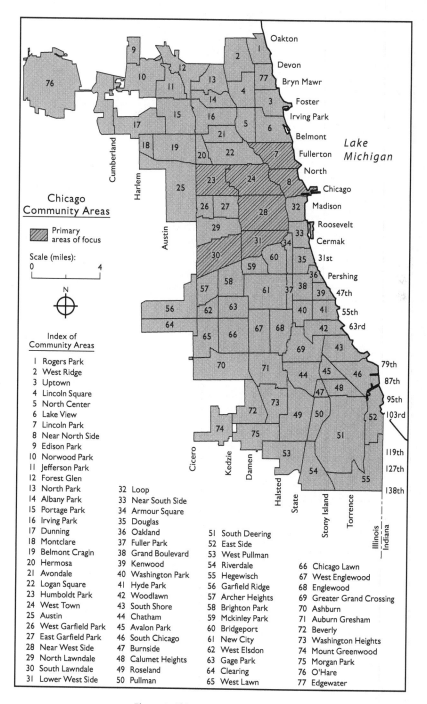

Figure 1. Chicago community areas.

Chicago
Community Areas

Primary
areas of focus

Scale (miles):
0   4

N

Index of
Community Areas

1 Rogers Park
2 West Ridge
3 Uptown
4 Lincoln Square
5 North Center
6 Lake View
7 Lincoln Park
8 Near North Side
9 Edison Park
10 Norwood Park
11 Jefferson Park
12 Forest Glen
13 North Park
14 Albany Park
15 Portage Park
16 Irving Park
17 Dunning
18 Montclare
19 Belmont Cragin
20 Hermosa
21 Avondale
22 Logan Square
23 Humboldt Park
24 West Town
25 Austin
26 West Garfield Park
27 East Garfield Park
28 Near West Side
29 North Lawndale
30 South Lawndale
31 Lower West Side

32 Loop
33 Near South Side
34 Armour Square
35 Douglas
36 Oakland
37 Fuller Park
38 Grand Boulevard
39 Kenwood
40 Washington Park
41 Hyde Park
42 Woodlawn
43 South Shore
44 Chatham
45 Avalon Park
46 South Chicago
47 Burnside
48 Calumet Heights
49 Roseland
50 Pullman

51 South Deering
52 East Side
53 West Pullman
54 Riverdale
55 Hegewisch
56 Garfield Ridge
57 Archer Heights
58 Brighton Park
59 Mckinley Park
60 Bridgeport
61 New City
62 West Elsdon
63 Gage Park
64 Clearing
65 West Lawn

66 Chicago Lawn
67 West Englewood
68 Englewood
69 Greater Grand Crossing
70 Ashburn
71 Auburn Gresham
72 Beverly
73 Washington Heights
74 Mount Greenwood
75 Morgan Park
76 O'Hare
77 Edgewater

INTRODUCTION

The Puerto Rican is not only a stranger to the land, but when he moves into one of the big cities, as most of them do, he steps into a complex of difficulties which are now commonly called metropolitan area problems. The decay of the inner city, the flight to the suburbs, the general population growth and the accelerated geographical and social mobility or internal migration, force the average working-class newcomer at least initially into the so-called "deteriorated neighborhood" or city-slum.

—Chicago Commission on Human Relations, 1960[1]

Despite the general tendency of the city to lose population, especially white population, Mexican areas have gained in population, and, what is very important, in young population which makes and will make these areas important centers of the urban labor force.

—Marta Isabel Kollman de Curutchet, 1967[2]

When Elvira Gonzalez de la Llata and Andres de la Llata arrived in Chicago from the quiet border town of Matamoros, Mexico, they could not have imagined the world they were entering. The young couple traveled to the Windy City in 1954 with their three small children (including a baby in arms) on the advice of Elvira's sister and brother-in-law, Rosa Gonzalez Torres and Francisco Torres. Rosa had reported to family members in Mexico and Texas that plentiful work was available in the city and encouraged them to come up north. The Gonzalez sisters and their parents were experienced transnational migrants, working on both sides of the US-Mexico border since the Second World War. Elvira had blazed the trail. As a teenager, she joined an aunt and uncle working on a ranch in south Texas to help support her mother, siblings, and disabled father back home. After a short time, she brought them across the border, and the family found varied employment shelling pecans, working in restaurants, and doing domestic work. Chicago, however, offered new possibilities they could not find in Texas or Mexico—namely, higher wages.

The social world the de la Llatas found in Chicago was surprisingly familiar but also unexpectedly new. First, they encountered many fellow migrants from Mexico and Texas on the city's Near West Side, where they arrived. The neighborhood had a small ethnic enclave established by Mexican migrants decades earlier. By the 1950s, it continued to be a port of entry for the latest Mexican arrivals and *Tejanos* (Mexican Americans from Texas). But the de la Llatas also met another incoming group—Puerto Ricans—who came to the city from similar backgrounds and with similar aspirations. As residents of a colonial possession of the United States, Puerto Ricans had US citizenship and thus, unlike Mexicans, were not technically "immigrants." Still, their cultural, linguistic, and ethnoracial distinctiveness hardly convinced most Chicagoans that they were in fact "Americans." Though Mexicans and Puerto Ricans had distinct histories, ancestries, and cultural practices, their futures in the city would be closely connected.

The de la Llatas encountered a number of other ethnic groups as well—Italians, Greeks, Poles, Germans, and Russian Jews. Despite their unique ethnic identities, by the postwar period they seemingly shared a social position with native-born "white" Americans. Nearby, African Americans had settled, especially those recently arrived from the South. Elvira had worked and developed friendships with African Americans in restaurant kitchens in Texas. She also had learned the harsh lessons of the country's racial hierarchy as evidenced in the segregated Greyhound bus stations of the South. The signs that read "Colored" confounded her, but her instinct to sit in such seats spared her the embarrassment of being challenged for sitting in "White" sections. In Chicago, fortunately, public accommodations would not create such dilemmas. Instead, racial hierarchies would manifest themselves in other ways—in the difficulty that dark-skinned Spanish speakers would face in securing housing, in the city's increasingly segregated neighborhoods, and the interracial and interethnic conflicts that would play out on the streets. As they encountered their new surroundings, the young de la Llata family could not have fathomed the great postwar migration they had just joined. Nor could they have anticipated how they and their children would fit into this environment and among their new neighbors.[3]

Chicago, like other industrial cities, underwent dramatic population shifts from 1940 to 1980 that literally changed the complexion and composition of the urban north. With few exceptions, this history has been viewed through a black and white lens. Scholars have focused their attention almost exclusively on this racial binary, concluding that "the urban North became a biracial society after the Second World War."[4] Black-white politics and relations certainly dominated the landscape, as these two groups constituted the overwhelming majority of the population. In Chicago, between 1940 and 1950, the black population grew 77 percent, from 278,000 to 492,000 people, making it the second largest black city in the country (see table 1). In the next three decades, African Americans grew to nearly 1.2 million, fully 40 percent of the city's residents. Their remarkable influx was matched by the equally dramatic exodus of white Chicagoans from the city. In 1940, both native-born and foreign-born whites together numbered over 3.1 million. In the next two decades, nearly 1 million had abandoned the city. By 1980, the population had shed more than half its numbers compared to 1940 figures. Less than 1.5 million whites lived in Chicago, constituting only one-half of the city's residents.[5]

Scholars have effectively dismissed the popular (and simplest) microlevel explanation of racial change in the nation's inner cities in the mid-twentieth century—that whites abandoned urban centers in large part because of racial animus toward and conflicts with incoming "nonwhite" (primarily understood to mean "black") people. Other macrolevel factors, particularly interventions by the state, they argue, contributed to transforming inner-city neighborhoods from being exclusively, 100 percent white to entirely, 100 percent black within a decade.[6] Urban historians have cited

Table 1　Black and white population of Chicago, 1940–80

	Black	White
1940	278,000	3,115,000
1950	492,000	3,112,000
1960	813,000	2,713,000
1970	1,102,000	2,208,000
1980	1,197,000	1,490,000

Source: Campbell Gibson and Kay Jung, "Historical Census Statistics on Population Totals by Race, 1790 to 1990, and by Hispanic Origin, 1970 to 1990, for Large Cities and Other Urban Places in the United States," Working Paper No. 76 (Washington, DC: US Census Bureau, February 2005).

structural factors such as rising taxes, declining infrastructure, the relocation of jobs, and alluring, subsidized suburban housing developments—as
well as the perceived threat of violence and crime in nearby nonwhite
communities—to help explain why so many left the inner city during these
years. As Thomas Sugrue, Amanda Seligman, Robert Self, and others have
noted, a convergence of economic, political, and other factors produced
the racially contrasting suburbs and inner-city ghettos of the mid-twentieth
century.[7] In his study of Brooklyn, New York, however, Craig Wilder has
persuasively argued that a centuries-old "covenant of color" lies at the heart
of the formation of urban black ghettos by the 1960s. Reflecting analytical
attention to space, place, and their embedded social relations, he writes:
"The ghetto is not so much a place as it is a relationship—the physical
manifestation of a perverse imbalance in social power." Race, he argues,
becomes the expression of that socioeconomic inequality and, in a circu-
lar logic, the ideology that helps explain it: "The formation of the Central
Brooklyn ghetto ensured that race would be propelled into the future; for,
the ghetto gave color an unmistakable, undeniable, and unavoidable daily
reality, a reality that black people were accused of creating."[8] By the 1970s
and especially the 1980s, the inner cities of the industrial north were characterized by impoverished black communities and ongoing tensions with
remaining white ones. Race had been inscribed into the very geography of
the city, and urban space reflected and reinforced the city's polarized racial
relations and inequalities.

Yet in cities like Chicago, the encounters, conflicts, and migrations of African Americans and whites into and out of the city tell only part of the story.
Our singular focus on the relations between these two groups has obscured
the complexity of racial dynamics and the postwar "urban crisis." The de la
Llatas and their contemporaries represent a wave of (im)migrants[9] whose
historical imprint on the urban north has gone unacknowledged. Indeed,
the migrations of Mexicans, Mexican Americans, and Puerto Ricans between World War II and the passage of the watershed 1965 Immigration Act
have been eclipsed by the waves of southern and eastern Europeans of the
early twentieth century and the Great Migrations of southern African Americans. Buried within census data, however, is the clue to an unremarked demographic shift in Chicago: the city's total population had declined only
slightly from 1940 to 1980—by fewer than 400,000 people—although it
had lost 1.5 million whites. African Americans did not entirely compensate
for the white population decline. What tempered white population loss,
and what only became visible for the first time statistically in the 1980 federal census, was the presence of hundreds of thousands of Latinos/as.

By 1970, Chicago reported nearly a quarter of a million "Spanish-speaking" or "Spanish-surnamed" people, as they were referred to collectively during these years. Mexican-origin people and Puerto Ricans constituted the overwhelming majority—nearly 75 percent of all the Spanish-speaking—numbering 106,000 and 78,000 people, respectively. Over the course of that decade, Chicago's mainstream media, political leaders, and the public more broadly were beginning to understand what many white and black Chicagoans in the inner city were witnessing firsthand—a dramatic number of Spanish-speaking migrants and their children had concentrated in central working-class neighborhoods. By 1980, over 420,000 Hispanic or "Spanish-origin" people called Chicago home, constituting a remarkable 14 percent of all Chicagoans.[10] The majority continued to be Mexican and Puerto Rican. This book explores the postwar origins of that population and the place they came to occupy in the central city.

Although Latinos/as have long surpassed African Americans as the nation's largest "minority" group, and number over 50 million people in the United States as of the 2010 census, perusing the index of the most lauded recent books on urban history or the history of race in the United States reveals little, if any, coverage of Mexicans, Puerto Ricans, or Latinos/as more broadly. Their presence in the postwar north specifically has gone almost entirely undetected by urban historians for several reasons. To begin with, Latinos/as have stood and continue to stand in the twenty-first century outside of our racial vocabulary, our historical memory, and our interpretations of the nation's past. The anachronistic construction of race in the United States as "black" and "white" has proved entirely inadequate in describing the history of Latinos/as as well as other "nonwhite," "nonblack" people. As a result, Latinos/as have not had a fixed or stable place within the nation's racial order. As sociologist Samuel Betances keenly observed in the 1970s, "Blacks see Latinos as honorary whites and whites see Latinos as honorary blacks, and that leaves Latinos in a racial no man's land [sic]."[11] This racial ambivalence has made Mexicans, Puerto Ricans, and other Latinos/as invisible as historical actors who have had experiences distinct from those of African Americans or European Americans. Instead, Latinos/as have presented a paradox: On the one hand, they are often referred to in the same breath with African Americans as "other minorities," suggesting that they share common characteristics or experiences with them. Yet they are rarely differentiated beyond that, leaving their "minority" status rather opaque. On the other hand, many scholars imagine that Latino/a immigrants' trajectory of migration, settlement, integration, and assimilation has resembled that of Europeans; like the Irish, Italians, and Poles, they were understood initially as distinct "ethnic" groups but eventually were accepted as "white." This paradox has made most scholars reluctant to address "the unanswerable question of whether Mexican Americans [or Latinos/as] were or 'really' are white."[12]

The obtuse way in which the nation-state has identified and officially counted Latinos/as has obscured their presence even further. Until 1980, most Latinos/as were officially classified as "white" on the US decennial census, thus making them undetectable as a distinct racialized group. Having the other options of "Black/African American," "American Indian/Eskimo/Aleut," "Asian/Pacific Islander," or "Other," many Latinos/as chose the category "White," either because they indeed believed that best reflected their racial ancestry or, perhaps more strategically, because it was the most attractive option in a society that historically has favored whiteness. (Others were simply classified as such according to the spontaneous racial discernment of census takers.) Mexican Americans specifically had been legally constructed as "white" as a result of the Treaty of Guadalupe-Hidalgo in 1848, which granted them US citizenship. Because US citizenship was limited to "whites," granting it to Mexicans made them "white" *by default*.[13] The social, political, and economic reality, however, revealed that Mexican Americans struggled to claim the privileges of whiteness, so that, as legal scholar Ariela Gross notes, "As a strategy, whiteness was used against Mexican Americans far more often than on their behalf."[14] Despite the efforts of some Mexican Americans as well as other Latinos/as, they have never as a whole consistently and resolutely been accepted as "white" by European Americans.[15]

In 1980, however, the Census Bureau dramatically shifted how it classified Latinos/as, making them more legible as a group demographically. Upon the urging of influential Hispanic leaders who advocated capturing the group's ethnic distinctiveness without limiting them to a singular racial identity, the Census Bureau added a question that allowed individuals to specify if they were of "Spanish origin," a precursor to today's more popular terms *Hispanic* or *Latino/a*, and changed how it classified Latinos/as racially. Whereas, in 1970, census editors routinely moved into the "white" category anyone who had marked his or her race as "other" and written in a Latin American signifier (Chicano, Spanish, Hispanic, etc.), in 1980, they discontinued this practice. Instead, editors allowed people to remain in the "other" category if they so identified. As a result, an unprecedented 6.7 million people identified as "other" that year, with 5.8 million of them also specifying being of "Spanish origin." Approximately 40 percent of Spanish-origin people nationwide identified themselves as "other." In Chicago, however, the number was significantly higher: nearly 55 percent of Chicagoans who called themselves "Spanish origin" said they were an "other" race.[16] By the penultimate decade of the twentieth century, the majority of Latinos/as in Chicago (particularly Mexicans and Puerto Ricans) *did not* identify and *was not* identified as white. Many had concluded that "white" was not the racial identity they had been assigned in the local social order nor one they wished to claim. This racial declaration changed the city's demographic data dramatically. The Windy City was no longer just black and white; it was also "brown."

What was it about Mexicans' and Puerto Ricans' experiences that had caused so many to conclude that they were not "black," not "white" but something else? How did Mexicans and Puerto Ricans find a place, both figuratively in the city's social order and physically in the city's geography? How did postwar dynamics and structural shifts shape this? What did it mean for Mexicans and Puerto Ricans to be "brown" in the Windy City, and what does this tell us about life in the postwar urban north? These are some of the questions this book seeks to answer.

Brown in the Windy City complicates our dualistic understanding of race in the urban north by examining the migration and settlement of Mexicans and Puerto Ricans in the postwar period. It illuminates the race-making process as evidenced in the sociospatial relations of everyday life in the city. I explore the meaning both the state and local actors assigned to Mexicans' and Puerto Ricans' social difference and that which they claimed themselves. The book begins with the parallel labor migrations of the two groups during World War II and ends with a flashpoint of their political activism in the mid-1970s.[17] Mexicans and Puerto Ricans arrived in Chicago in the midst of tremendous social, economic, and geographic change, and they added momentum to that restructuring. Over the course of these three decades, they bore witness to and were part of a dramatic labor migration wave, unprecedented demographic changes, declining industrial employment, massive urban renewal, racial succession, and social turmoil. Ultimately, I argue that through their experiences with these dynamics, Mexicans and Puerto Ricans collectively became an "other" race, subordinated to European Americans but sometimes favored in comparison to African Americans.[18] Despite their ethnic differences and individual variations, by 1980 a majority articulated a distinct racial subject position, one that was admittedly flexible and fluid, neither black nor white.

Race, Place, and Constructing "Brownness"

I analyze Mexicans' and Puerto Ricans' experience in postwar Chicago as interrelated and overlapping struggles over *place*—both an imagined position in the local social order and a concrete, physical location within the city's geography.[19] The meaning assigned to race is always historically contingent, relational, and tied to place. As geographer Laura Pulido notes, "Although all of the United States is informed by a national racial narrative, class structures and racial divisions of labor take shape and racial hierarchies are experienced at the regional and local levels."[20] Despite the state's provisional racial construction of Mexicans and Puerto Ricans through national immigration policies and the federal census, this meant little "on the ground" in the social relations of daily life. When Mexicans and Puerto Ricans first arrived in the city, they were racially unknown to most Chicagoans.[21] Assigning them a place in the local social order became contentious, particularly in a city in the midst of racial turmoil.

Latino/a migrants came to a starkly segregated city in which whites fought pitched battles to maintain their racial borders and African Americans regularly challenged them. In white neighborhoods where African Americans dared move, in public housing or public schools that blacks dared integrate, turbulent protests erupted on a regular basis. Widespread racial hostility has led historian Arnold Hirsch to call the 1940s and 1950s in Chicago "an era of hidden violence." The year after the de la Llatas arrived, Chicagoans voted into city hall Democratic machine boss Richard J. Daley, a man who ruled the city like "a feudal lord" for over twenty years. Under his powerful grip, Chicago became "the most residentially segregated large city in the nation," according to the US Civil Rights Commission.[22] The local political power structure (both the white machine and, to a lesser extent, its black submachine loyalists) had a deep investment in preventing the integration of black and white voters, and thus the potential defection of unhappy whites to the Republican Party. Daley thus pursued a policy of "building racial separation into the very concrete of the city." He corralled poor African Americans into high-rise public housing and built "new developments—housing, highways, and schools . . . where they would serve as a barrier between white neighborhoods and the black ghetto."[23] This was the racial and political geography that greeted Mexicans and Puerto Ricans when they arrived.

As Latinos/as came to the postwar city, the perceived racial difference they seemingly embodied would determine where they would be able to live. Those who could "pass" for Italian or Greek, for example, gained access to more desirable housing that was denied to darker-skinned Mexicans and Puerto Ricans unable to escape unfavorable racial judgments. Most found housing in some of the city's oldest and most deteriorated neighborhoods in the urban core—the Near West and Near North Sides, for example. These areas were economically marginalized and extremely heterogeneous, home to Mexicans who had migrated generations earlier, various ethnic whites—Poles, Italians, Germans, and Greeks—as well as African Americans, in some cases Native Americans, and white Appalachian migrants.

City officials considered these central neighborhoods "blighted" because of their physical condition and racial heterogeneity, and quickly targeted them for urban renewal.[24] "Slum clearance" and progrowth redevelopment relocated most white residents to more stable white communities in the city outskirts or suburbs, and warehoused poor African Americans in public housing projects, creating the "second ghetto." Urban renewal structured the city's social inequalities more sharply and exacerbated its racial polarization. The question of where Mexicans and Puerto Ricans fit in the postwar city proved complicated. Their ambivalent and elastic identity and their newcomer status made them simultaneously invisible in the local political landscape (e.g., they were a negligible constituency) but hypervisible socially. As midcentury state-sponsored urban renewal physically reshaped the city, Mexicans and Puerto Ricans became expendable populations, experiencing repeated dislocations that dispersed them across multiple neighborhoods and geographic communities in the urban core. Though they were not targeted for displacement necessarily *because* they were Mexican or Puerto Rican, their "racial" distinctiveness became amplified through the process.

In the "city of neighborhoods," where residents historically have looked upon outsiders with suspicion, Mexicans and Puerto Ricans learned the lesson of "the exclusive quality of urban space."[25] When these new (im)migrants moved to racially homogeneous, blue-collar, ethnic white neighborhoods, they often elicited hostility and, in the worst cases, violence from those who would keep them out. Beyond simply territoriality and parochialism, however, their presence precipitated a process of ethnoracial incorporation shaped by both the limited racial knowledge local whites possessed about Spanish-speaking groups and that which they actively began constructing. Many white residents did not know quite what to make of the newcomers, who bore the familiar signs of recent arrivals like the Italians and Poles of earlier decades, yet brought *new* cultural, social, and linguistic idiosyncrasies that made them incredibly conspicuous. Several decades after the last large wave of European immigration, most residents had already acculturated, assimilated, and embraced a shared whiteness. Moreover, Spanish-speaking people were arriving on the heels of the second great migration of African Americans. Were Mexicans and Puerto Ricans just like earlier European immigrant groups, whose ethnic/national characteristics would eventually become irrelevant? Or were they, like African Americans, perceived as *racially* different, a difference believed to be permanently and immutably present?

Latinos/as' racial flexibility forced both African Americans and whites to consider more carefully the boundaries of their own communities. Mexicans' and Puerto Ricans' racial ambiguity spared most from the more sustained racial exclusion or immediate racial turnover that African Americans experienced. As some scholars have suggested and as real estate brokers openly admitted in the 1960s and 1970s, Mexicans and Puerto Ricans often served as a "buffer" between blacks and whites, a liminal group that constituted the transitional zone between rigid racial borders.[26] Indeed, their presence in white neighborhoods reveals in urban housing history what Adrian Burgos has noted about Latinos in professional US baseball leagues: "Latinos were not at all tangential to the working of baseball's color line. To the contrary, in the face of African Americans' outright exclusion, Latinos were the main group used to test the limits of racial tolerance and to locate the exclusionary point along the color line."[27] In a similar fashion, Latinos/as in Chicago's neighborhoods tested the limits of residential integration. Because their "race" could be negotiated, contested, and reevaluated in a variety of contexts, this sometimes gave them access that was denied to African Americans, though not always.[28] Race in the urban north was not so black and white. Mexicans and Puerto Ricans complicated what has been perceived as a rather linear and dualistic narrative of postwar racial succession.

Mexicans and Puerto Ricans lived among ethnic and Appalachian whites for varying amounts of time. Some whites did not object to them vocally and remained in their "integrated" communities for a variety of reasons, in some cases for more than a decade. Others did swiftly reject their incursions and left almost immediately. With a diminishing white population, landlords (especially absentee property owners) rented to the Spanish-speaking in growing numbers. As Latinos/as concentrated in these neighborhoods, however, their social difference became spatialized. Geographers have taught us that space is not only the physical or discursive terrain on which social relations occur but it shapes those relations as well. Space produces subjectivity, and in a mutually constitutive fashion, acquires particular meaning(s) based on one's subject position.[29] The congregation of so many Mexicans and Puerto Ricans in these deteriorating areas intensified the negative racial characteristics that many whites ascribed to them, which in turn became anchored to those neighborhoods and to a subordinated class identity. White residents continued to abandon such communities and their diminishing social status for racially exclusive and more respectable suburbs.

Importantly, Mexican and Puerto Rican migrants (as well as other incoming groups) from the 1940s through the 1960s actually made the suburbanization of the central city's lower-middle-class white residents possible. In the mid-1950s, much of the urban core was in severe decay, loaded with nineteenth-century structures in varying stages of deterioration. As real estate development and investment rapidly shifted to the suburbs, lenders grew wary of loaning money in the racially transitioning inner city, and property owners became less likely to improve their buildings. Mexicans and Puerto Ricans who arrived in these crumbling neighborhoods freed white residents from aged real estate, making it possible for them to depart for better housing and an increased quality of life in the growing suburbs. Newcomers often took up the worst rental housing, bought deteriorated properties, and sent their children to many of the city's oldest and most dilapidated schools. They replenished the population in inner-city neighborhoods as so many blue-collar and upwardly mobile whites left.[30]

Mexicans and Puerto Ricans also arrived in the age of declining industrial employment. Along with other migrants, they moved to northern cities in hopes of securing high-paying factory jobs. Many did enter manufacturing, but they were latecomers to the industrial boom. Just as they gained access to the shop floor, those jobs quickly started dwindling. Between 1960 and 1970, the city of Chicago lost 211,000 jobs, a decline of 13 percent. The suburbs, in contrast, gained half a million jobs, an increase of 71 percent.[31] In 1947, the city held 70.6 percent of the metropolitan area's manufacturing employment (668,000 jobs). By 1982, that figure had dropped to 34.2 percent (277,000 jobs) while the suburbs gained in their share to 57.8 percent.[32] These were both geographic and sectoral changes in the economy. Unlike earlier waves of European immigrants, Spanish-speaking migrants found work opportunities shifting from the city to the suburbs, and from higher-paying, unionized industrial jobs to lower-wage, nonunion manufacturing and service industries. Automation further contributed to this deskilling of labor. By 1970, Latinos/as had found a niche in the city's industrial labor force: 56 percent of them worked in manufacturing, compared to only 30 percent of the rest of the city. While they often were favored compared to African Americans, they were still primarily unskilled workers: 50 percent of the city's Latino/a labor force worked as operatives and laborers.[33] Their exclusion from skilled labor markets would have tremendous implications for the upward mobility of successive generations, ensuring that most of the second generation would either stagnate economically or need much higher levels of education to get ahead.[34] The persistent economic subordination (and growing unemployment) of so many would inform ideas about their racial status and assimilability, which in turn would continue to circumscribe their economic mobility.

In contrast, the children and grandchildren of earlier generations of European immigrants overwhelmingly had secured their foothold in the middle class, in large part with the help of the federal government—New Deal liberal welfare programs; high rates of wartime industrial production and employment; the expansion of higher education to women and blue-collar veterans; increased home ownership—made possible by FHA and VA lending programs; and the growth of suburban communities—made possible by such lending programs but also by highway construction.[35] Many, though not all, white workers in higher-paid, unionized, skilled jobs enjoyed the mobility to escape these shrinking labor markets by leaving for the suburbs or moving south and west to the Sun Belt states. They also escaped a rapidly deteriorating city in distress—fleeing rising taxes, declining infrastructure, sinking property values, and increasingly isolated "nonwhite" communities—just as their departures exacerbated these conditions.

Some Latinos/as did indeed strive for whiteness—as European immigrants successfully had—understanding that their condition as workers, youth, tenants, and community members depended on how other Chicagoans interpreted who they were *racially*. They insisted that they were an *ethnic*, not a *racial*, group (hoping to distance themselves from the status assigned to African Americans as so many European immigrants had in the past). Being ascribed a denigrated racial identity by neighbors, police, or school officials certainly had tangible consequences (e.g., harassment, abuse, discrimination). This often occurred in gendered terms. The presence of thousands of "brown" men, whom police initially targeted for petty offenses and cultural misunderstandings on Chicago's streets, precipitated police mistreatment and what today we would call "racial profiling." By the 1960s, police declared war not only on African Americans on the South and West Sides of the city; they also did battle with Puerto Ricans, suspected "illegal" Mexican immigrants, and Latino youth gangs.[36] Ongoing tension and conflicts with police (precipitated as much by police efforts to uphold racial boundaries as by actual crimes committed by Mexicans and Puerto Ricans) reflected and reified local understandings of racial difference and affirmed the hardening views of many whites about their new neighbors.

Many Latino/a social activists, especially second- and third-generation youth of (im)migrant parents, increasingly understood that *claiming* whiteness had not shielded them from prejudice, discrimination, or their socioeconomic consequences. They began engaging in social protest to address the grievances they experienced at the hands of local institutions. Drawing on long traditions of activism within their own communities as well as the political energy of the times, activists embraced the language of Puerto Rican nationalism and the Chicano movement and drew attention to their populations' material needs. They began attracting social resources to communities that might not otherwise have received them. They forced federal, state, and local governments to expand the purview of social programs beyond the city's African American ghettos and allocate funding to the impoverished *barrios* that urban renewal had helped create. Most important, they turned the system of racial categorization on its head by embracing the racial difference they had been ascribed and using it to elaborate an autonomous identity and demand social justice. They recognized that in the context of civil rights and other political movements, speaking from the social location that local actors and the state had assigned them allowed them to demand remedies for their socioeconomic marginalization.[37]

Yet racial and economic marginalization were not the only factors shaping Latino/a people's lives. Women experienced urban life in distinct ways, and the intersectionality of their social identities made them sensitive to other forms of subordination. Their concerns, challenges, and opportunities as mothers, wives, and women shaped community relations in ways that I also aim to document. Women's gendered productive and reproductive labor made them aware of the limits of race-based politics and prompted some to bring attention to gender inequalities. They played a critical role in revealing the specific challenges that Latina women faced *within* their communities and in advocating on behalf of themselves and their families. They too sought to claim a place as community members and citizens of the city.

While Mexicans and Puerto Ricans had settled in various areas, by 1980, midcentury urban planning and neighborhood succession had concentrated them into four main community areas that became known as the

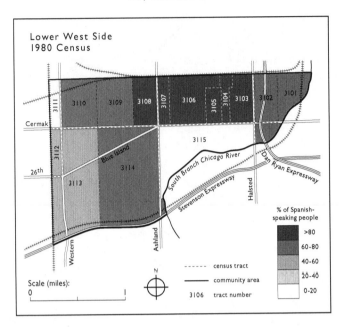

Figure 2. Spanish-speaking population, Lower West Side, 1980.

city's quintessential *barrios*—the Lower West Side (known more popularly as "Pilsen" or "Eighteenth Street"), South Lawndale ("Little Village" or "Twenty-Sixth Street"), West Town, and Humboldt Park (see figs. 2–5). These neighborhoods became burdened by the consequences of postwar deindustrialization and their accompanying social ills. The economically marginalized and neglected *barrios* seemingly embodied the negative racial conclusions about Mexicans and Puerto Ricans that had been forged over three decades. Yet they also became the site of vibrant community activism and campaigns for social and political change.

A Comparative Latino/a History

Scholars of Chicana/o, Puerto Rican, and the growing field of Latino/a history have been among the few to provide accounts of Latino/a people in the United States and fill important gaps in US historiography.[38] In the last three decades, social scientists also have begun documenting the experience of Latino/a immigrants, particularly how the state has "produced" them (especially Mexicans) as "illegal immigrants," thereby constructing a new form of social difference in the twentieth and twenty-first centuries.

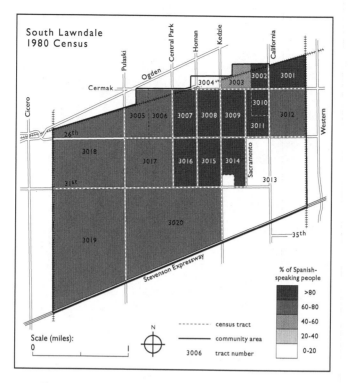

Figure 3. Spanish-speaking population, South Lawndale, 1980.

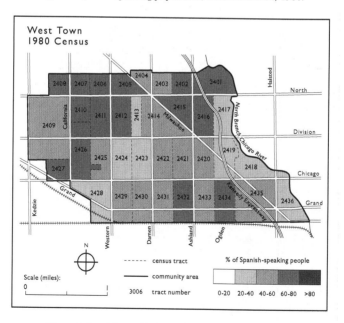

Figure 4. Spanish-speaking population, West Town, 1980.

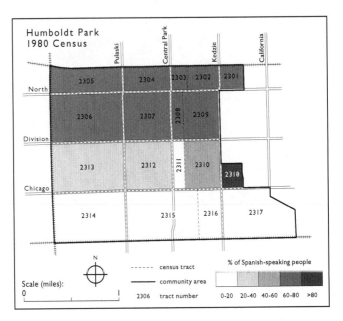

Figure 5. Spanish-speaking population, Humboldt Park, 1980

Very few, however, have written about Latinos/as in urban centers histori-cally before the 1970s, and even fewer have transcended the bicoastal focus on Mexicans in the Southwest and Puerto Ricans on the East Coast.[39]

Growing scholarship on Mexicans and Puerto Ricans in Chicago has be-gun to correct some of these omissions. Most of these studies, however, are contemporary ethnographies and/or explore individual national groups to the exclusion of others.[40] While these works provide useful analyses of these discrete ethnoracial groups, *Brown in the Windy City* contends that in postwar Chicago, Mexicans' and Puerto Ricans' parallel stories intertwined and resembled each other significantly and therefore must be told together. Chicago was unique in its ability to attract such large numbers of Mexicans and Puerto Ricans in the years during and after World War II, and it was the only major city in the country that contained such a distinctive ethnoracial mix. Thus, this text provides a history of the two groups that overlaps at particular moments just as it diverges at others.

I focus specifically on Mexicans and Puerto Ricans and not other Latino/a groups because these were by far the largest populations of Spanish-speaking people in the city (significantly larger than Cubans and Central or South Americans), and they shared similar experiences of settlement and displacement. Cuban immigrants, the third largest migrant group, numbered only fifteen thousand people in 1970, or 6 percent of the Latino/a population. They also had a much higher economic profile, as elite or middle-class exiles from Cuba's Communist revolution, and did not settle in the same neighborhoods or the same type of housing as frequently as Mexicans and Puerto Ricans, nor did they experience the same dynamics of urban renewal dislocation and ghettoization.[41] Moreover, based on skin color and ancestry, elite Cuban exiles were much more likely to be perceived as "white" and not racially distinguishable. Mexicans and Puerto Ricans, by contrast, more frequently shared a lower-class status, and although they brought distinct histories and racial origins, the process of assigning them a place in the city's racial and economic order unfolded in similar ways.

Given its comparative analysis, however, *Brown in the Windy City* does not advance a model of racial triangulation (*black-white-brown*) because of the tremendous variability, inconsistency, and recurring nature of Mexicans' and Puerto Ricans' racial formation. As scholars of race agree, the process of producing and sustaining racial categories requires a great deal of work: race must be constantly reproduced. Moreover, while the racial terms of *black* and *white* have been understood with some degree of certainty, the label *Latino*/a and the racial descriptor *brown* have been much more variable and difficult to define. These terms never have been static or fixed but differ in relation to specific contexts, social institutions, and actors. Latinos/as could be assigned vastly different racial ascriptions, for example, by church leaders, real estate agents, or landlords. Their racial formation has been much more uneven than the more uniform and absolute racialization of African Americans as *black*. Mexicans' and Puerto Ricans' subject position has historically been punctuated by class status, skin color, and location in ways that leave open the possibility for some to be accepted as *white*.

Furthermore, Mexicans and Puerto Ricans have not been ascribed racial identities in exactly the same ways. Although at times they embraced a shared identity as *Latinos/as*, their experiences were conditioned by their national histories, their distinct relationships to the United States, and their perceived legitimacy as (im)migrants and citizens in different ways. Finally, the term *brown* does not represent a universal *color* of all Mexicans and Puerto Ricans. Rather, in the racial taxonomy of the United States, *brown* stands in as a placeholder that captures the malleable meaning assigned to the social difference most Mexicans and Puerto Ricans are believed to embody. The term locates them between African Americans and whites on a racial/color spectrum whose center has been quite variegated and frequently contested.[42]

Layout of the Book

Brown in the Windy City moves through various neighborhoods of Chicago and shifts back and forth between primarily Mexican and primarily Puerto Rican populations in these areas. Chapter 1 traces the origins of these populations in the postwar city through their transnational labor migration during and after World War II. It underscores the similarities between both sets of migrants as state-sponsored and (un)regulated population flows and examines the position they and existing Mexican American workers occupied in the local labor market. Chapter 2 documents the settlement of these recent (im)migrants in one of the city's central community areas—the Near West Side—and explores their relations with others, and the organizational efforts they made to create community among themselves. Neither Mexicans nor Puerto Ricans stayed on the Near West Side for long, however, and chapter 3 explores the policies that displaced them. Here I examine race-based public housing policies, federal highway construction, and the progrowth imperative of urban revitalization. By the 1960s, these policies, and specifically the construction of the University of Illinois Circle Campus, expelled Mexicans and Puerto Ricans from the Near West Side and scattered them to other neighborhoods.

Chapter 4 follows the Puerto Rican population to the Near North Side, where many settled briefly before being relocated from there too. Many moved to West Town and Humboldt Park, where tense social relations and conflicts with law enforcement and other institutions eventually led to the eruption of riots in 1966. As developers and city planners continued to target Puerto Ricans in other neighborhoods, second-generation youth began resisting these dislocations with a nascent political consciousness. Chapter 5 documents the activism of the Young Lords Organization and how its members tried to fight urban renewal efforts to keep their place in their neighborhood. It also traces the importance of women as participants in and supporters of the YLO.

Across the city, Mexican Americans who were dislocated from the Near West Side turned to the Eighteenth Street (or Pilsen) neighborhood for refuge. Chapter 6 follows their settlement there and their encounters with ethnic white neighbors. Second-generation Mexican Americans began shaping their community with the discourse of the Chicano movement, initiating a flurry of protest and activist struggles from the late sixties through the early seventies. The nationalism and race-based identities that formed the backdrop to this activism, however, provided a limited vision of who constituted "the community." Chapter 7 thus explores the role of women in the community's new politics and how they engaged in local activism. Most significant, it documents the formation of a women's organization, Mujeres Latinas en Acción (Latina Women in Action). While gender analysis and women's stories appear in other chapters, this one devotes itself completely to these themes. Ultimately, the activism among Mexican Americans and Puerto Ricans laid the groundwork for more formal electoral participation, and it is here that the story concludes. By 1980, many Mexicans and Puerto Ricans—first, second, and third generations—seemingly embraced a new identity and sense of themselves that would demand greater representation from the local political structure to secure a more stable and visible footing in the city.

A Note on Terminology and Geography

Throughout the book, I use a number of terms to refer to various ethnoracial groupings of people of Latin American descent. When referring to people of Mexican origin or descent, I generally use the terms *Mexican*, *Mexican American*, or *Mexican origin*. The label *Mexican American* generally refers to individuals born or raised in the United States and thus generally does not refer to recent immigrants. The term *Mexican origin*, in contrast, includes both people who have migrated from Mexico and those born or raised in the United States. The term *Mexican* generally refers to the immigrant generation but at times encompasses people of Mexican descent regardless of generation. This was precisely an effect of the way in which whites racialized people of Mexican origin regardless of how long they have been in the United States (i.e., *Mexican* could mean a recent immigrant just as easily as it identified a third-generation descendant of immigrants). The term *Chicano*, which gained usage particularly among young political activists in the mid-1960s, appears in the book only when historical subjects actually used it to identify themselves. Thus, the term appears primarily in chapters 6 and 7. I identify both people who have migrated from the island of Puerto Rico and those who have been born or raised on the mainland as Puerto Ricans. If it is necessary to distinguish between the two, occasionally I qualify the term by specifying generation (e.g., "second-generation Puerto Ricans"). In addition, I use the terms *African American* or *black* interchangeably, and occasionally use the term *Negro* to accurately reflect the racial label applied to people of African descent in the 1940s, 1950s, and 1960s.

These terms are generally straightforward. What becomes more complicated, however, is discussing Mexicans and Puerto Ricans as well as others of Latin American origin collectively. Beginning in the 1950s, Chicagoans from these communities used the term *Spanish-speaking* to refer to themselves collectively. Thus, that term appears more frequently, rather than the more contemporary *Latino/a*, in order to reflect historical identities more accurately. The term *Latins* also began to emerge by the 1960s, and both whites and Latinos/as used that label. Some also called themselves *Latin American*, either to emphasize panethnic affinities or to avoid more racially denigrated terms. Finally, in the late 1960s and early 1970s, Mexicans and Puerto Ricans began using the terms *Latino* and *Latina*. In general, because even today the term *Latino/a* is ambiguous in its boundaries and specificities, I deploy it here as an *ethnoracial* label, at times signifying a multivalent, heterogeneous ethnic difference (i.e., encompassing the collective *ethnic and cultural* distinctiveness of Latin Americans broadly) and at other times signifying a broad *racial* location—namely, that of Mexicans and Puerto Ricans, who were more numerous than other Latin American groups.

There are no neighborhoods in Chicago where national origin groups live in complete, discrete isolation from one another. Thus, in predominantly "Mexican" neighborhoods, one will find a small number of Puerto Ricans, and in neighborhoods perceived as "Puerto Rican," there exists a considerable Mexican or other Latino/a population. It becomes necessary, then, to sometimes specify a given neighborhood or population as "Puerto Rican–Latino/a" to reflect that while it may be primarily Puerto Rican, it includes other Latinos/as. This is simply the reality of the city's geography and demographics.

An explanation of the geographical units used in this book is also in order. I use the broad "community areas" established by University of Chicago sociologists in the early twentieth century, which have endured until the present. When Chicago sociologists first set out to explore the social laboratory of the city, they established an organizational system for the city's many neighborhoods and identified "community areas" as geographical units (often separated by physical landmarks such as rivers and railroads). Each community area incorporated smaller neighborhoods and local communities and includes a varying number of census tracts, but the boundaries of the larger unit do not necessarily correspond to political units (i.e., aldermanic wards, state or congressional districts). While indeed many of the names given to a community area (such as *Lower West Side*) did not reflect how local people identified their neighborhoods at all (Pilsen, Eighteenth Street, Heart of Chicago), these names have endured for nearly a century by way of the *Local Community Fact Book*, published every decade and based on the US census. This may be confusing at times, when there are multiple, smaller neighborhoods within a community area—which there almost always are—but I try to specify these as needed. There are both advantages and limitations to using these geographical units, but they generally dictate the official mapping of the city and thus appear here as well.

ONE

Mexican and Puerto Rican Labor Migration to Chicago

In the spring of 1945 in the city of Chicago, a local Mexican American organization, the Mexican Civic Committee, alerted the Council of Social Agencies' Committee on Minority Groups about the presence of several hundred Mexican migrant contract workers (*braceros*) in the city. Most of the men worked on local rail lines while others labored in agriculture or on railroads elsewhere in the region and had made their way to the Windy City. By late 1946, the Committee on Minority Groups established a Subcommittee on Social Services to Mexican Migratory Workers to address the population's needs. At its first meeting in December of that year, the subcommittee discussed the status and social problems of the workers. Many *braceros* had poor working and living conditions, inadequate clothing for midwestern winters, inadequate food, and substandard wages. Some men had "skipped" their contracts and arrived in Chicago without money, a place to sleep, or a way to get back home. The subcommittee discussed how local social agencies could provide services to these migrants and help those who wanted to return to Mexico.[1]

That very same month, another group of Chicago residents also turned their attention to a different sort of *"braceros"* who were experiencing comparable conditions—Puerto Rican migrant female and male contract workers who had been placed locally as domestic servants and foundry workers, respectively. A group of students at the University of Chicago and other sympathizers began investigating worker complaints of employer abuses, unfair wage deductions, and overall bad experiences. What were these two different sets of workers doing in Chicago in the mid-1940s? What had brought them to the city? Although they garnered attention separately from each other, the simultaneous migrations and problems of Mexicans and Puerto Ricans were not coincidental. Their notable presence signaled the beginning of a dramatic postwar labor migration, one that in fact was solicited by the United States and coordinated with the governments of Mexico and Puerto Rico.

From World War II through the 1960s Mexicans and Puerto Ricans became subjects of state-sponsored mass labor importation programs in the United States. Both served as viable labor pools to fill American economic needs in the mid-twentieth century, but they were beckoned by the US government through contradictory and competing policies. The Emergency Farm Labor Program, or Bracero Program, called for the temporary recruitment of Mexican men for agricultural and railroad work. American government officials initially argued for the urgent need for such recruitment during the "wartime emergency" based on employers' complaints of severe labor shortages. Contract labor agreements between the United States and Mexico, however, were renewed repeatedly after the war, extending until 1964. Puerto Ricans became labor migrants under the auspices of the Puerto Rico Department of Labor's Migration Division, as part of the island's larger modernization and economic development campaign known as Operation Bootstrap / *Manos a la Obra*.[2] Broadly speaking, their migration had the two-pronged goals of alleviating the island's widespread unemployment and controlling its putative "overpopulation." The legal status of the two labor pools, however, differed sharply. Mexican migrants (whether *braceros* or not) entered the country as citizens of a sovereign nation and therefore were identified legally as "aliens" or temporary immigrants.[3] Puerto Ricans came as residents of an American colonial possession and therefore US citizens as established by the Insular Cases and the Jones Act of 1917. They were thus identified as "domestic migrants."[4] While these two migrant labor programs differed in significant ways, their end result was the same: both programs sent workers to do similar labor in the mainland United States for specified periods of time. Both populations were extremely vulnerable and exploitable in unprotected labor sectors. Though the majority of Mexican *braceros* labored in agricultural fields or on railroads in the Southwest, and most Puerto Rican labor migrants worked on the East Coast, the two converged in the fields, on the railroads, and, eventually, in the factories of the Midwest.

The same economic considerations that led Mexican men to take temporary labor contracts and Puerto Rican men and women to travel north also motivated Mexican American migrants and non-*bracero* Mexican immigrants (with or without visas). In the wartime production boom and the postwar era of economic prosperity, internal migrants from throughout the country—southern African Americans, southern whites, Native Americans—had begun abandoning agricultural labor and rural regions in search of higher-paying, industrial employment in urban centers. Mexican American migrant farm laborers, including many who had worked the seasonal circuit from Texas to the Midwest (Michigan, Ohio, Wisconsin, Indiana, Illinois), were particularly compelled to head north by the competition from the very *braceros* that farmers began hiring for lower wages. The Bracero Program thus drove increasing numbers of Mexican Americans out of the farm labor stream in search of more lucrative work in urban areas. The economic boom also inspired Mexican immigrants without *bracero* contracts—both men and women, authorized and unauthorized—to migrate north, especially by the late 1940s and 1950s, in search of reportedly plentiful work opportunities. In an era of European immigration restriction and at the end of the second Great Migration of southern African Americans, Puerto Ricans, Mexican nationals, and Mexican Americans came with the hopes of gaining economic security just as employers hoped to hire them for the lowest wages possible.[5]

Whether *braceros*, Mexican immigrants, *Tejanos* (Texas Mexican Americans), or Puerto Ricans, the majority came to occupy the same occupational stratum—unskilled or semiskilled labor in agriculture, on the railroads, in steel mills, meatpacking houses, or manufacturing. Like other immigrants of the past (Irish, Italians, Poles, Slavs, and others), the newly arrived generally occupied the bottom of the employment ladder—relegated to the lowest-paid, most dangerous, and undesirable work. Yet their labor migration differed in several important respects. As Chicano/a scholars of Mexican immigration have noted, Mexican immigration has carried with it the unique history of US-Mexican relations, the historical racialization of Mexicans that has accompanied those relations, and the continued (and often contested) racial ascriptions assigned to Mexicans and Mexican Americans throughout the twentieth century. Puerto Ricans brought with them a distinct colonial legacy. Yet for both Mexicans and Puerto Ricans who migrated to Chicago in these decades, their racial formation in the city was shaped both by their encounters with others and by the colonial pasts they carried. The role that the state played in recruiting them, moreover, made their migration that much more intriguing and paradoxical as the state sought to regulate and restrict their mobility once on the US mainland.

Prelude to Migration: Legacies of Colonialism

Numerous scholars have established that migrant labor has been a constitutive feature of the capitalist world-system. Indeed, "the relationship between capitalism, the nation-state, and human migration" has become a central feature of contemporary scholarship that has taken a transnational approach to the study of migration. Since at least the seventeenth century, colonizing nation-states have sought out low-wage workers in the colonies and later in the metropole for the production of goods for local and global markets. Such colonization of labor has occurred primarily through the distinct racialization of those populations as inferior and subordinate to the dominant group contracting them.[6]

Both Mexicans and Puerto Ricans have functioned as colonial labor in their respective places of origin—Mexicans as miners and petroleum workers for American and European corporations in Mexico, for example, and Puerto Ricans as needleworkers, or agricultural workers on US-owned sugar, coffee, and tobacco plantations on the island. Their migrations to the US mainland have also been a result of the economic, social, and political dislocations that such imperialism and colonialism have produced. Indeed, most studies of Puerto Rican migration analyze the phenomenon as part and parcel of the island's colonial relationship to the United States, interpreting "such a large-scale displacement [a]s an essential feature in the total process of colonialism, not only as it has operated in Puerto Rico, but as it manifests itself around the world today."[7] Chicano historians and other scholars have advanced this argument in relation to Mexican migrants as well. Gilbert González and Raul Fernández contend that "more than a century of economic domination of the United States over Mexico" has produced varying waves of migration to the United States since the mid-nineteenth-century conquest of Mexico's northern territory. This obtains for Mexican Americans as well, who either were folded into the nation through conquest in 1848 or are the descendants of subsequent immigrants. Indeed, Chicano scholars embraced the concept of "internal colonialism" in the 1970s to describe the subordinated status of Mexican Americans in the United States. Mae Ngai has likewise characterized the phenomenon of both Mexican and Mexican American labor migration in the United States as "imported colonialism," a dynamic that racializes ethnic Mexicans as laborers and positions them outside the nation-state regardless of their citizenship or birthplace. According to her, Mexican and Mexican American workers have essentially served as a colonized labor force under the guise of voluntary (im)migration and free labor conditions.[8]

These processes of colonization and imperialism have rested upon and reproduced racial logics that enable the economic, political, and social subordination of colonized groups. Mexicans and Puerto Ricans have had distinct histories of racialization vis-à-vis the United States. US conquest of northern Mexico in 1848 resulted in the racialization and proletarianization of Mexican people as an inferior, degraded, low-wage laboring class.[9] Such subordination allowed American colonizers to establish social, political, and especially economic control over the newly acquired territory and its seventy-five to one hundred thousand Mexicans.[10] The colonization of the island of Puerto Rico, exactly five decades later, similarly depended on the subordination of the island's people. Puerto Rico's much larger population, however, was racialized less as low-wage peons than as exotic, foreign, deficient, racial "others" in need of American paternalism and civilization. The ambivalence about incorporating the population into the nation translated into an ambivalent political condition, the island's "belonging to—but not part of—the United States." American hesitancy to incorporate islanders resulted in contentious debates over their constitutional claims to US citizenship.[11] Their colonial racialization vis-à-vis white Americans and their subsequent incorporation as subordinate citizens (much like African Americans and Native Americans) mutually reinforced each other and thus constructed Puerto Ricans as exploitable low-wage labor on both the island and the mainland. Rather than securing the full privileges and rights of white American citizens, the majority of the population was relegated to low-wage labor. Mexican and Puerto Rican racialization reflected the differing geographic locations, sociopolitical obstacles, and economic opportunities that they presented to American imperialist ambitions. Still, regardless of their local idioms, both populations were deemed unmistakably inferior to white Americans, and, thus, their incorporation into the national body as equal citizens would remain largely impossible.[12]

The migration of both populations to the mainland United States during the mid-twentieth century carried with it the legacy of this colonial past at the same time that it perpetuated and reinforced that colonial racialization, or "reracialized" those groups.[13] Americans had some knowledge of Mexicans and Mexico, remembering the recruitment of American soldiers to capture Pancho Villa in 1914, seeing film depictions of Mexico as a "barbarous" land, and seeking out the country for exotic travels. In the Midwest, specifically, white Americans had fewer encounters with Mexicans in the early twentieth century than in the Southwest, and they struggled to locate them among African Americans and European immigrants. As much as Mexicans complicated racial categories in the Midwest, however, Gabriela Arredondo argues that ultimately by the 1930s Chicagoans had ascribed this group a noncitizen/alien, nonwhite, and non-American racial location, marking them firmly outside the national body. Mexican immigrants represented a nonwhite "other." Their class status or "labor category," moreover, was decidedly inferior to that of native-born white Americans as well as European immigrants, who staked increasingly firmer claims to whiteness.[14] The Bracero Program and accompanying "illegal" immigration by the forties, fifties, and sixties perpetuated their subordinated socioeconomic status, a condition that seemed to improve little for second-generation Mexican Americans.

Puerto Ricans also presented a relatively new group of "others" to be incorporated into the racial and ethnic landscape on the mainland, and they complicated American racial taxonomies further. As Laura Briggs notes, "The work of incorporating new nationalities into modern racial categories change[d] in the post–World War II period with the implementation of policies encouraging the migration of Puerto Ricans to the mainland." If Mexicans were racial others, Puerto Ricans were even more indecipherable. They challenged Americans' categories of racial knowledge even further, being "Americans" and yet "foreigners" at the same time. Like incoming Mexicans, they confounded the nation's black-white binary at a moment when European immigrants had consolidated their "whiteness" and black migrants to the urban industrial north had been firmly cast in their "blackness." Puerto Ricans' heterogeneity in skin color and phenotype and their "racial" ambiguity marked them as some "other" nonwhite group despite their American citizenship.[15] Regardless of the differences in their specific histories of colonization and conquest and the particular technologies and local contours of their racialization, when both Mexicans and Puerto Ricans came to the mainland as labor migrants, they were unmistakably "subordinate with respect to the Euro-American population within the United States as a whole."[16]

The political status of the (im)migrant groups' respective homelands shaped the conditions of labor (im)migration and the contours of state-sponsored labor migration programs as well. As a sovereign state, Mexico had relative autonomy in negotiating with the United States compared to the colonial possession of Puerto Rico. Mexico's contract negotiations constituted part of the United States' foreign relations with its hemispheric neighbors. President Franklin D. Roosevelt's Good Neighbor Policy framed, at least discursively, the way in which American officials handled initial Bracero Program negotiations. Officials deployed Good Neighbor rhetoric to entreat Mexican cooperation with American labor demands and to emphasize that the United States wanted good relations with its southern neighbor. While Mexico was a sovereign, independent nation, it felt pressure from the Western Hemisphere's superpower to comply with its request for workers. Labor agreements thus were not marked by equity.

Although during World War II, Mexico had some leverage vis-à-vis the United States and was able to protect its laborers, over the years, this power waned and Mexican workers were left essentially at the mercy of American employers.[17]

In contrast, Puerto Rico had an explicitly colonial relationship with the United States. The much-celebrated change in Puerto Rico's designation to commonwealth status under the governorship of Luis Muñoz Marín in 1952 did little to change this colonial status. US citizenship made labor contracts much more informal and kept them outside the scope of foreign policy or diplomatic relations. Ironically, however, the United States had less official control over the movement of Puerto Ricans than Mexicans since the former could migrate freely like other American citizens. As a colonizing power, however, the United States played a more direct role in the social, political, and economic conditions and policies that prompted, even encouraged, unemployed or impoverished workers to leave the island in search of work.

By World War II, American economic conditions and needs made both Mexico and Puerto Rico viable choices for temporary, low-wage, low-skilled labor. Modernization and industrialization campaigns, agricultural displacement, environmental catastrophe, and government policies made Mexico and Puerto Rico ripe candidates for exporting workers. In the case of Mexico, it initially lent its citizens at the urging of American officials and employers.

Formalizing Labor Migration Policies

The World War II era propagated tremendous domestic migration within the mainland United States. Internal migrations of southern African Americans, southern whites, Native Americans, Mexican Americans, and Japanese American internees all contributed to increasingly diverse urban areas. Yet the drafting of soldiers, the upgrading of many Americans to lucrative defense jobs, the vacuum left by the restrictions on European immigration after 1924, and the urbanization of the American population during these years resulted in a dramatic decline in farm labor.[18] This reality collided with American imperatives for cheaper labor and increased food production during the war. Pressured for temporary workers by powerful agribusiness, manufacturing, and railroad companies, the United States government established agreements for temporary labor migrants from Jamaica, Mexico, the Bahamas, Honduras, and Puerto Rico. The largest number of workers issued from Mexico.

The Bracero Program

In the spring of 1942, American officials from the Departments of Agriculture, State, Labor, and Justice; the War Manpower Commission (WMC); and the Office of the Coordinator of Inter-American Affairs began exploring the possibility of importing temporary Mexican labor. Feeling pressure from agricultural lobbyists and California congressmen, the United States government began negotiations with the Mexican government that June and, by August, agreed upon the outline of the Emergency Farm Labor Program.[19] The initial program, popularly known as the Bracero Program, allowed employers to temporarily contract Mexican men for six months to a year at a time. The workers' contracts purportedly included free transportation from recruitment centers to the workplace, free sanitary housing, water, and nutritious meals provided at cost. Workers were guaranteed a minimum number of work hours during their contract period as well. They were to be paid the local prevailing wage, although local wage boards, composed largely of farmers themselves, established these at the beginning of each season. The Farm Security Administration (FSA) oversaw the certification process for farmers to acquire imported workers. The process required that farmers demonstrate that domestic labor was entirely unavailable, first through their own efforts, then with the assistance of the United States Employment Service (USES). If the USES could not find workers domestically, it would certify to the FSA that a labor shortage did indeed exist and farmers could proceed with their request for *braceros*. The first five hundred workers arrived in Stockon, California, on September 30, 1942. While initially *braceros* labored primarily in the Southwest, many began working crops and orchards in midwestern states like Michigan, Ohio, Minnesota, Illinois, and Wisconsin as early as 1944.[20]

The negotiation of labor contracts for Mexican workers also extended to the railroad industry. Like agribusiness, the railroads cited severe labor shortages during the war, although evidence suggests that the problem was not so much a dearth of domestic workers as it was the low wages that railroad companies wanted to pay for unskilled labor.[21] They also emphatically claimed that the nation's aging railroad system, an essential component of defense transportation during the war, was on the brink of collapse without additional track maintenance labor. In March of 1943, Joseph Eastman, director of the Office of Defense Transportation, communicated to the secretary of state "the great urgency of our railways in the Southwest to secure some four or five hundred track workers from Mexico."[22] Although

Mexico had initially opposed the exportation of contract workers to any industry other than agriculture, the railroads successfully made their claim, and the United States and Mexico signed an agreement on April 29, 1943, authorizing six thousand railroad workers for that year. Like the farm labor program, the railroad program required certification of labor shortages by the War Manpower Commission and the Railroad Retirement Board (RRB) before importing workers. Unlike in agriculture, however, the railroad program received significant opposition and intervention by railroad unions. In part as a result of union pressure, the program lasted only a short time.[23] Still, the railroad Bracero Program brought over one hundred thousand Mexican laborers in only two and a half years (from spring 1943 to late 1945). During their brief time in the country, Mexican workers traveled throughout the Southwest, East Coast, and Midwest.[24]

The Mexican government was initially skeptical and reluctant to have its citizens participate in the American labor program, citing criticisms and concern from various sectors of Mexican society. For one, it stressed its own labor needs both in its agriculture sector and on the country's very own aged and deteriorating railroad system.[25] Mexico feared losing too many of its nationals to the United States and creating labor shortages within its own borders. This in part motivated a gendered policy, which prohibited women and children from migrating along with men.[26]

The Mexican government also assumed a paternalistic stance in the protection and retention of its workers. The government expressed special concern about "difficulties" (racial discrimination and prejudice) that Mexican nationals had endured in the United States in the past, especially under a similar Bracero Program during World War I. As a result, it initially excluded Texas from the program because of its notoriety for discriminating against Mexicans.[27] The American government attempted to quell Mexico's concerns by abiding by Article 29 of Mexico's Labor Code and guaranteeing minimum work conditions, wages, and workers' rights. It also sought to assuage fears of discrimination by guaranteeing "nondiscriminatory treatment as enunciated in Roosevelt's Executive Order 8802," which established the Fair Employment Practices Commission (FEPC). This was merely symbolic, however, as the order "pertain[ed] only to fair treatment in defense industries and government employment; it ignored fair employment practices in agriculture or non-governmental operations."[28]

Mexico objected on various occasions to wage differentials and unfair treatment of workers, and made other complaints. In fact, in its negotiations with the United States after the war in early 1946, officials explained their government would consent to a new labor agreement only if the states of Illinois, Indiana, Michigan, Minnesota, Wisconsin, Colorado, Montana, and Wyoming were excluded from the program. Objections centered on poor wages, lack of medical care, and poor living conditions in those states. Further, the government specified it would not allow Mexican workers to labor in the sugar-beet industry, a crop that was particularly brutal in its physical demands because of the use of short-handled hoes. American officials successfully dissuaded Mexico from imposing the restrictions and persuaded it to send workers because of "the food situation throughout the world and the tremendous burden falling on the United States."[29] The US government appealed to Mexico's sense of duty and obligation to its northern neighbor in pleading for more workers.

The United States government frequently drew on the rhetoric of "hemispheric solidarity" and defense in the name of the Allied forces to persuade Mexico to lend its workers. President Roosevelt extolled Mexico's participation in the "war of (food) production, upon which the inevitable success of our military program depends."[30] Other American officials similarly applauded Mexico's contribution to the war effort and emphasized the country's gratitude for what it essentially characterized as Mexico's soldiers in the fields. When communicating with Mexican leaders, American officials labeled Mexican railroad workers a "division [on] the [war] front."[31] Throughout the mid-1940s, the United States continually implored Mexico to raise its ceilings on the number of workers it would export and emphasized how essential Mexico's workers were to victory. In 1944, the War Manpower Commission chief, John D. Coates, explained that labor needs for food processing in the northwestern United States "[could not] be fully met without the importation of additional labor from Mexico."[32] The United States depended desperately on Mexican labor.

In May of 1945, Mexico insisted upon reassurances that workers would be repatriated within six months of the end of hostilities. In August, when the war ended, the WMC began a staggered repatriation of agricultural and railway workers whose contracts started expiring that fall and winter. In September, however, the Department of Agriculture's Office of Labor began expressing concern over labor needs for current crops and called for extending existing agricultural contracts for an unspecified period of time. By that December, the department called for another fifty-four thousand agricultural workers for 1946.[33] Evidently, the United States' appetite for temporary Mexican contract labor was far from sated.

Throughout the early years, Mexico repeatedly expressed concern over "illegal" immigration across its borders into the United States, something that did not seem to concern US officials very much. Mexico charged that the American government was responsible for the widespread illegal crossing of Mexican laborers into the United States because of its lax and inconsistent border enforcement, and it opposed the existence of recruitment centers along the border rather than in the interior of Mexico.[34] The American ambassador in Mexico recognized the United States' complicity in creating a widespread illegal immigration problem. He noted in 1946:

> It may be argued too that the importation by the United States of several hundred thousand agricultural workers from Mexico during the last few years has contributed to the zeal of those now seeking continually to cross the border and find work in the agricultural sections of California. In other words, the need of the United States for additional agricultural labor has contributed much to creating the problem that now exists.

He further noted that Mexico was ineffective in preventing workers from migrating illegally and added, "Nor does it appear that this clandestine immigration will cease until employment is no longer available for these workers in the United States."[35] When Mexican officials continued to express apprehension over high rates of illegal immigration, American officials suggested that if Mexico renewed its labor agreement for 1946, the problem might be solved by deporting those unauthorized immigrants and legally readmitting them at a recruitment center along the border. This US practice of "drying out wetbacks," or legalizing illegal immigrants, would become common over the years.[36]

Many Mexican workers eagerly flocked to the United States given the lure of higher wages. Austere economic conditions prompted tens of thousands of Mexican farmers and laborers to make long journeys to Mexico City or other recruitment centers in search of work. Mexico faced widespread deprivation and poverty during these decades as a result of several factors. War and revolution had ravaged the land just two decades earlier; the effects of the worldwide depression lingered for many; the country witnessed a dramatic population increase between 1940 and 1950; and a severe five-year drought had struck northern Mexico. According to Juan García, the state of Durango had lost approximately 379,000 head of cattle worth $8.7 million in 1953. Mexicans found little relief from drought when floods destroyed many farms that year.[37] Many farmers, laborers, and even business owners and skilled craftsmen were eager to go north for work. Those who could not secure a *bracero* contract increasingly came on their own.

State-Managed Puerto Rican Labor Migration

In contrast to the Mexican government, which felt apprehensive about sending so many workers north, the Puerto Rican government was eager to participate in the war effort and send its residents to work on the mainland. As in Mexico, the dire economic conditions of the Depression continued to grip the island.[38] An ongoing employment crisis counted over 176,000 unemployed persons as of June 1942. Insular government officials urged the War Manpower Commission to hire Puerto Ricans (US citizens) for jobs that were being filled by imported foreign workers—Mexicans, Jamaicans, Bahamians, and Barbadians. The War Department raised various objections to such a plan but eventually agreed to a migration experiment. The program carefully selected more than one thousand skilled workers who could speak English, pay their own travel costs, and met other criteria. After six months, the WMC stopped recruiting skilled workers and turned to unskilled laborers for placement in the railroad, food-processing, and mining industries. In the late spring and early summer of 1943, workers traveled to the Baltimore and Ohio Railroad in Maryland, Campbell Soup Company in New Jersey, and copper mines in Utah. Not long after the program had begun, officials declared it a failure. Migrants complained about work and living conditions, and many skipped out on their work assignments. Employers bemoaned the unauthorized departures, with the B and O Railroad citing a 25 percent desertion rate within just weeks of importing the men. Apparently, neither employers nor the federal government had much control over the workers' mobility, as many chose to vote with their feet and leave unsatisfactory jobs. As a result, many employers chose instead to continue hiring foreign workers, who could purportedly be managed and disciplined more effectively with the threat of deportation.[39]

The WMC discontinued the recruitment project and instead allowed employers to seek workers on the island on their own. Mainland employers thus became part of the new "Operation Bootstrap," or *Manos a la Obra*, campaign aimed at dealing with the island's numerous economic, labor, and social issues. Operation Bootstrap had two goals—modernizing the island and addressing the putative "overpopulation" problem. The insular government sought to achieve this through two strategies—the movement of capital to the island and the movement of population off the island.

Island officials from both the Puerto Rico Economic Development Administration (EDA) / Administración de Fomento Económico (Fomento) and Puerto Rico Department of Labor worked intensively to attract manufacturing jobs to the island.[40] The EDA/Fomento designed elaborate publicity campaigns to lure American businesses, citing lower wages that could be paid to Puerto Rican workers (especially women), tax incentives, and lax labor regulations.[41] Offices in New York, Chicago, and Los Angeles carried out marketing campaigns through mass mailings to US companies and coordinated visits to the island for important manufacturers. The EDA succeeded in persuading some companies, which began relocating to Puerto Rico in search of lower production and labor costs. The EDA published monthly progress reports citing the number of plants that were operating or scheduled to open on the island.[42] The Department of Labor tracked the number of job placements it secured for unemployed workers (table 2). While such numbers increased significantly from 1947 to 1953, this did not provide adequate employment. The number of unemployed dropped from 104,000 in 1950 to 89,000 in 1958, going from a rate of 14.8 percent to 13.9 percent. Moreover, underemployment remained a serious problem.[43]

Nonetheless, the United States soon began showcasing Puerto Rico as a model of modernization and industrial development for the rest of Latin America. The island purportedly represented the promise that US investment could bring to other impoverished neighbors in the region. The irony of Puerto Rico's success, of course, was that while investors and elites reaped the profits of modernization and industrialization, such programs wrought irreversible changes on the island and its people. The economic development strategy displaced hundreds of thousands of subsistence

Table 2   Workers placed in Puerto Rico by Puerto Rico Employment Service

Fiscal Year	Placements
1947–48	8055
1948–49	6024
1949–50	3945
1950–51	5985
1951–52	12,263
1952–53	23,518
1953–54	31,744

Source: *Personas Colocadas Mediante Gestiones Realizadas por el Servicio de Empleos de Puerto Rico*, report, February 1955, box 30, División Técnica, 1955, A–C, tarea 61-55, Fondo Departamento del Trabajo, Archivo General de Puerto Rico, San Juan, Puerto Rico.

farmers. The residents displaced by the shift from agriculture to industry greatly outnumbered the newly created industrial jobs. Moreover, the jobs that did appear went largely to women at lower wages than those paid to men. These changes produced high rates of unemployment and widespread poverty throughout the island.[44]

Letters to the first democratically elected governor of Puerto Rico, Luis Muñoz Marín, in the late 1940s document the severe poverty and unemployment gripping the island. One group of women from the town of Vega Baja wrote the governor in March of 1949 explaining that 487 mothers and young women had been without work for over a year. As mothers responsible for families, they complained bitterly that locally available jobs went largely to women under thirty who did not have children to support. "In many cases, we find ourselves unable to send our children to school for lack of clothing and food," they protested. "What our husbands earn—those of us who have husbands—is not enough to support a home and at times our children go to bed without eating." They asked the governor to establish some type of industry in the area that would not discriminate against workers based on their age. They added that many men over the age of fifty—who also had families and children to feed—were without jobs as well.[45] The letter revealed the gendered concerns of women as mothers and, in some cases, wives and the widespread participation of Puerto Rican women in wage work outside the home.[46]

In contrast, another letter, from members of the United Evangelical Church of the Río Arriba *barrio* in the town of Fajardo, took a very different gendered perspective, that of male heads of households. The author informed the governor:

> The situation that the workers of this community and all the workers of Puerto Rico are facing is extremely desperate and anguished due to the scarcity of labor in the agricultural fields. It moves one to pity to see so many wretched, sickly, weak, and anemic, both workers as well as women and children. These heads of families ask for nothing other than work, work, and more work to earn a living. They do not ask for charity, food, medicine, or subsidies from the government.

The letter was signed by eighty-three men, congregants who demanded male employment and espoused a patriarchal solution to economic distress.[47]

The mayor of the town of Rincón, Manuel García, similarly supplicated the governor for assistance in several urgent telegrams. "The town's situation worsens every day because we lack industry," he explained. "I have between four and five thousand unemployed people who follow me day and night. . . . I am desperate in this situation." In another telegram, he again noted that "five thousand unemployed people beg for bread and local businesses have closed their doors to workers."[48] Many other letters to the governor described similar misery and hunger throughout the island during these years. It became clear that the infusion of American capital (i.e., modernization and development) did not deliver the much-promised economic panacea: it produced a surplus of workers who could not sustain themselves.[49]

As US economic policies failed to solve the unemployment problem, focus soon turned to the population itself. Officials began conjecturing that it was not a lack of employment but an oversupply of people that caused the island's problems. Puerto Rican women were held largely responsible for high fertility rates. The population needed to be dispersed in some way and population growth controlled. The temporary migration of workers (i.e., the separation of families) could theoretically slow population growth by delaying marriage or reproduction. Their migration as well as widespread sterilization campaigns promised to control the island's alleged overpopulation. As Laura Briggs argues, state-sponsored Puerto Rican migration was as much about controlling sexuality as it was about economic development. Siphoning off some of the island's unemployed assuaged the problem of providing jobs for so many.[50] The Puerto Rican government began small-scale migration experiments and began exploring migration as policy.

Contract Labor Arrives in Chicago

As a center of industrial production (steel, manufacturing), food processing (meatpacking, canning), and transportation routes (railroads), Chicago received many new workers during World War II. Mexican *braceros* began arriving shortly after the Bracero Program began. By May 1944, a reported six to eight thousand *braceros* were working on the railroads in the Chicago area. Between May 1943 and September 1945, over fifteen thousand *braceros* came to work in Chicago. They worked in the local area, and others came through on a number of lines, including the Santa Fe; the Illinois Central; the New York Central; the Pennsylvania; the Chicago, Burlington, and Quincy; the Chicago, Rock Island, and Pacific; the Chicago, Milwaukee, and Pacific; and the Chicago North Western.[51]

When they arrived, they found an established Mexican American com-

Figure 6. Mexican *braceros* doing railroad work. *Bracero Stories*, directed
by Patrick Mullins (Cherry Lane Productions, 2008), DVD.

munity that had lived in the city for more than two decades. In 1945, Mexican American leaders from the Mexican Civic Committee (MCC) brought attention to the population of several hundred contracted railroad *braceros* currently living and working in Chicago. At a May meeting of the Council of Social Agencies' Committee on Minority Groups, the chair, Horace Cayton, expressed concern over the men's work contracts and whether employers would allow local social service agencies to assist the men.[52] The committee invited Arthur Hillman of the Federal Security Agency to inform them about the workers. Hillman said that approximately eight hundred *braceros* currently worked in the Chicago area on the railroads. He explained that the War Manpower Commission made the initial arrangements, but that the Railroad Retirement Board was responsible for monitoring local work conditions. Hillman then shared a copy of the contract with the committee, "which indicated that the men were free to move about the community, make contacts with other groups, and bargain collectively."[53] This seemed to satisfy some of the committee's concerns, but it agreed to maintain communication with the Immigrants' Protective League and other social agencies to monitor the workers' status.[54]

That summer, local agencies such as the Immigrants' Protective League, Hull House, Henry Booth House, the Newberry Avenue Center, the Maxwell Street YMCA, Gads Hill Center, the University of Chicago Settlement House, and the South Chicago Community Center provided leisure activities and hospitality for the *braceros*. Horace Cayton noted at the Committee on Minority Groups' September 26 meeting, however, that "the committee had not yet been able to follow up [on] the question of the civil rights of this group."[55] By 1947, the Committee on Minority Groups had shifted its attention away from the now-defunct railroad Bracero Program and had established a more general Subcommittee on Special Problems of Mexicans in Chicago to address the more permanent Mexican and Mexican American population in the city.[56]

In addition to the men who worked under contracts locally on railroads, other *braceros* were often left stranded in the area and in need of help. In November 1945, Lucy Solano of the MCC reported on "the frequent calls coming . . . from Mexican workers stranded in Chicago, many of them . . . unable to speak English." Solano explained that local Mexican families temporarily took the men into their modest, crowded homes on the Near West Side. She identified four types of Mexican workers with which they had contact: "1. Contract laborers from farms who have broken contracts, and come to Chicago en route to another job or to Mexico. 2. Migratory workers, not on contracts. 3. Workers who have returned to Mexico and come back again to Chicago [undocumented return migrants]. 4. Residents of Chicago." The MCC did not track the number of people it served, however.[57] Frank Paz, head of the MCC, called an urgent meeting in June 1945 to respond to fifty workers who had been transported by rail from Mexico to the United States and were bound for agricultural work in Cedar Point, Wisconsin. Paz charged that their work contracts had been violated and they were stranded in the city without food.[58]

Throughout their tenure, *braceros* experienced many abuses. From uninhabitable converted chicken coops or shacks for housing to contaminated drinking water, verbal and physical abuse, and discrimination from employers and local residents, many *braceros* endured significant hardships while on contract. As early as March 1945, the Mexican consul general in Chicago complained to the president of Mexico "that the laborers were not being treated fairly in the region." Indeed, in 1951, President Harry Truman's Commission on Migrant Labor issued a report identifying severe problems with the agricultural Bracero Program, including employer abuses, lax enforcement of regulations, and deplorable living and working conditions. The commission's report ultimately recommended restricting the program. Labor activist Ernesto Galarza similarly noted in 1956, "In almost every area covered by the International Agreement, United States law, state law, and the provisions of the work contract, serious violations of the rights of Mexican nationals were found to be the norm rather than the exception." In the view of the growers and industries that profited from the use of low-wage Mexican labor, however, the program seemed to run fairly well.[59]

Kitty Calavita observes that for American growers, the Bracero Program was truly a dream. The program offered growers "a seemingly endless army of cheap, unorganized workers brought to their doorstep by the government."[60] Mexican laborers were essentially a captive population, required *by law* to work through their contracts. In a labor market that could be described as anything but free, workers could not compete with one another for wages, had little or no recourse for grievances or labor arbitration, and according to one union official, "no provision in [their] contract to join" a union.[61] Ironically, the President's Commission noted, growers had cried labor shortages for years, yet agricultural wages fell continuously during this period. They observed that during a labor shortage, wages should rise, not decline.[62]

Many workers chose to walk off, or "skip," their contracts rather than tolerate unbearable conditions. As one of the only alternatives available, this practice increased the circulation of undocumented Mexican workers in the United States.[63] Indeed, the number of "illegal aliens" circulating through the country grew commensurate with the number of contracted *braceros*. At times the difference between having a contract and working "illegally" could be negligible, as neither option provided many safeguards or protections. Indeed, the jobs offered to the majority of contracted labor migrants were also some of the least protected in the United States—agriculture and, as we will see in the case of Puerto Ricans, domestic work.[64] The imperatives of the Bracero Program resulted in contradictory public discourse and government policies. The nation injected essentially "unfree" temporary labor into its free market economy alongside the rhetoric of immigration control and restriction, especially by the 1950s.

Countless *braceros* whose contracts had ended or who had skipped their contracts came to Chicago, either in search of work or en route to other destinations.[65] Historian David Gutiérrez observes the irony that although American immigration policies aimed to restrict Mexican immigrants' mobility, the railroads gave workers more freedom to move about the country, skip contracts, or seek other jobs.[66] Some who eventually settled permanently in Chicago began on the railroad circuit. Twenty-year-old Felipe

Nava, for example, initially obtained a six-month contract to work on the New York Central Railroad in 1943 and was transported to Syracuse, New York, where he lived in a labor camp with approximately two hundred other Mexican men. After his contract expired, he signed up for others, including one at a roundhouse in Indiana. He later returned to Mexico to marry his sweetheart and eventually settled in Chicago, bringing his wife and oldest son to live with him.[67]

Many former *braceros* came to Chicago after returning to depressed labor markets in Mexico. Pedro Pineda had worked as a *bracero* on a ranch in Texas and had secured a visa after the Bracero Program ended. He came to the city on the advice of a cousin who was working there. Pineda found work, eventually married, and raised a family in Chicago. Countless other migrants in the 1960s, 1970s, and 1980s traced their routes to Chicago via the *bracero* migrations of fathers, grandfathers, or other male relatives who had spent time up north and thus facilitated subsequent family members' migrations.[68] Jesús García came to Chicago as a child in the 1960s because his father had migrated as a *bracero* in the late 1940s. When his contract expired, Mr. García returned north, working in California, Texas, and Kansas. He eventually secured legal residency in 1964, allowing him to bring his family to Chicago.[69] The number of Mexican immigrants legally admitted to Chicago from 1961 to 1965—less than ten thousand—belies a growing number who came without authorization.[70] As the United States increasingly restricted legal immigration from Mexico in 1965 and again in 1976, many continued following the paths worn by their predecessors, even without legal permits, and became part of the expanding class of "illegal" immigrants in the country.

Shortly after Mexican *braceros* began arriving, the first Puerto Rican contract laborers reached the city as well. In the fall of 1946, the Castle, Barton and Associates employment agency contracted nearly six hundred women and men as domestic, steel, and foundry workers.[71] Puerto Rican women began arriving in the city in stages beginning in September of that year. In total, well over three hundred women came to work as live-in domestics on such contracts. One married couple and one elderly man came among the group as well. With the cooperation of Puerto Rico's Department of Labor, the employment agency handled the arrangements and placements of the workers and outlined employment terms. The contracts for domestic work dictated the following: Workers were to be employed for a minimum of one year at a monthly wage of $60 (or $15 weekly). Room and board, and uniforms, if required, would be provided by the employer. Employees would receive one day off weekly and a half day on Sundays. Transportation from the airport in Chicago to the worksite would be provided free of charge. Both the employer and the employee would share the cost of air transportation from San Juan to Chicago ($150) and a $60 agency placement fee. The employee's share of the total costs ($105) would be deducted monthly from her paychecks. The women also had a requisite monthly deduction for return airfare after their contracts expired. In exchange for these terms, the worker agreed to present a medical certificate attesting to her good health and meet a number of other conditions. including relocating with her employer if the family moved away from the city.[72]

This employment resembled that of Mexican women as domestics in the Southwest, especially along the Texas-Mexico border. American housewives frequently sought Mexican women as household workers for their low cost, trainability, deferential character, and in some cases, deportability. The use of Mexican household workers was so common, in fact, that a 1959 publication entitled *Your Maid from Mexico* educated American women in the Southwest on how to train, manage, and handle their foreign housekeepers. In sharp contrast to the formalized importation agreements for Puerto Rican women domestics, however, Mexican immigrant women's domestic labor was not part of a large-scale state-sponsored program and was sometimes unauthorized.[73] The fact that the Bracero Program only recruited male workers revealed the concern over Mexican women's reproductive capacities—the possibility of their forming families in the United States and potentially staying there permanently. For Puerto Rican government officials, however, workers' permanent relocation to the mainland was generally desirable.

In Chicago, one newspaper writer positively endorsed the Puerto Rican domestic "experiment," praising the young women for their English language skills, their work ethic, and their cosmopolitan sophistication, contrasting these modern girls to the "drab old world matrons from Europe" who had traditionally been employed as domestics in the past.[74] The Puerto Rican women also received support from the local Young Women's Christian Association. When the Department of Labor in Puerto Rico initiated the work arrangements, the YWCA on the island contacted Chicago offices to alert them that several hundred women would be arriving in the city and would need assistance with urban adjustment and suitable social activities. The Chicago YWCA arranged for Thursday-afternoon teas and channeled the women toward acceptable forms of leisure.[75]

Nearly two hundred Puerto Rican men also arrived that September for industrial employment. The Chicago Hardware Foundry Company in North Chicago, thirty miles from the city, reportedly faced a labor shortage and struggled to find general laborers. The company's vice president flew to Puerto Rico and arranged to hire fifty-three men through the Castle, Barton and Associates agency. (An additional thirty-seven men came to work at a later date.) The men's contracts stipulated an hourly wage of 88.5 cents, the "standard American wage rate paid to other laborers in the plant."[76] The company also agreed to provide housing and meals for a fee. An article in the *Chicago Tribune* spoke highly of the workers, remarking that "many of the men speak English well" and many of them "were former GIs." Finally, a third group of approximately one hundred men contracted for work at the Inland Steel Corporation on the city's far south side. These workers received an hourly wage of 96.5 cents and had opportunities for overtime work as well. They were housed at a local hotel, for which they paid a fee, and were provided food at cost.[77]

In late October, Enrique Baiz Miró and forty-six of his fellow workers at the foundry sent a letter to the Puerto Rico Department of Labor complaining about living conditions and pay deductions. The Puerto Rico Department of Labor's commissioner, Manuel Pérez, responded to the letter noting that he had recently received a similar letter from another foundry worker and had explained the following: First, workers were free to provide their own meals if those provided by the company were unsatisfactory. The deductions about which workers complained had been set forth in their contracts; such deductions would pay for round-trip transportation from San Juan to Chicago and remittances to Puerto Rico, among other expenses that the workers might incur. Pérez explained that "the [Puerto Rico] Department of Labor . . . is happy to receive and handle all questions and complaints that our compatriots there may have at any moment, but workers are asked to read their contracts carefully once and again, before filing complaints or protestations regarding the conditions outlined therein." He further explained that prior to their departure, workers should have read the information provided regarding the vicissitudes of traveling to a foreign environment with new food, language, customs, and climate. "Acclimating to work such as that in a foundry, takes time even for those who are used to certain types of manual labor," he lectured. Pérez summarily dismissed the workers' complaints.[78]

By December of that year, however, complaints from the foundry workers and now the domestics mounted, and they had found local allies willing to help them.[79] A small group of Puerto Rican students and other sympathizers at the University of Chicago took an interest in the workers and publicly exposed their labor conditions. The group included Munita Muñoz Lee, daughter of Luis Muñoz Marín, then president of the Puerto Rican Senate and soon to be elected governor of the island. As the Senate president's daughter, Muñoz Lee had "promised [the workers] to personally get the information to [him] as soon as possible." The group also included two Puerto Rican graduate students, Milton Pabón and Elena Padilla, who would go on to become distinguished scholars in economics and anthropology, respectively. White students from a group called United Student Progressives joined the cause as well. The students investigated the workers' complaints and prepared a preliminary report based on their findings. They also joined more than fifty domestic workers, and supporters from the Workers Defense League in protesting and picketing Castle, Barton and Associates' offices. In a letter to a San Juan newspaper, *El Imparcial*, the students denounced the employment agency, the Illinois Department of Labor, and the Puerto Rico Department of Labor for the workers' appalling conditions.[80]

Their preliminary report outlined various problems. First, workers had been read their employment contracts for the first and only time at the Puerto Rico Department of Labor office in San Juan just minutes before leaving for the airport. Officials instructed them to sign the contracts immediately. Second, labor officials had failed to verify that workers met the minimum age requirement of eighteen years and thus allowed several underage girls to come on the work contracts. Officials had also failed to check health certificates attesting that migrants were in good health. As a result, company doctors at the foundry sent some men back to the island upon examining them. Finally, the men at the foundry suffered in horribly substandard housing: much like many Mexican *braceros*, they lived in railroad cars that had inadequate heating, dangerous conditions, and the barest of bedding.[81]

Also at issue were the workers' wages. While the Department of Labor stated that the work contract "is not written with the intention of establishing work norms or practices that are lower than the prevailing norms or standards in the city of Chicago," the domestic workers' weekly wage of $15.00 significantly undercut the going rate in the city. Contracts did not stipulate the number of work hours expected; thus, some women worked as many as fifteen hours a day. In the case of the foundry workers, excessive deductions were taken from their paychecks. The following deductions were taken from the men's standard weekly check of $35.40 for forty hours of work: $9.45 for meals, $3.50 for housing, $5.00 for airfare and employment agency commissions, $8.85 in family remittances, $2.00 held in escrow for return transportation to the island, and $0.35 for Social Security. This did not include federal and state income taxes and charges for clothing from the company store. Workers regularly received paychecks for as little as $1.00 for a week's work. Castle, Barton and Associates justified the workers' low wages "on the fact that they were earning much more than what they could ever earn in Puerto Rico."[82] The labor commissioner echoed this defense. Such arguments did not take into account the difference in cost of living from one location to another—in particular, the cost of buying winter clothes—or the airfare, agency commissions, and other costs that migrants incurred.

Munita Muñoz Lee forwarded the report to her father, San Juan's *El Imparcial*, and Labor Commissioner Manuel Pérez. In a letter to her father, she eloquently and astutely captured the dire conditions and unreasonable costs that labor migrants endured.

> None of the undersigned of this report are opposed in principle to emigration as a way of resolving the problems of Puerto Rico. We believe that such current emigration in which workers are sent under a contract that does not protect their rights, at such a personal cost that makes them unable to maintain a minimum standard of living according to the prevailing norms in the location where they migrated, and to the least protected jobs under the law (such as in the case of domestic workers), does not help resolve this problem.[83]

The students' exposé of the migration debacle became a public scandal in Puerto Rico and, indeed, an embarrassment to the Puerto Rico Department of Labor. *El Imparcial* published several articles on the issue, including excerpts from the students' report and editorials. In letters to his daughter, Muñoz Marín praised her and the Puerto Rican students for defending and advocating on behalf of their compatriots.[84] Labor Commissioner Manuel Peréz, however, was none too pleased with the students' impertinence. In a letter to Luis Muñoz Marín, Pérez expressed his disapproval of the students' activities, "supposedly in favor of the workers who come from Puerto Rico." He explained, "I fear that the actions of these youths, as well intentioned as they may be, might hamper the migration projects that were beginning to unfold quite satisfactorily."[85] As a Department of Labor official, Peréz was concerned primarily with keeping avenues open for further migration. The negative publicity might dissuade the state of Illinois's Department of Labor and prospective employers from contracting Puerto Ricans in the future.

When he responded to Munita Muñoz Lee's letter, Pérez asked for concrete evidence of the charges the students made—names and addresses of employees and employers, and detailed evidence of the workers' wages, hours, and working and living conditions. In a rather underhanded way of chastising their involvement in labor issues, Peréz challenged the students to

> inform this Department about the most advantageous employment opportunities that Puerto Rican men and women might be able to obtain in Chicago and if those jobs could be secured through contracts. This would be a great help that you would be making to our country, where we have so many people unemployed and living in misery, despite all the great efforts that the government is making.[86]

Finally, the labor commissioner wrote a lengthy letter to the newspaper defending the department and explaining its position on the entire case. Peréz explained that the agency negotiated the contracts for workers, clearly outlining proposed salaries, work hours, length of contract, and arrangements for food and lodging, among other provisions. The agency, he argued, had not failed in its duty to apprise migrants of the terms of their employment in the United States, nor had it neglected to ascertain that all workers were healthy and of legal age to work. The department did not know of any underage migrants working in the United States and demanded proof of this allegation. Peréz further claimed that "the Department of Labor ha[d] not received to date any specific and direct complaint or protest from workers who have gone to Chicago." On the contrary, he claimed, the department had received only positive, salutary letters from workers "expressing that workers were well and satisfied with their jobs." He conveniently omitted, of course, the letter from Baiz and forty-six fellow foundry workers.[87]

Commissioner Peréz further absolved his agency of any obligation to the migrants. He explained that workers signed contracts of their own free will, fully informed of what their contracts entailed. Instead, he explained, "the role of the Department is to see that contracts are made according to law and outline reasonable salary, work, and housing conditions." Peréz's letter included a homily on the widespread unemployment on the island and the significance of employment opportunities in the United States in alleviating the problem. He described the wages both domestic and foundry workers received, asking, "If some workers work few hours (due to sickness or any other reason, including being on a picket line) and if after covering their living expenses and sending remittances to family they are left with little or no money, whose fault is that?" Or, he asked sardonically, "do they have a better opportunity in Puerto Rico to cover their living expenses?"[88]

While the University of Chicago students had begun the investigation into the workers' conditions, they soon secured the help of a public official from the island. Carmen Isales, a social worker in Puerto Rico's Department of Health, Division of Public Welfare had been vacationing in Chicago when the labor problems unfolded. She decided to take a leave of absence from her post and stayed in Chicago for several weeks to assist in the matter. She followed up on the students' preliminary research, investigating the workers' case in greater detail, and produced a report of her own. Isales interviewed thirty of the domestic workers through the social gatherings at the YWCA and researched local wage rates and labor standards. Her reports echoed the students' initial observations. Isales explained that the wage paid to Puerto Rican women was significantly lower than the average wage of $25 to $35 advertised in local newspaper job listings. This represented a racially based wage differential, she explained. White women earned "no less than $35 and sometimes as much as $40 a week," she observed. "Colored" women earned $25 a week "because they are discriminated against." Puerto Rican women, however, earned only $15 weekly. Almost all of the women interviewed complained of excessive work. In one case, an employer gradually dismissed two other employees after hiring her Puerto Rican domestic. "Now, for $60 she does the work of three people: a nanny, a cook and a housekeeper," Isales remarked.[89]

Isales also visited the foundry workers and found their conditions to be deplorable. Workers lacked adequate clothing for the winter cold and were forced to buy it at inflated prices from a company store. The boxcars that served as their housing were dangerous and unfit for human habitation. "Who knows?" she wrote with acrimony. "Perhaps, as some have claimed, the men lived like this or even worse in Puerto Rico but the fact is that here they must pay $3.50 weekly for this hovel, in addition to $9.45 weekly for meals." After deductions, the men's weekly paychecks were a pittance. Isales testified, "I have held in my hand paychecks for 60 cents and 86 cents. One worker told me that after receiving a check for 26 cents he tore it into pieces." The local steelworkers union took an interest in the men, admitted them to the union without charging them dues, and began working on their case.[90] Unlike the women, the male foundry workers at least found some union protection and advocacy. Unfortunately, the union was unable or unwilling to help the workers, citing that no conditions in the contracts had been violated.[91]

Isales dissected the employment contract line by line, demonstrating that the contracts were not "worth the paper [they were] written on." First, the stated wage for domestics of $60.00 monthly or $15.00 weekly failed to account for the fact that each month includes approximately 4.33 weeks. The women were rightfully entitled to a monthly wage of $64.90. Second, Isales pointed out that the contract required employers to abide by all state and federal labor laws; yet "domestic labor is not protected in Illinois by any labor laws either at the federal or state level, such as social security, minimum wage protections, maximum work hours, medical care, or accident insurance. Nor is it protected by any labor unions." Third, Isales revealed that workers were not adequately informed about their work contracts and did not understand their terms. Isales highlighted the Department of Labor's complicity in promoting utterly worthless work contracts. "If the Department's purpose is to guarantee the best work conditions . . . and the contract was carefully examined, how could it possibly have accepted [such a faulty] agreement?" she asked.[92]

In January of 1947, Vicente Géigel Polanco, head of the Puerto Rican Senate's Labor Committee, traveled to the city to investigate the case of the workers and to mollify the public criticism that by now circulated around the issue of contract migration. Géigel worried mainly about maintaining good relations with the Illinois Department of Labor and potential future employers to keep migration avenues open. He also sought to develop appropriate legislation in Puerto Rico that would avoid such turmoil in the future. Initially, a Chicago newspaper reported that Géigel corroborated the findings of both the students and the social worker, citing that the domestic workers earned much less than local American maids. He commented, however, that other complaints about food being different and the weather being too cold were trivial. When Géigel cabled Luis Muñoz Marín, he noted that "living conditions [were] pretty good." A San Juan newspaper similarly quoted Géigel as saying that conditions in Chicago were "not that bad." He concluded that the main problem was the poor selection of workers and their lack of training. In other words, labor conditions were not to blame; the department simply needed to find Puerto Ricans who would more willingly accept these conditions. The Puerto Rican Senate subsequently developed stricter legislation to help control this issue.[93]

Since before the turn of the century, islanders had been migrating to New York City, and consequently, it was home to the largest Puerto Rican population on the mainland.[94] As migration accelerated, however, local officials and residents began blaming the swelling migrant population for various social ills. Puerto Ricans reportedly had high rates of dependence on public assistance; they had formed ghetto communities; and they proved difficult to "assimilate." A series of articles asserted this in New York papers in October 1947.[95] The Department of Labor quickly initiated a public relations campaign to refute such charges and resolved to disperse the migrant population to other parts of the continent. It looked to Chicago as a city that offered employment opportunities and still had low numbers of Puerto Rican migrants. It determined, however, that it needed a more systematic approach to large-scale migration.

In 1947 the insular government established a Migration Division, housed within the Department of Labor's Bureau of Employment and Migration. The first office and administrative headquarters on the mainland opened in New York City. There, social scientists and government bureaucrats embarked upon the scientific study of Puerto Rican labor migration. Publicly, the insular government took a neutral position, "neither encourag[ing] or discourag[ing] migration." Its Migration Division, it explained, only offered migrants information and assistance in adjusting to their new locales.[96] Despite the official rhetoric, however, migration figured prominently in its solution to unemployment and overpopulation.

The Migration Division opened a midwestern regional office in Chicago in January of 1949.[97] The office aimed to scout the area for employment opportunities and negotiate labor contracts to bring workers to the region. Public relations constituted an important part of migration campaigns. The Migration Division regularly publicized job opportunities, thereby channeling labor migration to particular industries and regions. It soon established offices in Cleveland, Hartford, Philadelphia, and Rochester. The division negotiated agricultural labor contracts in New York, Connecticut, Ohio, New Jersey, and Pennsylvania. As it secured more contracts, placement rates increased significantly. Within a span of five years, the Department of Labor had increased its placements over fourfold, from just over three thousand workers in 1947 to more than fourteen thousand in 1953.

Puerto Rico's Department of Labor, in cooperation with the United States Employment Service (USES), began placing Puerto Rican workers on farms in the continental United States to harvest tobacco, tomatoes, apples, cherries, sugar beets, onions, green beans, and other crops, mainly in the Northeast and Midwest. By 1953, the department increasingly began placing workers in industrial positions such as on railroads and in factories.[98] Through newspaper advertisements, educational films, and other forms of publicity, the Migration Division stressed the many advantages and benefits of traveling to the mainland on a state-issued labor contract.[99] Much like the government of Mexico and its *bracero* contracts, however, the Puerto Rican government could not or did not effectively protect its workers against abuses, low wages, and poor working conditions. Similarly, the jobs offered to the majority of contracted labor migrants were some of the least protected and most exploited in the United States—agriculture and domestic work. Yet workers made their own choices, leaving agricultural labor camps and live-in domestic situations for greater autonomy and higher earnings. Many continued looking to Chicago for better opportunities.

Mexican Americans, Puerto Ricans, and "Illegal" Labor in Chicago

Puerto Ricans, *braceros*, and other Mexican migrants arrived in Chicago to find an established Mexican American community that had been present in the city since World War I. Chicago's Mexican American community seemed welcoming to Mexican immigrant laborers initially. Local organizations such as the Mexican Civic Committee (MCC), the Mexican Welfare Council, and the Mexican Patriotic Committee took an interest in the welfare of recent arrivals. Indeed, they felt sympathies and affinities with the *braceros*. As leaders of the MCC noted, "The Mexican population of Chicago has long occupied the status of a labor reserve . . . utilized in times of need and displaced in times of low production."[100] This described quite accurately the present role of *braceros* in the United States, but it was a status that Mexican Americans in Chicago had held for over two decades. If the example of what earlier Mexican immigrants and their children could achieve within a generation was any indication of recent migrants' potential futures, then the outlook was bleak. Thousands of Mexican immigrants and their US-citizen children had been deported or repatriated during the Great Depression. Those who remained, however, had not fared very well in the local labor market. In 1935, one survey found that 66 percent of Mexicans occupied unskilled jobs compared to 31 percent of native-born whites, 35 percent of foreign-born whites, and 58 percent of African Americans. Only 5 percent of Mexicans held skilled positions compared to 35 percent of foreign-born whites. Mexicans had much higher unemployment rates as well: 30 percent were unemployed.[101] This racially based differential in employment seemingly affected Mexicans as severely as African Americans, if not more, at least during the Depression. Moreover, these figures reflected a Mexican labor force that had been reduced already by repatriation and deportation.

Nearly fifteen years later, the employment status of Mexican Americans had changed little. At a 1949 conference entitled "The Status of the Mexican American in Chicago," Mexican American leader Frank Paz described the position of ethnic Mexicans in the local labor market and the racial discrimination that kept them in the lowest positions. Why, he asked, were there no Mexican brakemen, conductors, firemen, or switchmen on the railroads? "There is nothing wrong with working as a railroad section hand," he asserted, "but when a group of people are branded for employment only in one particular task there is something radically wrong." He cited similar patterns in the steel mills and packinghouses: Mexicans worked only in the dirtiest, most dangerous, lowest-paid, and unskilled jobs. Why did they hold no positions within the Steel Workers Union? Citing a 1927 report, which stated that Mexicans occupied only unskilled jobs in these industries, he asked why they had not been able to move up the occupational ladder despite more than three decades in Chicago.[102] Paz magnified the subtle and often invisible systemic exclusions that Mexicans experienced as a population. While this may not have mirrored the experience of African Americans, who faced unabashed employment discrimination and exclusion, this contrasted dramatically with European immigrants, most of whom had education levels comparable to Mexicans and also started in the lowest entry-level employment but had gradually ascended into skilled work.

The existing Mexican population in Chicago, which included many second-generation Mexican Americans, faced a variety of obstacles. Mexican American leaders struggled to be recognized as a minority group in the city. They expressed sympathy and took on the cause of Mexican immigrants' welfare, but were ill equipped to help since Mexican Americans had lived in the city for years, adapted to American life, but still faced tremendous economic insecurity.[103] They also encountered many incoming *Tejanos*, or Texas Mexican Americans, who looked for work in Chicago as the competition from *braceros* in the agricultural fields pushed many out of the migrant labor stream.[104] Northern industrial employment offered higher wages, but the cost of urban living was also much higher (especially the cost of housing), and industrial work provided little job security in times of economic downturns or production slowdowns. For the most recently hired, layoffs could be all too common.

Many Mexican Americans had a long history of working on local railroads. Mexican men had been recruited by railroads as early as 1916. Mexican American women also became a labor source during World War II shortages. When the de la Llata family arrived in the city in 1954, Andres de la Llata found his first job at a nearby rail yard. After experiencing the harshness of working outdoors in Chicago's bitter winters, however, he left the rails and found work instead at a cold-storage facility that warehoused the city's incoming produce. The physical labor was demanding and it still required working in cold conditions, but it was significantly better than being outside.[105] Railroad work, particularly the track labor for which Mexicans were hired, could be extremely dangerous and even fatal. In March of 1944, the *Chicago Tribune* reported that four Mexican track workers were struck by a New York Central train in South Chicago. The men's names and addresses suggest that they might have been longtime residents. Despite such dangers, the railroads continued to be an important employer for the newly arrived.[106]

As undocumented immigration increased during the Bracero Program, Mexican Americans in Chicago began grappling with this new category of immigrant as well. Leaders seemed to remain sympathetic to *braceros* but were more ambivalent about "illegal" Mexican immigrants. In a February 1953 newsletter, the Mexican American Council (MAC) expressed its opinion regarding the distinctions between Mexican immigrants it considered to have a lawful right to be in the city and "illegal immigrants":

> The so-called "braceros" or contract laborers who came to this country to work but who decided to remain need the help and advice of an organization such as the Mexican American Council. Since this group came to the U.S. through contract they should be considered as legal entrants. On the other hand, there is the great number of "wetbacks" or illegal Mexican nationals living in the Chicago metropolitan area. According to Marcus T. Neeley, district director of immigration and naturalization, there are some 9,000 "wetbacks" residing in this area. Frankly, there is not much that can be done on their behalf. Nevertheless, there is a social, economic, and cultural problem which exists because of this group.[107]

The MAC drew a fine line between government-sanctioned labor migration and that which occurred organically. Like other Mexican American leaders of the time in the Southwest (the League of United Latin American Citizens [LULAC], the American GI Forum), MAC increasingly distanced itself from undocumented Mexican immigrants.[108] The irony, of course, was that they or their parents may very well have been undocumented immigrants just a generation earlier.

As citizens of the United States, Puerto Ricans enjoyed greater ease in migrating. A report on Puerto Rican migration published in 1955 made the argument that this movement of people was no different from the domestic migration of other groups:

> The mass migration of Puerto Ricans to the mainland of the United States is characteristic of the contemporary American pattern. In the past few decades we have been witnessing several mass movements of people within the boundaries of the United States and her territorial possessions [including American Indian reservations]. These are people whose homes, for the most part, no longer can sustain them economically. The drought-ravaged dust bowl made the "Okies" the nomads of the Southwest; the social inequities in the South have sent thousands upon thousands of Southern Negroes swarming to the Northern industrial cities, and Mexican-Americans whose employment waxes and wanes with harvest on Southwestern farms and orchards, also are seeking more permanent living conditions in the cities.[109]

Puerto Ricans could travel freely with or without labor contracts and did not have to register with authorities to seek permission for their travel. The Puerto Rico Department of Labor, however, did attempt to regulate migration by creating a category of "illegal labor recruitment" within its administration to privilege state-sanctioned migration arranged through the department's labor contracts over informal labor recruitment done on the island directly by employers, relatives, or friends. There was no enforcement, much less penalty, however, for islanders who headed to the mainland on their own without first stopping at the Puerto Rico Department of Labor offices for a work contract.

Mexicans, in contrast, either needed to have a *bracero* permit or other visa to cross the border legally or attempted to travel undetected by immigration officials or the Border Patrol. In fact, the regulation and supervision of their migration were often arbitrary, haphazard, and contradictory. At times throughout the Bracero Program, Immigration and Naturalization Service (INS) and Border Patrol officials practiced what Manuel García y Griego calls a "flexible approach to the enforcement of immigration law." Many employers, especially those in border regions, openly hired and recruited undocumented workers while the INS and Border Patrol officials simply looked the other way or relaxed enforcement practices. In other cases, officials violated their own laws by converting illegal immigrants into *braceros* as labor demands dictated. Mexican immigrants were thus at the whim of the state's immigration apparatus. The requirement of authorization for entry into the United States was irregularly and inconsistently enforced, and the Bracero Program operated within a nexus of fundamental contradictions in American immigration and labor policies: the guest worker program dramatically increased illegal immigration during its twenty-two-year existence. As has been well documented, many growers welcomed, even preferred, undocumented workers.[110] At the same time, the program was increasingly accompanied by stringent roundup and deportation procedures, especially in the 1950s.

When public outcry demanded control of the emerging "wetback crisis," government officials obliged with highly publicized campaigns. In 1954, officials initiated a large-scale effort to round up and remove "illegal aliens" (over 1 million total) from the United States. This massive deportation campaign, called "Operation Wetback," began in June in the southwestern United States. By the middle of September, it had reached the Midwest. On September 18, 1954, immigration officials in Chicago arrested fifty Mexican "illegal aliens" and flew them to Brownsville, Texas, for deportation. Walter A. Sahli, the district director of immigration and naturalization in Chicago, headed the campaign. His office set up 150 cots in a holding facility to house immigrants awaiting deportation. Such efforts served to quell public anxieties over "illegal" Mexican immigrants at the same time that they justified and reaffirmed national hysteria. This contradiction in United States immigration policy made it very clear that "Mexicans were welcomed as laborers but not as permanent residents seeking citizenship status."[111]

Deportation drives did not affect only recent unauthorized immigrants. Those who had crossed the border prior to 1924, when there was little to no regulation of Mexican immigrants, were completely unaware that they had become "illegal" as the laws changed. One man, Silverio N[a]varro-Jarco, had entered the United States without being processed in 1921 and had been living in Chicago for decades. Now fifty years old, Navarro-Jarco worked as a dishwasher and lived on Madison and Halsted streets, in the heart of a growing Puerto Rican enclave on the Near West Side. Immigrants like him who had lived in the United States for so long had the possibility of avoiding deportation and being repatriated "voluntarily" or seeking legal channels to stay in the country. When news of the deportation sweeps reached them, many chose to turn themselves in rather than be ambushed in raids (fig. 7). Immigration director Sahli reported that in one day, 172 Mexican immigrants appeared at his office "seeking letters to allow them to return voluntarily."[112]

Operation Wetback initiated a period of terror and harassment not only

Figure 7. "Mexican men in line at post office awaiting deportation [1954]. Immigration officer Walter Sahli and detention officer Carl Preston at right." ICHi-59815, Chicago History Museum.

for Mexican "illegal aliens," but for anyone who law enforcement officials suspected might be "illegal." Even years after the 1954 campaign, repression against Mexican immigrants continued. Local police indiscriminately harassed anyone who might appear to be an "illegal alien," including Puerto Ricans. Although Puerto Ricans were citizens, most Americans could not distinguish them from Mexicans. Police routinely stopped and questioned anyone who looked "Mexican." One Puerto Rican man, Roberto Medina, recalled that as a teenager in the 1960s, he and others experienced harassment regularly. He notes, "If the police saw you in a car (I have my own personal experiences of this) they would pull you out and ask if you were a 'wet back' because at that time everybody was a 'wet back.' . . . They would just pull you out of your car, totally violate your civil rights, search your car, hit you with their sticks, and just harass you."[113] Puerto Ricans could not be deported and did not face compulsory deportation after their work terms expired. Still, employers sometimes mistakenly threatened them with deportation, as in the case of one of the domestic workers in Chicago who complained about her work assignment. A staff person at Castle, Barton and Associates threatened to deport her, but ultimately, there was no legal basis for this. Puerto Ricans thus enjoyed some security in the fact that they *could not* be deported. In contrast, aggrieved Mexican workers left their jobs under penalty of capture and detention. In one case, *bracero* deserters were arrested and detained in a local Chicago jail for several weeks for having abandoned their jobs.[114] Regardless of their origins and legal status, Mexicans and Puerto Ricans both became subjects of surveillance by the very state that had so eagerly recruited them as workers.

Conclusion

Throughout the 1950s, 1960s, and 1970s, Mexican immigrants—both men and women—entered unskilled or semiskilled manufacturing work where many employers welcomed them regardless of legal status. The availability of workers became such common knowledge that local factories such as Zenith Corporation, Western Electric, Motorola, National Video Corp., National Radio Co., Florsheim Shoe, and food processors such as Nabisco, Jays Potato Chips, Wilson, Swift, and others, regularly approached pastors at Spanish-speaking Catholic parishes when they were hiring. They also employed US-born Mexican Americans and Puerto Ricans.[115] With notable exceptions in steel and meatpacking, Mexican Americans and Puerto Ricans were often excluded from unions and, in general, increasingly became part of a nonunionized industrial labor force. Ironically, however, industrial employment opportunities began diminishing. From 1955 to 1965, the Mid-Chicago Industrial Development Area lost four hundred companies (more than seventy thousand jobs).[116] Industrial flight to regions with even cheaper labor (both in the United States and abroad) meant fewer jobs, a growing surplus of workers, and precipitously declining wages.[117] This would make it more difficult for (im)migrants to achieve economic mobility and more likely that they would retain their racial and class location as low-wage laborers. How would they integrate among other Chicagoans? What kinds of relations did they encounter with longtime residents? Where did Mexicans and Puerto Ricans fit in the social landscape? These are the topics of the next chapter.

TWO

Putting Down Roots: Mexican and Puerto Rican Settlement on the Near West Side, 1940–60

The population of this area . . . has always been very heterogeneous. It has been occupied by successive waves of immigrants, as the older Irish and German groups moved farther west and northwest. They were replaced by Italians, Poles, Russians, Greeks, and Mexicans. The latter, since 1960 has been the second largest foreign group after the Italians. As the Puerto Ricans represent another important group, together they make this area a typical "Latin American district."

—Marta Isabel Kollman de Curutchet, 1967[1]

Our program consists of welcoming newcomers especially from Mexico, Puerto Rico and Texas in every way. Helping them adjust to their new neighborhood, interpreting letters, filling in applications . . . army questionnaires, offering them English classes, telling them of openings in factories. . . . These people are welcome to what little material resources are in our hands.

—Cordi Marian Settlement, 1957[2]

When the de la Llata family came to Chicago from Mexico in 1954, they arrived, like most immigrants did, at the home of relatives. Mrs. de la Llata's sister and brother-in-law received the family of five in their small apartment in the Taylor Street neighborhood on the city's Near West Side. The family would stay there until they could get settled, orient themselves adequately, and find housing of their own. They remarked at their good fortune when they found an apartment two doors down in the rear building of an Italian landlord. Finding housing among Italians was not always easy, as they sometimes did not have good relations with Mexicans. Moreover, housing quality in the neighborhood was not the best. The apartment did not have a private bathroom, for example, as many buildings still lacked full indoor plumbing. Still, the de la Llatas were grateful that they had found a place to live and would have relatives and friends nearby.

The Near West Side was also ideal because it was not far from the railroads where Mr. de la Llata had found work. While he worked at the rail yard, and later for another nearby employer, Mrs. de la Llata tended to the children and their home. Being a savvy woman, she quickly discovered local resources to help her in her role as mother and homemaker. She found the Infant Welfare Clinic, where she took her small children for vaccinations and medical care. She began learning English in adult education classes at a local elementary school. Perhaps the greatest treasure of all was Jane Addams's Hull House. The beloved local settlement house had provided assistance to immigrants for generations. When they were old enough, the de la Llata children began attending after-school and summer programs there. They took music and art classes, went on field trips, and skated at the settlement's roller rink. Rosa de la Llata, the family's oldest daughter, remembers her time in the neighborhood and Hull House fondly. "I loved growing up on Taylor Street and going to Hull House. We had wonderful experiences there," she recalled. "It gave our family the chance to learn new things, enjoy recreational activities, and spend time with other children and adults in the community."[3] The socialization immigrants experienced at Hull House and the contacts they made there would prove useful as they navigated their way through the multiethnic and rapidly changing neighborhood.

The Near West Side had been a port of entry since the mid-nineteenth century, shortly after the city consolidated and expelled native Potawatomi Indians. Germans, Irish, Poles, Bohemians, Russian and Romanian Jews, Gypsies, Italians, and others all settled in the area over the nineteenth and early twentieth centuries. As they secured upward mobility, most moved on to better accommodations, leaving the most recent ethnic colonies behind. By World War I, this included growing numbers of southern African Americans and Mexicans.

The Near West Side housed one of the oldest Mexican communities in Chicago. During World War I, nearby railroad yards began recruiting Mexican immigrants to the area. They and their children joined the throngs of southern and eastern Europeans who huddled near Hull House and tried to make the best of slum conditions. By World War II, the longtime Mexican American settlement had survived deportations and repatriations during the Great Depression and established various organizations and civic groups to improve their members' living conditions. The second generation, in particular, seemingly tried to follow the path of their Euro-American neighbors toward assimilation and acceptance by white Americans, but they faced serious obstacles to economic security. The majority of Mexican Americans had struggled for three decades and still had not achieved the stability that most European immigrants had attained. During the war, moreover, they began encountering growing numbers of new (im)migrants—Mexican *braceros* (recent Mexican immigrants both with and without papers), *Tejanos* (Texas Mexican Americans), and Puerto Ricans. As they arrived in the city, the Near West Side became their primary port of entry. The newcomers were drawn to the centrally located neighborhood by the ethnic familiarity of the Mexican American population and the availability of Spanish-speaking services—Catholic and Protestant churches, grocery stores, and other small businesses. Though they settled in other areas as well—the Near North Side, South Chicago, Back of the Yards, West Town, and Woodlawn—the Near West Side was the most prominent settlement. By 1953, the year before the de la Llatas arrived, the neighborhood had an estimated twenty-eight thousand "Spanish-speaking"[4] people. By the end of the decade, it housed nearly 20 percent of all Mexicans and Puerto Ricans in Chicago, the largest concentration in the city.[5]

When the postwar (im)migrants arrived, they found a worn and weary district layered with the grime of earlier generations. The Near West Side was also an extremely heterogeneous social environment. By the forties, Italian, Mexican, and African Americans and smaller numbers of Greeks and Eastern European Jews comprised the area's largest ethnic and racial groups.[6] Soon, Puerto Ricans arrived as well. Relations among such diverse people could at times be harmonious but just as often proved tense and volatile. Naturally, Mexicans and Puerto Ricans tried to fit into the frequently divided ethnoracial[7] landscape in the most advantageous ways possible. As they navigated the terrain of the neighborhood and the city, each experienced a variable and shifting social status and position vis-à-vis local institutions, social service providers, multiracial neighbors, and one another. They found a racial hierarchy that had very clearly defined poles of black and white but that had an ambiguous and unstable middle, where they sometimes could claim an ethnic identity much like "hyphenated" European Americans but could just as easily be perceived as racially distinct (foreign and *nonwhite*) and occupy a position closer to African Americans. The grounds on which these distinctions were made for Mexicans and Puerto Ricans could be rather opaque and contingent upon who was making these judgments. Ethnic and racial identity, as scholars have suggested, consists of "imputed" or "observed" race or ethnicity (that is, how others perceive and treat a group) as well as internal or self-fashioned identities (how an individual or group perceives itself).[8] Mexicans and Puerto Ricans thus had to make sense of their own identities in relation to others at the same time that they were being assigned sometimes competing and contradictory labels by their neighbors and by the state.

Unbeknownst to them, the de la Llatas arrived at a moment of increasing anxiety among city officials and the public over the growing number of Spanish-speaking (im)migrants in the city. In the midst of an economic recession after the Korean War, both Mexican and Puerto Rican migrants became targets of suspicion and scorn, though for very different reasons. The county welfare commissioner had decried the influx of Puerto Ricans, who, he claimed, put a strain on local relief rolls. Similarly, local newspapers regularly reported on the "wetback" invasion of Mexican "illegal aliens," who purportedly took American jobs and depressed wages. The crisis had gained national attention by 1954. The Immigration and Naturalization Service's nationwide "Operation Wetback" campaign reached Chicago, rounding up hundreds of unauthorized Mexican immigrants. As in other periods of distress, native-born Americans looked upon the most recent newcomers and foreigners as the cause of economic decline.

The Near West Side

The geographical unit designated by University of Chicago sociologists as the Near West Side (Community Area 28)[9] was one of the oldest sections in the city, located immediately west and south of the downtown business district, or "the Loop" (see fig. 1). As European Americans began colonizing the area in the nineteenth century, it rapidly became a port of entry for immigrants. As such, it was characterized by the layering of ethnic groups, each of which settled, worked for nearby employers, endured the slum conditions, and then moved on to better environs. Shortly after the city's incorporation in 1837, the swampy northeastern section became home to northern and western European immigrants (Irish and Germans). Dilapidated wooden shacks provided crude shelter for their teeming denizens. The impoverished and overcrowded conditions were so dangerous that they led to the first event that made the area famous, the Great Chicago Fire of 1871. The conflagration nearly obliterated the entire city, and newspaper accounts traced its origins back to a poor Irishwoman's shack in the congested immigrant district.[10]

In the late nineteenth century, Russian, Polish, and German Jews began forming an enclave around Halsted and Maxwell Streets. Over forty synagogues dotted the neighborhood. As Jews continued to move in and the area became a crowded ghetto, the wealthiest residents fled farther northwest, building luxurious brownstone mansions along Jackson Boulevard near Ashland Avenue. By the turn of the century, eastern and southern Europeans—both Jews and Gentiles—dominated the poorer sections. Greeks, continuing influxes of Russian, Romanian, and Polish Jews, and the latest group—Italians—crowded the neighborhood. These new immigrants settled in deteriorated tenement buildings, which lacked plumbing or sewage systems. The neighborhood soon became well known for social reformer Jane Addams, who chose it for her social settlement work and established the renowned Hull House in 1889. There, Addams, along with other upper-middle-class, white, Protestant women, advocated for the immigrant poor as they sought to Americanize them.[11]

Distinct areas of the neighborhood were known by their ethnic composition. By the early 1900s, the intersection of Maxwell and Halsted Streets became the heart of Jewish commercial activities, known in later years simply as "Jewtown." The center of business in the area, and the attraction that drew thousands of people from near and far, was the Maxwell Street Market, an enormous open-air bazaar. There, vendors set up stalls to sell fruits and vegetables, clothing, tools, and an assortment of other new and used goods, while nonambulatory businesses offered live poultry, fish, housewares, anything a person might need. Carolyn Eastwood notes that Maxwell Street provided a means of making a living as well as a central location for local residents to obtain low-cost necessities and other consumer goods. One man described the market as "'a poor man's [sic] paradise.'"[12] By the 1950s, Mexicans and Puerto Ricans walked among Italians, Greeks, Arabs, Gypsies, Jews, and African Americans in the public bazaar, where folks gathered to bargain, barter, sing, eat, preach the gospel, listen to music, and make a living (fig. 8).

Italian immigrants became associated with "Taylor Street," the main thoroughfare that bisected their settlement.[13] Their colony soon became famous (or notorious) for such contrasting figures as Prohibition-era gangster Al Capone and the lesser known Mother Cabrini, who established a hospital for Italian immigrants nearby and was named the first American saint. As it did with other national groups, the Chicago Archdiocese established Italian Catholic parishes, such as Holy Guardian Angel and Our Lady of Pompeii. By the mid-1920s, Italians had wrested some political power from the Irish and began to vote their own candidates into office. By then, they had become the most numerous and politically dominant group in the area, though they never quite reached a majority.[14]

Figure 8. Street scene of Maxwell Street Market, 1964. *And This Is Free*, directed by Mike Shea (Shanachie Entertainment Corp., 1965, 2008), DVD.

Greeks had settled at the turn of the century near Harrison and Halsted Streets in an area called "the Delta," but they moved farther north near Van Buren and Halsted Streets in later decades. Like others, they worked in nearby factories, as peddlers, and small business owners. Along with Italians and Jews, Greeks frequented Hull House for much-needed social, recreational, and health services; Americanization programs; and classes for children and adults.[15] Greeks purchased an imposing Jewish synagogue on Ashland Avenue when Jews had all but abandoned the area by the 1920s and converted it into a Greek Orthodox church.[16] Most immigrants struggled to raise their families and make a living in what was undoubtedly an urban "ghetto" in the early twentieth century, yet within a generation or two, many immigrants and their children amassed sufficient capital to move to more spacious and improved neighborhoods or suburbs.

When European immigration diminished dramatically after 1924, new migrants—Mexicans and southern African Americans—began arriving in large numbers on the Near West Side. The humble neighborhood was one of the least expensive places to live and one of the few areas that tolerated racial minorities. In the midst of the Great Migration, native and foreign-born "white" Chicagoans zealously contained newcomers in a highly concentrated and extremely overcrowded black ghetto on the South Side known as "the Black Belt." Southern black migrants continued to pour in over the following decades, pressing the limits and gradually expanding the boundaries of their highly segregated colony in their perpetual search for better housing. Yet whites adamantly opposed blacks permeating their neighborhoods and often reacted with violence.[17] African Americans began settling, however, in the area just east of Halsted and Maxwell Streets, near the Jewish enclave, which was losing its residents and was soon renamed "Black Bottom."[18] They also settled in the southwestern section of the area along Twelfth Street (later renamed Roosevelt Road, after President Franklin D. Roosevelt). African Americans formed a third enclave on the northern edge as well. Though the Near West Side housed a racially mixed population, this diversity belied the continuing physical segregation of African Americans. They lived *within* Near West Side boundaries but generally did not live *among* Italians, Greeks, or other European immigrant neighbors. In contrast, whites congregated in what were perceived to be ethnically exclusive enclaves but were actually much more heterogeneous in composition. The Near West Side denoted a fairly large region made up of multiple smaller communities whose racial boundaries held more firmly than their ethnic ones.[19]

The neighborhood included a number of important local institutions. Hull House figured among the largest social service agencies in the city and served as an anchor for recent immigrant families. The Institute for Juvenile Research, the Juvenile Justice Courts (the first courts for children in the nation, also founded by Jane Addams),[20] and a sprawling medical complex—consisting of Cook County Hospital, the University of Illinois Medical School and Hospital, and Rush-Presbyterian and St. Luke's Hospital—occupied the western end of the region. The Infant Welfare Society and Immigrants Protective League also provided services to local residents. Various Catholic and Protestant churches dotted the area as well, where, as was the custom, each national group worshipped among their own.

Mexicans Come to the Near West Side

Mexican immigrants first arrived in Chicago en masse in 1916 to work on the railroads. The largely male population settled in the northeastern quadrant, a transient and rooming-house district near Madison and Halsted Streets. By the 1920s, the city's steel mills and meatpacking plants began recruiting Mexican men as well, especially during times of labor strife.

Gradually, as immigrant families increased, they began moving farther south and west toward the intersection of Twelfth Street and Halsted, where larger apartments could accommodate bigger households. Mexicans came to a uniquely urban and industrial environment, unlike their compatriots who migrated to the Southwest and labored mainly in agricultural and rural communities. By 1930, they numbered somewhere between twenty and thirty thousand in the Chicago area.[21] They lived in three main colonies— the Near West Side, Back of the Yards / Packingtown, and the steel mill community of South Chicago. Several thousand also lived in the neighboring steel mill communities of northwest Indiana just across the state line. Much smaller numbers formed colonies in rural areas and small towns far beyond the city limits, such as Aurora, Waukegan, and Joliet.[22]

Their primary colony on the Near West Side formed directly around Jane Addams's Hull House at Halsted and Polk. During the 1920s and 1930s, Hull House's Americanization programs reached out to Mexicans among its multiethnic clients, incorporating them into its arts and crafts activities, especially its pottery-making program. The Henry Booth House at Union and Fourteenth Streets also served Mexican and other immigrant residents.[23] St. Francis of Assisi, located on Twelfth Street and Newberry Avenue, quickly became the neighborhood parish for Mexican Catholics. On November 20, 1925, the Claretian Missionary Fathers of St. Francis celebrated the first Sunday mass for Mexicans on the Near West Side. In the following year, 195 of the parish's 238 baptisms were Mexican, signaling that the former European immigrants were rapidly moving out. St. Francis also operated a grade school that soon began enrolling local Mexican children.[24] In addition to the church, an order of Catholic nuns (quoted in one of the chapter's epigraphs), the Cordi-Marian Sisters, who had fled Mexico during the Cristero Rebellion, began a nearby settlement in 1936. They served the community with a nursery, day-care center, and programs for children and adults. A handful of Protestant and evangelical churches ministered to local Mexicans as well.[25] Mexicans and a small number of other Latin Americans also began providing for themselves by opening businesses as early as the 1920s, including restaurants, boardinghouses, pool halls, and small grocery stores. They established the typical mutual aid societies, athletic and fraternal clubs, and patriotic organizations. They published a handful of Spanish-language newspapers and periodicals in the neighborhood that lasted for varying lengths of time during the 1920s and 1930s.[26]

During these years, historian Gabriela Arredondo argues, Mexicans in Chicago "became Mexican." Immigrants had left their home country during

Figure 9. Mexican girls in taxi on way to Hull House summer camp at Bowen Country Club near Waukegan, Illinois. "Bowen Country Club Arrival." Photograph by Wallace Kirkland, no date, Jane Addams Hull House Photographic Collection, JAMC_0000_0122-0963, University of Illinois at Chicago Library, Special Collections.

the Mexican Revolution, a period that had just begun expanding the nationalist project of making "Mexicans" out of the country's heterogeneous indigenous and *mestizo* peasant population.[27] Like other groups (e.g., Italians), upon arriving in Chicago, most immigrants had not developed a national identity but rather understood themselves and one another in local or regional terms. White Chicagoans struggled to locate Mexicans along the racial spectrum, even confusing them for African Americans during the bloody race riot of 1919.[28] But native-born whites and European immigrants soon identified them as a group distinct from African Americans yet not quite worthy of inclusion in the category of "white." Mexicans discovered their "Mexicanness" when they encountered blatant racism and prejudice in employment, housing, and police relations. In response, Arredondo explains, Mexicans turned inward and cultivated their Mexican identity as a source of moral strength and social support.

This local racial positioning of Mexican immigrants and their children shifted significantly during this period and had distinct meanings at the local and national levels. Until 1930, the federal census had classified Mexicans as "foreign-born whites," a result of the 1848 Treaty of Guadalupe Hidalgo, which guaranteed Mexicans US citizenship in the newly conquered territory. Since US citizenship was reserved exclusively for those legally classified as "white," Mexicans technically became "white" by default. By 1930, however, in the midst of the Great Depression and widespread nativism, the US census classified Mexicans in their own separate category apart from blacks and whites. The following decade, the census returned to classifying them as "foreign-born whites," after considerable pressure from Mexican American activists who insisted they were racially "Caucasian."[29] This inconsistent official classification has made it difficult to trace the population's growth accurately from one decade to the next. According to the 1940 census, for example, foreign-born Mexicans numbered approximately 2,742 people on the Near West Side. "Native whites" composed 59.6 percent of the neighborhood, with "foreign-born whites" constituting 21.2 percent and blacks constituting 18.9 percent. Italians constituted the largest foreign-born white group (making up 41 percent), while Mexicans came in second at nearly 10 percent.[30]

By 1950, the census counted Mexicans as nonwhite only if they had visible Indian ancestry: "Persons of Mexican birth or ancestry who were not definitely Indian or of other nonwhite race are classified as white."[31] This slippage and fluidity reveals Mexicans', and to a certain extent other Latinos/as', flexible, shifting, and contradictory racialization between "white" and "nonwhite." Hounded by the question of whether they constituted an ethnic or racial group, and classified according to how a census enumerator might interpret their physical appearance, Mexicans and other Latinas/os eluded racial categories, possessing "distinction-plus-duality"— that is, ethnic as well as racial difference. As sociologist Clara Rodríguez reminds us, however, ethnic and racial classifications are self-constructed, observer-constructed, and assigned by the state. Because of the racial mixture of most Latinas/os, and because of their phenotypical diversity, their racial classification has been "immediate, provisional, contextually dependent, and sometimes contested."[32] This was certainly the case in 1950s Chicago, when Mexicans and Puerto Ricans were identified locally as an "other" group—despite being officially classified as "white" by the census.

The Status of the Mexican American in Chicago

Mexican Americans had a long-standing presence in the city, but they occupied an ambiguous and barely visible "minority" status. Nonetheless, they had looked to local social service agencies like Hull House to help address their needs over the years. Still, Mexican American leaders were becoming restless with the limited resources and sociopolitical power they had acquired and the lukewarm responses they received from some agencies. In 1947, the Council on Social Agencies' Committee on Minority Groups established a Sub-committee on Mexican American Interests. It took on its first task of gathering information on the city's Mexican population. It also called on local service agencies to develop greater leadership and participation of Mexican Americans in their organizations. Mexican American leader Frank Paz prepared a report titled *Mexican-Americans in Chicago: A General Survey* in January 1948. The report aimed to inform local agencies about Mexican history in Chicago, employment, settlement patterns, and social needs. The subcommittee soon decided to plan and organize for a citywide conference. It hoped the conference would accomplish two goals—raise awareness among the general population about Mexican Americans in Chicago, and increase ethnic pride and leadership among Mexican Americans themselves. This two-pronged approach aimed to address both the structural barriers that prevented Mexican Americans from achieving social mobility and the individual prejudice that many Americans expressed toward the group. The former problem could be solved with more social services and resources (English classes, antidiscrimination policies in employment, etc.), but the latter would be solved only by educating whites and also teaching Mexicans to represent themselves with dignity and pride.

On May 22, 1949, the Council of Social Agencies (which by this time had renamed itself the Welfare Council of Metropolitan Chicago), along with the Chicago Commission on Human Relations, social and welfare agencies, and leaders of the Mexican American community, held a conference entitled "The Status of the Mexican American in Chicago." The guest list included both service providers and delegates from thirty of the city's Mexican organizations. Attendees heard speeches from distinguished guests such as a Mexican American member of the Denver City Council, and San Antonio School Board member and prominent Mexican American attorney Gus Garcia.[33]

Frank Paz opened the conference with provocative remarks and set the stage by examining the discrimination that Mexicans faced and how it had kept them at the bottom of the local socioeconomic order. He first addressed housing, noting, "There is no neighborhood, that I know of, which has a publicly announced policy which says 'We do not rent to Mexicans,' yet it happens—could it be accidentally?—that we find ourselves congregated in particular districts." Paz blasted employment discrimination against Mexicans, citing the inequalities in wages and opportunities for promotion and upgrading that left Mexicans largely impoverished.[34] He boldly made an incisive critique of settlement work as well, for failing to incorporate Mexican Americans into its leadership though it had worked with them for more than a generation. He did not name it explicitly, but he was clearly referring to Hull House, an institution where he had worked and lived in the past:

> Some of my friends in the settlement movement say, "Well, we have our doors open to your people (they are always *my* people). The doors are open to your people and there is nothing else we can do." . . . A settlement house on the West Side . . . has served the Mexican community for the last thirty years. During these thirty years there has *never* been a Mexican American on the settlement's Board of Directors. From time to time the settlement has had one Mexican on the staff. (emphasis in the original)[35]

Paz pointed to important disparities in power relations between Mexican Americans and the local "white" community: Mexicans were seen only as clients in need of social services but not as leaders capable of shaping agency policies and decisions.

Paz also commented on the contradictory ways that Americans acknowledged Mexican Americans' ethnicity by asking rhetorically, "When are we Americans and when do we cease to be Mexicans?" He provided this answer: "When somebody is accused of a brutal crime, then we are [identified as] Mexicans, but when we have a hero, a Chicago boy like Manuel Perez, who received the Congressional Medal of Honor [during World War II] . . . he is never mentioned as 'Manuel Perez, Mexican.'" Paz pointed up the inconsistent and harmful way Mexican Americans were identified as a distinct group only under negative circumstances but made invisible in moments of achievement or celebration. "The minute one of us is accused of a crime," he noted, "we cease to be an American and become a Mexican, in capital letters."[36]

The conference proceeded with workshops on employment; education; and health, welfare, and recreation. Participants concluded their sessions by making several recommendations in these areas and some general resolutions as well. In the end, they "proposed the formation of a citywide, self-directed, nonprofit organization for the purpose of serving as [the] representative voice for persons of Mexican American descent in Chicago." By the following June, the organization was incorporated as the Mexican American Council (MAC), with Paz as its first chair.[37]

The Mexican American Council

Like the conference that led to its creation, the Mexican American Council established as its mission "the better integration of the Mexican American into the life of his [sic] community in metropolitan Chicago." Interestingly, it had deliberately used the term *Mexican American*, signaling a desire for greater integration in American society. The group hoped to address both Mexican Americans who had lived in Chicago for more than a generation and recent immigrants who continued flowing into the city and faced a whole host of problems as well. MAC noted:

> The Mexican American is confronted with manifold inter-related social problems. As a recent immigrant his [sic] income is low, his employment security uncertain, and his "acceptance" by other ethnic groups in doubt. He faces numerous problems occasioned by his differences from his neighbors in language, culture, and educational opportunity. Judged by even the minimum of American standards of health and decency, he is in general "ill-housed, ill-clothed, and ill-fed."[38]

MAC established its operations on the Near West Side, a symbolic decision made both for the area's central location and because it was the oldest Mexican settlement and a continued port of entry. By 1950, MAC estimated that sixty-two thousand Mexican Americans lived throughout the entire city.[39]

Like Mexican American organizations in the southwestern United States during the forties and fifties, MAC initially emphasized assimilation and education as the means to Mexican Americans' social advancement.[40] Such groups strongly believed that the most effective way of combating racial prejudice and discrimination (as well as overcoming poverty and igno-rance) was to surpass Americans' low expectations of Mexican people. MAC and organizations like it stressed that individuals had much of the respon-sibility for how outsiders perceived their ethnic group. One newspaper ex-plained that "by showing them [Mexican Americans] what they can do for themselves, [MAC] has set out to see that the young people finish high school and that those who can go on to college, that the older and work-ing generations secure better working conditions, and that they all have an opportunity to learn English."[41] Accordingly, MAC quickly established committees on labor relations, housing, employment, and education. The group soon realized, however, that the multitude of social and economic problems that Mexican Americans encountered went beyond just individ-ual acts of prejudice and would require more than just highlighting group achievements. Mexicans were experiencing systematic subordination as im-migrants, workers, and residents in the city.[42]

By September 1951, MAC had obtained office space in the Hull House complex and hired a full-time director, Martín Ortíz, courtesy of the Chi-cago Area Project. MAC assembled a board of directors that included peo-ple from diverse class backgrounds, racial and ethnic origins, and neigh-borhoods in the city. Steelworkers, printers, insurance agents, and small businessmen represented blue-collar workers and business professionals. The organization also counted interested white academics affiliated with the University of Chicago, attorneys, and other professionals as allies. The growing Puerto Rican population also sent a representative, Anthony Vega, the director of the Commonwealth of Puerto Rico Department of Labor's Migration Division office in Chicago. MAC received criticism, however, from the local Catholic leadership, which allegedly disapproved of the group's affiliation with the Protestant-oriented Hull House.[43] As MAC de-veloped its activities, social services, and advocacy, its service population continued to grow. MAC encountered the tensions and dilemmas of serv-ing a large Mexican American population and its pressing social issues—poverty, employment and housing discrimination, language barriers, juve-nile delinquency—and representing the community in the city's broader sociopolitical environment.

Social service agencies, like the Cordi Marian Settlement, Hull House, and others, continued opening their doors to the most recent Spanish-speaking (im)migrants and Mexican American residents. The Cordi-Marian Sisters operated a nursery and day-care center to serve the needs of mothers with small children who worked outside the home. They offered classes and recreational activities for children and adults, including cooking, woodcraft, English, music, typing, and sewing. The local Infant Welfare Society offered a prenatal and baby wellness clinic. MAC also tried to provide assistance and referrals, though it did so with a paid staff of only two people. Still, with its skeletal volunteer force, its health committee helped translate information into Spanish; the housing committee assisted those who needed emergency shelter; the labor committee met with union representatives; the education committee awarded scholarships to Mexican American high school graduates; and the youth committee addressed the issue of juvenile delinquency.[44]

Puerto Rican Newcomers on the Near West Side

MAC quickly took notice of the newest migrant group. Puerto Ricans had started settling on the Near West Side in the late forties, lured by the proximity of jobs, the presence of an already established Spanish-speaking community, and the availability of relatively lower rents. In exchange, they found substandard housing, aging schools, high rates of tuberculosis, unemployment and underemployment, and generally poor conditions.[45] They brought with them their distinctive dialect of Spanish, foreign culinary and social practices, and more prominent African (rather than indigenous) ancestry compared to Mexicans. The Puerto Rico Department of Labor's Migration Division had begun funneling migrants to Chicago during the late 1940s. After the largely unsuccessful migration experiment in 1946, and with mounting pressures from New York City officials who bemoaned the constant influx of migrants to their city, the Migration Division began efforts to more carefully channel and manage its compatriots' movement to Chicago. In 1949, it established an office on Wabash Street in the South Loop area, on the eastern edge of the Near West Side.

The agency sought to manage Puerto Rican migration in a number of ways. First, it systematically recruited workers from the island through prearranged labor contracts with local employers. Second, when that was not possible, it operated as a placement agency, helping workers find employment once they arrived in the city. From July 1953 to June 1954, for example, in cooperation with the Illinois State Employment Service, it reported placing 5,358 Puerto Rican workers in the Chicagoland area.[46] Still, most workers simply departed from the island on their own without any government contact or assistance. Others had come to the mainland on labor contracts elsewhere (in agriculture, for example) and then headed to the Windy City on word of better wages from relatives and friends.[47] Thus, the Migration Division served in a third capacity, as a public relations office, issuing press releases to would-be migrants, warning them not to start out without English-language skills and ample money to subsist until they secured employment.[48]

The agency operated in a fourth capacity as well, offering Spanish-language assistance, an introduction to local resources, and referrals to social agencies and organizations to orient migrants and help them adjust to urban life on the mainland. The Migration Division, headquartered in New York, produced short educational films, including one 1956 title, *Un Amigo en Chicago* (A Friend in Chicago), introducing potential migrants to the Chicago office and familiarizing them with the services they could find there. In its efforts to educate migrants, the office regularly presented other educational films on topics as varied as marital relations, consumer credit, folk culture and superstitions, and individual and group relations.[49] Similar to the Urban League, which served southern black migrants, the Migration Division assumed the role of educating, assimilating, and urbanizing its largely rural, peasant compatriots. The agency engaged in community organizing, developing leadership among migrants through labor unions, fraternal groups, church groups, and neighborhood clubs. The office sought to train some men and women in the skills necessary to organize their fellow migrants and resolve many of the social problems they faced. Overall, the Migration Division served as an advocate for Puerto Ricans, defending their rights in employment issues, intervening with the public schools, the archdiocese, and other institutions.[50] Yet its capacities and will also had limits.

Puerto Rican migration to Chicago increased dramatically during the early fifties. In the first year of operation, the Migration Division office recorded 5,308 visitors (see table 3). By 1950, the number increased to 7,951. The following year, it counted 6,475 and another 8,879 in 1952. In only the first six months of 1953, it received a whopping 6,253 people. Of this last number, approximately 2,530 were newcomers to Chicago, recently arrived and in need of assistance.[51]

The Puerto Rican population grew dramatically in just a matter of years. In 1940, the census counted only 240 Puerto Ricans in Chicago; by 1947, that number had increased to 6,000, and by 1953, officials estimated 20,000 people. By 1960, approximately 32,000 islanders lived in Chicago. An estimated 6,200 of them lived on the Near West Side, the second largest concentration of Puerto Ricans in the city. It also had the second poorest Puerto Rican enclave in Chicago, with a median income of $3,680.[52] Like Mexicans, Puerto Ricans constituted only a small proportion of the area's

Table 3   Visitors to Chicago's Migration Division Office, 1949–53

	1949	1950	1951	1952	1953*
January	n/a	798	600	630	976
February	n/a	597	563	526	767
March	283	685	373	528	1064
April	394	532	215	581	1052
May	380	577	800	547	1023
June	462	473	716	782	1371
July	617	513	562	1466	n/a
August	485	559	532	721	n/a
September	581	779	505	850	n/a
October	663	954	557	704	n/a
November	671	915	570	650	n/a
December	772	569	482	894	n/a
Total	5308	7951	6475	8879	6253

Source: Commonwealth of Puerto Rico, Department of Labor, Bureau of Employment and Migration, Migration Division report, July 22, 1953, folder 10, box 147, Welfare Council of Metropolitan Chicago Collection (formerly known as Council of Social Agencies), Chicago History Museum.
* 1953 figures are for first 6 months only.

population—4.9 percent—but their concentration in certain census tracts made them highly visible.[53]

The Migration Division sought to manage and influence how Puerto Ricans would be incorporated in the local social order by initially discouraging them from settling "with any Spanish-speaking people," urging them instead "to distribute themselves all over the city in Polish, Italian, Czechoslovak and other areas so that they soon learn to speak English." Chicago's Migration Division director, Anthony Vega, reportedly "warn[ed] against the formation of colonies of residence with Mexicans."[54] Officials hoped to prevent the development of Spanish-speaking *barrios* or slums, such as those that had formed in New York City. Still, Puerto Ricans did not always heed the warnings of their leaders to avoid the Mexican colonies. A small number settled just west of Taylor and Halsted Streets, among the Near West Side's Mexican and Italian communities. Others settled just north of that, forming an enclave along Harrison Street. The largest concentration in the neighborhood comprised an area along Madison Street.[55] It was located across the physical barrier of the Congress Expressway, a federal highway under construction in the 1950s, which effectively separated them from Mexicans to the south. Despite the physical barrier, migrants were close enough to access Mexican grocery stores, St. Francis of Assisi's Spanish mass, and a Spanish-language theater, which screened Mexican movies.[56] St. Francis was so popular, in fact, that it held six Spanish masses on Sundays—the most of any parish in Chicago—in order to accommodate the city's Spanish-speaking faithful.[57]

Even if they had wanted to, Puerto Ricans found it hard to heed the Migration Division's instructions to live among ethnic whites. Many whites saw Puerto Ricans (especially those with dark skin) as racially foreign, in some cases rejecting them as fiercely as they did African Americans. Some frequently encountered racial discrimination from landlords, which was compounded by severe housing shortages in the years after World War II. As a result, one-third of Near West Side Puerto Ricans concentrated in census tracts with high numbers of African Americans (see fig. 10 and table 4). This may have reflected the way that white Chicagoans positioned them in the racial order but perhaps also reflected their own self-fashioned racial identities from the island. A small number of Puerto Ricans had settled in black neighborhoods such as Woodlawn when they had first arrived in the city in the late forties. As racially mixed people, some may have chosen black neighborhoods because they seemed racially, if not culturally, familiar and less hostile.[58]

As Puerto Ricans settled and acclimated to their new environment, they made efforts to create a sense of community. They faced a host of social

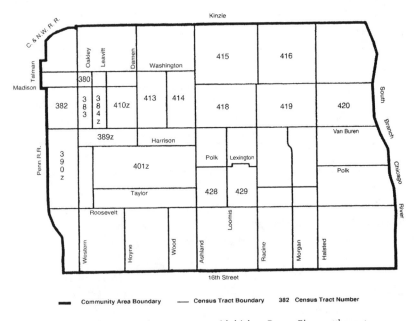

Figure 10. Near West Side census tracts with highest Puerto Rican settlement.

Table 4 Puerto Rican and black population of Near West Side, selected census tracts, 1960

Census tract	Total population	Puerto Rican population	% of total population	Black population	% of total population
All census tracts	126,610	6,204	4.9	68,116	53.8
380*	702	21	3.0	610	86.9
382*	6,314	303	4.8	5,613	88.9
383*	2,121	155	7.3	1,611	76.0
384z*	2,006	183	9.1	1,444	72.0
389z	954	111	11.7	243	25.5
390z	3,986	403	10.1	678	17.0
401z	8,111	316	3.9	1,541	19.0
407	3,194	661	20.7	29	0.9
408	1,833	213	11.6	20	1.1
410z*	4,223	190	4.5	3,665	86.8
413*	6,433	508	7.9	5,037	78.3
414*	4,531	358	7.9	2,809	62.0
415*	2,580	196	7.6	1,641	63.6
416	1,540	40	2.6	129	8.4
418†	6,201	1,066	17.2	1,724	27.8
419	2,952	47	1.6	115	3.9
420	3,898	129	3.3	78	2.0
428	5,068	639	12.6	593	11.7
429*	4,211	177	4.2	2,409	57.2

Source: Compiled from Kitagawa and Taeuber, *Local Community Fact Book, 1960*, 71, 167.
*Tracts where African Americans are at least 50 percent of the population.
†Tract with the largest Puerto Rican population.

issues—overcrowded, overpriced, dilapidated housing; racial tensions with neighbors; and language barriers. Migrants formed social bonds with one another and found ways to organize themselves and improve their conditions. By the midfifties, some had opened their own small businesses—grocery stores, taverns, and other shops along Madison Street such as Tropical Restaurant, San Juan Bar, El Marro, Casa Arzola, and Bodega Reyes. Many began affiliating with the Catholic Church and social service groups.[59] José Hernández was one such man who expressed concern over helping fellow migrants better adjust to life in the city. He lived on the 1700 block of West Roosevelt Road, among an African American enclave, and had decided to begin a "family club." Hernández reportedly was

concerned with the assimilation problems of Puerto Rican families (some 300, he says) in his neighborhood. His family and twelve others have formed the House of Puerto Rico, a "family club" which eventually hopes to embrace many other PR families in the area. He outlined certain contemplated projects, including instruction of housewives on how to buy and prepare American food, and informing members of programs of nearby welfare agencies in order to make all community resources known to them.

Hernández received a referral to the Welfare Council for assistance with his project and to direct him to appropriate social agencies that could serve the population.[60]

Puerto Ricans were especially encouraged to turn to the Catholic Church to help them adjust successfully in their new environment. In 1954, Puerto Rican men established the Caballeros de San Juan (Knights of St. John) under the sponsorship of Chicago's cardinal Samuel Stritch and Father Leo T. Mahon, an Irish priest who worked closely with Puerto Ricans in the Woodlawn neighborhood.[61] Because of their geographic dispersal throughout the city and perhaps because of the obstacles that ethnic enclaves would pose for assimilating Puerto Ricans, the archdiocese had decided against the national parish model that it had instituted for European immigrants in earlier decades and instead sought to minister to Puerto Ricans more diffusely.[62] Father Mahon and the church approached Puerto Ricans similarly to European immigrants, however, in assuming that by assimilating and Americanizing, the newcomers would be accepted by American society and no longer encounter prejudice and discrimination. The Caballeros thus promoted Americanization and acculturation—teaching Puerto Rican men in particular how to be good Catholics, and according to sociologist Felix Padilla, "to whatever extent possible . . . adopting the customs, attitudes, and language of white America."[63] The organization provided social services to its members and created a religious-based center for social activities and organizing. Perhaps its greatest contribution, the Caballeros developed leadership skills among Puerto Rican men. Mahon and Catholic leaders also hoped that this would help make them loyal Catholics.[64]

A group of men on the Near West Side soon established their own chapter, or *concilio*, of the Caballeros, as the organization expanded throughout the Near North Side as well. Perhaps reflecting the high number of Puerto Ricans in the area, the Knights held meetings at two nearby locations— the first near the corner of Roosevelt Road and Ashland Avenue, and the second a mile directly north, at Paulina and Jackson Boulevard.[65] The first group held its meetings in the offices of a newly formed entity, the "Cardinal's Committee for the Spanish-Speaking," established by the archdiocese in the mid-1950s. Although in name the committee ministered to its Spanish-speaking followers broadly, balancing its attention to varied Spanish-speaking national groups proved challenging. The committee later located its headquarters in the same building as the Puerto Rico Migration Division office, perhaps leaving the impression that it favored Puerto Rican followers.[66] The archdiocese fostered the formation of the Caballeros and the Cardinal's Committee to some extent because other Catholic priests and parishioners did not express enthusiasm for the newcomers. Many Catholic churches did not welcome or accommodate Puerto Ricans (or Mexicans, for that matter). Some parishes did so grudgingly, holding Spanish masses in basements and requiring Spanish-speaking parishioners to enter through side doors rather than the main entrance.[67] Many Puerto Rican Catholics chose instead to join the Mexican faithful at St. Francis, where they could at least attend mass in the main church and enter through the front doors.

Encountering the Local Ethnoracial Order

Chicago in the 1940s and 1950s was plagued with racial violence, particularly against the rapidly growing African American population who dared breech the boundaries of white neighborhoods. When Puerto Ricans and Mexicans arrived on the Near West Side, they quickly had to learn the ethnoracial order of the community and the city. As geographer Don Mitchell observes, in contrast to the homogeneity of rural life, "The city is the place where difference lives." This certainly held true for the diverse racial and ethnic landscape of the Near West Side. By the 1950s, according to one newspaper, the area was a "'Melting Pot' of Races [and] Religions." It noted, that "melting pot around famed Hull House," however, "was bubbling and the aroma was not very savory. Tension and tempers were running high."[68] Though the neighborhood was extremely heterogeneous, certain ethnoracial groups laid claim to particular sections of the area. The Spanish-speaking assimilated the lessons of urban space: those who were different or unfamiliar—outsiders—were generally viewed with suspicion. Inner-city neighborhoods in midcentury Chicago became sites not only of black-white racial conflict, as has been documented by other scholars, but of complicated social relations where the boundaries of blackness and whiteness were being worked out and where Mexicans and Puerto Ricans challenged those boundaries.[69]

By the 1950s and 1960s, Italians, African Americans, Mexicans, and Puerto Ricans constituted the largest populations in the neighborhood. Most Jewish and Greek neighbors had long since moved out. "Jewtown" had in fact become an entirely black community and was Jewish only in its commercial ownership. The construction of the Congress Expressway in the fifties displaced much of the Greek population as well. They maintained the remnants of a retail district along Halsted Avenue near Van Buren Street and came into the area to attend services at their Orthodox church.[70] The Spanish-speaking thus encountered Greeks and Jews mainly as merchants, employers, or absentee landlords. Their daily encounters with others on the front stoop, the street corners, playgrounds, and schools occurred primarily with Italians and African Americans.

Although the Near West Side had a very mixed population, Taylor Street was still known as an Italian community. As the oldest and largest ethnic group in the area, Italian Americans dominated the local political structure, and Alderman Vito Marzullo controlled the links to city hall and municipal jobs. Florence Scala, a local homemaker, shared her memories as a child in the Italian neighborhood in the 1920s and 1930s: "At the time, the neighborhood was dominated by gangsters and hoodlums. They were men from the old country, who lorded it over the people in the area. It was the day of moonshine." While locally Italians may have dominated the area, their broader political power was more fabled than real, especially vis-à-vis the city's established Irish political machine.[71] Still, Italians claimed domain over the territory, though they were rapidly being outnumbered by "others." In 1950, African Americans constituted 40.8 percent of the area's residents, more than doubling their numbers since the previous decade. By 1960, they represented over half the area residents. The influx of almost thirty thousand Mexicans and Puerto Ricans also unsettled many longtime residents. Italians were becoming increasingly anxious about their changing neighborhood.

Residents often maintained rigid ethnoracial boundaries with one another, but their alliances and affiliations could just as easily form along geographic lines. Nonetheless, in a community that firmly segregated African Americans, and sometimes relegated Mexicans and Puerto Ricans to particular blocks or buildings, geographic and ethnoracial boundaries often mapped onto one another.[72] Relations among these four groups could be complex, subtly nuanced, and varied depending on the context. Individuals developed their opinions about other groups based on perceived characteristics, popular stereotypes, and personal experience. Spanish speakers had varying experiences with Italians, for example. Some Mexicans, like the de la Llata family, remember positive relations with Italian landlords and neighbors who readily accepted them as just the latest immigrant group. Longtime residents who had been in the neighborhood for years tended to be more socially integrated with one another as well.[73] Relations between Italians and Mexicans were reportedly positive in the early 1920s. As time went on, however, friction between the two increased.[74] Italians who saw Mexicans as racially different, and therefore unfamiliar, adamantly strove to keep them out. Frank Paz's 1948 study noted, for example, that

> Mexicans live within this larger community in small islands. . . . Although they have been living there for the last twenty-five or thirty years, they are still looked upon by the Italian-Americans as outsiders and intruders. . . . There are sections in this large area where Mexicans are restricted. "They have been kept out," as someone from the Italian group has boasted.[75]

Some Mexicans did indeed encounter discrimination in trying to find housing among Italians, being turned away sometimes based on their appearance or demeanor. Some discovered that "passing" for Italian or Greek helped diminish the discrimination they frequently encountered. As more and more Spanish-speaking moved into the area, however, landlords had to decide if the difference between themselves and these recent migrants was more important than the rents they could collect. Absentee landlords, for example, were much less discriminating in selecting tenants, renting out run-down apartments at inflated prices to desperate new arrivals. Especially during the dramatic housing shortages of the forties and early fifties, many renters took whatever they could find. The aged and worn district often provided some of the worst housing in the city.[76]

Puerto Ricans faced similar problems in a tight, overpriced housing market and also learned that being ambiguous about their ethnoracial origins worked to their advantage. Just as some Mexicans, they also availed themselves of ethnic disguises. When landlords mistook light-skinned Puerto Ricans for Italians or Greeks, they did not correct them.[77] One man, for example, vividly remembered as a child visiting the home of a Puerto Rican family who lived in the Italian Taylor Street area. When he sat near an open window eating a traditional Puerto Rican dish of *arroz con gandules* (rice with pigeon peas), he was swiftly reprimanded. He did not understand at the time, but the family feared that the ethnic signifier would surely reveal to their neighbors that they were not Italians, and perhaps get them expelled from their apartment.[78] Italian hostility toward Puerto Ricans might also explain why so many settled in African American tenements, where absentee landlords seemed less concerned about tenants' racial backgrounds than they were about making a profit.

Aggressive policing of ethnoracial boundaries happened among young men who physically kept "others" out of their community with street gang violence. Some Puerto Rican men remembered that if they passed through the Italian district, for example, they would invariably be beaten. In the summer of 1954, the conflict on the Near West Side was so heightened that it drew the attention of the secretary of labor of Puerto Rico, Fernando Sierra Berdecía, during his visit to the city. A "wave of violence and racial tension" erupted again between Italians and Puerto Ricans just four years later.[79] Such tense relations occurred in other parts of the city as well. While we might interpret these conflicts as simply territorial rather than racial, historian Andrew Diamond has suggested that it was not just a sense of territoriality or "protecting the neighborhood" that motivated whites to employ violence to keep nonwhites out. Conflicts over space often carried explicitly racial meanings.[80]

If Italian Americans disparaged and harassed them, Puerto Ricans also faced battles on the other end of the color line. Puerto Ricans and African Americans did not always live in harmony either. The same young man who was reprimanded for eating by a window also recalled tensions with African Americans, in one case being chased by an African American teenager "swinging a chain with a padlock on it." Puerto Ricans occupied a precarious social position and could potentially receive assaults from all sides.[81] As the most recent group in the neighborhood and one with what anthropologist Elena Padilla called "color visibility," Puerto Ricans learned that their place within the social order was still being worked out; it was contextually dependent and often based on one's appearance rather than how one self-identified.[82] Their racial ambiguity occasionally shielded them, however. One dark-skinned man recalled escaping trouble from Italians (although they were especially hostile toward Puerto Ricans) because they mistook him for an African American, a racial group that they were not looking to quarrel with at that moment.[83]

Mexican American teenage boys often had conflicts with Italians and African Americans as well. At a younger age, boys of varying backgrounds attended summer camps together, ostensibly in an effort to cultivate human relations and prevent the rise of gangs, juvenile delinquency, and racial problems. By their teens, however, many young men had joined gangs, or "athletic clubs" as they were more innocuously named, which frequently fractured along racial and ethnic lines. These clubs regularly clashed with one another on area streets, defending neighborhood boundaries with displays of male bravado.[84] Yet interracial tensions among youth were not limited to young men. Young women also experienced friction with one another, and the Chicago Area Project hired female street workers to intervene with them as well. The famous Chicago writer Ana Castillo, who grew up on Taylor Street in the 1950s, depicts a hostile encounter between a young Mexican female narrator and Italian American teenage girls in a poem entitled "Dirty Mexican." She describes the seemingly routine neighborhood dynamics in graphic detail:

> "Dirty Mexican, dirty, dirty Mexican!"
> And i said: "i'll kick your ass, Dago bitch!"
> tall for my race, strutted right past
> black projects,
> leather jacket, something sharp
> in my pocket
> to Pompeii School.
>
> i scrawled in chalk all over sidewalks
> MEXICAN POWER CON/SAFOS
> crashed their dances,
> *get them broads, corner 'em in the bathroom,*
> in the hallway, and their loudmouth mamas
> calling from windows: "Roxanne!" "Antoinette!"
> And when my height wouldn't do
> my mouth called their bluff:
> *"That's right, honey, I'm Mexican!*
> *Watchu gonna do about it?"* Since they didn't
> want their hair or lipstick mussed they
> shrugged their shoulders 'til distance gave way:
> "Dirty Mexican, dirty Mexican bitch."
> Made me book back, right up their faces,
> *"Watchu say?"* And it started all over again.[85]

Castillo's poem reveals the enmity between some Italian American and Mexican American teenage girls that seemed to be part of everyday life. The narrator encounters problems at one of the local Catholic schools where both groups shared classrooms and came in direct contact with each other. Castillo points also to African Americans, who lived primarily in local public housing projects, and whom many Mexicans seemingly avoided. That the narrator carried a weapon also suggests an ever-present threat of violence.

In reality, Mexicans negotiated complicated racial hierarchies in the neighborhood, seeking to distance themselves from whichever group was

Figure 11. Spanish-speaking shoppers and famous blues musician Arvella Gray at the Maxwell Street Market, 1964. *And This Is Free*, directed by Mike Shea (Shanachie Entertainment Corp., 1965, 2008), DVD.

most disparaged at any moment and at times claiming a white identity alongside Italian Americans. Mexicans and Italians occasionally formed alliances against African Americans, but at other moments Mexicans sought to remain neutral in conflicts between Italians and African Americans. In an environment where a community's integrity was often the only social capital that working-class residents possessed, ethnic and racial difference took on paramount importance.

Despite the sometimes hostile climate, some residents did form close personal relationships across ethnoracial lines. Frank Paz noted in his study, "In spite of this feeling [of animosity] there have been a number of inter-marriages between Italians and Mexicans." Indeed, some Mexicans and Puerto Ricans intermarried with Italians as they did with African Americans as well.[86] They also married one another. While some residents may have been more socially tolerant and open-minded than others, such unions did not always go uncontested by family and community members. In an environment where people encountered "difference," negotiating space, resources, and social well-being could be complicated. Ultimately, each group had to look after its own, and interracial and interethnic alliances and cooperation more often represented the exception rather than the rule.[87]

Relations among the Spanish-Speaking

If contending with racial and ethnic others in their community proved complex and vexing, the Spanish-speaking on the Near West Side may have assumed that relations with one another would be easier. After all, both populations spoke a common, albeit differently inflected, language. Both included many recent arrivals in the city who had to adjust to urban life in the United States. Yet both groups also had inter- and intraethnic differences. As economic conditions took a turn for the worse in the early fifties, however, Chicagoans scrutinized Mexicans and Puerto Ricans more carefully. Both had to defend themselves from public criticism and attacks and had to defend their right to be present in the city at all. Joining together under a label that emphasized their shared characteristics became increasingly appealing to community leaders.

Economic Recession and the Status of the Spanish-Speaking

Opinions on Puerto Rican migrants fluctuated between positive endorsements and alarmist concerns as their numbers in the city rapidly increased. The press on the island, not surprisingly, published triumphant stories about their compatriots. Workers reportedly received glowing reviews from employers, from Puerto Rican government officials, and from the local media.[88] This masked a growing concern in some sectors that Puerto Ricans were becoming a burden on social welfare programs. By 1953, Puerto Rican officials estimated that the population in Chicago had grown to twenty thousand people. Like most new (im)migrant groups, they drew concern from service professionals for their potential social problems, delinquency, and cultural obstinacy. Would these newcomers assimilate successfully? Did they have the knowledge and skills to follow the path of European immigrants and achieve social and economic mobility? The Welfare Council of Metropolitan Chicago and other social and religious leaders decided they needed a study to collect demographic data and better understand the population. Both nonprofit and government social welfare agencies agreed that such information would benefit them tremendously in helping these most recent migrants adjust. They noted, "Although the Puerto Ricans are but a small segment of the population, they are viewed as making for serious problems in the community. They seem to be a back country people with virtually no comprehension of American mores and limited capacity to comprehend them. If most Puerto Ricans are like this, the agencies will have much difficulty developing programs to meet their needs."[89] Catholic leaders, board of education officials, the Illinois employment bureau chief, Chicago Housing Authority officials, and directors of charitable agencies and settlement houses all wrote letters in support of the study.[90]

Alvin E. Rose, commissioner of public welfare for Cook County, stood out among those who expressed concern over the new migrants. His agency had started taking notice of the growing numbers of Puerto Ricans seeking public assistance and the "problems they were creating."[91] Rose observed that many agricultural workers who went to neighboring states eventually arrived in Chicago at the end of the harvest season and struggled to find work. While the department had a one-year residency requirement in Illinois (six months in Chicago) in order to qualify for public assistance, Rose stated that he would make exceptions to the policy only to help needy families return to the island, and ostensibly relieve pressures on his agency. He would not help single men, however, nor families who wanted to stay in the city. Following this strategy would seemingly prevent what had happened in New York, "which now must deal with a Puerto Rican population of 450,000 which strains their public welfare system." Rose traveled to the island to discuss plans to "repatriate" migrants with local authorities. He also wanted to publicly discourage any other unskilled workers from coming to Chicago. He flew to Puerto Rico that February to meet with island officials and coordinate a publicity campaign to warn islanders not to come to Chicago.[92]

In a speech he made on the island, Rose apparently reassured listeners that neither he nor his agency were expressing racial prejudice: "Please believe me above all else that Puerto Ricans in Chicago are not now and never have been treated differently by the Chicago Department of Welfare than anyone else of any other race, creed, color or national origin." He explained further that his office was merely helping those who wanted to return to the island. "We are not sending anybody back," he said in defense of the "repatriations." In private, however, Rose expressed a very different policy. He reportedly told a staff member at the Welfare Council his policy to "ship them back in plane lots" and allegedly urged the agency "not [to] make it too easy for them to stay and bring others in."[93]

Rose's concerns about Puerto Rican welfare dependency were exaggerated, as Puerto Ricans made up less than 1 percent of the relief rolls in Chicago, a fact that he himself revealed. Out of over 18,000 cases of public assistance, Puerto Ricans accounted for only 148 cases. The island's Department of Labor cited this in a January 1954 press release, headlined "Puerto Ricans Go in Search of Work, Not Aid." Island officials adamantly defended them as labor migrants, not drifters in search of handouts. Former governor of Puerto Rico Rexford Guy Tugwell, who had since become a lecturer of political science at the University of Chicago, publicly criticized Rose's efforts to discourage Puerto Rican migration, stating that Puerto Ricans had as much right to migrate as "Texans, New Yorkers, and the mountain people of Mississippi."[94] Anthony Vega, of the Chicago Migration Division office, emphatically noted that the main issue in the city was one of economics, not Puerto Rican dependency. "This is a problem of unemployment, not a Puerto Rican problem," he explained. Indeed, economic recession and high unemployment rates strained the most vulnerable families and workers during this period. But Chicago officials singled out this population as a burden. In reality, very few Puerto Ricans received public assistance, although many more certainly must have been eligible.[95]

The years 1953 to 1954 were indeed difficult for the nation. With the end of the Korean War, the country slipped into economic recession. While it was mild in comparison to other periods of decline, it hit the manufacturing sector especially hard, resulting in high unemployment. Puerto Ricans (and Mexican immigrants) were coming to the city just as industrial jobs were declining. Since many of them found work in manufacturing, they suffered significantly during the downturn.[96] The Migration Division office did in fact observe a marked increase in the proportion of visitors to its offices who came in search of employment from 1953 to 1954. It noted an equally dramatic decline in employment placements, especially in industrial jobs (as compared to agricultural labor). While only 7,944 visitors came to the office seeking employment in 1952–53, the following year 16,686 did so out of a total of 17,487 visitors (table 5). Similarly, job placements decreased significantly overall. Though the office recorded a 67 percent placement rate for 1952–53, that figure dropped to just under 24 percent by 1953–54. The Migration Division struggled to find employment for those in search of work (table 6).[97]

At the same time that Puerto Ricans were receiving negative attention

Table 5   Visitors to Migration Division Office, 1951–55

Fiscal year (July–June)	Visitors	Visitors seeking employment	% of visitors seeking employment
1951–52	6,802	3,771	55
1952–53	11,538	7,944	69
1953–54	17,487	16,686	95
1954–55	16,555	14,553	88

Source: Migration Division, annual report, 1954–55, 76.

Table 6 Migration Division Office employment placements, 1951–55

Fiscal Year (July–June)	Visits for employment	Number referred to jobs	% of all visitors referred	Job placements	% of all visitors placed
1951–52	3,771	1,898*	n/a	2,783	n/a
1952–53	7,944	7,647	96	5,359	67
1953–54	16,686	5,500	33	4,039	24
1954–55	14,553	5,108	35	3,684	25

Source: Migration Division, annual report, 1954–55, 76.
*This figure is for the last 6 months of the fiscal year only.

for their unemployment rates and being encouraged to "repatriate," unauthorized Mexican immigrants were increasingly becoming the targets of public hysteria and facing official deportations. The simultaneity of these phenomena could be gleaned on February 2, 1954, on the pages of the conservative *Chicago Tribune*, which carried stories on that day about both the Puerto Rican welfare "menace" and the Mexican "hordes" invading the border.[98] The 1924 immigration law, which had established quotas for European immigration and created the Border Patrol, also created an "illegal" status for Mexicans.[99] The INS had been deporting illegal aliens from Chicago, including those who overstayed *bracero* contracts, for several years. While Americans did not seem to mind the *braceros* during World War II, many increasingly insisted on removing illegal aliens in the midst of economic decline. In 1954, the federal government unveiled an aggressive nationwide roundup campaign it called "Operation Wetback." The sweeps of Mexican immigrants started on the West Coast in January and reached Chicago by that September. Community agencies like the Mexican American Council (MAC) tried to educate potential deportees on their legal rights and their options should they be arrested. Still, the INS deported as many as one hundred people a day (see chapter 1).[100]

Negotiating Alliances

As both populations became targets of public concern and criticism, community leaders struggled to gain support from local social service agencies. While the Welfare Council continued discussing the need for a study on Puerto Ricans, it decided to establish a Subcommittee on the Integration of Spanish Speaking Citizenry. Like the Cardinal's Committee, the group's chosen name suggested it might address all "Spanish-speaking" Chicagoans. In practice, however, the subcommittee continued discussing how best to document the Puerto Rican population.[101] This troubled Martin Ortíz, director of MAC, who met with Anthony Vega in anticipation of a Welfare Council meeting to discuss how they might cooperate in addressing the problems of *both* their communities. In a letter to Miss Hollis Vick of the Welfare Council, Ortíz expressed his dissatisfaction with the invidious dynamics of social service provision. He wrote, "I suppose I'm going to be rather selfish in making this inquiry but . . . might it be possible to make a few comments . . . on the current status and some of the major problems of persons of Mexican descent in Chicago which number about 60,000?"[102] Mexican American leaders acknowledged the growing presence of Puerto Rican migrants in the city, but they also recognized that Mexican Americans had lived in the city much longer and faced persistent social issues. Moreover, their community was much larger and continued to grow. Furthermore, Puerto Ricans seemingly came with one significant advantage compared to Mexican immigrants—citizenship. Ortíz was quick to point this out. Still, he saw an opportunity to join Puerto Rican leaders and lobby on behalf of their constituents together. He explained, "Mr. Vega [of the Puerto Rico Migration Division] and I were in full agreement on the fact that it's not merely a problem of Mexicans and Puerto Ricans but rather, a problem facing persons of Spanish-speaking background."[103]

This tension between advocating for one's own national group or joining forces under the umbrella of "Spanish-speaking" emerged repeatedly on the Near West Side. At key moments, for example, both groups did everything possible to distinguish themselves from each other. Puerto Ricans were advised to carry birth certificates or documentation in case they encountered INS officials in search of suspected illegal aliens. Mexican Americans also tried to distance themselves from Puerto Ricans when Nationalists carried out a sensational attack on Congress. In March 1954, four Puerto Rican Nationalists stormed the United States House of Representatives while in session and opened fire, wounding five congressmen. The story received front-page treatment in newspapers across the country. Ironically, the assembly had just voted on the Mexican Bracero Program seconds before the shooting began. The Nationalists were reported to have shouted "Viva Mexico!" and "Free Puerto Rico!"[104] Police soon alleged ties to local Puerto Ricans in Chicago, including several living on the Near West Side. Their connection stemmed from death threats reportedly made against Welfare Commissioner Alvin Rose during the welfare controversy the previous year.[105]

The arrests must have affected the Mexican community, if not directly at least morally, as Martin Ortíz soon joined Anthony Vega in protesting the "mass arrests of Spanish-speaking citizens." Ultimately, authorities delivered six local men, most of whom were living on the Near West Side, to the FBI for allegedly conspiring in the attacks.[106] Still, local newspapers soon quoted MAC as denouncing the Nationalist action. The *Chicago Sun-Times* published a photograph of a MAC meeting, calling the organization "Spokesman of the Latin-American colony of Chicago" and describing the group's disapproval of the attack. A local Mexican radio announcer, Jose E. Chapa, took offense at MAC's moral pronouncement and the claim that it represented the city's entire Latin American community. In a letter to the council, he asked what authority it had to make such statements and whether the whole Latin American colony had agreed that MAC spoke for them. Chapa disagreed with the denouncement of the Nationalists, pointing out that they would be dealt with by the American justice system. "I do not see reasonably [*sic*] for the Council to use this moment to speculate in the columns of the *Prensa* [press]," he noted. "Nor could I judge the town [*sic*] of Puerto Rico for the conduct of one group, as well as we can't judge the town of Mexico for the massacre committed during our revolutions."[107] Chapa's opposition to MAC's denouncement of the Puerto Rican Nationalists signaled a diversity of political opinions among Chicago's Mexican American community and the complexities of inter-Latino relations.

Relations among the Spanish-speaking ebbed and flowed. The year after the debacle over the Nationalist attacks in Washington, the Puerto Rican Congress of Mutual Aid donated over six hundred dollars to the Chicago Mexican Chamber of Commerce for the benefit of hurricane victims in Tampico, Mexico.[108] The two populations seemed earnest in their efforts at cooperation. The Migration Division office initially seemed enthusiastic about working with Mexican Americans and MAC. In 1954, it noted, "The Midwest Office has worked closely with this group. In doing this, friction that existed between Puerto Ricans and Mexicans in this city has been eliminated. The difficulties created between these two groups have been resolved, allowing both groups equal participation on the radio, in meetings, and conferences." But the goal of cooperating across ethnic lines may have simply proved too much. Just two years later, the Migration Division appeared frustrated with biethnic efforts, declaring "We can not nor do we wish to be all things to all the Spanish-speaking people of Chicago. We have to mobilize all the human resources and materials in the city for the permanent wellbeing of the Puerto Ricans living in Chicago."[109] In a period of economic distress and social crisis, interethnic cooperation seemed viable and appealing. In the long run, however, it was much more difficult to sustain.

Conclusion

By the late 1950s, Mexicans and Puerto Ricans had spent several years in the neighborhood. They had learned the lessons of how urban space was divided and protected along ethnoracial lines and the imprecise place they occupied within it. Some residents got along fine and had little friction, and others certainly promoted interracial understanding and harmony. Still others, especially male youths, fought furiously to repel newcomers. Mexicans and Puerto Ricans also learned the fragility of their status as some of the most recently arrived people in the city. Not all Chicagoans welcomed them. Whatever relations they established, however, would soon change. The social and economic dynamics transforming the postwar city would affect residents' ability to remain in the neighborhood where they had begun setting down roots. Though their time on the Near West Side would be brief, Mexicans and Puerto Ricans had made significant strides in perhaps their most important challenge—becoming Chicagoans.

THREE

Race, Class, Housing, and Urban Renewal: Dismantling the Near West Side

Not everyone can or wishes to live in a suburb. The [p]hysical rehabilitation of central Chicago must include an area for good integrated private housing to supplement the overabundance of public housing where some of the estimated one-third of Chicago's working force can live. On the Near West Side one such development is under way—the Harrison-Halsted Project of the Chicago Land Clearance Commission and one under consideration [by] the Conservation Board of Chicago. . . . If the bold, creative plans Mayor Daley and Planning Commissioner, Ira J. Bach, have presented for the improvement of Chicago becomes a reality, the value of the Near West Side as a close-to-the-loop, non-segregated residential area is inestimable.

—Near West Side Community Council, *October 1958*[1]

One way to indicate the pressures on the Harrison-Halsted neighborhood is to say that it is within sight of Chicago's downtown business district, the Loop, and has been alternately sought after for its convenience and location and despised for its crowded, and often unsanitary, living conditions.

—Carolyn Eastwood, *Near West Side Stories*[2]

Mexicans and Puerto Ricans who settled on the Near West Side of Chicago in the 1950s found themselves in a city undergoing profound social, economic, and spatial transformations. Their neighborhood faced increasing physical decay, dramatic population changes, massive federal highway construction, and the rapid expansion of public housing. As one of the oldest and most crowded sections of the city, it had housed poor immigrants for nearly a century. Earlier generations of European transplants had exhausted the life span of worn housing structures. Once new migrants arrived in the mid-twentieth century amid severe housing shortages, many buildings were beyond repair. With the exception of six public housing developments, the area had not built any new housing since the 1920s.[3] The community was also witnessing dramatic racial changes—Latina/o (im)migrants and, more significant, the influx of African Americans after 1940. Over that decade, forty thousand African Americans, part of the second Great Migration from the South, had settled in the vicinity, now constituting over 40 percent of the area's population. Meanwhile, by 1953, an estimated twenty-eight thousand "Spanish-speaking" (im)migrants lived in the area. White residents who had the desire and means to escape the run-down district did so in growing numbers, thereby exacerbating the racial change. If racial fears or upward mobility did not prompt others to move, federal highway construction did. Thousands of residents were excised as the city made way for expressways that would bring suburbanites into the city more quickly, and, the hope was, keep them from abandoning it altogether.

Urban planners and downtown executives considered the city's central region "blighted" and "near blighted" and saw it, and especially its growing African American population, as a threat to the vitality of the metropolis, and especially its downtown department stores, banks, insurance companies, and railroads. Fortunately for downtown business interests, they had a friend in newly elected Democratic mayor Richard J. Daley. When Daley moved into city hall, he quickly developed an agenda that included modernizing the city, improving services to (some) neighborhoods, and cultivating powerful allies among the downtown (almost entirely Republican) elite. Daley was keenly aware of the value that the city's most powerful Republicans symbolized for him politically. Thus, he began a modernization and redevelopment plan for the city that would ease their fears of a rapidly declining downtown. Clearing the overcrowded, dirty slums of the Near West Side and other nearby areas would potentially attract commercial and residential real estate investment and thereby help stabilize a downtown economy that was rapidly being eclipsed by new suburban markets. Urban renewal would also attract millions of federal dollars, and it would mean huge patronage contracts and jobs that the Democratic machine would happily dole out in exchange for political loyalty at the polls. Redevelopment would be made possible by the large-scale construction of public housing, meant to replace deleterious dwellings and improve the appearance of the central city. But urban renewal would also be guided by racial concerns. As journalists Adam Cohen and Elizabeth Taylor observe, "Daley's most lasting legacy was . . . building the modern city of Chicago. . . . Daley's modern Chicago was built, however, on an unstated foundation: commitment to racial segregation. He preserved the city's white neighborhoods and business districts by building racial separation into the very concrete of the city. New developments—housing, highways, and schools—were built where they would serve as a barrier between white neighborhoods and the black ghetto."[4]

Many Near West Side residents agreed that their neighborhood was extremely deteriorated, undergoing dramatic population turnover, and in need of municipal resources. A number of area residents—Italians, Greeks, Mexicans, African Americans, and others—were concerned enough to form a grassroots organization, the Near West Side Planning Board, to solicit community participation in shaping the area's future. The group sought to direct the conservation, improvement, and redevelopment of the neighborhood's housing, infrastructure, and public works (streets, alleys, parks). By 1960, the grassroots democratic, multiracial experiment looked promising: the group had succeeded in getting forty-five acres of land at Harrison and Halsted Streets designated for new affordable housing and a revitalized multiethnic shopping district. The plans of a small neighborhood group, however, would prove no match for city hall, powerful business interests, and state officials. The Near West Side would go the way of other urban communities—Lincoln Square in Manhattan, Chavez Ravine in Los Angeles, and Boston's West End—working-class communities that were each displaced by grand urban renewal projects.[5]

In the postwar era, when housing and urban planning initiatives aimed to increase the numbers of middle-class whites and solidify the city's racial boundaries, Mexicans and Puerto Ricans became casualties of such policies. They experienced a pattern of successive displacement that relocated them from one neighborhood to another just ahead of urban renewal bulldozers. This chapter and the two that follow trace the story of such displacement, revealing how race and class converged to determine the future of Mexican and Puerto Rican communities in the central city. These narratives form an important part of the collective memory of many Mexican and Puerto Rican Chicagoans. Their imprint on official archives is rather faint, as is their presence in the dominant narrative told about the urban renewal, in large part because most Spanish-speaking residents were relative newcomers and did not wield much political power. But their historical presence has also been overshadowed by displaced white ethnic groups—Italian and Greek Americans—and African Americans who remained. Nonetheless, the memories of so many former Puerto Rican, and especially Mexican American, residents reveal that they were at the center of such physical restructuring—not much able to change it but burdened with its consequences.

Urban Planning, Racial Change, and Public Housing

The condition of Chicago's central city neighborhoods—the Near West, Near North, and Near South Sides—in the mid-twentieth century provoked great consternation among public officials and the city's urban planning advisers. As early as 1943, civic leaders and business magnates who formed the membership of the Chicago Plan Commission (CPC) deemed these areas immediately surrounding the central business district or downtown "blighted" and "near blighted" (see fig. 12). This decay was particularly troubling because many members of the CPC (department store barons, bankers, real estate investors) held business interests downtown and thus were concerned with the area's economic viability. The CPC was established in the early 1900s with one hundred "leading citizens" of Chicago, including renowned architect Daniel H. Burnham, and served as an advisory board on urban planning affairs. With a stream of seemingly unruly immigrants flooding the metropolis, the city's elite needed a plan for taming urban squalor and disorder. In 1909, Burnham and the CPC produced the "Plan of Chicago," which projected an idealized vision for the city's future. Though the body changed in form and composition over the years, in the 1940s and 1950s, it continued expressing concern over the city's future. The commission recognized that much of the central city was in extremely aged and deteriorated condition. Many buildings dated back nearly one hundred years, and still lacked plumbing and sewage lines. The region also had the city's highest population density—over thirty-five thousand people per square mile.[6]

The CPC sketched out plans for a renewed and revitalized central area of the city. Urban planners, downtown business leaders, and politicians thought that offering the amenities that made the suburbs so attractive—larger plots of land for homes; cleaner, safer, homogeneous neighborhoods; decreased traffic; and overall, aesthetically pleasing surroundings—would help retain middle-class whites and restore economic stability. Ultimately, city leaders sought "the maintenance of the Loop and its environs as a safe and environmentally congenial locale for business activities, cultural institutions, and affluent residents."[7]

Concerns about physical decay were compounded by striking population trends that were reshaping the metropolis. Between 1940 and 1950, the nonwhite population of Chicago more than doubled, from 232,000 to 510,000 people. Chicago had the second largest nonwhite population in the country. Of those classified as "nonwhite," 492,000 were "Negroes," most of them recent migrants from the South. (The 13,000 other "nonwhites"

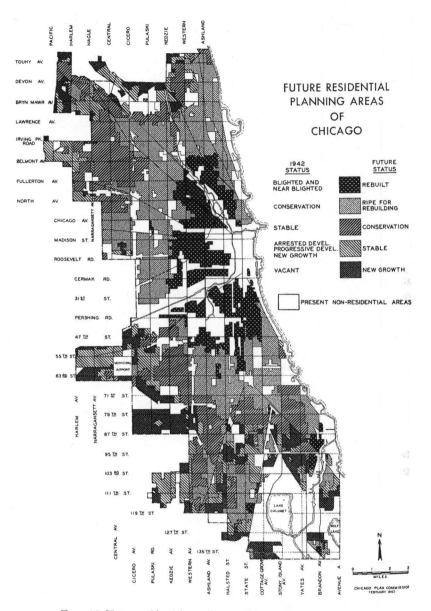

Figure 12. "Future residential areas," 1943. Chicago Plan Commission,
Chicago Looks Ahead (Chicago: Chicago Plan Commission, 1945).

included Chinese, Japanese, American Indians, and Mexicans who were identified as having visibly "Indian" ancestry.) This new black populace was pressing out of the historically segregated Black Belt and settling directly west of the Loop, on the Near West Side.[8] At the same time, the city was experiencing rapid white population loss. In 1941, the CPC recognized that white families were leaving for the suburbs. Soon the downtown business district began losing retail sales to newly built suburban shopping centers. The CPC began strategizing ways to attract middle-class white professionals back to the central city and revitalize the downtown shopping corridor.[9]

The Home Owners Loan Corporation (HOLC) had given the Near West Side neighborhood a grade of "D" in 1940, noting "the future of this blighted neighborhood is hopeless." Although African Americans made up less than 20 percent of local residents, the HOLC bluntly expressed its opinion about the racially mixed community: "The entire area is just as bad, if not worse, than the large colored blighted area where Chicago's three hundred odd thousand colored people live [the Black Belt]. . . . [It] is becoming, increasingly, a serious problem and a menace."[10] The Chicago Plan Commission echoed this assessment, objecting not only to the racial diversity but to the diversity of the built environment: "The population today is one of the most heterogeneous in the city. . . . This area is among the worst near the core of the city from the point of view of size and variation of blocks." The Near West Side was also one of the poorest in the city, after the segregated all-black communities of the South Side. The median family income measured only $3,984, compared to neighborhoods of the city outskirts, which averaged $7,000–$8,000. The area had some of the oldest school buildings in the city, some dating back to the 1850s and 1870s.[11] Many buildings were in desperate need of repair, some even beyond salvaging, and others lay abandoned and vacant.

The area had numerous absentee landlords and a low number of homeowners. In 1960, only 10 percent of all housing units were owner occupied. Single-family homes were uncommon: 46 percent of housing structures had three to nine units, and 30 percent had ten units or more.[12] Many apartments were regularly subdivided into smaller "kitchenettes," or one-room dwellings with shared bathroom and sometimes shared kitchen facilities. Slumlords, including local politicians such as State Senator Roland Libonati (D-17th), maintained buildings with faulty plumbing, exposed wires, broken fire escapes and stairways, and leaking roofs. Trash heaps and rodents added to these serious hazards. Tenants such as the Hernandez family, who lived in a single room (formerly a saloon), without a bathtub or kitchen sink, paid Libonati sixty dollars a month for the space. A single cardboard partition divided the room for the couple and their ten children. Such unsafe, substandard housing was not uncommon in the central city, where landlords tried to extract the highest rents possible with the most minimal improvements. Unless local media brought attention to these slum conditions, as the *Chicago Daily News* did in the 1950s, most landlords operated with impunity from building inspectors and fire officials.[13]

Urban renewal would ostensibly eliminate such types of inadequate housing and conserve that which still appeared viable. State legislation provided the legal basis for these plans, and federal funding soon supported such ambitions. In 1941, the state passed the Neighborhood Redevelopment Corporations Act, allowing community groups or other entities to effect plans for renewal in slum and blighted areas. Entire communities would be targeted for "slum clearance," meaning that older housing structures would be razed and residents (usually low-income and often nonwhite) removed. In their place, the city or private developers would erect new housing units to provide more sanitary and structurally sound living environments. On the face of it, this seemed good policy. According to housing commissioner Charles E. Slusser, public housing represented "an important example of an 'island of resistance' to the blight which threatens so many of the nation's large cities."[14] Although public housing was not in itself the end goal, it became a constitutive element of urban redevelopment. As Arnold Hirsch notes, "Public housing . . . bec[a]me the cornerstone of private redevelopment, and in turn, was dominated by it." Profit-driven redevelopment for middle- to upper-income white residents took priority over constructing sound, suitable dwellings for the city's poor, predominantly nonwhite citizens.[15]

The nation's first public housing developments had emerged during the Franklin D. Roosevelt administration. Initially designed to improve shelter for the poor and, more important, to create jobs during the Depression, a 1933 federal housing law established the Public Works Administration (PWA) to lead this effort. The PWA made loans to local housing authorities or private developers, or initiated projects on its own. Chicago desperately needed new housing: in 1933, in the midst of the Great Depression, only twenty-three new apartments had been built in the entire city.[16] By 1937, the PWA, along with the recently formed Chicago Housing Authority

(CHA), completed the city's first public housing development, a collection of neat, low-rise brick row houses on the Near West Side called the Jane Addams Homes (JAH).[17]

The JAH initially served an almost exclusively white population. Administrators had correctly anticipated white objections to racial integration and thus planned to rent only 26 of the 1,027 units to African Americans. Once black leaders publicly protested, however, JAH officials acquiesced by admitting slightly more black tenants but restricting them to less than 10 percent of the population until the 1950s. Housing officials were beholden to the "neighborhood composition rule," an inelegant but expedient solution to deal with the problem of racial segregation. Introduced by federal housing administrator Harold Ickes, it required that public housing projects maintain the existing racial composition of a neighborhood once they began to admit tenants. Thus, projects built in predominantly white areas should remain white, and those in black areas remained black. This policy would later guide public housing placement: CHA officials would be careful to select sites for future projects that would match the intended racial occupancy of developments. At JAH, the CHA used a very restrictive definition of the surrounding neighborhood so that African Americans would be represented in limited numbers. In particular, it did not count the large black population concentrated to the south of Twelfth Street (Roosevelt Road). Once it felt pressure to admit black tenants, it restricted them to only certain buildings in the complex.[18] As a solution to calls for black occupancy, in 1942 the agency opened the Robert H. Brooks Homes, named after the first black World War II hero. This became the city's second segregated predominantly black housing development.[19] The 834 units lay just across the street from the Addams Homes, on the south side of Twelfth Street, where African Americans were more numerous. The racial segregation was shockingly apparent—Brooks was almost 82 percent black while Addams was over 90 percent white.[20]

Mexicans occupied public housing from the beginning as well. Because Mexicans were not classified separately at this time, they seem to have been counted as "white." They were not officially excluded from JAH as stringently as African Americans. JAH resident newsletters occasionally mentioned Spanish-surnamed tenants such as the Melendez family, the Valles family, and the Lunas as early as 1939. Still, their numbers were surprisingly low given the high rates of poverty and their population numbering over twenty thousand citywide. That year, they comprised 1.9 percent of Addams tenants, although they represented 3.8 percent of the neighborhood's population.[21]

By World War II, Chicagoans faced a desperate need for shelter as thousands of war workers crammed into the region. For many whites, the housing crisis was resolved by the postwar construction of private housing (federally subsidized with FHA and VA mortgages), especially in the city's outskirts and suburbs. Seventy-seven percent of all new housing in the Chicagoland area was in fact built in the suburbs in the postwar era, and 76 percent of it consisted of single-family homes.[22] African Americans were effectively excluded from such housing. They put increasing pressure on city officials to provide them more accommodations. If the private housing market made little room for them and relegated them to slum neighborhoods, however, the city's policy of clearing black slums did not offer a solution either. The Urban League pointed out the consequences of urban renewal, or what some called "Negro removal," and the "neighborhood composition rule." The group astutely observed that the pattern of slum clearance "displace[d] Negro homes" and added a subsequent "load . . . to the already intolerable overcrowding in Negro housing."[23] Other housing leaders noted, "The eradication of blight inherently did nothing to increase the supply of low-income housing and inevitably created the problem of relocating uprooted slum dwellers."[24] Instead, as substandard and condemned buildings were dropped to the ground, the CHA erected public housing in the same segregated slum areas. Arnold Hirsch has noted that the government's tacit endorsement of segregation created a "second ghetto" in the forties and fifties, reinforcing black isolation and doing little to address chronic and crippling poverty and unemployment, often caused by employment discrimination. Unfortunately, though perhaps not surprisingly, new housing was woefully inadequate. Chicago architect Barry Byrne observed, "Slum clearance hasn't improved [the slums]. They have substituted a more sanitary type of squalor." New York housing advocate Catherine Bauer similarly noted, "Life in the usual public housing projects is just not the way most American families want to live."[25]

The Near West Side became increasingly heterogeneous in the postwar years as a result of the influx of African Americans and Latinos/as and the departure of many whites. Population data clearly reveal the apparent "white flight"[26] of the neighborhood in the mid-twentieth century (see table 7). Though the neighborhood had witnessed a population decline beginning in the 1920s, it experienced a significant population increase between 1940 and 1950 as a result of black in-migration. Mexicans and Puerto Ricans began moving in, but their numbers were masked under the racial label

Table 7   Near West Side white and black populations, 1940–70

	1940	1950	1960	1970
Total population	136,518	160,362	126,610	78,703
% change		(+17.5)	(−21.0)	(−37.8)
White population*	110,274	93,934	57,676	19,833†
% change		(−14.8)	(−38.6)	(−65.6)
Black population	25,774	65,520	68,146	56,836
Blacks as % of population	18.9	40.9	53.8	72.2

Sources: Kitagawa and Taueber, *Local Community Fact Book, 1960;* and Chicago Fact Book Consortium, *Local Community Fact Book, 1970 and 1980.*
*White population figures also included Mexicans and Puerto Ricans during these years who were not visibly identified as some other race (Negro, other) or who self-identified as white or whom census enumerators chose to classify as "white."
†An estimated 6,989 "Spanish Language" persons (mainly Mexicans and Puerto Ricans) were included in this number. Thus, the total non-Hispanic white population by 1970 actually numbered only 12,844.

of "white." In fact, whites continued to decline, so that between 1940 and 1970, the area lost fully 82 percent of its white population.

Some residents had been pushed out by highway construction; others were motivated by opportunities for better housing, lured by the construction boom of the city's outer neighborhoods and suburbs. More than a few, however, must have considered the area's changing racial dynamics in making their decisions. While they most likely did not consult census records, white residents could see a shifting balance in the neighborhood's racial composition. With a startling decline of over 52,000 whites by 1960, African Americans became the majority of the population. Mexicans composed the second largest foreign-stock group in the neighborhood (after Italians), and Puerto Ricans numbered over 6,000. By 1970, the area's population had contracted to half its figure two decades earlier. Fewer than 13,000 non-Hispanic whites remained in the area, from a peak of 110,000 three decades earlier. African Americans constituted the overwhelming majority, 72.2 percent.[27]

As elsewhere in the city, race played a pivotal factor in urban renewal and public housing policy decisions. Architect Wolf Von Eckardt has noted, "Overtly or covertly, race is the predominant issue of urban renewal and urban life. Racial design dictates just about all city planning."[28] Indeed, the growing black population on the Near West Side made city leaders increasingly uneasy. Officials responded by corralling African Americans into public housing.

The "second ghetto," however, was not limited to the South Side, epitomized in the iconic four-mile stretch of the Robert Taylor, Harold Ickes,

Dearborn, Hilliard, and Stateway Gardens Homes.[29] Rather, the Near West Side, a politically weak, blue-collar, expendable, and most important, *racially mixed* area, also became concentrated with predominantly black public housing projects by the early sixties. The CHA proceeded apace to construct segregated public housing in the neighborhood under the cover of the Ickes neighborhood composition rule. Loomis Courts, twin seven-story buildings constructed just steps from the segregated Robert H. Brooks Homes, opened in 1953 with 126 units. The Grace Abbott development at Fifteenth Street and Blue Island Avenue solidified the local racial geography. The 1,200-unit complex opened its doors in 1954, adjacent to the Brooks Homes and Loomis Courts, where "Negro families now constitute over 90 percent of the total population."[30] These three developments, along with the Addams Homes, were collectively known as "the ABLA Homes"—an acronym for Addams, Brooks, Loomis, Abbott. All together, ABLA had over 3,500 units, a dense congregation of predominantly poor and working-class African Americans mostly south of Roosevelt Road. In 1950, the CHA also built two seven-story high-rise buildings with the idyllic name "Maplewood Courts" two miles away on the northwestern edge of the community along Western Avenue and Van Buren Street, adding 132 more public housing units on the Near West Side.[31] Finally, from 1957 to 1961, the housing authority opened the Henry Horner Homes, a mix of low-rise and multistory buildings, to the west of the huge medical complex. By the 1960s, the Near West Side had six major housing projects within its boundaries, and African Americans predominated in all of them.[32] The Near West Side stood out as one of the only racially mixed community areas in the city with such a high concentration of public housing. Apart from the massive ABLA Homes, the density of the units was alleviated by the physical dispersal of the Maplewood and Horner projects, far enough to exist beyond the imagination of most residents who lived in the "Taylor Street" or Harrison-Halsted area (see fig. 13). In its efforts to rid the Near West Side of deleterious and condemned housing, the city had dismantled local community life and created a "second ghetto."[33]

Not all white leaders supported such policy. CHA director Elizabeth Wood had gained a reputation for promoting integrated public housing during her time at the agency. White opposition stymied her efforts, however. In 1948, the state legislature granted the city council the power to veto CHA decisions on where to locate housing projects; thus, aldermen could pander to their constituents' "NIMBY-ism"[34] and prejudice against black-occupied public housing in their wards. Wood's efforts were completely crushed when she was fired by Mayor Martin Kennelly in 1954. At that

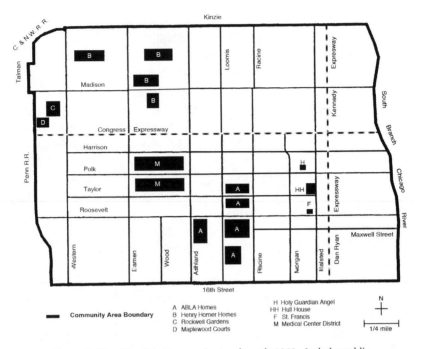

Figure 13. Near West Side Community Area by early 1960s. Includes public housing projects, newly constructed highways, and the locations of the soon-to-be-demolished Hull House and Holy Guardian Angel parish and school. Note that the Near West Side measures less than six square miles.

point, the dream of ever integrating public housing evaporated.[35] New leaders appointed by Kennelly and, later, Daley ensured that the CHA would no longer pursue racial integration as a policy. Locating public housing, especially for African Americans, involved careful political calculations. Since Mayor Daley faced political resistance to public housing projects in the "Bungalow Belt" areas of the city, he and his planners chose instead to build vertical high-rise projects to contain the city's large African American population in as limited an area as possible.[36] When he entered office in 1956, he grabbed hold of federal urban renewal dollars but assured white machine loyalists in the Bungalow Belt, especially those in his own neighborhood of Bridgeport, that African Americans would not penetrate their boundaries. Daley did not dare upset the racial order of the Bungalow Belt. He sacrificed the Near West Side instead.

What appeared to be all-black housing developments initially included other "nonwhite" people. Perhaps because of their extant US citizenship and familiarity with federal social programs on the island, some Puerto

Rican migrants soon settled into public projects. An estimated 150 families occupied the Jane Addams Homes in 1953.[37] The local Puerto Rico Migration Division office facilitated access to apartments by assisting many new arrivals with completing applications. In the 1956–57 fiscal year, for example, it helped over 600 people apply for apartments throughout the city.[38] Dark-skinned Puerto Ricans blended in with African Americans and were perhaps indistinguishable to outside observers. Light-skinned migrants, however, who were technically classified by the census and many institutions as "white," conveniently served as replacements for outgoing white tenants and thus provided the illusion of racial integration.[39] While Puerto Ricans lived in public housing in other neighborhoods as well (see chapter 4), more than a few found themselves in projects on the Near West Side. The Ramirez family, for example, obtained housing in Maplewood Courts in the 1950s. The concentration of urban poor and the racial tensions that festered in the cramped quarters, however, eventually forced the family out of the building. By the late fifties, the Puerto Rican Catholic fraternal group the Knights of St. John became vocal critics of public housing conditions, warning "all Spanish-speaking in-migrant families to 'stay out of public housing projects.'" Mexican families who occupied the ABLA Homes likewise struggled with tensions and violence, particularly among young men. Such families grappled with the difficult choice between remaining in their low-cost apartments and risking their children's safety or paying higher rents for lower-quality housing elsewhere in exchange for less hostile conditions.[40]

To be sure, public projects provided affordable living for families who otherwise could afford only the most dilapidated and deleterious accommodations. Public housing also provided an alternative to the racial discrimination of the private housing market, which prevented many African Americans, and some Puerto Ricans and Mexicans, from securing better homes. Sparkling new CHA buildings in their modern concrete and brick splendor seemed promising at first to new tenants. Indeed, anything would have been a marked improvement for families who had endured some of the city's worst slum conditions. Buildings, however, rapidly revealed design, planning, and social engineering flaws. Some observers have argued that income regulations and lax tenant selection policies drove out stable working-class families of all races, leaving behind only the most marginal and troublesome residents. Yet with few employment opportunities, many tenants not surprisingly turned to the informal economy and illicit activities to support themselves. As a result, drug dealers, gang members, and other criminalized people soon dominated and ruled over remaining residents (especially single mothers) who lacked the means to escape communities that became seized by terror.[41] Only a few critics in the early years predicted the disaster that such public housing policies would produce. Elizabeth Wood had presciently observed, "The next generation will have to cure the slums created by this generation's official blindness."[42]

African Americans soon became synonymous with public housing and vice versa, an association that quickly stigmatized the developments with a racially undesirable population and stereotyped its tenants as welfare dependent, lazy, and criminal. Many whites increasingly viewed blacks as the undeserving beneficiaries of federal and local entitlement programs, granted subsidized housing while they (whites) had to pay higher rents or rising property taxes.[43] Whites who initially occupied JAH were usually blue-collar, two-parent households, the "deserving poor." As income qualifications for public housing increasingly excluded most working families and since African Americans experienced higher rates of poverty, residents overwhelmingly consisted of those who relied on public assistance (i.e., Aid to Dependent Children). This further cemented white views that black people received social benefits that hardworking whites paid for but were denied. These twin racial and class aspersions stigmatized public housing and ensured that most nonblack families and economically stable black families quickly fled the projects.

Some African Americans worked hard to dispel this characterization and develop interracial cooperation and understanding in the neighborhood. The Near West Side Community Council (NWSCC), formed originally as the Interracial Council in 1939, sought to improve neighborhood relations in the multiracial, multiethnic community. William Jones, a southern African American educated at Morehouse College, led the organization beginning in 1946. Jones and his staff worked to foster interethnic and interracial harmony, inviting a wide range of groups and individuals to join his organization. He secured participation from over ninety churches, schools, social welfare agencies, veterans' groups, and public housing tenant councils. Mexican American groups, such as the Mexican Civic Committee, the Mexican American Council, and the Manuel Perez American Legion Post, joined the council along with many others. The NWSCC recognized the need to develop and provide services for impoverished area residents, hopefully to improve living conditions and therefore the climate. The work of the NWSCC reveals the ways in which black leaders tried to carve a place in the neighborhood for the black community. Rather than just shadowy interlopers or anonymous occupants of public housing and slum buildings, black residents associated with community institutions (i.e., churches, clubs, the NWSCC) made an effort to integrate themselves into the Near West Side and establish good relations with their diverse neighbors.[44]

Grassroots Neighborhood Planning

In the years after World War II, Near West Side residents recognized that their neighborhood sorely needed rehabilitation and improvements and was showing "fractures in [its] physical infrastructure."[45] Italian Americans, one of the oldest groups in the area, became especially concerned about the neighborhood's future and began discussing these issues in the late 1940s. They soon turned to Hull House for guidance on how to preserve and improve their community. Eri Hulbert, nephew of Jane Addams and the former executive director of the public housing development named after his aunt, began meeting with community residents to discuss the neighborhood's condition. The ad hoc group created the Near West Side Planning Board (NWSPB) in 1949, identifying as its purpose "to plan and effect legal foundations for basic land use and street requirements; to stimulate private and public rehabilitation and redevelopment according to plan; [and] to effect with present occupants, a stable, modern enduring Near West Side."[46]

The NWSPB included small business and property owners, representatives from large manufacturing concerns in the area, churches and public housing projects, and Hull House staff members such as Jessie Binford. Italian Americans represented the largest ethnic group, including local residents such as Ernest Giovangelo and his sister, Florence Scala. In 1950, the organization reportedly claimed "128 Italians, 70 blacks, 15 Mexicans, 5 Greeks, and 122 others."[47] The NWSPB tried to be inclusive in reaching its multiracial and multiethnic neighbors, working closely with William P. Jones of the Near West Side Community Council.[48] The board was truly an experiment in democratic urban planning and impressed federal administrators so much that it was featured in a national publication of the Housing and Home Finance Agency, *Approaches to Urban Renewal in Several Cities*. Remarkably, the NWSPB represented a proactive initiative of local residents (homeowners, renters, and business owners) to contribute to the city's planning in their neighborhood. It truly distinguished itself as a model of community-controlled development long before such approaches gained wider popularity.[49]

The NWSPB developed a multilayered plan for neighborhood improvement—calling for razing certain areas, conserving others, and building new housing. Its work was made possible by local, state, and federal legislation that had begun promoting urban renewal. The Illinois legislature's 1947 Blighted Areas Redevelopment Act granted authority to land clearance commissions to designate areas as "blighted" and "slum" and to acquire such land to clear and sell to private developers.[50] The city council established the Chicago Land Clearance Commission (CLCC) to carry out these duties. In 1953, the state created the Urban Community Conservation Act, extending cities' power of eminent domain to conservation projects in addition to slum clearance projects. In anticipation of the law, the city had formed an interim Commission on Neighborhood Conservation, to identify areas that qualified for preservation rather than clearance and to oversee the process. The temporary commission was later renamed the Community Conservation Board (CCB), operating from 1955 until 1962, when it was merged with the CLCC into the new Department of Urban Renewal.[51]

In the 1940s, the Near West Side had been designated as an entirely blighted area, thus marking it for complete demolition and redevelopment under city guidelines. The NWSPB succeeded in reversing that designation so that it could more carefully identify which areas were eligible for conservation and which needed to be razed completely. This would help preserve many people's homes and assist them in securing private bank loans to fund property improvements.[52] The NWSPB also began preparing for other dramatic changes in its built environment. In the years after World War II, highway construction accelerated throughout the nation. Local authorities made plans for various expressways and toll roads around the Chicago area and suburbs, connecting the city to far-reaching rural areas. The interstates would provide faster routes for moving goods and foodstuffs and would make it easier for suburbanites to come into the city and hopefully contribute dollars to the local economy.[53] In 1955, the state passed a massive bond issue that helped fund highway construction. The next year, the Federal Interstate Highway Act pushed local highway projects forward. The Near West Side, with its central location and proximity to downtown, became the central interchange for three federal expressways that fanned out to the north, south, and west. In 1955, a nearby section of the Congress Street (later renamed Eisenhower) Expressway, which for several years had been undergoing expansion to convert it from a parkway to a "superhighway," was finally completed.[54] The North (Kennedy) Expressway opened that same year, and the South (Dan Ryan) Expressway opened in 1961–62. Such massive federal highway projects had a much higher price tag than their financial cost. They deformed the neighborhood by excising thousands of residents. The Congress Expressway, for example, removed sixteen thousand families in its path, thus contributing to the area's population decline.[55]

In conjunction with the Chicago Plan Commission, the Near West Side Planning Board held open forums for community residents to provide input for future plans. Since its early days, the planning board sought the cooperation and participation of local businesses, churches, and other community organizations. An open meeting in March 1952 announced the support of over eighty neighborhood groups, including churches, the Jane Addams and Robert Brooks Homes, schools, social service agencies, and civic groups. Mexican American organizations participated, including the Cordi Marian Settlement, the Mexican American Council of Chicago, the Mexican Civic Committee of the West Side, the Mexican Methodist Church, the Manuel Pérez American Legion Post 1017, and St. Francis of Assisi Church. As the planning board met with the city about new housing and the expressway construction, it invited neighborhood organizations and institutions to share their views. A public hearing in May 1956 to decide whether to designate a section of the community as a "conservation area" drew a crowd of more than four hundred people.[56] At one community forum, invited guest speaker James C. Downs, the city's housing and redevelopment coordinator, applauded the residents and encouraged their efforts: "Here you have tremendous resources. You have here not only commercial . . . industrial . . . residential resources . . . but you have spiritual . . . cultural . . . social resources. . . . There is a direction to what you are doing."[57] Most urban planning projects did not have such community involvement, but the Near West Side Planning Board was determined to play a role in its own future.[58]

The group faced an uphill battle, however, in securing funding and maintaining relations with the neighborhood's most important institutions—the Catholic churches and the political establishment. As institutions vying for power and influence, such groups were always wary of one another. On the one hand, some Catholic priests did not approve of Protestant Hull House wielding so much influence over its parishioners. On the other hand, the NWSPB did not always have complete cooperation from Hull House, especially after the suicide of Eri Hulbert in 1955. Without his advocacy, the NWSPB lost its most important champion at Hull House. Since Jane Addams's death, the board of trustees no longer had her intimate connection with area residents and expressed much less interest in the community's development. Eventually, the NWSPB encountered friction with the trustees. At one point, Hull House even withdrew funding from the planning board and instead funded its own competing Citizen Participation Project, in which it incorporated Italian, Greek, and Mexican Americans in neighborhood planning projects.

By 1956, the community also obtained a "blighted" designation for the Harrison-Halsted sector, approximately forty-five acres covering ten blocks from Harrison to Arthington Streets, and Halsted to Morgan Streets, which contained some of the neighborhood's worst housing. The area secured approval for clearance and redevelopment.[59] The site encompassed 835 dwelling units and approximately 3,500 people, or 700 families. This included the heart of the Mexican settlement and many of the groceries, restaurants, and other businesses that served it. The Harrison-Halsted site had a projected cost of $6.2 million, over $4 million of which would be paid by the federal government. The Community Conservation Board had also approved conservation projects in other parts of the neighborhood with an additional projected cost of $4.6 million. The federal government was expected to cover three-fourths of this expenditure, and the project would require the relocation of 1,700 families. In the neighboring streets just to the west of the Harrison-Halsted site, the CCB estimated that 1,807 units would have to be cleared because of slum, deleterious, or unsound environmental conditions. Mexicans occupied 18.9 percent, or 343, of those units. An additional 106 Mexican households would need to be displaced for street widening and other public works. Puerto Ricans occupied 84 units, and "other Spanish" residents held another 28 apartments. Altogether, the Spanish-speaking comprised 25 percent of the dwellings to be displaced. Many of these families were large and included small children. Redevelopment and clearance plans would have an especially hard impact on them, as they often struggled most to find new housing.[60]

Some observers have suggested that the neighborhood revitalization efforts of the NWSPB were spurred by fear of racial change. Sociologist Gerald Suttles implies that the community's Italian Americans (and some Mexican Americans) wished to expel the growing population of poor black and brown people. According to him, "It was hoped that rental and property values would be raised out of the reach of the low income members of the other ethnic groups [Mexicans, Puerto Ricans, and African Americans]." Italian Americans were certainly apprehensive about how "their" neighborhood was changing. Undoubtedly, the Near West Side was being dismantled bit by bit, disfigured by expressways, abandoned by those who had means, and increasingly relinquished to poor, predominantly African American, public housing residents. Community leader Florence Scala recognized the racial implications of the broader urban planning policies taking place around her: "We were inexperienced and unschooled and yet we knew that unless you began to renew and redevelop the city, that it would become a black ghetto, in—we thought at that time—25 years." Though Scala's comments suggest racial fears, other statements she has made and her record of community activism reveal a strong commitment to interracial cooperation and pluralism. Her concerns seemed more focused on the compounded effects of race and class. Like some others on the Near West Side, she hoped to sustain the racial mix of the neighborhood and prevent the complete turnover occurring in other parts of the city. Residents fought to stay in their neighborhood rather than flee the area in fear.[61]

Certainly some community residents did express racist impulses. For some, for example, the community's southern boundary lay at Roosevelt Road and its eastern boundary at Halsted, thus excluding the large African American population in the Robert Brooks Homes and later the Loomis and Abbott Homes. For those individuals, the boundaries of such an "imagined community" revealed a racially exclusive vision.[62] But the NWSPB clearly outlined its area boundaries at Sixteenth Street, the railroad tracks that separated it from the Pilsen neighborhood to the south. Thus, African Americans in both private and public housing were included. The fact that the NWSPB worked with William Jones of the Near West Side Community Council and had many black members suggests that at least some neighbors sought to work cooperatively with the black community to combat neighborhood decline. Still, some whites were clearly not interested in an experiment of racial integration.[63]

By 1958, the city council and the Illinois Housing Board had approved Harrison-Halsted as a renewal site. Illinois Project R-10, as it was known, called for new affordable housing that would be made available to local residents for purchase and a "small international kind of shopping center."[64] The project would cost the city only one-third of the total price, as federal urban renewal funds would cover the remainder.[65] The project's inclusion in the city's formal *Central Area Plan* that year (as cited in the chapter's first epigraph) signaled to the NWSPB that its plans had met approval and reassured it of the city's commitment. The Chicago Land Clearance Commission thus began appraising and purchasing lots and clearing them. Families and business owners began moving out. Nothing could have prepared them, however, for what happened next. The area's urban renewal designation inadvertently led the neighborhood in an entirely different direction. The land clearance commissioner, Philip Doyle, was fully aware of the Harrison-Halsted plans and had even met with the NWSPB in late 1960. Yet both James Downs and Doyle were aware of and complicit in promoting other plans for the area. By the fall of that year, the mayor was considering scrapping the Harrison-Halsted plans and offering the half-cleared site for the construction of a state university.[66]

A Place for the University

After World War II, the University of Illinois, located in the towns of Champaign and Urbana, two hours south of Chicago, opened a two-year campus at Chicago's Navy Pier. As a public institution meant to serve working- and middle-class students, the campus attracted those who sought a less expensive education than that offered by local private colleges.[67] Students, primarily GIs, attended the lakefront campus for two years and then had the option of transferring downstate to the four-year institution in Urbana-Champaign. Many complained, however, that relocating to central Illinois proved unfeasible, especially for those with work or family obligations. The Navy Pier location (recently an actual functioning pier for the US Navy during the war) was sorely inadequate for expansion to a four-year university. The university needed a new site. Chicago officials soon saw an opportunity for locating a new four-year undergraduate campus within the city.[68]

Beginning in 1951, the board of trustees began discussing the need for a permanent location for a Chicago-area, four-year branch. As George Rosen describes, the decision to build a northern Illinois campus involved a number of political actors and received support and criticism from various sectors. The board of trustees, state legislature, state board of education, city government, nearby private universities, other public colleges throughout the state, and even the University of Illinois's Champaign-Urbana campus either supported or opposed the proposal based on their varying interests and concerns over the construction of a new campus.[69] By 1955, the board of trustees and the University of Illinois president agreed on the need to actively begin searching for a Chicago-area location. An initial report identified sixty-nine potential sites, both within the city and in the suburbs. Among three types of sites that might be considered—a suburban location, a lakefront site, or a slum clearance project—the first would be the least expensive. Miller Meadows, a tract of the Cook County Forest Preserves, became the board of trustees' first choice. The dean of the Navy Pier campus, C. C. Caveny, made known his preference for a suburban site and his endorsement of Miller Meadows. He hinted at the greater desirability of a suburban campus in terms of space and safety compared to the crowded, unsanitary, and dangerous conditions of the inner city.[70] Yet legal restrictions on land use and the county's opposition to using public park space blocked the Miller Meadows option.

Recently elected Mayor Richard J. Daley initially remained neutral on the site selection. He soon realized, however, that downtown business leaders strongly advocated that the university be built within city limits, and preferably downtown. The Chicago Central Area Committee (CCAC), a group of business leaders whose interests lay in the commercial transactions and real estate values of the city's central business district, was deeply invested in the conditions of the surrounding areas. It recognized the significance of the Near West Side's location, "within a stone's throw of the most valuable property in Metropolitan Chicago." CCAC and Chicago Plan Commission memberships overlapped considerably. Daley needed the political support of downtown Republican business magnates as a new mayor who would seek reelection. He quickly aligned himself with their cause and aggressively promoted a central city location for the campus.[71]

In 1957, the CCAC proposed three central city sites, including one on the northeastern end of the Near West Side, an underutilized railroad yard. CCAC chairman Holman D. Pettibone tried to make a persuasive case for how the university's location close to downtown would benefit the city and inversely how the area could offer so much to the university, its students, and faculty. The board of trustees initially dismissed the site, ostensibly because of cleanup costs and the time required to begin construction. It turned instead to a golf course in the suburb of North Riverside. The local community opposed the plan, however, so the trustees moved on to their next choice—land on Northerly Island, a lakefront parcel that included a small private airport, Meigs Field. Relocating the airport seemed too cumbersome, however, and the Chicago Association of Commerce and Industry objected to the proposal. The university thus looked next to parkland in the West Side neighborhood of Garfield Park, a blue-collar white community on the brink of racial turnover. Many residents there welcomed the campus, as it would repurpose a deteriorating park that formed a boundary with the racially transitioning East Garfield Park community. Residents of East Garfield Park, social service providers, conservationists, and the park district itself, however, opposed the loss of public recreational space. Still, supporters of the campus launched an aggressive letter-writing and publicity campaign in hopes that their neighborhood would be selected.[72]

The racial barrier that the campus symbolized was not lost on Daley and downtown businessmen. They very clearly saw a location on the Near West Side as an optimal way of blocking the African American population from moving too close to downtown. Real estate developer Arthur Rubloff baldly expressed the racism that many shared toward the presence of African Americans: "I'll tell you what's wrong with the Loop [downtown]. . . . It's people's conception of it. And the conception they have about it is one word—black. B-L-A-C-K. Black." Rubloff went on to explain that since ghettos had few businesses, African Americans went downtown to shop and eat out. Rubloff and other businessmen wanted desperately to keep African Americans away so that whites might return to the area instead.[73] The mayor and the CCAC thus insisted on a Near West Side location. The Department of City Planning's *Central Area Plan* in 1958, which included the Harrison-Halsted redevelopment project, clearly indicated the mayor's plan for the campus to be built on the proposed nearby railroad terminals. To keep the university's interest in the city and deter it from choosing a suburban location, the mayor actually offered to pay any difference in the cost of acquiring land in the city rather than in the suburbs.[74] The university thus returned to the original proposal of the idle railroad yards. The time and expense to clear the yards, however, would make it impossible to have the campus operating by the target date of 1963. More important, the railroads themselves were reluctant to negotiate a fair price for the land and terminal consolidation elsewhere. They were clearly dragging their feet and unwilling to provide the mayor his highly coveted central city location. Growing increasingly desperate, the mayor kept searching for alternatives.

In early 1959, Phil Doyle, executive director of the Chicago Land Clearance Commission, had raised the possibility of the fifty-five-acre Harrison-Halsted site. He cited the fact that the city already owned title to much of the land, much of it was cleared, and it had been approved for federal urban renewal funding. Because the Garfield Park and railroad terminal sites were still under consideration, Doyle's recommendation stirred minimal interest. By the end of that year, however, when those sites continued presenting legal and financial obstacles, Doyle raised the Harrison-Halsted option again with the mayor.[75] This new location was kept quiet, as university officials were still studying, deliberating, and hoping for a final resolution on the other two sites. By early 1960, the university's president informed the mayor that the board of trustees had decided against the railroad site and was opting for Garfield Park. The university and park district decided to pursue a legal test (a "friendly" lawsuit) to see if the sale of parkland would stand up in court. A circuit court judge ultimately ruled that acquiring parkland for a state university was unconstitutional.[76] The university then appealed to the Illinois Supreme Court. In the meantime, the mayor and his advisers continued exploring the Harrison-Halsted option.

James Downs, one of the mayor's closest urban planning advisers, became a key player in this maneuvering. Downs also sat on the Hull House Board of Trustees, even serving as president until 1960. In the midst of the NWSPB's redevelopment projects, Hull House had proposed rehabilitating some of its own buildings and developing a cooperative housing program. Downs seemingly supported these plans, but at a meeting in the spring of 1960, he relayed local news reports that the Harrison-Halsted site was being considered for the university campus. He likely knew of this possibility long before its public disclosure, since he was intimately involved with the mayor in city planning matters. Nonetheless, he reassured the Hull House board that the proposal was only rumored and not cause for concern. Downs clearly had several conflicts of interest that compromised his position as a decision maker at Hull House. As a prominent alumnus of the university and also chair of the Real Estate Research Corporation—the company that the university had hired to conduct various feasibility studies of other sites—his interests lay with the university. As a friend and trusted adviser to an increasingly powerful mayor, Downs also wanted to stay in his favor. He had the least amount of loyalty to or interest in the Hull House neighborhood. Unlike the founders and early reformers at the settlement who felt personally invested in the community, Downs had no commitments to area residents. Both the Harrison-Halsted project and Hull House's future plans now stood in jeopardy. If the city did indeed offer the urban renewal site for the campus, the rehabilitation of the settlement house facilities would also have to be halted.[77]

By May, rumors swirled in the press that the Harrison-Halsted site might be considered as the next possibility for the campus. The mayor had in fact asked the Department of City Planning to present the university with formal plans. The city apprised the university of this new option, and by the summer it had retained Downs's Real Estate Research Corporation to conduct a preliminary site study.[78] Downs was tasked with evaluating whether the community and institution that he served were expendable for the purpose of a college campus. In the meantime, the University of Illinois publicly continued to express interest in the Garfield Park site while awaiting a decision on its appeal to the Illinois Supreme Court.

By that September, the mayor publicly and officially recommended 145 acres on the Near West Side for the university's campus—the NWSPB's 58 acres, an additional 45 acres abutting the site, and another 42 acres for residential construction. The mayor cited the advantageous location and the urgent need to find a place for the university within the city immediately. The NWSPB learned of the decision through the newspapers. Within a few weeks, the Chicago Plan Commission formally replaced its proposal for the railroad terminal in its 1960 *Central Area Plan* with the Harrison-Halsted site.[79]

The university's board of trustees next had to vote on whether or not to accept the proposed site. It first awaited news of a higher education bond issue, which received voter approval in November.[80] After that, it decided to study Harrison-Halsted closely, in comparison to the only other remaining option, Garfield Park. By January, the Illinois Supreme Court reversed the circuit court's decision, allowing the university to purchase the Garfield Park land. Despite the legal green light, the university's board of trustees remained leery of rumored continuing challenges. Opponents intimated they might appeal to the US Supreme Court, which would mean further construction delays. Thus, in February the university publicly announced its decision to accept the Harrison-Halsted location.[81]

The plans immediately drew opposition from various sectors. Near West Side residents who had painstakingly participated in their neighborhood's grassroots redevelopment felt betrayed. Their hard work and planning were completely obliterated with a wave of the mayor's hand. Garfield Park residents objected vociferously as well, pointing out the irony—the Near West Side did not want the campus and they overwhelmingly did.[82] One outspoken leader of a south suburban municipal association rang a racist alarm against the inner-city site, still trying to persuade the university to choose a suburban location. Karl Treen couched his objections in concerns over crime, congestion, and traffic: "Industrial workers, students, nurses and doctors are being attacked. Professors are fearful of attacks on themselves and families." He cited the high numbers of "criminals" (in the increasingly black and Latino neighborhood) and concluded with a final admonition: "The Harrison-Halsted Street neighborhood is not only loaded crime-wise now, but will be hostile because of being up-rooted. I do not think we should antagonize 200,000 Spanish descent people."[83] The writer laid bare the explicitly racist fears of so many in the suburbs. Most tellingly, they were not directed only at African Americans but at "Spanish descent people" as well.

The Fight for the Near West Side

When NWSPB members and local residents initially learned of the mayor's decision on the Harrison-Halsted site, they did not respond publicly. Perhaps they simply could not believe that such a deal would pass: they had too much faith in their alderman, who they expected would block the proposal. They were indeed extremely naïve about how city politics worked and just how much power their Italian American alderman wielded within the Irish-dominated Democratic machine. Moreover, they did not anticipate that Hull House would passively consent to the decision or that the president of its board of directors had helped facilitate the deal. They assumed that the settlement house, which had faithfully served the neighborhood for decades, would defend them.[84] Area residents did not react to the decision until the university publicly accepted the site that February.

At that point, community residents prepared to fight for their neighborhood. Shortly after the University of Illinois's public announcement, over three hundred neighborhood residents gathered at the Holy Guardian Angel Church. They felt insulted because they had not been offered even the courtesy of public hearings to voice their opinions on the proposal.[85] They planned for fifty women—mostly mothers of children who attended Holy Guardian Angel School—to picket and protest the next morning at city hall. The group was primarily Italian American but included Mexican women as well. Interestingly, they were to be joined by Garfield Park residents who still held hopes of wooing the university there. The next morning after the picket, ten of the women met with the mayor, who told them there was nothing he could do.

The following Monday, a reported five hundred people gathered at Hull House to discuss their next steps. Residents objected to the change of plans on a number of grounds. Those who had moved out of the Harrison-Halsted area so their buildings could be razed were promised the opportunity to buy newly built homes and move back into their neighborhood. Business owners and homeowners in the conservation area that would now be demolished had invested money in rehabilitating and improving their properties. Others cited not only the financial costs but also the psychological investment people had in their neighborhood. Mrs. Carmela Zucker explained, "'My 90-year old father [has] lived in his house for 50 years. How can I explain that he has to leave this home he worked for so hard?'"[86] The mayor defended his decision as a wise choice and offered assurances that displaced residents would be relocated "in a humane and proper way."

Italian Americans primarily led the struggle against the university since they were most numerous in the area, owned the most properties and businesses, and held the most political power. At the first community meeting at Holy Guardian Angel Church, residents decided to form the Harrison-Halsted Community Group (HHCG) to protest the city's decision. The group eventually included nearly one thousand members. Reverend Italo Scola of Holy Guardian urged Florence Scala to head the group, as she had been a visible community leader.[87] Scala had been treasurer of the NWSPB in 1952 and served as a board member on the Near West Side Community Council in 1959. She was well known and well liked. Although her home specifically would not be displaced by the construction, she had helped persuade many people in the area to rehabilitate their homes and businesses under the community redevelopment plan.[88] Residents turned to her for leadership. She recalled:

> People knew I was active on the Near West Side Planning Board, and one woman came and knocked on my door. This was when I was in the middle of mopping my kitchen, and she said, "Florence, what are we going to do about our houses? Are we going to fight? Are we going to do anything?" I was mopping my floor and not thinking about anything except finishing the mopping. . . . I said, "I don't know."[89]

Italian Americans felt particularly betrayed by the mayor's decision because of their emotional, spiritual, and financial investment in one particular institution, Holy Guardian Angel parish and school. Only a few years earlier, they had relocated the church and school because it stood in the path of the South Expressway. Parishioners' contributions helped build a new school and church at the cost of six hundred thousand dollars. The mayor himself had been at the dedication ceremony and praised the community's efforts.[90] But the buildings would now have to be torn down for the planned university. Father Scola explained, "We were assured in 1958 that this would not be the college site. That is why we went ahead with this new church and school."[91] Italian Americans soon called upon their (coethnic) political representatives to oppose the university construction. State Representative Peter G. Granata expressed his opposition to the plan. The neighborhood alderman, John D'Arco, opposed it as well. He noted that his constituents were not opposed to progress; "they have given the most of any neighborhood for progress"—five public housing projects, three expressways, and the medical center.[92]

Spanish-speaking residents, particularly Mexican Americans, expressed similar opinions. Although they were less numerous and most were recent immigrants, older, more established, and second-generation Mexican Americans represented the community in the HHCG. Mexican American leader Pete Guerrero of the Manuel Perez American Legion Post 917 echoed Alderman D'Arco's point: "Some residents of the area have already been relocated for the construction of the South Route Expressway and other land clearance projects."[93] Arthur Velasquez, a former Taylor Street resident, vice president of the Mexican Chamber of Commerce, and a member of the Illinois Federation of Mexican Americans and St. Francis of Assisi parish, spoke out publicly as well. He appeared before a board of trustees meeting in Champaign-Urbana in early February 1961 and decried the dislocation that Mexican Americans would suffer.[94] In 1960, there were approximately forty-eight hundred Mexicans in the six census tracts that would be taken for the university and related construction. Although most were not homeowners, Mexican Americans were visibly present in the public protests and marches. They voiced their opinions in newspaper letters to the editor.[95] Mexican business owners who had their shops along Halsted Street joined the fight to protect their livelihoods as well. While Italians gathered primarily at Holy Guardian, Mexican Americans held their meetings at St. Francis. On a Sunday in mid-March, approximately six hundred of them gathered at the church and then marched in protest carrying signs reading "Down with Daley," "Daley Sold Us Out," and "*Respeten Nuestros Hogares*" (Respect Our Homes). A mariachi band led the protesters, playing music along the way. They distributed leaflets in Spanish and English inviting residents to another mass meeting and to a city council meeting that week.[96]

Throughout March, HHCG members, primarily women, picketed and protested outside city hall.[97] They began attending city council meetings in anticipation of the council hearings to officially approve the redesignation of the site. The hearings were merely a formality, however, as the city council had increasingly become a rubber stamp for the mayor. The day that Daley officially announced the approved city ordinance, about two hundred people in the audience, mostly women, booed him. They included folks from the HHCG and residents of Garfield Park who stubbornly insisted on their location for the campus. Scala next attended a Chicago Plan Commission meeting at which, not surprisingly, members approved the university location as well.[98]

Residents next descended upon hearings of the city council's Housing and Planning Committee and, for three days, gave emotional testimonies as to why the university should be located elsewhere. A planning consultant hired by the HHCG noted that nearly eight thousand people would need to be relocated. Mrs. Ana Guerrero, a mother of six, testified on the hardships it would cause. Many elderly Italian residents would not be able to afford to buy in newer, better neighborhoods. A thirteen-year-old student from Holy Guardian Angel testified, "Just two years ago we moved into a new school. We were proud of it. We don't consider ourselves underprivileged and we don't consider our neighborhood undesirable or a slum. It may not be as fancy as some, but it's ours and we love it. We're proud of

Figure 14. Aerial photo of Harrison-Halsted neighborhood / UIC campus,
no date (but pre-1960). The bottom right quadrant was the area demolished for
the university construction. The wide parkway running left to right through the center
of the photo is the Congress (Eisenhower) Expressway. The circle on the right border
is the interchange between the Congress, Kennedy, and Dan Ryan Expressways.
UA90–999_2156, University of Illinois at Chicago Library, University Archives.

our parents and of the homes they have made for us."[99] Despite three days
of impassioned testimony, the committee voted in favor of the site. Forty
women then marched upstairs to protest outside Daley's office, where they
clashed with Navy Pier students who staged a counterprotest. When news
of the Housing and Planning Committee's decision reached the neighborhood, residents of the 1000 through 1100 blocks of South Newberry Street
whose homes would be demolished made up impromptu signs to display
on their buildings: "THIS HOUSE NOT FOR SALE TO U OF I."[100] The street
ended at the doorstep of St. Francis Church, where many Mexican residents
attended mass; celebrated baptisms, weddings, and first communions; and
performed other sacraments. Although the historic church itself would be
spared, most of its parishioners would not.

In addition to the churches and their parishioners that would be affected, residents feared for Hull House, which would also be demolished for the university's plans.[101] The settlement held a very dear place in the hearts of many Chicagoans who had grown up in the neighborhood and partaken of the center's services. Florence Scala expressed the sentiments of more than a few:

> I grew up around Hull-House. . . . My father was a tailor, and we were just getting along in a very poor neighborhood. He never had money to send us to school; but we were not impoverished. When one of the teachers suggested that our mother send us to Hull-House, life began to open up. . . . It gave us . . . well, for the first time my mother left that darn old shop to attend Mother's Club once a week. . . . Hull-House gave you a little insight into another world. There was something else to life besides sewing and pressing.[102]

Prominent leaders, many with close connections to the neighborhood, joined the protest, including US Senator Paul Douglas, who charged that tearing down Hull House amounted to "historic vandalism." Other prominent figures such as State Representative Abner Mikva, authors Nelson Algren and Studs Terkel, and journalists Jack Mabley and Georgie Ann Geyer joined in protesting the destruction of the settlement.[103] Scala reportedly told newspapers, "We don't want a plaque to replace Hull House. The neighbors will not let a wrecking crew destroy it. Bulldozers won't knock down Holy Guardian Angel School unless they run over people to do it." Mrs. Ana Guerrero warned, "When those bulldozers come they're going to have to run over the bodies of women and children."[104]

Yet Hull House itself had a mixed reaction to the university's decision. Most staff members, including Jessie Binford, opposed the plans. It had been Eri Hulbert, Hull House staff member and nephew of Jane Addams, who had originally spearheaded community planning and the Near West Side Planning Board. Executive Director Russell Ballard, an early supporter of the NWSPB's activities, opposed the university as well, but he had since been replaced by a new director, Paul Jans, who seemingly accepted the university's plan and announced that the agency would relocate and continue its programs elsewhere. Many felt the settlement house had turned its back on local residents, an irony given all the community engagement that the settlement house practiced. Ultimately, however, the board of trustees had been compromised: board president James C. Downs had played a role in the selling of the Harrison-Halsted site. Several months after he had originally informed the board of trustees that the city might offer the site for the campus and the six-decades-old settlement house would have to be demolished,[105] the board called a special meeting to discuss the matter. For whatever reason, Downs did not attend. The board drafted two motions, one in favor and one against the university's decision. It met again two days later without Downs. When it delivered a rather mixed vote, the board decided to abstain from taking a public position on the matter. In the meantime, Downs decided to step down as board president, perhaps in belated acknowledgment of his conflict of interest or perhaps for entirely unrelated reasons. He stayed on nonetheless as a regular board member.[106] In the end, a majority of Hull House's board of trustees opposed the decision. "For decades," a representative noted, "Hull House has been standing for Democratic [sic] processes, and has been endeavoring to teach them to thousands of new Americans. . . . In the tradition of Jane Addams, Hull House cannot stand by while a project is undertaken which, however worthy in itself, completely ignores these processes, and must oppose governmental actions which fail to consider the rights of the people affected."[107] Many felt that Jane Addams and the early founders of the nation's most famous social settlement house would never have stood by and watched the beloved institution and community destroyed.

Not all local institutions supported the residents' fight against the city and university, however. Local Catholic clergy had rather mixed responses. St. Francis priests opposed the university construction, and certainly Holy Guardian Angel priests did as well. But St. Ignatius College Preparatory School and its companion Holy Family parish supported the city and university. Their buildings would not be affected by the construction. Local politicians beholden to the Daley Democratic machine also supported the mayor.[108]

The struggle to save Harrison-Halsted ultimately was a very gendered one. On a larger scale, it was a battle between powerful men—the mayor, city planners, businessmen, university trustees—and the legacy of women who had given over half a century of social service to the immigrant neighborhood. Social reformers like Jane Addams, Ellen Star Gates, Edith Abbott, and Jessie Binford had made a lasting impact on the city and its people. The construction of the university on the Harrison-Halsted site now threatened their legacy. These gendered dynamics echoed on the ground. Housewives seemingly led the battle to defend their place against the city. These included women like Sara Avalos, a Mexican American widow and grandmother who lived directly across the street from St. Francis of Assisi Church and whose residence would be demolished. Women organized fund-raising events and sold food—"pizzas, tamales, tortillas, Mexican chocolate, and cookies to try to save their community."[109] Women presented the public face of protests and picket lines, as Scala noted, because,

> whenever they photographed any event that took place during the day downtown, it was primarily women. A few men might be around on the marches and picketing, but most of the men were working. . . . As far as demonstrations, they were mostly women because they were the ones who were available.[110]

The women received criticism from some politicians, such as Alderman Vito Marzullo of a neighboring ward, who called them "a bunch of crazies." Others disparagingly referred to them as "caterwauling Italian fishwives."[111] Female protesters made male politicians, especially the mayor, quite uncomfortable. Such men were unaccustomed to dealing with visible, public opposition from women picketers making their claims as mothers, wives, neighbors, and community residents. Although community men may have agreed with them, for various reasons many, especially Italian American men, did not participate publicly. Some suggest this was on account of many holding city patronage jobs and thus being indebted to the political establishment.[112]

Despite the pickets, protests, and sit-ins, by May the city council approved the campus site as an audience of over four hundred citizens watched. The political cards were stacked against the neighborhood. Even local labor unions, including the American Federation of Labor, the Chicago Federation of Labor, and the Building Services Employees International, supported the construction at Harrison-Halsted, as it promised many jobs.[113] Daley in the meantime continued to absolve himself of any responsibility for the campus location decision, claiming it was the university and not his office that had chosen the site. Not long after, protesters began picketing his home.[114]

Throughout the summer, the Harrison-Halsted Community Group pursued various legal means to challenge the site selection. It tried to get the federal government to intervene since it had approved the urban renewal designation and would contribute two-thirds of the funds for the project. The federal government abstained, however, claiming this was a local matter.[115] HHCG sought recourse at the state housing board, which held two meetings to hear the protesters' demands. Still, by August, the Illinois Housing Board added its endorsement for the new campus. Throughout the fall of 1961, women continued protesting and picketing at city hall. They took their case to the circuit court but lost.[116] Business owners and homeowners then filed individual lawsuits against the condemnation of their properties, but ultimately the suits were all defeated. The group then tried to argue in federal court that the university's construction would disrupt the neighborhood's "ethnic character." The judge, however, dismissed this argument as well, observing that it smacked of "provincialism" and could be used to defend racial segregation.[117] Although the area was racially mixed, a decision in the group's favor would have established a dangerous precedent for upholding housing discrimination.

By August, HHCG had two court cases pending—one in the US Court of Appeals and the other in the US Supreme Court. The city proceeded with soliciting bids for the university construction. HHCG legal appeals delayed construction plans for two years. In February 1963, the Illinois Supreme Court affirmed the lower courts' decisions in favor of the university. The United States Supreme Court turned down the case that May. HHCG

Figure 15. Protest signs and a coffin on a vacant property in the Harrison-Halsted area. Note that the signs propose two alternative sites for the university—one at city hall, located between Clark, Randolph, LaSalle, and Washington Streets, and the other on Thirty-Fifth and Lowe Streets, the location of Mayor Daley's home. ICHi-14396, Chicago History Museum.

Figure 16. Demolition of Hull House. Photograph by Wallace Kirkland, 1963.
Jane Addams–Hull House Photographic Collection, JAMC_0000_0122_0963,
University of Illinois at Chicago Library, Special Collections.

had exhausted all legal avenues. Shortly thereafter, the university began groundbreaking for the new campus.[118]

In the end, the university paid only $4.6 million for the land at Harrison-Halsted, nearly less than a third of the city's actual cost to acquire and clear the tracts.[119] The university purchased the Hull House complex for $875,000 and Holy Guardian for $510,000. The church and school were destroyed. All of the Hull House buildings were demolished except for one—the original Hull mansion, which stands as a museum on the university's campus. When the bulldozers came to demolish Hull House, Florence Scala, Jessie Binford, and the settlement's janitor cried as they watched the wrecking crew remove trees from the courtyard.[120]

The Demise of a Neighborhood

The construction of the university and accompanying urban renewal efforts destroyed the area's existing community life. Between 1950 and 1960, before the university's construction, the area had lost over thirty-four thousand residents. Some of them were surely lured to the expansive new homes of the suburbs, but others were victims of public housing and expressway construction. In the following decade, it lost an additional forty-seven thousand people, over one-fifth of whom were Mexican American. Certainly not all moved directly as a result of the university, but the majority of families had in some way or another been dislocated by the construction and urban renewal plans.[121] All told, an additional thirteen hundred families were displaced for university construction in addition to those who had been displaced for the original Harrison-Halsted site.[122] Many more were removed for the neighboring residential conservation and clearance projects. Carolyn Eastwood estimates that "approximately 45 percent of the families and 33 percent of single residents displaced by the university were Mexican." Families who lived in the now-redesignated clearance tracts received visits from a Department of Urban Renewal (DUR) relocation specialist who offered financial assistance with moving and would help families apply for public housing if they qualified. The DUR offered each household up to two hundred dollars for moving expenses. It also provided assistance to small business owners. The case of "Mr. and Mrs. Z" was typical. The Mexican couple, who had been in the country only two years, lived in a dilapidated four-room apartment with their nine children. DUR staff person Gus Miller paid them a visit trying to convince Mrs. Z that she and her family must move. He handed her a pamphlet in English, *Facts You Should Know about Relocation*. Though her apartment's hot water boiler had broken down, the heater was not working, and one wall had "a rat hole the size of a baseball," Mrs. Z refused to leave her familiar surroundings. "Why I got to move?" she asked defiantly. Miller later commented to a reporter, "Of course she doesn't want to move. She feels safe [in the neighborhood] . . . knowing there are other Mexican families nearby."[123]

By the early 1960s, most Mexican families in the university zone had been pushed farther west toward Polk and Laflin Streets. Within a short time, they were displaced from there also, as the university and medical center expanded their appetite for student, faculty, and staff housing.[124] In 1964, Near West Side Community Committee staff member Frank Delgado Jr. noted that only a few Spanish-speaking families remained in its service boundaries: "The community is in a state of disarray because of the knocking down of sections of the neighborhood for the University of Illinois site and for Urban Renewal [sic]." The Mexican business district on Halsted Street, which provided Mexicans throughout the city, suburbs, and even farther away with imported food products, *tortillerías* (tortilla factories), *panaderías* (bakeries), and other ethnic shops, closed its doors. Some businesses moved elsewhere; others never reopened.[125] The Puerto Rican population, which was not displaced directly by the Harrison-Halsted construction, eventually felt the effects of upscale residential redevelopment along Harrison Street. Their numbers declined by 9,104 persons between 1960 and 1970.[126]

Communities of neighbors who had known one another for decades, or more recent arrivals who had just begun making homes for themselves on the Near West Side, dispersed throughout the city. By 1970, fewer than seventy-nine thousand people remained in the area, 72 percent of whom were African American.[127] A small Italian community stayed on in the remnants of what was once a thriving "Little Italy," though it had lost many of its social institutions, community organizations, and much of its commercial vitality. Most Italian Americans who remained did not accept the new reality very well. They had believed themselves the custodians of the neighborhood, with the greatest moral and political investment there. While some lamented their defeat at the hands of the city and the university, others interpreted the neighborhood changes in racial terms. Community worker Frank Delgado Jr. encountered apathy in his work with residents in 1962 and found racial explanations for the neighborhood's changes: "The small Italian community fails to respond . . . for several reasons: 1) The people do not want to take interest in the area because they feel that sooner or later they will be forced out by the University of Illinois plans or by Urban Renewall [*sic*]. 2) They feel that the Negro people are getting the benefit of all improvements in the neighborhood."[128] Another researcher noted in the early sixties, "The Italians in the area are especially apprehensive and often blame the other groups for 'ruining' the area's prospects." Since African Americans had begun moving into the area in the 1940s, and had come to dominate public housing, some Italians blamed them for the neighborhood's destruction. Moreover, some perceived "portions of the urban renewal program and even the University of Illinois . . . as 'something for the niggers.'"[129] Such perceptions may have stemmed from the fact that most black people in the neighborhood occupied new public housing developments, which were very clearly not in danger of demolition. Whites saw them as the beneficiaries of new apartment homes, subsidized by the federal and local governments. Such observations failed to acknowledge, however, the tremendous amount of social welfare programs and benefits that white Americans had received from government munificence since the New Deal era. And they overlooked the fact that public housing was not exactly prime real estate: it was inferior in quality, poorly designed, and soon collapsed into a dangerous environment for the families who lived there. Italians saw themselves as victims of policies that benefited blacks, but they failed to see how structural racism, unequal employment and housing opportunities, and even their own prejudice kept black people isolated, impoverished, and marginalized. Rather than directing their anger and resentment toward the powerful institutions that had actually orchestrated or consented to the neighborhood's destruction—the city government, the university, the archdiocese, and the business elite—they blamed poor black residents who had secured modest low-income housing in their community.

Certainly, many of those residents who lamented the demise of the area held romanticized memories of "the old neighborhood." Others took a longer and more realistic view. Florence Scala, for example, recalled the Italian crime syndicate that controlled much of the local economy and politics, especially during Prohibition years. She acknowledged as well the cramped and modest conditions of the area. As she explained, "This . . . is not a neighborhood that any of us loved. . . . We didn't love it because we wanted to keep it the way it was; but what was so important . . . was a kind of plan that could have come out of this, and what we wanted was to change all these things we hated all our lives. . . . The environment, it was stifling here. What was terrible was that the possibilities were absolutely removed."[130] The university, while a noble endeavor of its own, had foreclosed the neighborhood's future as a community of multiracial and multiethnic working-class families.

Once the university opened in February 1965, relations with the campus remained tense. Its imposing, modernist architecture and layout were unintelligible to most residents.[131] They saw the campus as a cold, sterile, concrete fortress, insulated from the surrounding community by its high walls and vast stretches of parking lots. Students, well aware of the opposition the neighborhood had posed to its construction, sometimes took a combative stance and derided the community. City and especially campus newspapers featured cartoons portraying area residents as ignorant obstacles to education and progress. Residents took offense at such characterizations and felt even more alienated from the campus.[132]

In light of the urban renewal explosion throughout the city, many white Chicagoans, especially those in the city's outlying neighborhoods, began registering their objections to such projects and their costly tax hikes. In April of 1962, voters defeated an urban renewal bond issue, forfeiting $66 million in federal funding. HHCG campaigned against the bond as well, since city hall and downtown power brokers had clearly demonstrated that they did not take ordinary people's interests into consideration in the city's redevelopment. The following month, news stories surfaced that Chicago urban renewal officials were involved with private appraisers and lawyers in financial scandals, including inflating land prices, further diminishing the public's faith in government urban renewal projects.[133]

Conclusion

The destruction of the Harrison-Halsted neighborhood resembles similar stories of other working-class urban communities. Italian Americans in Boston's West End found themselves displaced by upscale, luxury high-rise apartments in the late 1950s. The diverse working-class residents of Manhattan's Lincoln Square were forced to sacrifice their community for "the greater good of the arts" in the form of Lincoln Center. In Los Angeles, city officials relocated Mexican Americans from the Chavez Ravine community, on the promise that they would be able to return to new public housing—only to abandon that project and offer the site instead for the Los Angeles Dodgers baseball stadium.[134] On the Near West Side, the "life space" of the Taylor Street community evaporated as well.[135] Neighborhood institutions such as social agencies and ethnic organizations dispersed or folded altogether. Hull House closed its doors and turned to citywide, rather than neighborhood-specific, social services.[136] Those who left the neighborhood lost not only their homes but their communities and social networks as well. While some residents remained, their neighborhood would never be the same, and the consequence of such population decline meant that African Americans in public housing found themselves more isolated than ever.

The battle between a working-class community and a public university seemed paradoxical in some ways. Like residents of New York's Lincoln Square who found themselves pitted against a public arts center, Near West Side residents found themselves doing battle against an institution purportedly established for the public good. The arresting images of women picketers with signs that read "Homes, Not Education" must have puzzled many observers. Why would anyone object to expanding higher education opportunities for young people? If we understand this episode as simply a power struggle between provincial blue-collar people and a public university, we miss the nuances and complexities of the matter. Most residents did not oppose education in principle, but neither could many have imagined that the university would serve their children or grandchildren in the decades to come. Perhaps most blue-collar and immigrant workers did not dream so ambitiously. Or perhaps residents simply wanted to hold on to what was left of their vanishing community.

The Harrison-Halsted struggle revealed the tensions between "use value" and "exchange value" in the city.[137] It brought to light the true costs of urban renewal and raised the question of who pays "for the public good." As a number of leaders pointed out, Near West Side residents had already surrendered so much of their neighborhood for expressways, public housing, and other projects. Why did they need to give up even more? As one observer astutely remarked, city "planners rarely stop to ask, 'Who is sacrificing what for whom?'" Working-class residents, including racial minorities who would face discrimination in finding housing elsewhere, bore the brunt of urban renewal, expressway construction, and civic improvements that largely benefited downtown business interests, politicians, and powerful institutions. One group of policy analysts has summarized Chicago's urban renewal in this way: "Poor and working class communities were neglected, if not altogether destroyed, as resources were focused on downtown commercial development, on the expansion of institutions serving the middle class, or on luxury waterfront housing."[138] As the logic and mechanisms of urban renewal unfolded, critics began to observe that the policy of redeveloping the city's core yielded benefits for the wealthiest residents, not for the most marginal. The investment in private capital projects inversely reduced investments in public services—education, housing, mass transit—thereby driving poor neighborhoods into further decline. Thus continued the uneven development and the growing "urban crisis" that made places like Chicago objects of fear and disdain among white suburbanites in the sixties and seventies.[139]

Despite the impoverished and difficult conditions of the Near West Side, Mexican Americans had made it home for several decades, and recent arrivals had found it an amenable port of entry. Countless families tell stories of growing up in the neighborhood and eventually being forced to move as apartments were torn down for classroom buildings, athletic fields, parking lots, or housing for university and medical students. The de la Llata family, for example, who had lived in the neighborhood less than six years, found themselves displaced from their apartment for the university's construction. After moving a few blocks west, they were pushed out once more for the construction of student housing. The de la Llata children were perhaps most affected by the closing of Hull House and losing access to many nearby resources for local families.[140] The loss of their community had a tremendous impact on the neighborhood's children. María Ovalle remembers as a child coming home from the fourth grade every day to see which buildings on her block had been marked for demolition. This experience became part of the neighborhood children's daily life. She recalled, "I have a very, very clear recollection of this, of sitting outside . . . because at that time we knew that all the houses were gonna be leveled. It's like, you would come home and if your house had been . . . was ready, it would have a circle with a cross on it, is my recollection. And so, it would be really, really sad! You'd come home and the kids would look, 'Oh, our house is going next,' and you'd have to move."[141]

As bulldozers razed area apartment buildings, the majority of Taylor Street's Mexican families reluctantly packed up and moved just south to the neighboring Lower West Side, known popularly as Pilsen or "Eighteenth Street" (see chapter 6). While some Puerto Rican families joined them, the majority of them moved to the city's Near North Side neighborhood. There, they joined other Puerto Rican migrants who had recently settled in the area. Their presence would be temporary, however, for urban renewal was targeting that community as well. As urban renewal displaced them and pushed them into neighboring blue-collar white ethnic communities, they would face a new set of challenges.

FOUR

Pushing Puerto Ricans Around: Urban Renewal, Race, and Neighborhood Change

The spatial structure of the Chicago metropolitan region is not a spontaneous expression of natural forces, contrary to the theories of some ecologists. And residence is not just coincidentally related to race, ethnicity, and class distribution of populations in the metropolitan area. This spatial structure is the result of decisions made by key institutional actors about where various kinds of housing will be constructed. Banks and savings and loan institutions determine where mortgage money will be made available and which neighborhoods will be denied credit; municipal zoning regulations determine the kind of housing that can be constructed. . . . Government agencies make decisions about what kind of public housing will be built and where it will be located. . . . The federal government enforces or relaxes its guidelines about what housing projects will be funded under urban renewal. . . . The Chicago Housing Authority decides on locations for public housing.

—Squires et al., *Chicago: Race, Class and the Response to Urban Decline*[1]

Our data show that there is no excessive juvenile or adult Puerto Rican crime incidence for Chicago. Many of their violations are slum-conditioned, related to their cultural background . . . or their inadequate command of the English language.

—Chicago Commission on Human Relations, *Mayor's Committee on New Residents*[2]

They do not treat us like human beings. The Americans, because they are white and speak English better, think they are superior to us. It was necessary to act even though I think that it may now be worse for us.

—Felix Padilla, *Puerto Rican Chicago*[3]

When Puerto Ricans came to Chicago in the 1940s and 1950s, many of them settled in the neighborhoods closest to the city's downtown—the Near West Side and the Near North Side—areas with relatively cheap rents, racially mixed populations, and also the most aged real estate in the city. On the Near West Side, the Congress Expressway, the residential redevelopment precipitated by the construction of University of Illinois Circle Campus, and urban renewal made their stays there rather brief. By the early 1960s, many Puerto Ricans were relocating elsewhere. Many went to the Near North Side, where newly arrived families had settled in the fifties. Migrants formed an enclave in the area of Clark Street and Superior Avenue, close to downtown hotels and restaurants—which employed many of them as busboys, housekeepers, and janitors—and factories that hired others in the industrial corridor to the west.[4] Apart from its convenient location, the area had little to offer. Tightly packed with crowded, multistory structures that had mixed commercial and residential uses, the district was in severe decline. Shops and stores occupied many first floors while transient hotels and kitchenette apartments filled upper floors, bursting at the seams with tenants. Families started in such buildings near Clark and Superior Streets, then moved farther north as budgets allowed for better housing, once conditions became intolerable, or when slum clearance forced them out. Migrants eventually dispersed across an area that covered Dearborn to Halsted Streets and Superior to North Avenues (see fig. 17).[5]

The midcentury in-migration of Puerto Ricans (as well as Mexicans and African Americans) to central city neighborhoods in the industrial north signaled a dramatic change in the urban social landscape. Their growing presence led to increasingly complex and multilayered racial and ethnic encounters between residents who contended with one another's social difference and sought to define the boundaries and limits of their "communities." Yet the interpersonal dynamics that occurred in the city's neighborhoods were not simply a human drama decided by individual actors. Capital interests and the state (as represented by federal and local urban planning policies) also played a role in determining those encounters—with whom people would come into contact, and under what circumstances—by reshaping the physical landscape. City planners and real estate developers were targeting the very neighborhoods where Puerto Rican migrants could afford to settle—some of the oldest and most dilapidated in the city. Puerto Ricans thus found themselves repeatedly displaced by urban renewal, highway construction, and public housing projects that

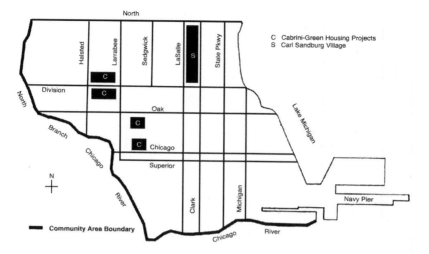

Figure 17. Near North Side Community Area map.

spurred them into neighboring white working-class areas. In contrast to the aggressive efforts at containment and segregation of African Americans, theirs was a story of constant mobility: the population continued to migrate farther north and west just steps ahead of the bulldozers. Puerto Ricans thus occupied simultaneous and constantly shifting settlements in a number of neighborhoods. As wrecking balls demolished the apartment buildings and hotels where they lived on the Near West Side, Near North Side, and later Lincoln Park, they fled to West Town, Humboldt Park, and Lakeview. Newly arriving migrants joined them.

When they moved into those blue-collar white neighborhoods, they initiated a process meant to assign them a place in the local social order. European immigrants and their children ("ethnic whites") had largely assimilated, become "American" and, more important, "white." While they retained some degree of ethnic differences (Polish, German, Italian, Russian), they held firmly to their highly coveted racial status.[6] They had secured their whiteness in the context of dramatic European immigration restriction after 1924, which sharply reduced the number of recently immigrated, unassimilated coethnics who might tarnish their status.[7] Yet ethnic whites also had constructed and won their whiteness in the midst of an influx of hundreds of thousands of southern African Americans. European immigrants and their children had attained whiteness by brazenly rejecting blackness.[8] Puerto Ricans, however, were a new and unfamiliar group. They seemed like immigrants because of their foreign language and culture, yet they brought with them US citizenship. Moreover, they presented tremendous phenotypical diversity, ranging from the fairest skin to the darkest complexions. When whites began encountering them in their neighborhoods, they tried to make sense of just exactly who they were. Were they black? Or a group closer to the Italians and Poles? White residents began making racial judgments about this new group, trying to discern the meaning of their social difference and what consequences it would have for their own social status.

White residents had mixed reactions to Puerto Ricans. They did not rebuff them as universally and unequivocally as they did African Americans. Nor did they abandon neighborhoods almost immediately where Puerto Ricans moved in. Instead, many remained among them for a more protracted form of racial succession, one that lasted as long as two decades. White residents seemed to be interpreting Puerto Ricans' social difference differently than they did that of African Americans. That whites lived among them for longer periods of time, however, does not mean that they accepted the migrants as racial equals. Most Puerto Ricans encountered tensions with white residents and often understood that they were not welcome.

City leaders, researchers, residents, and Puerto Ricans themselves all varied in their understandings of the group. In the late 1940s, anthropologist Elena Padilla contended that Puerto Ricans had high "color visibility": their physical features made them distinctive among white Americans, thus making them the target of prejudice at times.[9] Twenty years later, a University of Chicago study claimed, "We recognize that Puerto Ricans are not a separate 'race' from all whites. But, the cultural lines drawn around this minority group are so well defined that we feel that it is important to discuss the plight of the Puerto Rican in the United States in terms of the problem of race relations."[10] Indeed, the group's experience in the city's neighborhoods—marked by displacement; housing discrimination; racial hostility from neighbors; police brutality; high rates of unemployment; widespread poverty; and overcrowded, substandard housing—resembled that of urban African Americans more closely than that of their white neighbors. In turn, whites interpreted Puerto Rican deprivation, deplorable living conditions, and participation in the informal economy as innate cultural preferences, further heightening their disdain for the group.[11]

Puerto Ricans' racial diversity and ambiguity made them even more conspicuous on neighborhood streets, and this was precisely where their social position was worked out most visibly—in public encounters with police. The events of the summer of 1966 made them hypervisible not only among their neighbors but throughout the entire city. On June 12, hundreds of Puerto Rican residents took to the streets after police shot a Puerto Rican teenage boy. Law enforcement and area residents skirmished in the streets for several days. The 1966 Division Street riots marked a boiling point in police-community relations. Some scholars have documented the story as a turning point in the politicization of Chicago's Puerto Rican community. Indeed, the riots brought to light the conditions that Puerto Ricans were enduring in rapidly declining, neglected neighborhoods.[12] The standoff between a predominantly white police force and overwhelmingly Puerto Rican participants, moreover, magnified their racial difference. Although the city did not recognize them as a distinct group with legitimate grievances, their experiences in the city's working-class white neighborhoods suggested otherwise. Over the next several years, whites abandoned the increasingly undesirable neighborhood. By 1980, Puerto Ricans found themselves heirs to terribly impoverished, deteriorated, and economically marginalized communities. Although they included Mexicans, African Americans, and some remaining whites, West Town and especially Humboldt Park became known as Puerto Rican *barrios*. The area lost most of its white population not only through the actual departure of European American residents but through the more visible identification of Spanish-speaking residents as an "other" race. West Town and Humboldt Park were no longer "white" neighborhoods.

Arriving on the Near North Side

When Puerto Ricans settled on the Near North Side (Community Area 8) in the late forties and early fifties, they came to a neighborhood much like the rest of the central city, layered with the residue of so many previous generations. Since the late nineteenth century, the Near North Side represented the epitome of urban contrasts and inequality. The eastern edge of the area, known as the Gold Coast, housed some of the city's wealthiest residents. Stately homes and well-appointed apartments accommodated Chicago's elite—doctors, bankers, industrialists, and real estate barons. By the mid-twentieth century, the Gold Coast had the highest concentration of wealth in the city. Only blocks away, impoverished southern and eastern European immigrants lived in the most squalid slums close to the North Branch of the Chicago River, where factories, railroads, and the shipping industry employed many of them. The Near North Side held a mix of residential, commercial, and industrial districts that spilled over onto one another. In the early twentieth century, the southern edge held rooming houses, "single room occupancy" hotels (SROs), and a vice district.[13] The area had a preponderance of such housing: 38 percent of all units were one-room apartments; over half had two rooms or fewer. Residents had a median of 2.3 rooms per housing unit, one of the lowest ratios in the city.[14]

By the 1950s, Puerto Rican families began settling along the southern edge, where Superior Avenue intersected with LaSalle and Clark Streets. Eugenia Rodríguez, mother of Young Lords leader José "Cha Cha" Jiménez, recalled how she first arrived with her family in 1951. She had reunited with her husband in Concord, Massachusetts, where he worked as a migrant farm laborer. The couple decided to try their luck in Chicago, where they had heard that higher-paying jobs abounded. They made the journey by train along with their four-month-old baby girl. Mrs. Rodríguez vividly remembered arriving on a Sunday to a one-room apartment she had secured for fifteen dollars a week. She recalled not sleeping at all that night after discovering the conditions of their accommodations. "I put the baby on the bed, but she kept crying. When I turned on the light, the bed was black [with bedbugs]." The very next morning she sent her husband out to look for another apartment. He found a two-room unit on the seventh floor of the nearby Water Hotel, a building like many others that had served as a transient hotel. Mrs. Rodríguez noted that they were the first Puerto Rican family on that floor, but shortly after they moved in, other migrants from their village of San Salvador joined them. Like immigrants of earlier generations, extended Puerto Rican families, including married couples and their brothers, sisters, uncles, aunts, and cousins, crowded into small two- or three-room apartments in similar hotel buildings nearby.[15]

The Near North Side held an extremely heterogeneous population. During the 1950s, the black population had increased by 29.8 percent to twenty-three thousand people, approximately 31 percent of the community area's residents. Puerto Ricans constituted nearly twenty-seven hundred persons, ethnic Mexicans numbered about seven hundred persons, and whites made up the majority (over fifty thousand people). A number of Japanese Americans, resettlers after internment, also lived in the area.[16] It was home as well to many rural southern white migrants who had left small Appalachian towns after "the mines [we]re all worked out" and to Native Americans who had migrated from reservations as part of federal urbanization programs.[17] One young Native American woman in the neighborhood noted during this time, "It was a League of Nations. All my girlfriends were from different ethnic groups—Greek, Japanese, Spanish, Puerto Rican, Polish."[18] A titillating guide to the city's nightlife and vice crassly described the district as home to "'gambling houses, neighborhood gangsters, Negroes, Poles and prostitutes.'" East of Clark Street, wealthy white residents worked assiduously to keep the "undesirable element" out of their neighborhood. They formed groups such as the Greater North Michigan Avenue Association and the Dearborn Improvement Association to ensure that the boundaries between their genteel community and the disorderly tenements of the poor held firm.[19]

With some of the most crowded and least expensive housing available, the Near North Side was home to the poorest Puerto Ricans in the city, whose yearly family income averaged $3,475.[20] Still, they managed to establish a thriving community life in their humble, less-than-ideal quarters. By the late 1950s, island migrants opened small grocery stores that, in addition to being provisioners of food and other goods, served as neighborhood meeting centers, especially for men. Businesses like the "Spanish American Foods" grocery on the corner of Clark and Superior Streets provided a place where men gathered to play dominoes and discuss the politics and news of the day.[21] In a neighborhood with few public parks, adults and children escaped the suffocating summer air of crowded walk-up apartments by congregating on front stoops and street corners (fig. 18).

Figure 18. "Puerto Rican residents on steps." These women were photographed in the area marked for redevelopment on the Near North Side in the 1950s. Apf2-09033, Mildred Mead Photographs, Special Collections Research Center, University of Chicago Library.

Such public spaces provided refuge from unbearable conditions in the often condemnable apartments. In 1960, 34.8 percent of all housing units in the area were in substandard condition. Of the neighborhood's nearly seven hundred Puerto Rican households counted that year, 60 percent of their units were classified as either "deteriorating" or "dilapidated." Less than half occupied "sound" housing with at least *some* private plumbing facilities. Forty-one percent of Puerto Rican households had two rooms or fewer, although over 70 percent of them had three or more people. Puerto Ricans were relatively new in the area, but they were also experiencing high turnover: the 1960 census noted that 75 percent of households had been in their apartments two years or less.[22]

Revitalizing the Near North Side

The very conditions that made the Near North Side affordable for recent migrants also precipitated its destruction. City leaders and business elites had long recognized that it was an eyesore and liability so close to the downtown business district, which was increasingly alienating middle-class white residents and shoppers. In the early 1940s, the Chicago Plan Commission (the city's planning body until 1959) mapped out the city, noting the "blighted" conditions of central neighborhoods like the Near West, North, and South Sides. The CPC sketched out plans for renovating and revitalizing the Near North area and improving its socioeconomic profile. By 1947, wealthy real estate developer Arthur Rubloff publicly stated his interest in making North Michigan Avenue a "Magnificent Mile," the nickname that has stuck with the boulevard ever since.[23] When federal funds for urban renewal became available, Chicago's leaders quickly sought to avail themselves of the monies. Within a few years, the city announced plans for the redevelopment of Clark to LaSalle Streets, and Division Street to North Avenue. The Greater North Michigan Avenue Association recommended that the easternmost edge of the area, the Gold Coast, be designated as "stable." It would not require much attention. Clark Street, from which Puerto Rican settlement extended west, was marked for redevelopment, while the area around the low-rise Cabrini Homes was identified as "High Priority Residential Redevelopment," foreshadowing the construction of the Cabrini-Green high-rise developments. Farther south, planners designated the heart of the Puerto Rican enclave (LaSalle and Superior Streets) as "Commercial Rehabilitation and Renovation," thus eliminating possibilities for future residential occupancy.[24]

At the center of Near North Side renewal plans stood the North-LaSalle project, a middle- to upper-income residential development of thirteen hundred new units. The land designated for the project (almost thirty-four acres) was officially identified as a "slum" (fig. 19). It was home to various businesses but also to thousands of Puerto Ricans, Appalachians, and others. Arthur Rubloff acquired the prized deal to develop the project. It would eventually be named "Carl Sandburg Village," after the state's premier poet, a name meant to evoke small-town charm within the inner city.

Figure 19. "Overall view of the Department of Urban Renewal's North-LaSalle project on the Near North Side." This view looks north from Division Street on the area that would be razed for the Carl Sandburg Village project. ICHi-64808, Chicago History Museum.

The "Village" would span four square blocks, from Clark to LaSalle Streets and Division Street to North Avenue. Fourteen-story towers would contain smaller apartments for single residents or couples without children, while three-story town houses would be suitable for families. Carl Sandburg Village and similar private commercial and residential developments represented what Don Parson has called "corporate modernism."[25] In their structure, the dense collection of high-rise apartments would resemble the public housing towers rising elsewhere in the city to warehouse the displaced poor. Unlike those projects, however, these luxury apartments would have upscale amenities, attractive landscaping, and other accoutrements that sharply contrasted with the sparse, bare silos erected for low-income people. The "Village" was planned to have all the attractions of a small community, including a grocery store, dry cleaner, tennis courts, off-street parking, and other services (see fig. 20).[26]

Such plans were made possible by federal and local legislation. Chicago received $75 million in federal housing aid for the year ending May 1,

Figure 20. Carl Sandburg Village, looking south, over the same area shown in figure 19, after the towers were completed. Photograph by Calvin Hutchinson, 1964. ICHi37474, Chicago History Museum.

1957. City and state matching funds brought the total amount available for urban renewal to $160 million. Of this amount, $35 million was earmarked for slum clearance, $50 million for public housing, and the largest amount, $75 million, for private investors such as Rubloff. By 1958, the city had secured the federal government's approval, with passage of the 1957 Housing Act, to pay three-fourths of the project costs. The city estimated a total cost for the Carl Sandburg Village of $7.5 million, of which the federal government was expected to pay $5 million. The federal Urban Renewal Administration also agreed to offer the city an $8.1 million loan in addition to the $5 million capital grant. Plans thus moved ahead for the Carl Sandburg project. Five other projects had been completed in the area already, with a total of 854 units for middle- to upper-income residents. Two additional projects in progress would create another 322 units, for a total of over 2,400 luxury apartments.[27]

The city anticipated that nearly nine hundred families would need to be relocated from the North-LaSalle site. By 1960, the Chicago Land Clearance Commission had taken charge of the project, meaning that current residents had been removed and acquisition and demolition were under way. The question of providing for those displaced proved problematic, however. The city prided itself on being a leader in urban renewal nationwide. It boasted that it had cleared seventy-five thousand dilapidated housing units from 1952 to 1962. It did not explain the fact that housing erected in its place was usually not affordable for previous occupants (unless it was public housing), nor did it explain where those previous residents went. The Chicago Plan Commission publicized its policy of providing *permanent* relocation housing for people displaced by urban renewal, in accordance with federal urban renewal guidelines.[28]

Chicago, like other American cities, promoted "uneven development," the inequitable distribution of both public and private resources and capital along racial and class lines. The redevelopment of the Near North Side reflected the favored position that affluent areas enjoyed on the city's political agenda and the priority that downtown interests claimed in the distribution of public funds.[29] The federal Housing and Home Finance Agency's objective could not have been any clearer: "The intention is to combine conservation, rehabilitation, and clearance for redevelopment in a program calculated to arrest and reverse deterioration and to make the area a valuable asset, rather than a potential liability, to Chicago."[30] Indeed, Carl Sandburg Village would sit in a "buffer zone," meant to block the blight and deterioration farther west from creeping into the Gold Coast. City planners and developers in fact accomplished this goal. By 1980, the Gold

Coast was the second wealthiest urban neighborhood in the entire nation, with an astounding per capita income of $27,000, compared to only $7,200 for the nation and $6,933 for the city as a whole. The area west of LaSalle Street, called the "Lower North Side" by some, continued to project back the city's socioeconomic inequalities: it became increasingly segregated, not only by class but by race. The population, which was 85 percent white in 1940, became 89 percent black by 1970. It remained extremely poor as it had always been, but now distinguished itself as well by the high concentration of poor African Americans in public housing, the notorious Cabrini-Green Housing Projects.[31]

Temporary Life in Public Housing

City plans for slum clearance did not usually call for rehousing current residents on the same land. Renovated buildings were designed to attract middle- and upper-income residents and upscale commercial tenants. The entire Puerto Rican enclave on the Near North Side would be completely displaced. When city officials came to board up and condemn buildings, many families packed their belongings and moved directly north or west in hopes of staying nearby.[32] Their new homes, however, were often next on the planning board's agenda. Puerto Rican families thus began a continuous journey north and west in the city as the imperatives of urban redevelopment followed them from one neighborhood to another.

The Flores family represented a typical example of repeated dislocation: first settling along LaSalle and Superior Streets, the family of seven then moved farther north and west to Willow and Larrabee Streets before finding a more permanent home along Armitage Avenue. The Rodriguez family followed a similar path, starting first on Clark Street, then going to the area of North Avenue and Larrabee before settling for several years on Armitage Avenue and Clifton Street. Countless other residents had similar experiences.[33] Most families simply searched for alternate housing on their own. Some, however, particularly those who met income qualifications, took the option the city offered of relocating into public housing.

The Near North Side had first welcomed public housing on the western edge of the neighborhood before World War II. In 1940, the Home Owners Loan Corporation (HOLC) had graded the community bordering the Chicago River along Chicago Avenue—one of the most deteriorated areas occupied primarily by impoverished Italian Americans and African Americans—with a "D" on its A–D scale. Authorities wrote, "The section has no future and . . . is definitely blighted." The newly formed Chicago Housing Authority (CHA) thus decided to clear the local slums and build low-rise row houses. The Cabrini Homes opened in late 1942, at the height of the wartime housing shortage. CHA director Elizabeth Wood was sympathetic to racial integration and tried hard to maintain a balance between the local Italian population and nearby black residents. Wood assigned 20 percent of the Cabrini units to African Americans, but white tenants vocally objected. Nearby working-class white homeowners protested the integration as well, preferring that African Americans remain segregated in their own enclaves as far away as possible. As a result of such opposition, apartments assigned for white tenancy were left vacant by whites who refused to move in alongside African Americans, while black families languished on waiting lists desperately enduring the housing shortage.[34]

After the war, public housing was meant to provide "permanent standard relocation housing" for those displaced by slum clearance. In the late 1950s, the CHA expanded the Cabrini projects dramatically to relieve nearby urban renewal displacement. It chose the area north of the original Cabrini Homes, close to the Chicago River and industrial sites, to expand public housing into vertical communities. The Cabrini Extension, fifteen high-rise buildings that held over nineteen hundred units, opened in 1958. Three years later, the agency erected the William Green Homes, another eight towers that added eleven hundred apartments. Altogether, the projects had more than thirty-five hundred units and housed over eighteen thousand people. The modern concrete towers that economized land and space with the design of "superblocks" symbolized the latest in urban architectural design, much like the high-rise luxury apartments for wealthier tenants farther east. Their similarities, however, ended there.[35]

Families who first walked into the modern new buildings certainly felt overjoyed to secure such ideal low-cost housing. Indeed, many were relieved to leave behind dilapidated, unsafe apartments for brand-new, secure accommodations. But the sparkle of these buildings soon faded. Shoddy construction quickly led to mechanical failures in elevators and other maintenance problems. Buildings began to break down under the wear and tear of so many tenants, especially children.[36] Chicago's public housing projects were among the most expensive in the nation, with construction costs topping those in New York City. The high price tag had little to do with the quality of construction, however, and more to do with the excesses of corruption and greed so rampant in city politics.[37] In sharp contrast to the luxury towers of Carl Sandburg Village, public housing packed residents in tightly, especially large families with many children. Moreover, the bleak and barren design of buildings and grounds, and geographically isolated location stretches of blocks away from "regular" neighborhood housing left residents feeling even more alienated in their "sterile silos" and stark environment.[38]

Approximately one hundred Puerto Rican families lived in the low-rise Cabrini Homes by the mid-1950s. An estimated one thousand Puerto Ricans lived there and in the new high-rises by 1960, constituting 7 percent of the development's fourteen thousand residents. Many, like the Lucas family, came to the projects after being displaced by the Sandburg Village construction. Monse Lucas-Figueroa and her family lived in Cabrini-Green from 1960 to 1965. She described difficult living circumstances in the dense collection of high-rise buildings that packed so many poor into close quarters. She explains, "It was a very sad thing. They stuck everybody in a hole. And with the project [urban] renewal, there was no other way because they were moving people out of sections for them to build these apartments [Carl Sandburg Village] or renovate these apartments where the people [existing residents] could not afford to pay the [increased] rent. So they decided, 'Okay, we're gonna have to put these people somewhere!' . . . It was very, very bad."[39] Contrary to the view that public housing was initially "paradise," families like the Lucases recognized the social engineering flaws of housing developments, especially high-rise buildings, from the very beginning.

Parents soon realized that high-rise living did not suit families very well. Letting their children play outside became more precarious than it had been in smaller buildings. The narrow fenced walkways or "galleries" outside high-rise apartment doors hardly provided suitable play space, and neighbors frequently complained that children made too much noise. Instead, parents had to either accompany their children down multiple flights of stairs to outside playgrounds on the ground floor or let their children venture unsupervised all the way down on their own. The sheer number of children and the high youth-adult ratio, as historian Brad Hunt has shown, meant that children were not well supervised. Moreover, children and teens often discovered tense racial dynamics among themselves. As a young girl, Monse Lucas-Figueroa and her brother and sisters constantly fought with other (mainly African American) children and teens in the project. "We were always fighting," she explained. "People were always teasing my dad, 'You know, your girls are never gonna get married 'cuz they do nothing but fight!'"[40]

Certainly the influx of new, unfamiliar tenants in restricted quarters created enough tensions, but Lucas-Figueroa noted that the CHA exacerbated racial conflict through its policy of segregating tenants within the housing developments. She recalls, "What they did . . . from the first to seventh floor were *familias Latinas*. From the seventh floor to the tenth floor belonged to the *blanquitos*, the hillbilly families. From there on up were all black families. That's why all the fights started!" She added:

> The *prietos* [blacks] knew that they were being . . . they stuck them all on the [top floors]. . . . That was not correct. We used to say it was not correct. . . . [The CHA was segregating] within the housing projects. And the person that says, "Oh, that's [just] how it worked out," oh, please! Every project building that you went to, the first five or seven floors were all Latinos. In between you had your hillbillies, and the top floors was all *los negros* [the blacks]. So, *entre el círculo de los residenciales había racismo* [there was racism within the residential complex].

Even children clearly recognized the racial segregation policies under which they were forced to live. Such arrangements did not bode well for community life.[41]

The Puerto Rico Migration Division, which had a regional office in Chicago, tried to organize Puerto Rican residents in Cabrini-Green, assigning community workers to help integrate tenants into the projects and improve their living conditions. Community organizers worked with residents to develop social and recreational activities for youth, to address social needs, and to acculturate migrants. Still, many tenants complained. The fraternal group Caballeros de San Juan (Knights of Saint John) publicly denounced the "'human slums'" that public housing created and warned migrants about moving in.[42] Within a matter of years, conditions and race relations worsened. Most Latino/a families, including the Lucas family, abandoned their subsidized apartments, citing poor race relations, lack of a sense of "community," and high crime.[43] White and black families who had the option moved out as well, leaving it a hypersegregated "ghetto" of only the most severely impoverished African American residents. Those who remained generally did not have the means to leave or refused to return to more expensive substandard private housing. The experiment in public housing was failing miserably. Though some placed blame exclusively on the poor themselves, more critical observers recognized the flaws in a policy that privileged private interests and capital imperatives over the humane provision of shelter for the city's poor and that obeyed the racial imperatives of segregation and exclusivity for white communities nearby. Lawrence Vale writes that "public housing projects became seen not as progressive enclaves of slum reform, but as discredited visions that carried many of the worst aspects of slum conditions to a new degree of degradation and isolation." Indeed, the Cabrini-Green housing complex gained nationwide notoriety in the following decades as a symbol of the worst in public housing—a toxic concentration of crime, danger, and chronically unemployed and disenfranchised African American residents who had little recourse to escape the miserable conditions. In 1981, in response to complaints about crime, Mayor Jane Byrne created a media spectacle by moving into the Cabrini-Green projects herself. She and her husband, the only white tenants in the entire complex, occupied an apartment for three weeks accompanied by a heavy police presence meant to curb the recent double-digit homicide rates. Her short stay did little to improve conditions, however, as the Chicago Housing Authority administration continued to be fraught with corruption, scandal, and mismanagement, and murders continued occurring on a regular basis after her departure.[44] Public housing of the kind built in Chicago in the 1950s and 1960s proved to be a terribly flawed urban policy. Families and children who had little option but to stay in developments like Cabrini-Green became human casualties of a massive urban planning mistake.

If life in public housing for Puerto Ricans was characterized by racial tensions with African Americans, private housing offered tense relations with white neighbors. As urban renewal refugees pressed into white neighborhoods, many ethnic white residents were outwardly hostile to the newcomers. European immigrants and their children, who only in recent decades had successfully become "white," continued to mold and shape that identity in the 1960s not only vis-à-vis African Americans but increasingly in relation to Puerto Ricans and Mexicans as well. This was evident across a number of encounters.[45]

Housing discrimination provided one means of keeping groups that threatened the racial order out of a particular neighborhood. Puerto Ricans observed that "real estate agencies and private owners of buildings refuse to rent houses or apartments to Spanish speaking families."[46] Landlords often discriminated based on skin color, something that families of varying skin tones quickly discovered. Monse Lucas-Figueroa recalled a time when her mother had found an apartment for the family but then lost it once her husband arrived at the building:

> Lucas . . . sounds more Italian than Puerto Rican. So my mom went to look for an apartment, and they thought that her accent was due to an Italian accent. My mom was very white because her family was from Spain. . . . The guy was willing to give [her] the apartment, so [she] gave him the rent and the deposit. . . . When my mom took my dad—my dad is Puerto Rican, but *el es trigueño* [he is brown-skinned/mixed]—the guy said no. He gave my mother back her deposit, and we were without an apartment. . . . When he saw my father, [he must have thought] "Ahh! He's black!"[47]

Another dark-skinned Puerto Rican man recounted a similar story of having trouble securing an apartment for his family. As soon as he appeared to answer an ad, the landlord would reject him. Finally, a friend recommended he send his wife instead of going himself, since "'she looks more white [sic] than you.'" The man observed, "Do you know that the first time she went out to look for an apartment, she found one?"[48] For many white Chicagoans, deciphering Puerto Ricans' ethnoracial identity became an exercise in determining their "blackness." Gender certainly informed such racial determinations, as landlords objected most vociferously to dark-skinned men.

In cases where landlords did rent to Puerto Ricans, neighboring whites often resented and intimidated the new arrivals. One community worker clearly articulated neighborhood dynamics on the Near North and Northwest Sides: "As soon as they [Puerto Ricans] move to this particular neighborhoods [sic] they feel the old residents do not like and want them as neighbors."[49] This was common among European immigrants in the early twentieth century, who often encountered tension with other existing European residents. But Dominic Pacyga and other historians have dispelled the "myth of ethnic succession." As Pacyga notes, European nationals did not move out en masse when new European ethnics arrived. Instead, they lived "spatially integrated, but socially segregated."[50] It is difficult to determine just how rapidly existing ethnic white residents moved out when Puerto Ricans moved in because Appalachian whites were often an incoming group as well. Thus, Appalachians may have replaced some ethnic whites who abandoned the neighborhoods. As recent (and relatively poor) newcomers to the city as well, Appalachians were limited in their options for seeking affordable housing. Many followed the same paths that Puerto Ricans did to declining neighborhoods. This helps explain why they might have lived among them for longer periods of time.

Puerto Ricans found ways to develop a sense of community among themselves and provide for their own social needs despite experiences with prejudice and discrimination. They initiated traditional hometown clubs and societies, and groups such as the Puerto Rican Congress of Mutual Aid; the Latin American Association of Mutual Aid; and the Borinquen Health Club, a men's group dedicated to recreation and exercise. These groups often sponsored social events such as boxing shows, domino tournaments, beauty pageants, dances, and family activities. Throughout their various efforts, emerging community leaders believed that personal self-improvement and acculturation to American ways would promise better lives for Puerto Rican migrants and their children.[51]

The Catholic Church, settlement houses, and the Puerto Rico Migration Division tried to assimilate the islanders and facilitate more organized contact with whites (*norteamericanos*) to break down racial barriers. The Migration Division, in fact, made strenuous efforts to manage and control Puerto Rican migrants' image among continental Americans, publishing educational pamphlets meant to convince whites that Puerto Ricans were "Americans" just like them. While some local newspaper accounts praised Puerto Ricans' assimilation and success as new migrants, the radical activities of nationalist groups sullied their reputation. The assassination attempt by a Puerto Rican man on President Harry S. Truman in 1950 and the shootings at the US House of Representatives by Puerto Rican Nationalists four years later alarmed many.[52] The Migration Division vigorously fought to counter the negative portrayals of Puerto Ricans in the media.

The church often initiated efforts out of its own evangelical concerns. Priests discovered that Puerto Ricans, especially men, did not attend church regularly or observe Catholic sacraments. This may have been a result of laxer religious standards of devotion on the island that did not stress regular attendance at mass or the result of Puerto Ricans' exclusion from many white Catholic parishes. The traditional national or ethnic parishes established for European immigrants in the late nineteenth and early twentieth centuries generally did not welcome Puerto Rican worshippers, only begrudgingly permitting them to hold services in church basements, for example.[53] To address their pastoral concerns, the archdiocese sponsored the creation of fraternal clubs—Los Caballeros de San Juan—throughout Puerto Rican settlements. Through the Cardinal's Committee for the Spanish Speaking, the archdiocese took the lead on integrating the migrants, educating and indoctrinating them, and as a result, making them more devoted and active Catholics. Puerto Rican men on the Near North Side established two local councils and organized social and recreational activities for adults and children, held fund-raising events, and operated much like a traditional ethnic and religious social club. In an unexpected reversal of traditional gender expectations, men rather than women became the target of evangelization. While in some cases churches, especially Protestant ones, pursued women as the purveyors of a family's spirituality, the Catholic Church focused on Puerto Rican men as heads of households to direct the family's religious engagement and provide its moral leadership. Still, the male-centered Caballeros depended upon women, particularly the labor of members' wives and relatives, in preparing food, organizing events, doing clerical tasks, and sustaining social networks.[54]

West on Division Street: West Town and Humboldt Park

The Puerto Rican population on the Near North Side declined nearly 58 percent to fewer than fifteen hundred people between 1960 and 1970. Many families who had been displaced by urban renewal began migrating north and west to join a large and growing enclave in the West Town and Humboldt Park community areas, and to a lesser extent in neighboring Logan Square.[55] West Town (Community Area 24) and Humboldt Park (Community Area 23) lay directly west of the Near North Side and Lincoln Park, separated from those community areas by the Chicago River and the industrial corridor that flanked it on both sides. Much like the rest of the central city, West Town had been a port of entry for European immigrants and was layered by established families and waves of newer arrivals. Germans and Scandinavians began their settlement in Wicker Park, a small neighborhood in West Town anchored by a tiny park of the same name. At the turn of the twentieth century, the fashionable district was home to business families whose elegant homes stood as a testament to their wealth. Polish, Italian, Ukrainian, and Russian Jewish immigrants soon crowded into the area (one section became known as "Ukrainian Village"). Better-heeled Germans and Scandinavians continued moving farther west into neighboring Humboldt Park, which became the reserve of those who had ascended to the upper-middle class. As southern and eastern Europeans improved their lot, many, especially Russian Jews, also followed the migration westward to Humboldt Park, with its more substantial brick and limestone homes. Most homes in the area, however, were much more modest frame houses, two- and three-flats, and larger apartment buildings. By the 1950s and 1960s, these neighborhoods still maintained a large European immigrant population, though most of their children and grandchildren had joined the exodus for the city outskirts and suburbs. Whites who remained in these neighborhoods were generally the older immigrant generation, those who had fewer means to pursue better living, or those who simply preferred to stay in longtime residences.[56]

Economic changes began to affect these West Side neighborhoods even before Puerto Ricans began moving in. Declining property values and rising taxes in the city were both cause and symptom of urban disinvestment and the shift of the regional economic base to the suburbs. As the city lost revenue with the flight of industry and homeowners and as property values sank, the Daley administration responded by raising taxes for remaining residents. According to one newspaper, taxes had increased 116 percent from 1952 to 1962. One building in the nearby Garfield Park neighborhood, for example, was assessed a property tax bill of $1,800 in 1948; by 1962, the yearly bill had increased to $4,400. Rising taxes and the growing exodus of whites to the suburbs compounded the effect of sinking property values. Another building in that same neighborhood, which reportedly sold for $390,000 in 1955, was not worth half that amount seven years later when African Americans had begun moving in. Racially biased property appraisals valued black-occupied housing lower than that of whites. In the midst of these economic changes, the boom of expanding suburbs continued to lure away many young white families.[57] The demographics of these neighborhoods changed dramatically over the next the two decades.

West Town began receiving Puerto Rican migrants as early as 1953 but by 1960 counted more than seventy-nine hundred islanders and their children, constituting a full 25 percent of the city's entire Puerto Rican population and making it their largest settlement in the city. A smaller group of first- and second-generation Mexicans (over twenty-two hundred) and an equal number of African Americans resided in the neighborhood. All together, the three groups were less than 10 percent of the area's total population (see table 8).[58] By 1970, "Spanish-language" people constituted more than 39 percent of area residents; by 1980, they made up 57 percent. More significant, Spanish-speaking people were concentrated in particular enclaves: they were the majority in at least two-thirds of area census tracts and numbered over 62 percent of the population in nearly half of all tracts.[59]

Humboldt Park experienced similar change (see table 8). In 1960, it was home to fewer than three hundred Puerto Ricans and fewer than seven hundred Mexicans, and 99 percent of its population was classified as white.

Table 8 Population changes by race, West Town and Humboldt Park, 1960–80

	West Town		
	1960	1970	1980
Total population	139,657	124,800	96,428
White (may include Spanish origin)	136,445	114,941	53,132
% of population	97.7	92.1	55.1
Black	2,374	5,491	8,679
% of population	1.7	4.4	9.0
Other nonwhite races*	838	4,368	34,617
% of population	0.6	3.5	35.9
Spanish language / Spanish origin[†]	n/a	48,900	54,675
Puerto Rican	7,948	33,166	28,469
Mexican	2,232	n/a	23,477
% of population	7.3	39.1	56.7

	Humboldt Park		
Total population	71,609	71,726	70,866
White (may include Spanish origin)	70,964	56,807	24,803
% of population	99.1	79.2	35.0
Black	430	13,915	25,228
% of population	0.6	19.4	35.6
Other nonwhite races*	215	1,004	20,835
% of population	0.3	1.4	29.4
Spanish language / Spanish origin[†]	n/a	11,189	28,848
Puerto Rican	286	7,153	17,769
Mexican	683	n/a	8,876
% of population	1.3	15.6	40.7

Sources: Kitagawa and Taueber, *Local Community Fact Book, 1960*; and Chicago Fact Book Consortium, *Local Community Fact Book, 1970 and 1980.*

*The dramatic increase in "other nonwhite races" in 1980 reflects a shift in that year's census procedure. See the following note. The drop in "white" population reflects not only the departure of ethnic whites but the shift of many Latinas/os from "white" to "other" racial status.

[†]The term *Spanish language* was used in 1960 and 1970, while the term *Spanish origin* was used in 1980. The label "of Spanish origin" was assigned independently of race, under the assumption that Spanish-speaking people could be of any race. Most Spanish-origin people were counted as "white" in 1960 and 1970, though a small number who self-identified as "black" are enumerated as such. By 1980, a dramatically larger number of Spanish-origin people chose to identify as "other race." Still, Spanish-origin people continued to make up a significant number of those enumerated in the "white" population.

A decade later, 15.6 percent of its population was Spanish-speaking. African Americans, who were segregated in the southern part of the community area close to racially transitioning West Garfield Park, numbered nearly 20 percent of residents. By 1980, however, whites had declined to less than 24 percent. African Americans made up 36 percent, and the Spanish-speaking were nearly 41 percent. Again, Latinos/as concentrated in particular enclaves, constituting over 60 percent of the population in over half of census tracts. Although Puerto Ricans were not necessarily the majority of the population, in the span of two decades, West Town and Humboldt Park became identified as Latino/a, and more specifically, Puerto Rican *barrios*.[60]

In the face of these demographic changes, policing the boundaries of one's imagined and physical community took on paramount significance for white residents. They imparted the lesson of "the exclusive quality of urban space" to the newcomers.[61] The threat of Puerto Ricans, African Americans, and Mexicans, whose numbers were rapidly growing, prompted many to express their disdain for the foreigners and their encroachment on their territory. Conjuring up images of white settlers under siege, one Italian resident of West Town complained about Puerto Ricans, "They are making a circle around us." Some residents lamented their presence almost as much as they did the sighting of the first African Americans on the block. Yet, ironically, a declining white population and the vacancies they left meant that increasingly "landlords . . . reluctantly rented to Puerto Ricans."[62] As much as some residents may have tried to keep them out, others, especially absentee landlords and those selling their properties, abandoned their commitment to the neighborhood's racial exclusivity. Humboldt Park and West Town neighborhoods continued emptying out their white populations.

Puerto Ricans (and Mexicans) were not segregated or discriminated against in housing as fiercely and unequivocally as African Americans were. Still, their accommodation in white areas was hardly harmonious. To a certain extent, the racially ambiguous Spanish-speaking served as a "buffer" of sorts against what whites perceived to be the more objectionable threat of growing numbers of African Americans on the southern edge of their communities, next to racially shifting East Garfield Park and West Garfield Park.[63] Resigning oneself to accepting Puerto Rican neighbors meant not having to accept black ones perhaps. The fact that racial succession in areas of Puerto Rican settlement proceeded more slowly than in areas penetrated by African Americans suggests that white residents were willing to tolerate Puerto Ricans longer. Some whites actually may have been Appalachian migrants who had also been displaced with Puerto Ricans from other neighborhoods and now relocated in these communities alongside them.[64] Regardless of whether they were European immigrants or Appalachian migrants, white residents maintained an uneasy détente with their Spanish-speaking neighbors that sometimes lasted well over a decade.

The presence of Puerto Ricans challenged working-class ethnic whites in unprecedented ways. Puerto Ricans faced the harsh socioeconomic conditions of most recent migrants, but their cultural particularities, phenotypical diversity, and American citizenship were perplexing. The bevy of voices speaking Spanish on neighborhood streets seemed foreign to "Americans" who quickly forgot their own immigrant origins and insisted the newcomers "speak English." The pungent aromas of Caribbean cooking (*arroz con gandules, alcapurrias, pasteles*) wafting out of kitchen windows sharply contrasted with the olfactory and culinary predilections of Russians, Germans, and Poles. And the contemporary Latin rhythms of popular bugalú, cha-cha, mambo, and rumba music emanating from apartments and automobiles jarred white residents' aural sensibilities and musical consumption standards. Newcomers unsettled blue-collar communities that had established cultural accords, if not social harmony, among their ethnically diverse European American residents. Historical ethnic tensions and national conflicts that divided European Americans in the past diminished as they increasingly identified with one another in their opposition to newcomers.[65]

White residents and Puerto Ricans experienced cultural tensions with each other, but age disparities in the two populations fostered intergenerational conflict as well. Many white residents who stayed on were often elderly people who refused to leave their long-standing homes or were unable to sell or improve them because of depressed real estate markets and redlining. "Old-timers" resented the new migrant population that was changing their neighborhood. Incoming Latino/a families were much younger and frequently included many children. In 1960, 33.9 percent of West Town was under eighteen years old. Among Puerto Ricans, however, over 50 percent were in that age range. In that year, only twenty-five hundred Puerto Rican children and youth (both boys and girls) aged five to nineteen lived in the area along with more than seventeen thousand white adults over the age of sixty.[66] In contrast to the preponderance of children in predominantly African American public housing—where there was a shortage of adults to supervise youngsters—in West Town and Humboldt Park, there was an overabundance of older white residents who policed Puerto Rican children on neighborhood streets at a ratio of nearly seven to one. Scholar Marixsa Alicea remembers vividly, "As a child I was constantly being yelled at by white Anglo-Americans and European immigrants for sitting on their front steps, walking on their grass, or just simply coming too close to their house."[67]

The number of Latino/a children in West Town and especially Humboldt Park saw a dramatic increase over that decade. A community summer program documented the changes in public school enrollments:

> The great increase in the Latin-American population is indicated most dramatically in the school statistics. Whereas in 1960 Puerto Ricans accounted for only 14 percent of the population in our intensive service area and Mexicans another 2 percent[,] by November 1967, the eleven public schools serving our area indicated the following ethnic composition: Latin American— 50.0 percent, White—42.7 percent, Negro—4.9 percent, Other—2.4 percent.

Latin American students went from constituting 53 to 74 percent of the population at Von Humboldt Elementary School in the 1966–67 school years. Latin American children made up 72 percent of Sabin Elementary, 70 percent at Wicker Park Primary and Intermediate Schools, and 34 percent at Tuley High School.[68] The proportional growth of Latino/a students in local schools occurred in part because so many white children were vacating classroom seats. Many white families who remained in the area chose to send their children to local parochial schools, abandoning the crumbling public school system as more Latina/o and African American children moved in.

Intergenerational dynamics changed within a decade. Though Puerto Rican children initially found themselves in a community of elderly white residents, by 1970 seniors found themselves outnumbered. Puerto Rican children and youth numbered over eighteen thousand while whites over sixty had decreased to eleven thousand. In 1960, 34 percent of West Town's population was under the age of twenty. By 1980, children and youth made up 41 percent of the area's population (see table 9). In census tracts where the Spanish-speaking concentrated (numbering over 60 percent of residents), children and youth were nearly 50 percent of the population.[69]

The growing number of Puerto Rican and other Spanish-speaking youngsters provoked hostile reactions from white adults who increasingly saw the neighborhoods' demographic changes in racial terms. The community summer program noted, "There are many Puerto Rican children who live on the south side of Armitage between Hoyne and Damen. Some of these come to this caravan. An old Polish lady who lives near the caravan site complained vehemently [about] our causing the Puerto Rican kids

Table 9   Population changes by age, poverty, and unemployment, 1960–80

	West Town		
	1960 (%)	1970 (%)	1980 (%)
Under 20 years old*	33.9	42.0	40.8
Overall poverty rate†	14.4	19.4	27.2
White poverty rate	n/a	16.6	26.4
Puerto Rican / Spanish-speaking poverty rate	n/a	28.4	37.7
Overall unemployment rate‡	6.1	6.0	10.9
White unemployment rate§	6.1	5.9	9.1
Puerto Rican / Spanish-speaking unemployment rate	9.2	8.0	12.4
	Humboldt Park		
Under 20 years old*	30.2	40.8	44.6
Overall poverty rate†	9.8	13.0	25.9
White poverty rate	n/a	9.3	21.4
Puerto Rican / Spanish-speaking poverty rate	n/a	18.2	30.6
Overall unemployment rate‡	4.6	4.8	12.9
White unemployment rate§	4.5	4.4	10.5
Puerto Rican / Spanish-speaking unemployment rate	12.9	7.8	13.0

Sources: Kitagawa and Taueber, *Local Community Fact Book, 1960*; Chicago Fact Book Consortium, *Local Community Fact Book, 1970 and 1980*; and 1960, 1970, and 1980 census data tables at http://www.socialexplorer.com.

*In 1960, the figure represents those under the age of 18.

†In 1960, the census measured the number of people with a median family income of less than $3,000.

‡In 1960, unemployment rate represents only the male labor force.

§"White" unemployment rate includes Puerto Rican / Spanish-speaking people, as most were classified under that category in 1960 and 1970. The unemployment rate for non-Hispanic whites, then, is presumably even lower.

to come down 'white' Homer St."[70] White residents attacked Puerto Rican children because of the social change they represented and the disorder that they felt such children were bringing to the neighborhood. The distinction the Polish woman made between the children and her "white" street clearly expressed the view that Puerto Ricans were unquestionably *not* white.

White residents often judged Puerto Ricans' racial identity in relation to African Americans, sometimes collapsing the two under the same racial slurs and revealing their suspicions that Puerto Ricans were in fact black

Figure 21. Children with social worker John Russell from the Chicago Commons Association. This photo, whose original caption reads, "All Puerto Rican children except boy by car," captures a typical street scene in the West Town or Humboldt Park neighborhood in the mid-1960s. Note the conditions of area buildings, sidewalks, and the empty lot where children are playing. ICHi-36255aa, Chicago History Museum.

or at least stood very close to blackness. One man recalled entering a white tavern in the area during the 1950s: "We were always considered black. I remember this one time, I went to a tavern with a friend and the owner of the bar refused to serve us. I said to the guy, 'We want two beers,' and he said, 'We don't serve niggers here.' I replied that we were Puerto Ricans and he just said, 'That's the same shit.'"[71] The carelessness of using slurs normally targeted at African Americans to denigrate Puerto Ricans did not reflect racial ignorance on the part of whites as much as it revealed the limited vocabulary they had at hand and the fact that they were locating Puerto Ricans closer to blackness.[72]

Racial objections to Puerto Ricans were not limited to verbal assaults or insults but could become violent just as they did for African Americans and some Mexicans who were the first to breach white neighborhood boundaries. Male youths often became the protagonists in these physical conflicts. In 1960, Puerto Rican male youths were clearly outnumbered by white male youths by nearly eighteen to one, making them easy targets for white attacks.[73] The most extreme forms of resistance, however, included the fire-bombing of automobiles and homes by white youth gangs who sometimes were commissioned by neighborhood residents to scare nonwhite interlopers away.[74] Community activist Obed López explained that because of such violence, "some [Puerto Rican] families at one point or another would rent an apartment in the buildings where they were living for the[ir own] gangs to come and be there as a defense, a counter force to the people that were harassing them or using violence against them." While it is difficult to confirm evidence of this, López's comment suggests that some Puerto Rican adults may have condoned or at least tolerated Puerto Rican youth gangs in the neighborhood. Apart from the fact that the teenagers were their own children and kin, they served an important function of defending the community against white attacks. Just as white male youths served as the physical enforcers of community boundaries for white families, Puerto Rican youth gangs often originated or initially served as a defensive body to protect

Figure 22. "One of Viceroys who had been attacked by older whites telling story to Russell." The scene captured regular neighborhood dynamics in the 1960s and the formation of Puerto Rican gangs. ICHi-61163, Chicago History Museum.

themselves from white hostility (see chapter 5). Escalating violence between white and Puerto Rican youth increased residents' anxieties about newcomers and the effect they were having on the neighborhood. Moreover, for Puerto Ricans, just as for African Americans, "Years of harassment by 'white' youths had created a tradition of antiwhite sentiment on the streets."[75]

The media fueled such antagonisms and perpetuated the idea that Puerto Ricans were a dangerous racial group. The *Saturday Evening Post* prominently featured a lurid story in 1960 that grabbed national attention. In a one-sided account of racial hostility, the magazine recounted the tale of two Puerto Ricans who killed an Italian American in the West Town neighborhood. The article explained that the Puerto Ricans "had never met Guido Garro; they murdered him only because he happened to be an Italian." The author described the two suspects as vicious and depraved (one was a philanderer who regularly beat his wife, the other drifted aimlessly, committing senseless crimes). The story presented an extremely disparaging image of Puerto Ricans as a whole.[76] On the heels of the successful Broadway musical *West Side Story*, such sensational media accounts circulated the image of Puerto Ricans as violent, bloodthirsty, immoral people and depicted whites as their helpless victims. This narrative oversimplified and distorted the complex racial dynamics of rapidly changing urban neighborhoods. It failed to acknowledge that racial attacks often originated with whites (in particular, male youths) who directed it at much smaller numbers of newcomers. Such media stories reinforced negative stereotypes of Puerto Ricans and depicted them alone as the perpetrators of violence. The highly publicized shooting of Guido Garro and the threat of danger motivated even more white residents to leave the neighborhood. Many white homeowners sold out as quickly as they could.

The long sojourn of those who chose not to leave the area, however, sometimes reflected more tolerant social attitudes. Edward Stefaniak, a Polish American resident, for example, had lived for over twenty years next to "friendly blacks."[77] Stefaniak apparently tolerated the influx of Spanish speakers "with bland acceptance." Unlike most other Poles, "he found it hard to understand the fear and hatred many of the other Polish residents of Wicker Park expressed from time to time." As far as Stefaniak was concerned, "A neighboring Puerto Rican family had proven to be pleasant and solid." Puerto Rican homeowners, perhaps because of their perceived higher class status, seemed to enjoy better relations with white neighbors than did renters.[78]

Responses to neighborhood change could be colored by unrealistic nostalgia. The Reverend Henry Murray, director of Wicker Park's local settlement, Association House, explained, "'As these people [European immigrants and their children] move on, they think of Wicker Park as the neighborhood they remember from the old days, and they forget that it was pretty well used up by the time they abandoned it to the Puerto Ricans.'"[79] To be sure, earlier generations of immigrants romanticized the neighborhood of their childhoods. They seldom considered that they had exhausted the aged housing supply, leaving it dilapidated and in dire need of repairs.

Residents like Stefaniak and members of the Northwest Community Organization, which he led, seemed to understand the larger structural dynamics that were reshaping their neighborhoods. They realized that urban renewal on the Near North Side had pushed so many Spanish-speaking migrants into the area. They recognized that their community would be next on the chopping block for urban renewal initiatives. Some even capitalized on that renewal. But most white residents failed to understand that the privileging of private interests, public disinvestment, an uneven distribution of political power in the city's wards, and shifts in the economy all contributed to the decline of their neighborhoods and the racial change. They failed to recognize that public expenditures on private development (in the form of tax breaks and direct funding to developers and corporations) left less money for the improvement of streets, trash removal, and other public services, thus causing their communities to deteriorate. Few were aware of the practice of "redlining," lending discrimination by banks that accepted neighborhood people's deposits but denied them home improvement loans or mortgages if their communities were threatened by or already experiencing racial change. Real estate brokers profited enormously by selling decaying buildings at inflated prices to Puerto Rican, Mexican, and African American buyers, many of whom could not buy elsewhere. Instead of blaming "banks, corporate interests, and the political machine," many white residents focused their ire on "the blacks," "the Spanish," or "the Puerto Ricans." In reality, their neighborhoods were already being propelled into decline by growth-driven urban planning initiatives.[80]

Relations with Police and the Division Street Uprising

If relations between Puerto Ricans and white neighbors were tense, local law enforcement generally offered state sanction for most white residents' response to neighborhood change. This was the result of the racial composition of the police force, which was almost exclusively white, the age gap between white residents and incoming Puerto Ricans, and the impunity with which officers committed misconduct. In the 1960s, the Chicago Police Department (CPD) was an agency fraught with corruption and abuse. *Life* magazine declared that Chicago "probably has the worst police department of any sizable city."[81] In 1960, local newspapers ran an exposé on pervasive police collusion with the organized crime syndicate, links to corrupt machine politicians, and widespread police criminal activity. Police had close ties to the city's mob bosses, who paid off numerous captains and other officers for protection. Police often received a cut from the city's gambling parlors, taverns, prostitution rings, drug trade, and burglars. At least two separate burglary rings confessed to being shaken down by officers for jewelry, electronics, furs, golf clubs, and other stolen goods. One young burglar described in detail how officers from one North Side district actually helped commission burglaries of liquor stores and butcher shops, taking home thousands of dollars in alcohol and meat. The CPD was actually contributing to increased rates of burglary in some neighborhoods rather than reducing them.[82]

Corruption and lack of integrity coursed through the department's ranks. The *Chicago Tribune* revealed how local politicians often pulled strings on department promotions and plum assignments. Officers seeking to advance in rank often had to endorse machine candidates or do other political favors, thus making them beholden to machine politicians and Democratic Party leaders rather than their supervising officers. In other cases, those who had to take written exams for promotion could purchase answer sheets for a fee, thus revealing the fraud behind an ostensibly meritocratic system. Police were even accused of taking bribes to stand in place of suspects for lineups when witnesses came to identify suspected criminals.[83] All told, police corruption, misconduct, and malfeasance ran rampant through the department and stretched all the way to Richard Daley's city hall and the Cook County Democratic Party. Rather than fighting crime, many of Chicago's men in blue frequently aided and abetted or perpetrated it themselves.[84]

In a climate of widespread corruption and wrongdoing, then, it would not be hard to imagine that such a police force carried its bad behavior to neighborhood streets, particularly in relation to people perceived to be intruders in white neighborhoods. As political theorist Susan Bickford notes, "The presence of police . . . signals safety for some and danger for others."[85] For Puerto Ricans, Mexicans, and African Americans, the CPD had a long history of regularly harassing and brutalizing them with impunity over the years. Officers had reportedly killed several young men of color in the mid-sixties. Andrew Diamond notes that "youths hanging out on the streets in the late 1950s and early 1960s found themselves increasingly running up against antagonistic police officers."[86] Conflicts between police and young men of color were fueled in part by the fact that Puerto Ricans and African Americans were generally much younger than whites. (The median age of Puerto Rican men in West Town in 1960 was 20.9 years old.)[87] Over the next two decades, the Puerto Rican population remained significantly younger than white residents. As young people became increasingly alienated from school and dropped out in high numbers, and increasingly found themselves unemployed, they filled neighborhood streets, where they clashed with law enforcement.

Police-community conflicts, however, were also an extension of the racial antagonism in changing neighborhoods and the racial affinities of a predominantly white police force. Rather than assuaging racial tensions, local law enforcement perpetuated such conflict. Obed López observes, "The police in a real sense reflected the prejudices of the communities they came from." Police, after all, often shared ethnoracial and class backgrounds with the communities they worked in, communities that resented the newcomers and wanted them out of their neighborhoods. Like many residents, they harbored enmity against people they viewed as unwelcome outsiders. And they abused and harassed them with fervor.[88]

Community worker José Muñiz reported regularly that Puerto Ricans complained of problems with authorities. According to many, police routinely harassed them, often for innocuous behaviors such as congregating on public streets, a social practice whose cultural and class underpinnings clearly disrupted bourgeois ideals of more privatized leisure pursuits. Families organized to discuss police abuse and mistreatment. In 1960, a survey of Puerto Ricans in a section of West Town revealed that the majority of them felt discriminated against, particularly by police.[89] But the responses to address such tense relations surprisingly put the burden on the Puerto Rican community. That summer, after informally surveying members of a fraternal group (likely the Caballeros de San Juan), Muñiz reported, "I found out that at least 90% of this group had the idea that the police and the other neighbors hate and persecute the Spanish-Speaking people, especially the Puerto Ricans. I gave a long talk to them about the law and ways of living in this city. After the meeting was over, I can say that at least 75 or 80% of them agreed with me and will try to adjust themselves to the way of living in their community." Like some in the Puerto Rican community and in the social service professions, Muñiz seemed to believe that cultural differences and ignorance of American laws and way of life (*not* prejudice) caused poor relations with police. Muñiz tried to educate migrants and their children on what kinds of behaviors were unlawful. Working from another angle, the Migration Division helped establish Spanish classes and other programs for police officers and other public employees to familiarize them with Puerto Rican culture and language. They created an exchange program for Chicago policemen, funding trips to the island so they could visit with law enforcement there. Such efforts did not seem to stymie police mistreatment, however.[90]

Even when they walked alone, Puerto Rican men became targeted as suspects. Carlos Alvarez related to the famed oral historian Studs Terkel that he was unjustly arrested while leaving work one day. In the early-morning hours as he came off his shift as night watchman at a local museum, Alvarez was stopped and eventually surrounded by as many as fourteen squad cars. Officers refused to believe that he worked at the museum (though they allegedly did not bother to verify either) and instead mocked and mistreated him, fracturing his arm before taking him to jail. Although he tried to explain himself to a judge, he was found guilty of charges he did not understand (he did not speak English fluently) and lost his job as a result of the incident. Other young men likewise complained that police harassed them when they walked through neighborhood parks.[91] Relations with police revealed the gendered dynamics of race relations: white policemen made assumptions about Puerto Rican men's criminality and regularly persecuted them for even the smallest offenses.

Of course police responded to actual crimes, especially those committed by young men, who as a demographic commit the highest proportion of crimes. Male participation in certain activities, such as alcohol consumption, gambling, street fights, and gang feuds, certainly prompted many arrests. Still, as researchers noted, "The general public, including law enforcement authorities, have an exaggerated view as to the involvement of Puerto Ricans in crime and law violations."[92] Officers' encounters with actual offenders quickly colored their judgment and biased their views against the larger community. At the same time, given the violence from white male youths, deplorable living conditions, and shrinking employment opportunities, young men joined street gangs in growing numbers during these decades. Still, as a predominantly white police force encountered growing numbers of brown and black men, their clashes became contests over masculinity and manhood. Andrew Diamond notes that Chicagoans witnessed a campaign of gratuitous harassment waged by police against youths hanging out on the streets. According to one West Side youth worker, police repeatedly roughed up youths, forced them to remove scarves they wore on their heads, tore up their cigarettes, confiscated their money, and subjected them to verbal abuse. Such tactics clearly went beyond law enforcement: they indicate that the police had entered into the logic of a struggle for dominance predicated on emasculating their young rivals.[93]

Puerto Ricans were acutely aware of the abrasive relationship they had with local law enforcement. As Felix Padilla notes, "Residents of the Division Street area shared a pervasive belief that policemen were physically brutal, harsh, and discourteous to them because they were Puerto Ricans."[94] Over more than a decade, many Puerto Ricans grew to mistrust police.

In 1966, Mayor Richard J. Daley designated the first week in June "Puerto Rican Week." Community leaders cheered the gesture of ethnic inclusion, and planned enthusiastically for the weeklong celebration. Islanders from throughout the city gathered to celebrate and publicly show their cultural pride, culminating in a gathering of ten thousand people along the famous downtown State Street. The event's location on the prominent boulevard held great significance: it symbolized the mayor's and the city's public acknowledgment of this newest ethnic minority group.[95] The celebration culminated Sunday evening, June 12, in Humboldt Park. That night police allegedly answered a call about youths fighting in the street. As they approached a group of young men, they proceeded to chase two of them down an alley. In the pursuit, Officer Thomas Munyon shot a twenty-year-old man, Arcelis Cruz, claiming that he had drawn a gun. Witnesses disputed the accusation.

Since many people were out on the streets because of the festival, they soon began gathering to see what had happened and eventually to protest Cruz's shooting. Growing numbers of officers began arriving on the scene, and they brought police dogs to control the crowds. As they used the dogs to keep people back, one of them reportedly bit a young man, incensing the crowd further and escalating the hostilities. A local Spanish-language radio personality, Carlos Agrelot ("*El Argentino Boricua*," or "The Puerto Rican Argentine"), had been broadcasting live from the events throughout the day. When the tension and violence began, Agrelot continued coverage, providing regular updates on the police-community standoff. The radio broadcast attracted still more people into the streets, drawing listeners from neighborhoods even farther away. Word spread quickly throughout the community, and soon hundreds of people (newspapers claimed it was a thousand) took to the streets expressing outrage against this latest episode of police abuse. Women and children were among the crowd, which began pelting authorities with rocks and bottles. Police armed themselves with riot helmets and batons. Some rioters began turning over squad cars, setting property on fire, and looting stores. Between thirty-five and forty-four people, including the wounded Arcelis Cruz and four women, were arrested. Community leaders tried to quell the outburst and send people home, but the riot continued long after midnight until heavy rain finally dispersed the crowd. Chicago's Puerto Rican population had erupted in one of the growing "civil disturbances" spreading through impoverished inner-city, minority communities around the country.[96]

Residents had witnessed several incidents of police injustice in the previous summer. In June and July of 1965, officers savagely beat several Puerto Rican men over neighborhood use of fire hydrants. In a third case, the community accused police of inciting interracial violence between Puerto Ricans and African Americans and then refusing to intervene. While such cases often went unnoticed by the mainstream and more conservative press (like the *Chicago Tribune*), incidents of police brutality were more frequently reported in more liberal papers and the Spanish-language press.[97] The case of Celestino Gonzalez and Silvano Burgos, for example, appeared in *El Puertorriqueño* in August of 1965. Officers had reportedly responded to a call on West Division Street about an open fire hydrant. When they arrived, Gonzalez and Burgos, who stood near the hydrant, ran into a nearby building where they both lived. Police pursued and arrested them both in their homes. Gonzalez described the following:

> They handcuffed me in my room and took me to their car by pushing me and threatening my life. They took me to a hospital . . . where the policeman who broke the glass of my door was going to be treated. They pulled us out of the car and took us to a washroom in the hospital. There we were beaten savagely. The next stop was a park near the hospital where I was, once again, beaten up. Finally, I was taken to a police district where several policemen hit me like crazy; I fell to the floor and everyone that passed by hit me. I was bleeding terribly and I lost my consciousness, when I woke up, I was in Cook County Hospital with my hands and feet tied to a bed.[98]

Community leaders tried to bring the matter to the attention of the mayor and his relevant commissions, but the city seemed reluctant to acknowledge that the police department had a community relations problem with the city's Puerto Ricans.

The night after Arcelis Cruz's shooting, a crowd of people marched to the local police station to demand his release and that of thirty others who had been jailed. Looters and rioters continued breaking storefront windows and taking merchandise, especially from white-owned businesses. Authorities reported approximately ten thousand people in the streets defying "hundreds of police who attempted to restore order." That night officers shot seven more Puerto Rican men, most of whom were local residents, including one man who was fifty-six years old. A photograph taken during the evening's events captured the violence that police visited upon local residents: a lone youth stood in the street surrounded by at least six officers, several of whom wielded their clubs, and one of whom fiercely shouted at the boy. All told, thirty-seven individuals were arrested on the second night. The city's leading newspapers focused on the minor injuries that several officers suffered, as they frequently did when police faced off with civilians or protesters.[99]

On Tuesday, police officials met with church leaders, including Father Don Headley of the Cardinal's Committee on the Spanish-Speaking, and Puerto Rican ministers and lay leaders, to discuss the turmoil. Mayor Daley, who also attended, allegedly reported that "he had heard of no grievances from the Puerto Rican community that could have accounted for the violence. 'The problem seems to be mainly one of communication.'" Indeed, city officials seemed caught completely by surprise in responding to the riots because police had conducted intelligence operations to identify potential riot "hot spots" the month prior and reportedly had not anticipated any problems among Mexicans or Puerto Ricans. City leaders and social service providers claimed to be completely unaware of the high concentration of Puerto Ricans in the neighborhood. City officials, and indeed some Puerto Rican leaders, began blaming "outsiders" (Communists and gang members from other neighborhoods) for agitating the crowds and inciting the violence. Dr. Martin Luther King Jr. and the Southern Christian Leadership Conference (SCLC) had come to the city that year to help lead the Chicago Freedom Movement. As King was organizing peaceful marches for open housing and reaching African Americans on the West Side, his movement was having a tremendous impact, including among Latinos/as. Obed López recalls inviting acquaintances from the SCLC to serve as observers and witnesses to the uprising. Although the SCLC espoused nonviolence, some community leaders and the Daley administration began blaming them as the outside agitators.[100]

On the third night, five hundred officers patrolled the streets to maintain the peace. Perhaps in light of the accusations of police abuse, the acting deputy chief of patrol who led the officers ordered his men, "We'll lock up anyone we have to in order to clear the streets. But do it with a smile." They proceeded to arrest twenty-five adults and fifteen teenagers.[101] Over the course of the three days, some observers noted that undercover police (provocateurs) had incited some of the destruction themselves. Father Headley, who worked closely with the Caballeros de San Juan, recalled standing on top of a police car trying to dissuade an angry crowd from setting it on fire. He noted, "I was pointing out to them the fact that I knew this was a plot. There is something going on here because the two guys that are telling you to burn this car are cops.' I knew them from the Monroe Street district, I had been at St. Patrick's [parish] for five years and I knew that they were policemen." Once he stepped down from the car, he recalled, "Out of the gangways, police poured out. They were everywhere, they had dogs, they had helmets and they were beating the hell out of everybody on the street." The violence finally died down by June 15, with official reports citing dozens arrested, various injured, over fifty buildings destroyed, and millions of dollars in damages. While the mainstream press had barely noticed the festivities of Puerto Rican Week, the Division Street riots were featured in front-page headlines for several days.[102]

Observers soon tried to analyze the psychology and sociology of the riots. The nation had witnessed a number of black riots in Harlem, Watts, Detroit, and Philadelphia the year before. Some interpreted the uprisings as an enraged reaction from a frustrated, marginalized, and oppressed population.[103] Others vehemently disagreed. The *Chicago Tribune* denounced the Division Street rioters and opined, "The usual sentimental drivel is coming forth in an effort to excuse the rioters who for two successive nights engaged in shooting, looting, burning, and fighting with the police on the near northwest side. . . . Apologists for the rioters also have been looking for reasons to blame unemployment, interracial friction, and 'the ghetto.'" The editors incorrectly claimed that unemployment was not very high in the community and falsely asserted that "there has been little friction between Puerto Ricans and older residents." In another editorial, they staunchly defended police, stating they "had provocation to use force." They wrote, "The evidence has been overwhelming that the police in northern cities bend over backward to be gentle with members of minority groups." Despite the fact that police had shot seven people, the editors applauded: "It is greatly to their credit that they managed to disperse the mob and restore order without causing serious injury to any of the rioters."[104] A letter to the editor praised the *Tribune*'s response: "The Puerto Rican coming to our city presumably comes here to improve his lot in life (and judging by the thousands flocking here he does improve his standard of living) and to make his home. If this is so, then he should be prepared to adopt our customs and our language, the same as other immigrants have done in the past."[105] Another reprinted commentary remarked, "When these were Polish and German communities they weren't riot breeders. They were simply neighborhoods where these people felt at home while they and their children were becoming a *real* part of America" (emphasis in original).[106] Such critics were entirely unsympathetic to the plight of Puerto Ricans and denounced their behavior. The letters revealed the distinctions local white residents made between violent Puerto Ricans and earlier peaceful European immigrants. They failed to remember the mob violence that some of their own had committed against African Americans since the early 1900s, and especially since the Great Migration of World War II. According to these letter writers and others, Puerto Ricans were deficient "immigrants" who were failing to assimilate and become "Americans" as they had.

Making sense of the riots became a thorny issue for the community itself. The Migration Division's Chicago office repeatedly referred to the four days of rioting as a "disturbance," minimizing the extent of the violence and unrest in its communications with New York headquarters. Indeed, the Chicago office's annual report that year made no mention of the uprising at all.[107] Some in the Puerto Rican community expressed shame and embarrassment that so many had taken to the streets in such an unrestrained manner. Many lamented the violence and destruction and felt that the riots achieved nothing politically and instead worsened relations with police. Others, like Obed López, a Mexican immigrant who witnessed the riots firsthand, believed that they "were a spontaneous reaction to the police brutality and to discrimination of the residents of the area, [from] the Polish, Ukrainians, Italians. . . . I think . . . the riots took place . . . because . . . over the years, the pattern of attacks against Puerto Rican families had existed."[108] The most strident community leaders in the neighborhood used the riots as a starting point from which to demand greater attention to the poverty of Puerto Ricans and the need for culturally sensitive community services.

One month after the Division Street uprising, the city's black West Side erupted in response to police brutality. When black teens opened a neighborhood fire hydrant for local black children who were barred from three of the area's four public swimming pools, police responded with force and, in the ensuing struggle, "clubbed five youths bloody." The following day, the community broke out in violence, which the CPD reportedly could not suppress. The National Guard ultimately stepped in to restore order. After the guard had established peace, however, local police came back into the community and "shot up several homes in retaliation." This was the second riot among Chicago's black residents since 1965. Mayor Daley's notorious "shoot to kill" order against rioters hardly calmed community anger.[109]

Just three days after the black West Side uprising, the Chicago Commission on Human Relations (CCHR) began open hearings to address the Puerto Rican community's issues and concerns. The CCHR had originally formed in 1943 in response to the race riots that rocked Detroit and Los Angeles. Hoping to pacify the community now, Mayor Daley appointed Claudio Flores, publisher of the Spanish-language newspaper *El Puertorriqueño*, as the first Puerto Rican on the commission. The CCHR hearing was attended by over 250 people. Leaders and other community members testified to the conditions of police brutality, high rents and substandard housing, racial discrepancies in union wages, and credit schemes that defrauded consumers. They complained that city hall and the political structure were out of touch with the community and that the city fostered "apartheid, Chicago-style." Juan Díaz of the local Boys Club, one of the more vocal and militant leaders on Division Street, blasted city antipoverty programs for failing to reach Puerto Ricans. A local clergyman pointed out the fact that the hearings could not truly capture the opinions of most Puerto Ricans because they were held at a time and place that working people could not easily attend. Various speakers offered potential solutions for a number of problems, citing the need for greater political representation at the precinct level, and more parks and recreation facilities.[110] None of the suggestions offered, however, thoroughly examined two key underlying factors: the decline of well-paid manufacturing jobs was leading to growing unemployment, and working-class whites and the police who protected them resented Puerto Ricans in their communities.

Over the summer, residents, including some active in the Caballeros de San Juan, continued to hold meetings to address police abuse and submit grievances to the mayor and to the police internal affairs department. Their efforts at mending police-community relations, however, did not stop policemen's use of excessive force. In August, police killed Ismael Laboy at his home in front of his wife and eight children. Nearly fifteen hundred people reportedly gathered and began stoning squad cars before heavy rain dispersed the crowd. During that call, officers also shot seventeen-year-old Rigoberto Acosta in the back. Acosta had reportedly gone to see the gathering crowd with other youths and was fleeing the scene when police took aim at him, leaving him paralyzed for the rest of his life. The next month, an officer fatally shot a fourteen-year-old boy, Nelson Rivera, for stealing a car. Two hundred people gathered in the Woodlawn neighborhood immediately after the incident to protest. Community leaders managed to defuse the tension, just barely averting another violent face-off with authorities.[111] In another case, Ismael Solano Nieves died as a result of burns suffered while in custody at Cook County Jail. Community leader Carlos "Caribe" Ruiz noted, "Ever since the Division St. disorders of 1966, we've been preaching to our people that they should submit to arrest and then defend themselves according to law in court. But if this is the kind of thing that happens in the jail, then it is useless for us to go into the streets and try to talk about obeying the law."[112]

The year after the riots, University of Chicago researchers conducted a study on Puerto Ricans and race relations in West Town. Although almost 90 percent of the people surveyed believed that the riots did not help Puerto Ricans improve their situation, many respondents continued to have misgivings about police. An astonishing 71.4 percent agreed that Puerto Ricans had problems with law enforcement. Asked to choose from a list of topics which was the most important problem affecting the group, respondents ranked employment first followed by police relations.[113] More extensive verbal responses revealed that the longer Puerto Ricans lived in the city, the more likely they were to believe that police discriminated against their population and treated them unjustly. One fifty-four-year-old woman who had lived in Chicago twelve years and responded in Spanish explained, "The police abuse the Puerto Ricans. They are always looking and searching and, when they catch one, they strike him." A thirty-five-year-old male skilled worker, who had lived in Chicago over seventeen years and spoke English fluently, echoed this: "Police discriminate against Latins. You have to avoid them because, if they catch you, you will be in trouble."[114]

Five months after the CCHR public hearings, the commission produced an official report, which concluded that the problems of the Puerto Rican community stemmed from cultural causes—the language barriers of rural migrants coming to an urban society. To put it bluntly, Chicago, like other East Coast cities, had a "Puerto Rican problem." The report recommended bridging this cultural divide by offering more Spanish-language classes for local police and printing traffic laws and other publications in Spanish, among other things. The entire uprising and community protests had been reduced to a matter of cultural difference. The burden fell on Puerto Ricans to assimilate and change their behavior. This would ensure better relations with law enforcement and better conditions in their neighborhoods.[115]

Conclusion

Little has been written about the urban uprisings of Puerto Ricans in the 1960s. Still, the analysis of Chicago's black riots points to some parallels that are useful for understanding the Division Street uprising. In the case of African Americans, the Chicago Urban League, for example, noted how the influx of recent migrants, the city's urban renewal policies, and racial succession had fomented social unrest.

> The West Side was the newer of Chicago's two [black] ghettos, comprised of neighborhoods that had been white not long ago. Compared to the South Side, it had fewer community organizations, less-established churches, and fewer black-run businesses and institutions. Its residents were also different from blacks on the South Side. More of them had personally made the Great Migration from the rural South. They were more likely to be poor and undereducated, to have loose ties to the city, and to still be experiencing the disappointment of the gap between what they expected when they moved north to Chicago and what they found there.

The assessment captured the phenomenon of recent migration, but the league also noted the simultaneous impact of urban renewal displacement:

> Another large group of West Side residents were uprooted migrants from closer by. West Side neighborhoods were home to many blacks forcibly displaced by Daley's urban renewal programs—a Chicago Urban League report called them "dumping grounds for relocated families." In a 1958 series on urban renewal, the *Chicago Daily News* compared "Chicago's DP"—for the most part poor blacks pushed out by urban renewal—to European "displaced persons" uprooted by world war. Chicago's DP's were "made homeless not by war or communism or disaster but by wreckers," the *Daily News* reported, and were "refugees of the relocation that inevitably accompanies redevelopment. They are people, angry, indifferent, resentful, resigned." It was the kind of alienation, the Chicago Urban League's report concluded, that made an area a likely site for civil unrest.[116]

Much of what observers noted about the conditions of African Americans accurately applied to Puerto Ricans as well.

Omar López, a community activist and former member of the Young Lords, explained that as Puerto Ricans were displaced from the Near North Side and moved to West Town and Humboldt Park, the resistance and hostility they encountered from whites were reinforced by the police and civil institutions (schools, welfare department, etc.). As a result, López explained, "there was a lot of discontent building up in the community because the structures were not responding."[117] That so many women and children participated in the riots suggests that these dynamics had a direct impact on them as well. Women and girls came out on the streets, vocally defending their husbands, sons, boyfriends, and brothers, hoping to protect them from abuse, incarceration, or deadly violence. They were also expressing their own frustrations with local institutions and the inhospitable treatment they repeatedly faced.

In the following years, economic conditions in West Town and Humboldt Park remained bleak. Growing deindustrialization devastated Puerto Rican workers who felt the brunt of this in manufacturing layoffs. Unemployment statistics gathered by the Cardinal's Committee for the Spanish-Speaking revealed that 18 percent of the labor force in the Association House service area was unemployed. Puerto Ricans constituted two-thirds of those individuals. The Cardinal's Committee further reported that 76 percent of Puerto Rican heads of households were employed, but 13 percent earned below the poverty level of three thousand dollars a year. The study noted that "among the Spanish-Speaking persons employed, 44% work in factories, 15% are machine operators, 12% are engaged in general service type jobs (restaurants, bus boy, etc.), and 3½% are engaged in small business." Even among those employed, however, "21% received additional aid through welfare."[118] As the population became younger, it also became poorer. The decline of the city's industrial sector was increasingly manifested in growing unemployment rates, especially among the working class. In 1970, local labor markets were still relatively strong, but by 1980, 10.9 percent of West Town's workforce was unemployed, while Humboldt Park measured 12.9 percent unemployment. Poverty rates followed the upward trend, reaching 27.2 percent in West Town and 25.9 percent in Humboldt Park by 1980.[119] Spanish-speaking residents experienced significantly higher poverty and unemployment rates than whites, reinforcing growing ideas about their dependency, inadequacy as workers, and inability to assimilate and integrate economically.

Conditions continued to decline in West Town and Humboldt Park as absentee landlords extracted rents from poor tenants but let buildings fall into disrepair. The number of vacant housing units in Humboldt Park increased nearly tenfold from 1950 to 1980, going from only 1 percent of all units to nearly 10 percent. In West Town, the vacancy rate went from less than 2 percent to nearly 13 percent during the same period.[120] In a community of declining property values, buildings in disrepair or with severe code violations mysteriously burned down at high rates. The Northwest Community Organization counted thirty-five buildings razed by fire in Wicker Park and twenty-six in adjoining East Humboldt Park between 1969 and 1971. These fires cost the community approximately 198 apartments previously occupied largely by Spanish-speaking families. Throughout the 1970s, fires continued to claim dozens of buildings. In eleven months of 1978, there were three thousand fires in the area, over one-third of them officially determined to be arson. It is unclear how many lives such fires claimed. Whether these fires were caused by the faulty conditions of aged buildings, by negligent tenants, or by premeditated arson, a surprisingly high number of property owners disposed of real estate by collecting insurance claims.[121] The Near Northwest Side became riddled with vacant lots and boarded, charred, or hollowed-out buildings. Although it had sizable Mexican and African American populations, it became known as a "Puerto Rican ghetto."

Puerto Ricans initially found themselves unintelligible as an ethnic/national, racially heterogeneous, US-citizen, migrant group. Despite finding themselves in a social context that could not accommodate for their difference, they were unwilling initially to identify themselves as a distinct racial group, as this might mark them as socially inferior to whites and thus incapable of attaining equality. They did recognize, however, that they experienced prejudice and discrimination from whites as well as conflict and tensions with African Americans. Eventually, many realized they were being assigned a nonwhite identity that carried negative consequences. As a result of these experiences, the second generation began shifting its own self-perceptions, taking the racial lesson to heart and embracing a nonwhite identity, a *Puerto Rican* one. In the aftermath of the riots and in the context of late-sixties social movements, Puerto Ricans formed a new ethnoracial identity, one that allowed for nationalism, encouraged cultural pride, reconciled the racial diversity of the population, and was intersected by class. Their political awakening is the subject of the next chapter.

FIVE

The Evolution of the Young Lords Organization: From Street Gang to Revolutionaries

We were pushed out of Old Town. By the city. By the real estate developers. And we didn't know what was happening to us. . . . It happened once, it happened twice, it happened three times. Each time the family had to move. . . . And this is why the kids have become more political. The kids now realize what has happened to us, to our families.

—"Rodriquez [*sic*] on gangs"[1]

The Young Lords' approach was based on the premise that the only significant resource Puerto Ricans possessed was the capacity to make trouble—to disrupt institutions of the established system and produce sufficient political reverberations to force the authorities to respond.

—Felix Padilla, *Puerto Rican Chicago*[2]

The Division Street riots that rocked the West Town neighborhood in 1966 left an indelible mark on the Puerto Rican population in Chicago. Whether they had participated in the events or condemned them, Puerto Ricans had become more closely associated with crime, lawlessness, and social disorder.[3] The front-page headlines of local newspapers reinforced for several days that Puerto Ricans were a "problem" for law enforcement and the city more generally. Yet few told the story of the pressures that Puerto Ricans had been under for more than a decade. The compounded effects of poverty, prejudice, and displacement had made conditions difficult. Families weathered the instabilities of their households as urban renewal continued to dislocate them from the Near North Side and, by the midsixties, from Lincoln Park. Displacement forced families to move to other neighborhoods, which in turn created conflicts with new white neighbors and the local police force charged with protecting them and their property.

A Puerto Rico Migration Division report in 1960 captured the dynamics of neighborhood relations quite well: "The Lincoln Park Conservation Commission, an agency seeking to preserve the neighborhood, has been greatly disturbed by the overcrowding condition that has begun to prevail in some tenements in this area. . . . This is making itself felt in regard to a definite anti–Puerto Rican prejudice."[4] Some whites scorned the newcomers for crowding into small apartments with so many children and occupying public space in ways they found distasteful. Urban planners and private developers—usually supported by middle- and upper-class white residents—had plans to gentrify Lincoln Park. Poorer families (not only Puerto Ricans but poor whites and African Americans) who continued moving into the neighborhood after losing housing farther south disrupted the genteel visions of developers, planners, and well-to-do neighbors.

Puerto Ricans in Lincoln Park, youth in particular, however, had had enough of urban renewal. As the first epigraph notes, many young people had become critically conscious of their families' constant displacements and the physical and emotional disruptions in their lives. They became aware also of what they felt was racially based mistreatment at the hands of police, slumlords, social workers, and other authorities. Despite community pleas, police continued to use excessive force in their arrests of Puerto Rican men and boys, and community members continued to protest. Young people began fighting against displacement of the poor by urban renewal and vocally protesting the rampant brutality that police visited upon them on neighborhood streets. They formed a group called the Young Lords Organization (YLO). The group emerged initially as a street gang in the late fifties, to defend Puerto Rican boys in the neighborhood from white youths. Within a matter of years, however, the group adopted a politically conscious agenda and transformed itself into a militant, leftist, revolutionary organization. While it represents but one example of Puerto Rican (and Latina/o) social activism of the civil rights era, the Young Lords Organization has also drawn the most attention for its romantic, idealized, and fabled history. The militant young men and women who proudly donned purple berets became a historic icon of Puerto Rican radicalism.

The legendary Young Lords have long been perceived both in academic circles and in the popular imagination as an East Coast organization, associated most frequently with the much larger Puerto Rican population of New York City. Although New York became the most visible center of Young Lords activism, the group originated in the streets of Chicago.[5] Popular perceptions of the Young Lords and the Puerto Rican left have also understood the group as a primarily nationalist movement.[6] This provides an incomplete picture of what was a rather complex political and ideological terrain and diverse social reality. The YLO included Mexican American and other Latina/o members at the same time that it espoused independence for Puerto Rico and solidarity with Latin American people, both in the United States and throughout the hemisphere.

A convergence of multiple factors shaped youths' growing political consciousness. This included the social context and composition of the Lincoln Park community, as well as national trends and movements. First, Puerto Ricans in the neighborhood had been displaced by urban renewal multiple times. Many had been relocated by the Carl Sandburg Village project a few blocks south. Second, young Puerto Ricans had been harassed by white gangs and police for years. The Division Street riots in 1966 certainly brought home the realization that the Puerto Rican community's frustration with the indignities of racism and classism had reached a boiling point. Third, generation and experience played a role in the politicization of Puerto Rican youth. They had grown up attending the social events and celebrations of their parents' hometown clubs, mutual aid associations, and church groups. But they experienced different kinds of indignities than their parents, ones that they perhaps did not understand—with police, with schoolteachers, with neighborhood gangs. Some parents watched their dreams of a better future for their children wither as they saw youth increasingly alienated from public schools, turning to street gangs and, occasionally, drug use. Youth were also assimilating and acculturating to an American political climate that increasingly included radical activism among young people. Like other teens of their time, many were growing dissatisfied with the moderate and modest politics of their parents. This was closely tied to a fourth element—the Black Power and white radical movements unfolding both locally and nationally. Puerto Rican youth in Lincoln Park found themselves in a political atmosphere in which white leftists and radicals (especially college students) called for revolutionary class struggle and an end to the war in Vietnam, and militant African Americans advanced black liberation. These struggles reverberated in the neighborhood, broadcasting militant politics, ideologies, and demands onto the urban landscape. Though most YLO youth had not completed high school, much less attended college, they absorbed fragments of leftist political theory and Marxist analysis from the varied militant social movements in their midst. Finally, Puerto Rican youth drew on a tradition of Puerto Rican nationalist politics. They educated themselves on the island's rich anticolonial heritage and used nationalist symbols and icons to represent their political consciousness. They gathered the overlapping political strands that crisscrossed around them and developed a politics that was nationalist, panethnic, anti-imperialist, multiracial, and grounded in the working class.

Puerto Rican youth were also forming their own identity. In a racially polarized atmosphere of black and white conflict in which they had been increasingly racialized as a distinct group, Puerto Rican youth were coming to understand that they too had a place in the social hierarchy. A 1967 survey by a University of Chicago sociologist explained Puerto Ricans' racial awareness as such: "Puerto Rican is not racially homogeneous [sic]. But if this fact discourages a racial consciousness as strong as that found in North America, it does not make the people blind to color differences."[7] Puerto Rican youth were becoming educated in American meanings of race on the mainland, but they were also learning the language of class consciousness. In response to their experiences as a racially denigrated and economically marginalized group, they began asserting a political identity that embraced their ascribed racial difference and demanded rights as economically oppressed and colonized people within a capitalist, imperialist society. This formed the basis of the Young Lords' platform.

The Changing Community of Lincoln Park

Puerto Ricans first arrived in Lincoln Park in 1946 and 1947 when some of the earliest labor migrants were temporarily housed in the area. As migration increased, many newcomers continued settling there in the 1950s.[8] As families found themselves displaced by urban renewal projects nearby, especially the Carl Sandburg Village, their numbers in Lincoln Park grew. By 1960, the community area included nearly twenty-two hundred first- and second-generation Puerto Rican migrants. They were a fraction of the total population of eighty-nine thousand people (see table 10), along with nearly fourteen hundred people of Mexican origin, fourteen hundred African Americans, and another twenty-nine hundred people categorized as "other races"—namely, Japanese Americans and Native Americans.[9] A tremendous amount of racial/ethnic and economic diversity characterized the neighborhood, as middle- to upper-class residents occupied higher-end housing to the east and "hippies," artists, college students, Appalachian whites, Puerto Ricans, and others claimed lower-cost housing farther west. Myrna Rodriguez remembers Lincoln Park being very integrated in the area where her family lived. There were a lot of "hippies," so she says,

Table 10 Population changes by race and other selected data, Lincoln Park, 1950–80

	1950	1960	1970	1980
Total population	102,396	88,836	67,416	57,146
% change		−13	−24	−15
White	100,543	84,604	59,731	47,603
% of population	98.2	95.3	88.6	83.3
Black	205	1,358	4,921	4,915
% of population	0.2	1.5	7.3	8.6
Other nonwhite races	1,648	2,874	3,169	4,629
% of population	1.6	3.2	4.7	8.1
Spanish language / Spanish origin	n/a	n/a	9,880	6,000
Puerto Rican	n/a	2,181	5,114	2,117
Mexican	n/a	1,373	n/a	2,963
% of population	n/a	4.0	14.6	10.5
Median school years completed	9.7	9.8	12.2	15.7
Median family income ($)	n/a	6,195	9,652	24,509
% below poverty level	n/a	15.4*	12.6	12.0
% with income over $10,000/$15,000/$30,000†	n/a	16.7	24.0	41.2
% white-collar workers	n/a	34.7‡	39.8	78.5
% 1+ person per room	14.9	10.5	6.4	2.9
Median rent ($)	n/a	78	111	269
Median value, owner units ($)	n/a	14,500	19,500	123,700

Sources: Kitagawa and Taueber, *Local Community Fact Book, 1960*; and Chicago Fact Book Consortium, *Local Community Fact Book, 1970 and 1980*.
*In 1960, figure is for percentage with income under $3,000.
†1960 figure is for income over $10,000, 1970—over $15,000, and 1980—over $30,000.
‡Includes only males.

"I can't tell you that I suffered from racism from our neighbors, because it was all liberals. They didn't have any problem living with all of us. It was very mixed."[10] While on her block, Rodriguez felt well integrated with her neighbors, boosters and developers had plans to transform the deteriorated sections where most Puerto Ricans lived, thereby extending the Gold Coast farther north.

In the 1960s, Lincoln Park was a neighborhood "in transition"—described as "both an advertisement for city living and an example of the urban environment at its worst." Named after its prized lakefront recreational space, the neighborhood contained a strip of affluent residences along the eastern edge closest to Lake Michigan. Elaborate Victorian graystone and brownstone homes with towers, spires, and stained-glass windows accommodated well-to-do families. Fashionable high-rise apartment buildings and hotels, built in the teens and twenties, provided homes to retirees and other single residents without children. More modest immigrant workers' homes farther west imitated the European-inspired architectural features favored by wealthier neighbors (mansard roofs, ornamental ironwork), a testament to their hard work and class aspirations. Housing shortages, economic decline, and the flight of wealthier families eventually transformed many buildings into smaller apartments and kitchenettes, leading to more crowded conditions.[11] Similar to the Near West Side and the Near North Side, Lincoln Park had a high proportion of rentals: only 14 percent of its housing units were owner occupied, and 39 percent of all buildings had ten or more units.[12] The area certainly contained specimens of the city's finest residential architecture, but many buildings had fallen into disrepair. As the Near North Side began to realize the fruits of its urban renewal plans and established itself as a trendy urban destination for professionals and cultural connoisseurs, middle-class Lincoln Park residents, local business leaders, and ambitious developers began to see an opportunity for revitalizing their neighborhood, restoring many of its buildings, and improving its demographic profile. Both the Near North Side and Lincoln Park represented prime residential locations, steps away from scenic parks and the shores of Lake Michigan. The area also provided a short and easy commute to downtown office buildings and cultural amenities such as theaters, restaurants, and the city's museums. The North Michigan Avenue district, now nicknamed the "Magnificent Mile," was being redeveloped with upscale shops, hotels, and art galleries, thus dramatically improving the area's economic profile and soon overshadowing downtown State Street as the city's central shopping destination for the wealthy. Lincoln Park seemed the next logical target for residential redevelopment.

Renewal Redux

Puerto Ricans had become very familiar with the effects of urban renewal initiatives that had been displacing them from the Near North Side since the mid-1950s. Some of the families dislocated by the Carl Sandburg Village had begun moving to westerly neighborhoods like West Town and Humboldt Park. In the late sixties, however, a small enclave still remained in Lincoln Park centered around Armitage Avenue (see fig. 23). In the mid-1950s, middle- to upper-class community groups began working with city planners to revitalize the area. Residents established the Lincoln Park Conservation Association in 1954, to help preserve and improve the community. The group soon approached the Department of Urban Renewal to get support for its efforts.[13] Two years later, the city's Community Conservation Board (CCB) designated over one thousand acres of Lincoln Park a "con-

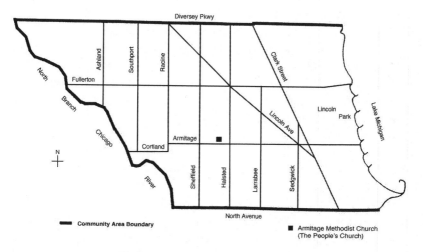

Figure 23. Lincoln Park Community Area.

servation area."[14] It would be eligible for funds to help restore sections of the neighborhood and preserve it from further blight and deterioration. The city council approved the conservation plan with an estimated cost of over $43 million. The federal government would pay $1 of that amount for every $2 paid by the city. By January of 1962, the CCB had submitted part 1 of the *General Neighborhood Renewal Plan for the Lincoln Park Area* to the United States Housing and Home Finance Agency and awaited federal approval. The plan for the entire neighborhood would proceed in four stages and would take ten years to complete. It called for clearing blighted and slum areas, conserving those that were still viable, and constructing new housing. The majority of new residential units in the area would be priced in a range intended for middle- to upper-income residents.[15]

At a time when most middle-class, white professionals had deserted the dangerous city for the safety and comforts of the suburbs, only an intrepid few dared to buy property among "minorities," bohemians, artists, and the poor. Urban "pioneers" began moving to the neighborhood, hoping to invest in real estate and grow equity. Couples like George and Mary Thrush began renovating and rehabilitating modest brick homes and apartment buildings. With aspirations to make Lincoln Park as fashionable and attractive as "Old Town" on the Near North Side had become in recent years, other young professionals entered the restoration business. The neighborhood's older German delicatessens and British pubs had a certain charm and appeal that suburban tract communities simply could not duplicate.

But the human elements that gave such urban neighborhoods "color" and "character"—the poorer residents and their social characteristics—gradually became superfluous to the quaint community that the homesteaders wished to create. As one white resident described, "Lincoln Park has changed a lot since I moved here, I'll tell you that. We renovated an old place because we wanted to live in a diverse neighborhood. Now so many people want it to be a suburb in the city."[16]

The neighborhood began removing its low-income population, clearing land of deteriorated apartment buildings and houses deemed unsalvageable. The city's bulldozers were aimed at many of the dwellings where Puerto Ricans lived. New development did not always come quickly, however, and vacant lots scarred the neighborhood, sometimes for years. One magazine noted in 1970, "Entire blocks on Armitage, Halsted, and Larrabee streets now lie bare where Urban Renewal has leveled the homes of Puerto Ricans and poor whites."[17] These gentrification efforts began meeting stiff resistance, however. In the wake of the Division Street riots and similar uprisings in black neighborhoods, young people in Lincoln Park began developing a political consciousness around the issue of urban renewal that threatened once again to uproot their lives.

Origins of a Street Gang

When Puerto Ricans moved into modest sections of the Lincoln Park community in the fifties and sixties, they were usually not well received by existing residents. Just like their cousins in West Town and Humboldt Park, many experienced hostility and racial antagonism from some working-class whites who felt threatened by and uncomfortable with the newcomers. One document described it well: "Moving into an area predominated by one of the older immigrant groups, they sense the hostility and antagonism with which they are greeted. Suddenly, violence and gang warfare begin to erupt."[18] Indeed, as Andrew Diamond, Jim Barrett, and David Roediger have shown, neighborhood conflict between existing residents and newcomers (especially ethnically distinct groups) often played out as physical contests among male youths. Street gangs might start innocuously enough, as neighborhood athletic clubs, meant to structure male youth recreation. This occurred throughout the city's working-class neighborhoods among various European ethnic groups, African Americans, southern whites, and Latinos. With time, however, some rivalries grew increasingly violent.[19] Since male gangs were much more visible in public space compared to the activities of girls, and since girls' conflicts did not as frequently result in contact with law enforcement, the preponderance of historical evidence documents relations among boys.

Gangs had occupied an important place in the social structure of urban immigrants for decades, according to historian Andrew Diamond, and offered a means through which youth negotiated Americanization. Invariably, working-class Irish, Italian, Czech, Polish, Russian Jewish, and other youth encountered gangs in the city's immigrant neighborhoods. As immigrants became more established and acquired political power, gangs became an integral part of political machines and ethnic politics and were rewarded for their cooperation by precinct captains and aldermanic leaders. Young male gangs also became the enforcers of community boundaries.[20]

When Puerto Rican boys and teens came to the city—migrants themselves or the children of migrants—many followed the same pattern of organizing to defend themselves as the most recent newcomers.[21] In 1960, Puerto Rican children and youths in Lincoln Park, both boys and girls aged ten to nineteen, numbered fewer than 500. White children of the same ages numbered well over 10,000. The ratio of boys—who often had more freedom to be in public compared to girls—hints at the potential for conflicts among them on neighborhood streets. In the entire community area, there were over 4,800 white boys between the ages of ten and nineteen, compared to fewer than 175 Puerto Rican boys of the same ages, a ratio of 27 to 1. Within census tracts where the Puerto Rican population was concentrated (100 persons or more), there were fewer than 17 Puerto Rican boys on average compared to a mean of 287 white boys. Puerto Ricans were literally the new kids on the block and found themselves outnumbered nearly 17 to 1.[22] Such disparate proportions do not translate into youth conflict necessarily, but they capture the sheer magnitude of Puerto Rican boys' minority status in the area and provide an empirical basis for the harassment they regularly described. They also provide a context to the rise of Puerto Rican and Latino gangs.

Puerto Rican youths frequently cited conflict with other neighborhood youths, especially with Italian Americans and "Billigans (hillbillies)." In 1959, Orlando Dávila and seven other young men decided to form the Young Lords "to counter the mounting antagonism against Puerto Ricans by other youth gangs."[23] Like other teenage boys, the group chose a name that asserted macho bravado and regal status. In its early years, the group defended itself from rival teens and engaged in the usual youth gang fare—social activities, petty crimes, and turf wars. Social workers from the local YMCA tried to recruit them and funnel them toward positive and productive activities. The Chicago Area Project, a juvenile delinquency prevention program, also dispatched community workers to intervene with local teens. Such efforts had limited influence on young people who were becoming hardened by the poverty and prejudice in their lives and cynical about their position in society.[24]

By 1964, many of the original Young Lords members were either in jail, on parole, married with children, consumed by drugs, or had left the city. José "Cha Cha" Jiménez, one of the group's early members, had assumed leadership of the gang. Like most of his peers, Jiménez was the son of migrants. His father had worked as a farm laborer on the East Coast before coming to Chicago with his wife and oldest child. Jiménez had grown up on the Near North Side and Lincoln Park, and had experienced the multiple dislocations of urban renewal. He had also served time in prison and had just returned to the neighborhood. In 1965, he established a young women's auxiliary to the Young Lords, the Lordettes. The group consisted of neighborhood young women, many of whom dated, were married to, or were relatives of the male members of the Young Lords. Jiménez soon returned to prison, but he began encountering the influence of black Muslims and started reading about Martin Luther King Jr., Malcolm X, the Puerto Rican nationalist hero Pedro Albízu Campos, and the massacre of Ponce, Puerto Rico. He began developing some awareness of the inequalities that Puerto Ricans had suffered and the colonial status of the island. When he was released from jail in January 1968, he had a newfound emerging consciousness. He and another Lord, Ralph Rivera, reorganized the gang, incorporated the women's group, and renamed the larger body the Young Lords Organization. They also expanded to include black, white, and other Latino members. They hoped to transform themselves from a simple street gang to a legitimate community organization.[25]

Developing a Political Consciousness

Armed with a growing consciousness of inequality and poverty, the Young Lords Organization started coordinating various fund-raising events and social services for the needy. According to its newspaper, however, the Young Lords soon realized "that often they were acting like social workers, not getting at the root causes of the community problems."[26] Other youth gangs had similarly made this turn to social reform. A number of African American gangs, such as Chicago's Blackstone Rangers and the Vice Lords, had begun capitalizing on the availability of public and private funds for helping "underprivileged" youth in inner cities. They started to institutionalize themselves as organizations that served the community and were doing "good" among the African American urban poor and called upon fellow inner-city black youth, who were already on the streets, to reconceptualize their war against one another to one against inequality.[27]

The political climate of 1968 and the local activist scene began shaping the Young Lords' consciousness as well. Nationally, the debate over police violence and repression versus civil disobedience and free speech had riveted the public's attention. Such dilemmas were materializing in the Young Lords' own backyard. Lincoln Park was a seat of leftist activity and home to many students and burgeoning activists. That summer, police clashed with white antiwar and leftist protesters in what many observers described as a police riot during the Democratic National Convention just a few miles away. During the convention, the neighborhood also witnessed confrontations between police and white demonstrators who tried to camp overnight in Lincoln Park. The area was also a principal site in the Students for a Democratic Society's "Four Days of Rage" in the fall of 1969.[28] Local radical white leftists (students, SDS members) and anarchists protested an array of issues—the Vietnam War, US imperialism, racism, police brutality, and urban renewal that displaced the poor. Jiménez was influenced by two white leftist activists in the neighborhood, Pat Devine and Dick Vision, who reportedly had shared a Black Panther Party (BPP) newspaper with him.[29] Jiménez had also met Fred Hampton, a young African American from the West Side who in the summer of 1968 established and became the leader of the Illinois chapter of the BPP.[30] Through his contacts with Hampton and other informal political education, Jiménez and Ralph Rivera developed their understanding of race- and class-based inequalities and began sharpening their political awareness. In October of 1968, they participated in a citywide meeting with other Latino/a groups and learned about activism elsewhere in the city.[31] The Young Lords distinguished themselves from other Latino gangs in other neighborhoods in that they found themselves more deeply immersed in a radical political environment in Lincoln Park. They boasted of being "the first of these youth groups to move in a positive, conscious political direction."[32] Jiménez and Rivera attended lectures at the Presbyterian Church's Urban Studies Institute, where they heard a minister from Puerto Rico talk about the island's political status. Gradually, they began to analyze the conditions of the neighborhood's poor and believe in the need for radical politics.[33]

Jiménez and Rivera did not immediately convert members of their group to their newfound politicization. Fellow Lords had approved of the social programs for the poor, but not all had taken the ideological leap to revolutionary consciousness. Some of the young men were more interested in continuing their gang activities than becoming activists.[34] Yet the menace of urban renewal was bearing down on them and promised to disrupt their lives once more. In December of 1968, the YLO learned that three real estate agencies in the area had plans to evict Puerto Rican families to renovate buildings and raise rents. One leftist neighborhood newspaper summed up the scenario: "Fat Larry from Bissell Realty says he has nothing against Puerto Ricans. Moving them out is just good business. He can make a lot more money renting to rich whites."[35] Groups such as the Lincoln Park Conservation Association endorsed the plans to renovate and rehabilitate the area's old stone and brick buildings to their original grandeur and attract white-collar renters and homeowners. The Young Lords decided to take action. They responded to the news by allegedly smashing the windows of the realty offices and reportedly ransacking the local urban renewal headquarters.[36]

The Concerned Citizens for Lincoln Park, a white leftist group, had charged that the Lincoln Park Conservation Association was not protecting the rights of area poor people. Landlords evicted tenants from their apartments, and realtors used scare tactics to get homeowners to sell their modest homes for less than their actual value.[37] Eugenia Rodríguez, Cha Cha Jiménez's mother, recalled that during these years, she paid $140 a month for her apartment but that developers raised rents to $300 monthly after renovating area buildings. This happened to the entire block, she noted, and not only Latinas/os but also poor whites who could not afford the rents were forced to move out.[38] Monse Lucas-Figueroa and her family (who had been displaced by the Carl Sandburg Village) settled near North Avenue by the time she was a teenager. She attended nearby St. Michael's Catholic High School and recalled, "It was everywhere, they were tearing buildings down. . . . After I graduated and a few other classes graduated, the school [St. Michael's] was sold and turned into condos. . . . But then [poor] people couldn't live in them! . . . It was not intended for the people that were living there for years because if you were paying [so much] rent, here comes this guy, he renovates your apartment. Now he wants to charge [double]!"[39]

The Lords adamantly opposed the top-down decision making and planning in their neighborhood that utterly disregarded the well-being of the poor. In January 1969, they flooded a meeting of the Lincoln Park Community Conservation Council with Latino/a participants and questioned why the board did not include any low-income people. They demanded that the group cease meeting until it added black, Latino, and poor white representatives. Felix Silva, the LPCCC's only Latino member, soon resigned in sympathy. He wrote, "Personally, I too feel that there is not adequate representation of the poor in the Lincoln Park Community Conservation Council. On a board of 15 members, I am the only Latin. . . . The poor of the area deserve better treatment than this. They should have a greater share in the decisions which are affecting their families and lives. . . . I cannot in [good] conscience, be a part of what my people feel to be a conspiracy against them."[40] For several months, the YLO, a poor white group called the Young Patriots, and a local gang named the Cobra Stones continued to disrupt LPCCC meetings, voicing their objections to the composition of the council's board. Mayor Daley ultimately interceded, appointing two African American men and one Latino to the board.[41]

"The People vs. the Police"[42]

As the YLO embraced a politicized agenda, it struggled to shake its reputation as a street gang. In an age of strident politics and civil disobedience, many wondered if "revolutionaries," especially black and brown ones, were simply gangsters hiding behind the cloak of radical activism. More than a few street gangs in Chicago had successfully transformed themselves into social service activists and secured War on Poverty funding from the federal government and monies from private foundations for social programs for the poor. Critics viewed their political conversion to revolutionary nationalism and radical politics with a great deal of cynicism. Police persecuted and arrested YLO members, convinced that they were simply "thugs." They mocked the uneducated, street-raised youths' attempts to cloak themselves with the mantle of social justice and revolution. Certainly, a number of Lords had long arrest sheets and had spent time in jail for various offenses. Whether they continued to engage in the same criminal activities after they became radicals or whether police were simply biased against them is debatable. Still, police found ways to arrest YLO members for the most minor infractions. The Chicago Police Department (CPD) targeted Jiménez in particular, arresting him regularly for participating in protests and rallies.[43] The police were at war with the Lords and skirmished with them constantly.

The Chicago Police Department, like other police forces across the country, regularly used informants and plainclothes policemen to do surveillance and infiltration of "subversive" organizations. At meetings, rallies, and public and private events, undercover agents often snapped photographs to document participants, took copious notes on suspects, and followed their movements.[44] The CPD employed surreptitious tactics, including using rival street toughs against one another to collect intelligence, disrupt gatherings, and stymie political organizing. On a number of occasions, the Young Lords had conflicts with the Latin Kings, the Latin Eagles, and the Cobra Stones, who tried to disrupt a march on a local police station and commandeered another march to a welfare office.[45] While many in radical, leftist, and minority nationalist groups were fully aware of the CPD's Red Squad in the sixties (because they realized they were under surveillance and being infiltrated), officials would not confirm its existence.[46]

As a rule, antiestablishment groups such as the YLO saw police as repressive agents of an exploitative capitalist and imperialist state. They regularly referred to them as "pigs." YLO members' quarrels with police were not limited to white officers; they had just as much contempt for black and Latino policemen.[47] Officers reciprocated the contempt through the use of excessive force and abuse. The Chicago Police Department during the Daley administration was notorious for its abuse and brutality, in one period killing more Chicago citizens than the police departments of New York, Los Angeles, and Philadelphia combined.[48] The Lords took pleasure, therefore, in confronting police, such as at one community-police workshop in early 1969, which they filled with nearly three hundred people. Young Lords and their supporters brought posters and signs protesting police abuse, defending Cha Cha Jiménez, and promoting their organization. In a satirical retort to youth delinquency prevention programs, one member carried a poster that cleverly read, "PIGS NEED SPORTS CENTERS TO KEEP THEM OFF THE STREET AND END VIOLENCE."[49] The group vocally condemned the abuse and mistreatment its members faced at the hands of law enforcement and regularly documented stories of police misconduct and brutality in its newspaper.[50]

The Young Lords adopted a structure similar to that of the Black Panther Party. Cha Cha Jiménez served as chair of a central committee that included a field marshal and various ministers of different programs—information, defense, education, and health. The group included several levels of membership—a core who devoted themselves full-time to YLO activism, members who were less involved but participated regularly, and those who only came out to support rallies. Like the BPP, the Lords also created a party program and platform. The New York chapter authored the following:

1   We want self-determination for Puerto Ricans. Liberation on the island and inside the United States.
2   We want self-determination for all Latinos.
3   We want liberation of all third world people.
4   We are revolutionary nationalists and oppose racism.

5 We want equality for women. Down with machismo and male chauvinism.

6 We want community control of our institutions and land.

7 We want a true education of our Afro-Indio culture and Spanish language.

8 We oppose capitalists and alliances with traitors.

9 We oppose the Amerikkkan military.

10 We want freedom for all political prisoners and prisoners of war.

11 We are internationalists.

12 We believe armed self-defense and armed struggle are the only means to liberation.

13 We want a socialist society.[51]

Each of these points was elaborated in greater detail, further clarifying the YLO's position. The Black Panther Party's influence on the Young Lords and their affinities were unmistakable: the *YLO* newspaper published the BPP's ten-point platform, photos of BPP leader Huey Newton, and advertisements for Panther pamphlets and writings. The BPP certainly inspired the Young Lords, as it did other groups that adopted a militant, paramilitary style and revolutionary leftist politics.

The Murder of Manuel Ramos

If the YLO had not yet won the hearts and minds of most community youths and adults, the events of early May 1969 unexpectedly unified the group and dramatically galvanized support for its cause. Late on the night of Saturday, May 4, a number of YLO members attended a party at the South Side home of founder Orlando Dávila. An off-duty police officer, James Lamb, who was painting an apartment across the street from the party, went to Dávila's home and began arguing with some YLO members. In the ensuing altercation, Lamb shot Manuel Ramos in the face and Rafael Rivera in the neck. Lamb claimed that he identified himself as police and that Ramos was armed, though witnesses disputed both points. Four men—Orlando Dávila, Pedro Martinez, Jose Lind, and Sal De Rivero—then allegedly attacked Lamb. When squad cars arrived, Lamb identified himself as an officer and ordered the four Lords arrested. Ramos and Rivera were taken to the hospital, where Ramos died minutes after arriving. Rivera survived his gunshot wound. Though the YLO called for Lamb's arrest, a coroner's jury ultimately concluded that Lamb had shot Ramos in self-defense, claiming that Ramos had high levels of alcohol in his blood. Lamb escaped any criminal charges, and instead, the four arrested Young Lords faced trials for assaulting an officer.[52]

The murder of Manuel Ramos and the arrest of four Young Lords became a rallying point for the group and served as a powerful catalyst for politicizing members and others in the community. The night after the shooting, the YLO along with the Black Panthers, the Students for a Democratic Society, the Latin American Defense Organization (LADO), and other sympathizers held a rally at an empty urban renewal lot on the corner of Armitage and Halsted Streets, the symbolic center of the YLO movement. They reportedly drew nearly one thousand people on a three-mile march to the site of the wake. After hearing members of the Ramos family speak, a crowd of young people led a caravan of thirty-five cars to the Deering police station in the neighborhood of Ramos's shooting, to protest his murder and demand Lamb's arrest. A force of one hundred officers immediately gathered and prepared to do battle with the crowd. Undercover police provocateurs attempted to lure protesters to attack Mayor Daley's home, just blocks away, but the crowd ignored them and violence was averted.[53] The following night, the Lords and their allies held a memorial service, which attracted over six hundred people. At St. Theresa's Catholic Church on Armitage Avenue that Wednesday, Young Lords—dressed in black and donning their signature purple berets—and Black Panthers in their regalia, carrying the BPP flag, stood at attention outside the doors of the church where the funeral mass was being held. When "the coffin was carried through two lines of Young Lords who stood with clenched fists raised," the imposing, quasi-military display of masculine defense and power stopped more than a few onlookers. One observer wrote, "As the funeral motorcade moved out to the cemetery, fists were raised by people in the motorcade and answering salutes came from blacks, Latins, and some whites all along the route." The funeral brought out several hundred people, including many parents from the Lincoln Park community, such as Cha Cha Jiménez's mother and father and others who knew the Ramos family.[54] Regardless of what his legacy may have been in life, Ramos had become a martyr for the cause.

With the death of a Young Lord, many members who had not yet fully embraced Cha Cha Jiménez's and Ralph Rivera's political stance became much more militant. Jiménez himself credited Ramos's murder as a turning point, the moment in which he "became a real revolutionary." The second issue of the newly established *YLO* newspaper was dedicated to Ramos's memory, showcasing all the recent activities the Lords had carried out in his name (fig. 24). The tragedy also consolidated their interracial alliances.[55]

The YLO's interracial coalitions with other militant groups were key to its development. The group initially shared office space with the Concerned

Figure 24. *Young Lords Organization* newspaper, vol. 1, no. 2.
Special issue dedicated to the memory of Manuel Ramos.

Citizens' Survival Front, a white leftist group in Lincoln Park, and the neighborhood branch of the Young Patriots, a southern white group based primarily in the Uptown community. The YLO collaborated regularly with the Panthers, the Students for a Democratic Society (the RYM II faction), the Young Patriots, and another white youth group from Logan Square, Rising Up Angry.[56] YLO members attended the SDS conference in May of 1969. The following month, the YLO, BPP, and Young Patriots announced they were forming a *Rainbow Coalition*, a term that Panther leader Fred Hampton is said to have coined.[57] The task of bringing together African Americans, Puerto Ricans and other Latinos/as, and poor southern whites—many of whom wore Confederate flags with pride—presented a real challenge, but such alliances were nurtured on multiple levels. Jiménez and Hampton personally cultivated an organizational alliance with each other; the YLO and the Young Patriots in Lincoln Park communicated regularly in their shared office; and Bobby Lee, an African American VISTA organizer who had come to Chicago from Houston and became a BPP field marshal, impressed upon the Young Patriots the poverty they shared with African Americans and the political potency of their union.[58] The YLO and its allies exchanged strategies and information, and, most important, supported one another in their protests and demonstrations. Fred Hampton and other Panthers, for example, marched with the YLO, LADO, and other organizations in support of welfare rights for poor mothers. Likewise, YLO members attended "Free Huey" rallies in support of jailed Panther leader Huey P. Newton.

After Ramos's murder, the YLO and Rainbow Coalition allies demanded justice for the dead man and his family. On May 13, they organized a march from the corner of Armitage and Halsted Streets to the Eighteenth District Police Station, where State's Attorney Ed Hanrahan was scheduled to hold a police-community workshop. The march began with six hundred people, but as the marchers crossed through the Cabrini-Green housing projects, they drew hundreds of African American youths. By the time they reached the police station, over one thousand people reportedly surrounded the building. Marchers protested both Ramos's shooting and the arrest of the four Young Lords. Hanrahan failed to appear, allegedly because of a scheduling conflict, but sent an assistant in his place. When march leaders demanded Lamb's arrest and Hanrahan's representative responded that the case was under investigation, the crowd booed him loudly. The group eventually dispersed, but not before breaking nearby shop windows and looting them for soda pop, chips, and cookies, which they distributed to the crowd.[59]

Takeover of McCormick Seminary

The loss of one of their members had a tremendous impact on the YLO and strengthened its commitment to political struggle. A week after Ramos's murder, the Young Lords joined the Poor People's Coalition (PPC) in holding a rally on the grounds of the Presbyterian McCormick Theological Seminary. The coalition consisted of several local groups—among others, the YLO; the Young Patriots; LADO; a group from the Cabrini-Green housing projects called "BAD" (Black, Active and Determined); the Concerned Citizens Survival Front; and the Welfare and Working Mothers of Wicker Park. They targeted the seminary because of its involvement in and support of urban renewal projects in the neighborhood.[60]

The Poor People's Coalition had initially approached McCormick seminary in early May with a list of ten demands. The seminary reportedly had $600,000 available for investment, and the Poor People's Coalition demanded that the money be used to fund low-income housing, a day-care center, a health clinic, a low-income law office, and a Puerto Rican cultural center. It also demanded that the seminary support the Wicker Park Welfare Coalition in its demands for just and humane treatment for mothers on welfare, and that it make its facilities more accessible to the local community. As one paper described it, "Iron fences 7 feet high keep the neighborhood people away from its beautifully manicured lawns, libraries, and playground."[61]

When a May 12 meeting with the administration did not yield a positive response, the PPC decided to occupy the seminary's brand-new building on the corner of Halsted and Fullerton Streets. Approximately seventy-five protesters seized the building at midnight on May 14 and renamed it the Manuel Ramos Memorial Building.[62] At its height, the occupation included as many as three hundred people. Angie Navedo, a young mother at the time, remembered taking her two toddlers when she participated in the occupation. She recalled the strict orders from coalition and YLO leaders against vandalizing or defacing seminary property. "There was real [discipline], you know—you don't take anything, you don't touch anything, you don't go into people's offices. It was real disciplined," she remembers. When the director of the seminary refused to negotiate and threatened to send in police, protesters responded in kind by threatening to occupy the seminary library, which contained a collection of rare religious books. A number of radical seminarians supported the takeover, warning protesters when police attempted to enter the building. After occupying the grounds for five days, the protesters finally succeeded in getting most of their demands met.[63]

The YLO and PPC had not made abstract and intangible requests. They hired a local architect, Howard Alan, to draw up plans for the low-income housing development.[64] The PPC even secured the Lincoln Park Community Conservation Council's endorsement of the plans. When the project went before the city's Department of Urban Renewal, however, it was rejected, despite the LPCCC's approval. The DUR instead endorsed a project brought forth by a private developer for middle- to upper-income housing. The defeat demoralized PPC activists, who realized that the city would reject even well-developed, architecturally sound plans for low-income housing if they came from the poor themselves and if they would not provide someone a profit.[65]

Survival for the Poor

The YLO soon turned to providing desperately needed basic human services to its community. In late 1968, the Young Lords approached the pastor of a local church, the Reverend Bruce Johnson, about using the church basement for an office and survival programs modeled on those of the BPP—a food pantry, health clinic, day-care center, and a children's breakfast program. The Armitage Methodist Church stood in the center of Lincoln Park's Puerto Rican community, at the corner of Armitage and Dayton Streets. The progressive pastor and his liberal white congregation reportedly sympathized with the Young Lords' goals. But the church also had a Cuban congregation, composed largely of exiles from Castro's revolution. This second congregation vociferously objected to the Young Lords' use of the building.[66] By June 1969, growing impatient because they had not yet secured permission to use the church, the YLO decided to simply take it over, reasoning that it was a neighborhood institution and should therefore serve the community's needs. They occupied the building, called a press conference, and renamed it "the People's Church." They made it their new headquarters and began a free breakfast program for children. They also distributed free clothing and tried to start a day-care center.[67]

The YLO's most effective and most promising project was the free health clinic at the People's Church. Poor residents had complained for some time that local hospitals failed to serve them. Of six hospitals located in Lincoln Park, only two operated low-income clinics. The YLO thus opened the Emeterio Betances Health Center in the People's Church in late February of 1970. Alberto Chivera, a third-year medical student at Northwestern University and YLO minister of health, headed the clinic along with his wife. The Chiveras enlisted progressive doctors, fellow medical students, and nurses as volunteers. The clinic initially operated on Saturday afternoons and provided a free alternative to the prohibitive costs of nearby Grant Hospital and to the overcrowded and understaffed Cook County Hospital, to which most of the city's indigent patients were referred.[68]

Educating its constituency became central to the YLO's mission. The Young Lords sought to expand their knowledge and develop a critical analysis of capitalism and imperialism to understand Puerto Ricans' conditions. Thus, they educated their core members through classes on Maoist political theory and the history of Puerto Rico. They also informed the public through their newspaper, the *Young Lords Organization*, which first appeared in March of 1969. The newspaper carried stories on local protests, YLO events, and the Young Lords' regular encounters with Chicago police. While the newspaper focused primarily on local issues, it also sought to teach readers about the colonial history of Puerto Rico and important historical Latin American leaders, as well as educate them on national and international issues, such as the political status of the island, the war in Vietnam, and revolutionary struggles around the world.[69] It also featured letters, stories, and poetry from local youth who had turned on to the YLO and were beginning to embrace its message.

In making the shift from street gang to political activism, the Young Lords drew on a history and consciousness from two different but interrelated sources. First, they drew on a local history—that of their own lived experiences of poor urban youth in rapidly changing neighborhoods. While most of their families were renters, not homeowners, with a relatively short history in the neighborhood, they based their claims on the right of working-class people to affordable housing, safe communities, and social services. Former minister of information Omar López stressed the importance of the organization's roots as a neighborhood group in its decision to take up urban renewal as a political issue. The YLO's politicization emerged organically out of immediate local concerns in a specific community, not from studying ideology or political theory but rather from the lived experience of material dislocations. Angie Navedo, a Young Lord and the widow of fellow Lord Pancho Lind, explained, "The change for us really wasn't theory. The change for us was reality. We lived through urban renewal. . . . The housing issue really made us become a political organization. . . . It was survival."[70] Cha Cha Jiménez and his family had been forced to move four times by late 1968. Carlos Flores and his family had moved repeatedly before they finally bought their own home in the area.

Monse Lucas-Figueroa and her family's repeated displacements began in the late 1950s. With constant urban renewal relocations, attempts to build a stable, enduring community had been elusive for Puerto Ricans. Yet the YLO began to establish a sense of place and belonging in the neighborhood and a more abstract imagined community as poor people living in oppressive conditions. They drew on their collective memory of earlier displacement and insisted on their right to the community they had finally begun to cultivate.[71]

Inasmuch as the group grounded itself in localized struggles, it also drew on a transnational history. The Young Lords expressed solidarity with global causes, such as liberation for all colonized people, an end to the Vietnam War, and independence for Puerto Rico. The YLO's commitment to revolutionary struggle was indeed internationalist. The newspaper became an important organ for educating its readership on anticolonial struggles in Africa, Asia, and Latin America. Lords even traveled internationally to support such causes. Some members participated in the Venceremos Brigades in Cuba in 1971. YLO women attended the International Women's Conference with Vietnamese women in Toronto that same year. Members demonstrated their solidarity with and support for a number of international causes.[72]

Most Young Lords had never been to the island, or had left it at a very young age. Yet they understood Puerto Ricans as colonized subjects. As migrants or the children of migrants who had fled a US territory whose economy could not sustain its citizens, the Young Lords articulated a political nationalism centered on the island's status. Moreover, they drew parallels between the colonial status of the island and their "internal colonialism" on the mainland. They perceived their condition in mainland cities like Chicago and New York as a direct result of the island's colonial condition and saw their liberation as intertwined. This nationalism was embodied in the group's ubiquitous logo, a silhouette of the island with a raised arm and rifle in the foreground and the phrase "Tengo [a] Puerto Rico en Mi Corazon" (Puerto Rico Is in My Heart).[73] Pedro Albízu Campos, the quintessential Puerto Rican nationalist hero, became perhaps the most celebrated figure in the YLO newspaper's pages, and his image was a constant presence at rallies and marches.

Reaching the Women

The YLO represented a predominantly male organization. Though it publicly supported gender equity in its platform, it did not easily bridge the distance between this principle and the group's practices. From the beginning, the YLO was masculinist and androcentric in its posture, its politics, and its leadership. The handsome and charismatic José "Cha Cha" Jiménez stood center stage. His image appeared regularly in the *YLO* newspaper, though it was not as ubiquitous as Huey Newton's in Panther publications. Still, Jiménez's celebrity certainly contained an element of egotism and macho bravado. Many articles were either written by him or defended and promoted him as a revolutionary figure in the community. To a certain extent, such a strategy made sense: as a key leader who was continuously under attack by police and the city power structure, Jiménez had to win the people over to his cause. (At one point, he had eighteen grand jury indictments against him in a six-week period.) He made public appearances, including a local television news program that dedicated an episode to the Lords during their takeover of the seminary and Armitage Methodist Church. Although women participated in the group's activities in growing numbers, its origins as a male youth street gang were hard to miss.[74]

Supporters often wrote letters to the *Young Lords Organization* newspaper explaining why they supported the group and why they were committed to the movement. One letter signed by "Isabel, revolutionary sister and wife," revealed the gender dynamics of the group and gendered perceptions within the community. Isabel began, "I have been married for two months to a member of the Young Lords Organization. In those two months I have learned why he wants to stay in the Y.L.O. He wants his people to be free." The Young Lords wife noted how she often worried when her husband stayed out late at night, but she knew that he was doing important work. "There are many reasons why I do not mind him staying in the Y.L.O.," she continued. "One reason is because he helps people. The poor people who do not know how to speak English or to fight back and defend their rights." The letter established YLO activism as men's work and underscored the danger they faced, particularly at the hands of abusive police and gangs. It also gave men license to be away from home until late at night. Letters such as Isabel's relegated women to secondary supportive roles in the movement and encouraged other YLO wives to be understanding of men's behavior because of its revolutionary purpose.[75]

Struggles over gender roles played out both in people's personal relationships and within the organization. Women provided labor for the YLO in multiple forms—at rallies and marches, in survival programs, and in administrative roles. Still, the face of leadership remained largely male. News reports and photographs often featured men; they were the ones quoted and sought out at the negotiating table after protests and rallies.

Undoubtedly, the political terrain the YLO navigated *was* male dominated. YLO members had to negotiate with local street gangs, call for truces, and request cooperation for marches and protests. Gang members, politicians, and police officers used to squaring off with other men were hardly eager to meet with women. The YLO reflected the mainstream gender norms of its time. Inasmuch as revolutionary nationalists operated within an extremely sexist and male chauvinist environment, most were not quite ready to liberate their minds and challenge society in that respect. While the Young Lords articulated many admirable principles, they did not easily discard their own machismo. As a result, they kept women from becoming fully equal participants. Hilda Vasquez-Ignatin, a Mexican American who was one of the most active women early in the organization, was one of the few who actually spoke publicly. She shared the stage with Cha Cha Jiménez, for example, at a march in October 1969 in honor of nationalist hero Pedro Albízu Campos.[76] She also wrote articles for the newspaper and received byline credit. On most other occasions, however, both the public face of leadership and the actual central committee were male.[77]

Part of what prevented some women from participating more fully was gendered child-care responsibilities. Many of the YLO's women were young mothers who were caring for small children, and thus had limited opportunities to become involved. Still, the fact that so many members did have children meant that, for some, the Young Lords was a family affair—people brought their children to the People's Church, to rallies and marches. The constant threat of violence, however—from either police or gangs—kept some away. Perhaps for this reason, women and children became most involved in the survival programs. Women played key roles in the health care program, for example. Monse Lucas-Figueroa, a high school student when the clinic opened, fondly remembered her experience as a volunteer. She oversaw the intake of patients, managed their files, and prepared them to be seen by doctors. She recalled that the clinic provided checkups and regular doctor's visits, optometry services, dental care, and prenatal care to people who had limited access otherwise. The clinic even had basic laboratory facilities but referred patients to local hospitals for more advanced medical attention. Lucas-Figueroa recalls that if a patient did not have transportation to the hospital, she would accompany the person and get another YLO member to help: "If they needed a ride to the hospital, there was always someone around. [I would say] *'Dame pon'* (Gimme a ride). . . . There was always an available person to take us to the emergency room with a referral from the doctor that was there." Although she did not support all of the YLO ideologies, such as independence for Puerto Rico, she thought, "The free clinic was an excellent concept." Angie Navedo similarly expressed great pride in the health center. "We ran a very, very good health clinic. . . . I was really proud of it," she recalled.[78]

The YLO women who volunteered served as translators for patients and made sure that doctors' and nurses' instructions were communicated clearly. They provided pamphlets and medical information in Spanish as well. Doctors saw as many as fifty patients each Saturday afternoon. Importantly, the clinic detected conditions and prevented the spread of diseases in a population that did not receive regular medical care. Lucas-Figueroa recalled, for example, an elderly woman who came in with various symptoms. When the doctor ran a simple blood sugar test, he found dangerous sugar levels. The woman had never been diagnosed as a diabetic. The clinic made people aware of previously unknown medical conditions and put them on the path to managing their health.[79]

Some neighborhood residents, especially older women, were initially apprehensive about visiting the health center. Many continued to perceive the YLO as a gang and worried about associating with the group. But the social programs and young women's involvement became critical to developing community support. As more and more community members came in contact with YLO programs and benefited from their services, this softened the Lords' image. One older woman bore witness in the *YLO* newspaper to their many good works. Anselma Benitez explained in Spanish that she used to believe that the Young Lords were a gang like everyone else, but after seeing how much they helped people, she had changed her opinion. She noticed how they helped families move when evicted from their apartments, and she noted the many children who gathered at the People's Church every day for the breakfast program. Gradually, as the clinic reached out to neighborhood residents through door-to-door canvassing, many women began to see the organization in a different light.[80]

The health clinic presented perhaps the greatest potential to develop a community movement in Lincoln Park, according to journalist Frank Browning. In an article in October 1970, he commented, "The fact that the clinic does work primarily in the neighborhood means that it is tying itself very effectively into the social structure of the community. If the Lords can continue that direct relationship with the Puerto Rican women, who form one of the strongest sources of traditional stability, then their chances of growing into an effective community-wide political organization are greater than ever before." Indeed, the clinic did provide a remarkable model of community programming. Its effectiveness came from the personalized care and attention that the clinic provided, characteristics traditionally associated with women's work. In contrast to the violence of encounters with police, negotiations with neighborhood gangs, and the general machismo of the YLO and its allies, the clinic provided a safe and inviting space, particularly for women. Browning noted, "The camaraderie and sensitive care that the clinic has come to offer have probably become the Lords' most successful organizing tool." The community-focused work of the clinic, the day-care center, and the breakfast program—activities largely organized and accessed by women and children—served an important function. They addressed women's concerns, and as the Lords learned, women formed a critical constituency of the organization.[81]

Unfortunately, the survival programs did not last very long. Like the children's breakfast program and the day-care center, the clinic soon came under attack by city officials. Board of Health inspectors cited various violations and ordered the clinic shut down. The board targeted similar clinics operated by LADO, the Black Panthers, and the Young Patriots. Lucas-Figueroa took personal offense at Board of Health charges that the YLO facilities were not sanitary. She recalled, "I was furious! I used to go and clean the bathrooms. Before I started interviewing [patients] I would clean the bathrooms with a couple of the kids. And the bathrooms were spotless. The area where the blood was [drawn] was spotless. There was nothing dirty." She remembered having fire extinguishers, requisite signs, and all the necessary equipment the city required. Still, she believed that Board of Health officials searched for excuses to close them down. On one occasion when inspectors visited, she recalled, "I told this one guy who came, I says, 'What is it of this that you don't like? These people are getting help, they're getting checked up. What don't you like?'" Regardless of the clinic's good work, or perhaps precisely because of it, and the potential power that the YLO might gain as a result, city officials wanted the operation closed. As one doctor remarked, the city harassed free health clinics because the organizations that operated them "[we]re creating energies from people who were powerless, and this power may be a harbinger of further democratic processes in the cit[y]."[82]

The YLO's sympathies and alliances with other leftist and militant groups stretched across the country. In 1970, Jiménez and a YLO member from Puerto Rico visited American Indian activists who had occupied Alcatraz Island. They met with Black Panthers and Brown Berets in Oakland. Their first introduction to Chicanos in the Southwest came through the Chicano Youth Liberation Conference in Denver. They learned about Corky González's conference perhaps through their links with other Mexican American gangs and activists in the city's Pilsen neighborhood. Together, Chicago Latino/a activists sent at least two busloads and several cars to Denver. For the YLO, the experience exposed members to the ways in which others were "liberating" themselves elsewhere in the country. It also sharpened their political position. One participant observed their differences, for example, with some Chicanos from the Southwest who were reportedly "too nationalistic and saw everything from a racial or cultural point of view." This writer commented, "We tried to explain that culture isn't the whole answer and that the reason we are treated the way we are is usually because we are poor, not because of our race." While the YLO sympathized with the Chicano struggle, some members rejected strict cultural nationalism and advocated a broader vision of justice for all oppressed peoples.[83]

The YLO promoted a multiracial class consciousness. The group aspired to become the vanguard of the revolution, and saw its members as the "lumpen proletariat" who would lead the struggle. The Young Lords imagined themselves part of a multiracial movement: Jiménez was quoted in the *Black Panther*, stating, "'We feel that we are revolutionaries and revolutionaries have no race.'"[84] A number of factors contributed to this expansive vision. First, the group's local social context played a critical role. The YLO included white members, such as Angie Navedo, an Italian American woman who was married to a Puerto Rican member. The group also counted upon white leftist allies who provided technical support for its operations. A strictly race-based vision was not politically strategic. Second, Puerto Ricans' own physical/phenotypical diversity made a rigid understanding of race and racial boundaries absolutely untenable. As Jeffrey Ogbar notes, "Cha Cha Jimenez and other Lords were careful to refer to the range of colors among Puerto Ricans as an instructive tool to inveigh against race-only discourse, while celebrating an identity that was not white. Jimenez, for example, would not make reference to even the lightest Puerto Ricans as 'white.' In discussing the importance of class struggle, he insisted that 'we relate to the class struggle because there's Puerto Ricans that are real black, then there's Puerto Ricans that are light-skinned like myself.'" Jiménez's own very light skin—he could have passed for white—as well as that of other Puerto Ricans made it difficult to argue that Puerto Ricans were discriminated against because of the color of their skin. Instead, they understood Puerto Rican inequality and oppression as a result of American imperialism, colonialism, and capitalism. For this reason, for example,

Jiménez "insisted that it was inefficacious to insist on more 'Puerto Rican' police to replace 'white' police, when the fundamental job of the police was to operate as 'bodyguards for the capitalists.'"[85]

The presence of Mexican Americans and other Latinos/as in the Lincoln Park neighborhood and the city more broadly further stymied any kind of strict cultural nationalism from dominating the organization. That the YLO espoused "self-determination for all Latinos" reflected the heterogeneity of Chicago's Latino/a population and the panethnic reality of their lived experience. Puerto Rican youths in Lincoln Park had Mexican American friends, including several YLO members—Sal de Rivero, Omar López, Luis Chavez, and Hilda Vasquez-Ignatin, among others. Chicana artist Felicitas Nuñez, who painted murals at YLO headquarters, included icons of the Mexican Revolution, such as Emiliano Zapata and La Adelita. Zapata appeared also in the *YLO* newspaper. Most surprising, perhaps, was that a Mexican American member, Sal de Rivero, had created the group's nationalist logo.[86] From its inception as a political organ, the YLO identified itself as a pan-Latino entity. The *Young Lords Organization* issue of May 1969 announced: "The Young Lords . . . see the need for unity with other Latin groups, and seek to implement it. They are seeking to build an organization that can build mass consciousness and prepare the way for fundamental, necessary changes. They understand that to be relevant and effective they must be both politically advanced and prepared to defend the Latin colony and its people."[87] Just as some politicized African American gangs began calling for an end to internecine conflicts with one another, the YLO urged Latino gangs to cease warring and unite to fight the common enemy that oppressed them all—a capitalist, fascist American state and its law enforcement arm.

The YLO soon gained attention throughout the country. Iris Morales, a young Puerto Rican woman from New York City, had met Jiménez in March of 1969 at the Crusade for Justice's Chicano Youth Liberation Conference in Denver, Colorado. Other New York Latinos/as soon heard of the YLO as well. That June, a group of New York Latino/a college students read an interview with Jiménez published in a Black Panther newspaper. As Pablo Guzmán remembers, he and two other activists decided to drive to Chicago to find out more about the Lords and their Rainbow Coalition. After meeting with them, Jiménez gave them permission to organize a YLO chapter in New York. The chapter began similar serve-the-people programs, occupied a local church in Spanish Harlem, and took over a local hospital and a tuberculosis testing truck. It gained significant media attention in a short period of time and became the subject of a documentary and several books. The two groups operated independently, each addressing the concerns of their local communities. But the affiliation did not last. Over time, the alliance fractured and the New York chapter broke away and changed its name to the Young Lords Party. The Chicago YLO, meanwhile, developed chapters in other parts of the country, among Chicanos in San Diego and Hayward, California, and Puerto Ricans in Milwaukee and Puerto Rico.[88]

The Decline of the YLO

By late 1970, police harassment of the YLO had reached a crescendo. Jiménez had several warrants for his arrest and decided to leave Chicago. The most recent charge involved the theft of twenty-three dollars' worth of lumber that he allegedly stole from an urban renewal site. When city inspectors visited the People's Church to approve it as a licensed day-care facility, they charged that ceilings needed to be lowered, floors raised, and partitions erected. Jiménez approached a neighborhood lumberyard for donations but was given only scraps of wood. Infuriated, he decided to take lumber from a local urban renewal construction site and was arrested immediately. After his release on bail, he fled the city and went underground with several other YLO members. He resigned as chair of the organization and left the central committee in charge.[89]

By the early to midseventies, police repression and surveillance were bearing down on many militant activists. Some radical leftist groups had disbanded, gone underground, or been effectively infiltrated and destroyed. In December of 1969, Chicago police had brutally murdered Panther leader Fred Hampton and a member from Peoria, Mark Clark, allegedly upon orders of notorious Cook County state's attorney Ed Hanrahan. Evidence later revealed that the FBI had played a key role in the assassinations as well.[90] Hampton's murder had a chilling effect on activists, who felt increasingly fearful of state-authorized violence. The Young Lords were continually being harassed, arrested, and jailed and constantly used up their meager funds for bail money. During the two years that Jiménez and other YLO leaders went into hiding, publication of their newspaper shifted to Milwaukee, Wisconsin, and became sporadic. Organizing against urban renewal all but disappeared. The group had also lost support from some white liberals in Lincoln Park because of rumors that linked its members to the murders of the Armitage Methodist Church pastor Bruce Johnson and his wife, Eugenia Johnson, just months after the YLO had occupied the church.[91] During the time that Jiménez and others were underground, neighborhood clearance and development plans continued displacing Puerto Rican families. When Jiménez came back to Chicago in December 1972 to surrender himself for the theft charges, few Puerto Ricans remained in the Armitage neighborhood. Some had moved to West Town and Humboldt Park while others had moved north to the neighboring Lakeview community.[92]

Jiménez and his associates chose to regroup in Lakeview and attempted to renew their community work. Because so much of their base had dispersed throughout the city, the YLO faced the challenge of organizing and politicizing an entirely new neighborhood. It moved to the corner of Wilton and Grace Streets, the heart of a new Puerto Rican enclave but also a heavy drug-trafficking center. Though the Lords claimed they moved there to organize the community and combat drugs, some interpreted their choice of location as evidence of their intimate involvement in the drug trade. Nonetheless, urban renewal had crept northward into Lakeview. The city planned to gentrify the East Lakeview neighborhood just as it had done in Lincoln Park, to attract young professionals and push Puerto Ricans and other poor people out once more.[93]

Jiménez and the Lords attempted to revitalize their coalitions with poor whites, held rallies in support of the United Farm Workers, and worked with local Native American activists. But they also changed their strategy. Both locally and nationally, some African American activists and white leftists had begun shifting from direct action to electoral politics. In 1974, Jiménez made a bid for alderman of the Forty-Sixth Ward, which included sections of Lakeview and neighboring Uptown. He and his associates registered thirty-four hundred low-income and minority voters and developed a base of support. While he garnered a significant number of votes, he lost the election by a wide margin.[94] Jiménez's personal life began to decline as well, as he allegedly became consumed by drug addiction. He left the city shortly thereafter, abandoning a movement that he could no longer lead and that had effectively dissolved.

The YLO as a social movement suffered many shortcomings. It was a male-dominated organization that had started as a street gang, and its young male members continued to espouse a gang mentality and tactics. Indeed, this was cited as one of the causes for the rift between the Young Lords in New York City and the Chicago headquarters. Unlike the street-bred Lords of Chicago, many of whom had not completed high school and considered themselves the "lumpen proletariat," the New York activists consisted largely of college students who seemingly had a more sophisticated grasp on politics. The Chicago chapter called them "intellectuals" because of their educational backgrounds and their emphasis on theory and ideology. This key difference eventually splintered the two chapters.[95] By late spring of 1970, the New York chapter broke from the national organization, citing Chicago's lack of organization, discipline, and professionalism.

The organization was indeed fraught with internal problems. Local and federal law enforcement (FBI COINTELPRO) kept the group under constant surveillance. They harassed, intimidated, and terrorized members, which scared some supporters away. Cha Cha Jiménez was, of course, the main target and like other militant organizational leaders was constantly in and out of jail. Infiltrators and provocateurs caused disruption and dissent within the group as well. YLO members themselves shared some of the blame for their shortcomings. As Omar López noted, most of the YLO members had known one another as neighborhood friends since childhood. As a result, imposing discipline when members failed to show up to meetings, arrived late, or did not complete their assignments proved difficult. Few members wanted to enforce rules on one another. Some clung to their street gang attitudes and did not completely assimilate the political platform. A number fell victim to drug addictions and struggled with a variety of other personal problems. For multiple reasons, the group's effectiveness diminished.[96]

Conclusion

The period of the 1960s proved a pivotal moment for Chicago's Puerto Rican community. As many felt the consequences of city planning imperatives and the dire social conditions in impoverished, neglected neighborhoods, such conditions began to take their toll. The brief rise of the Young Lords as a social organ for youth activism provides but one example (perhaps the most visible) of how some tried to cope with this reality. Their short-lived success and their significance cannot be understated: when Bobby Seale came to speak in Chicago, Cha Cha Jiménez spoke alongside him, making Puerto Ricans visible on the local political stage beside Black Power advocates and radical leftist whites.[97] Although they may not have been as prominent on the national scene as other leftist, radical groups, at the local level, they commanded a large audience.

Laura Pulido has noted that "Black Power . . . is key to understanding the development of the New Left, nationalist struggles, and the Third World Left." Indeed, the civil rights movement and the shift to Black Power opened up a space politically for other racialized minority groups; if African Americans could make claims against the state about racism, oppression, and the denial of their civil rights, then perhaps Chicanos/as, Puerto

Ricans, American Indians, and Asian Americans could too.[98] The BPP dem-onstrated that militant revolutionary politics were *possible* in the contem-porary political climate, although of course the strength of its movement was met with an equal amount of repression. Yet we should not conclude that the Young Lords and other militant Latino/a groups merely imitated black political mobilization, because this erases a rich history of political struggle among Latinos/as (e.g., Puerto Rican nationalist movements of the early twentieth century, Mexican American labor struggles).[99] It also reduces a much more complex exchange of political influence during this era. Just as the BPP shaped other racialized minority movements, the activism of Latinos/as, American Indians, and colonized peoples throughout the Third World informed the development of the BPP's political position as a US Third World Left organization. The *Black Panther* regularly published stories on the Young Lords, the Brown Berets, the United Farm Workers, and other Chicano causes and campaigns. The BPP remained constantly attuned to the political battles fought by other racial minority groups, something that strengthened its support among the Third World Left and further edu-cated other leftists on the vast landscape of racialized populations fighting against capitalism and racism.[100]

As historian Johanna Fernandez has noted, the Young Lords stood some-where "between social service reform and revolutionary politics."[101] While they developed from a street gang into a politicized militant community group, they straddled the line between providing basic human services to their needy constituents and working for radical social change. Choosing to organize as a pan-Latino, leftist, and simultaneously nationalist Puerto Rican organization, the YLO espoused a nuanced and complex class-based politics that sought to eliminate inequality, colonialism, poverty, and social injustice. The Young Lords were a product of their local social environment and a rich anticolonial heritage, and traversed a complicated and volatile political terrain.

The sight of hundreds of Puerto Rican youth and their allies occupying the streets of Chicago in the late sixties was surely arresting for many Chi-cagoans and Americans throughout the country. At their peak, the Young Lords could summon over a thousand people to their marches. Critics were disgusted by their insolence while sympathizers applauded their stridency. Though many critics characterized the Young Lords simply as disaffected youth who latched onto the popular protest movements of the times, the members themselves were moved to action based on their lived experi-ences of material deprivation and social marginalization. The continual menace of urban renewal, the reality of inner-city gang life, rampant police brutality, the presence of political allies in the Black Panthers and others in the black community, the Young Patriots and white leftists, and the charismatic leadership of José Jiménez and countless men and women gave birth to a social movement that left an indelible mark on Chicago's Puerto Rican community and let the city know that Puerto Ricans were a population to be reckoned with.

SIX

From Eighteenth Street to *La Dieciocho*: Neighborhood Transformation in the Age of the Chicano Movement

Over the years this community [the Mexican community of Eighteenth Street] has been ignored by federal, state, and city agencies that have been established to meet some of the needs of inner city residents. . . . There has been little interest on the part of city agencies to expand [*sic*] energy or monies to provide needed services for our community. [El Centro aims] to provide an atmosphere which encourages adults to use their civil rights and responsibilities and which enables youth to realize their full potential.

—El Centro de la Causa press release[1]

On a Thursday evening in April 1969, over one hundred residents of Chicago's Pilsen / Eighteenth Street[2] community gathered for a public meeting of the organization ALAS, Alianza Latino-Americana para el Adelanto Social (Latin American Alliance for Social Advancement). The organization regularly met at Howell House, the neighborhood settlement house that had long served "Middle European"[3] immigrants in earlier decades. ALAS was one of a number of organizations recently formed in the neighborhood, since growing numbers of Mexicans and Puerto Ricans had moved into the neighborhood in the past decade. At its public meeting, ALAS addressed a variety of issues affecting the Mexican/"Spanish-speaking" population.[4] First, the organization officially endorsed a Mexican American candidate, Arthur Vázquez, for executive director of Howell House.[5] The group also discussed parents' ongoing grievances regarding the neighborhood's woefully inadequate schools. It sought a new principal at a local middle school and appointed a committee to meet with the city board of education on the matter. ALAS also discussed the problems many Mexican and other Latino/a students faced at Harrison High School, the only area high school, located on the western outskirts of the neighborhood.

Latino/a students had walked out of the school in protest the previous fall and had issued a "Latin American Student Manifesto."[6] Since ALAS's membership consisted of many community parents, the organization had begun negotiations with the district superintendent to meet the students' and parents' demands, including appointing Latino/a counselors, recruiting two Latino/a assistant principals, hiring Latino/a teacher's aides, increasing the number of teachers of English as a Second Language, providing tutoring, and implementing a full-scale bilingual education program. A group of young men from the area's street clubs (gangs) addressed the audience as well, seeking support for a young man named Jesse Maldonado who allegedly had been brutalized by police while facilitating a truce between neighborhood gangs. The crowd unanimously agreed to support Maldonado's cause. The final item on the agenda addressed Chicano issues beyond the community. The group discussed the nationwide United Farm Workers grape boycott, voted unanimously to endorse the campaign, and established a committee to support the effort locally.[7] As a rule, ALAS conducted all of its meetings in both Spanish and English to make them accessible to all members of the community and printed all of its flyers, meeting minutes, and announcements bilingually.[8]

This gathering in early 1969 marked a critical moment of transition in the Eighteenth Street / Pilsen neighborhood. The area's white population had begun declining in previous decades as the children and grandchildren of middle European immigrants left the crowded district for better living elsewhere. At the same time, Mexicans had been moving in. In the late 1950s and early 1960s, expressway construction, urban renewal, and the construction of a new University of Illinois campus displaced the Mexican settlement just north in the neighboring Taylor Street area. Many simply crossed the train tracks that divided the two communities, into the predominantly Polish and Czechoslovakian Eighteenth Street / Pilsen neighborhood. Pilsen soon became the new port of entry for incoming Mexican immigrants and *Tejano* migrants (Mexican Americans from Texas) who continued arriving throughout the sixties and seventies. Several hundred Puerto Ricans added to the Spanish-speaking population as well. As a result of these demographic shifts, Eighteenth Street and the neighboring South Lawndale community to the west underwent dramatic racial succession.

In 1960, Mexicans[9] and other Spanish-speaking people made up less than 14 percent of Pilsen's residents. By 1970, they constituted 55 percent of the population (although local researchers claimed the census severely undercounted and the figure was closer to 80 percent). Neighboring Little Village counted almost no Mexicans or Spanish-speaking people in 1960 but identified 32 percent of its population as Spanish-speaking in 1970. A decade later, 74 percent of Little Village was Mexican/Spanish-speaking, as was 78 percent of Pilsen. Together these two communities contained over one-third of the city's Mexican population and represented the largest concentration of Mexican people in the entire Midwest. Nearly one hundred thousand Mexicans and a small number of other Latinos/as crowded into less than eight square miles, amid a rapidly disappearing white community and a large neighboring African American population.[10] By 1980, these neighborhoods had become Mexican *barrios*.

The ALAS meeting underscores two other interrelated developments. First, Mexicans were becoming more publicly visible social actors in the neighborhood, actively creating community, sometimes in the face of outright hostility from neighbors. As their numbers increased, they struggled to get local institutions to serve the needs of their rather young, growing population. Mexicans thus began organizing themselves to claim a place and resources in their new community. Second, the Mexican residents of Eighteenth Street had a growing consciousness of the Chicano movement spreading throughout the Southwest, and many increasingly saw themselves as part of it or at least sympathetic to its ideals. The growing Chicano movement provided inspiration for activists in Pilsen and elsewhere in the city. As Leonard Ramirez has observed, the "educational, economic, and political marginalization [of Pilsen's Mexican community] was reinforced by their national exclusion from public policy discussion."[11] The movement brought visibility on a national scale to a population that long had been "a forgotten minority." It offered a response to the racial prejudice that Mexicans had historically experienced vis-à-vis the nation's social, economic, legal, and political institutions. It nurtured a sense of pride in oneself, one's history, and one's indigenous roots, and it challenged the European immigrant model of assimilation that most Mexicans simply could not and would not emulate. The movement took hold in Chicago as well, circumscribed by the local political context and social conditions. Just as Puerto Ricans were becoming politically active in West Town, Humboldt Park, and Lincoln Park; African Americans were increasingly demanding Black Power after years of civil rights struggles; radical white leftists and student groups were challenging liberalism; and women were demanding equality, Mexicans on Eighteenth Street also began making sociopolitical and economic claims against the local political structure.

From 1968 to 1974, Mexicans in Pilsen initiated a period of intense social activism, making it the center of Chicago's Chicano movement. Scholar-activist Carlos Muñoz notes that throughout the country, "activists with quite diverse ideologies [who were never really engaged in the movement] have claimed their political projects to be part of the Chicano movement." While certainly not all efforts in Pilsen's Mexican community should be classified under this label, the breadth and heterogeneity of activism in Pilsen deserve attention.[12] Neighborhood activism and protest represented a wide range of political views, strategies, and goals. Mexican and Puerto Rican workers had formed a coalition called Asociación pro Derechos Obreros (APO; Association for Workers' Rights), which, among other things, staged bus boycotts and sit-ins to protest employment discrimination against Latinos/as by the Chicago Transit Authority. Mexican American participants in the Pilsen Neighbors Community Council (PNCC), a Saul Alinsky / Industrial Areas Foundation organization, successfully challenged the long-standing white leadership, which had refused to relinquish its power despite changing community demographics. Meanwhile, young men in local street gangs embraced Chicano nationalism and formed a chapter of the Brown Berets. One wing of Chicano/a activists began La Raza Unida Party chapters in the city and put forth a Mexican American congressional candidate in the neighborhood in 1972. Mothers and other residents fought for a day-care center and the construction of a much-needed high school in the community. Another group established an alternative school for students who had been expelled or "pushed out" of the local high school. Leftist organizations such as Centro de Acción Social Autónomo—Hermandad General de Trabajadores (CASA-HGT), or Center for Autonomous Social Action—General Brotherhood of Workers, waged campaigns for immigrants' rights, competing for ideological space on Eighteenth Street with other leftist organizations.[13] One group of Mexican American women decided to form an organization to address specifically the overlooked needs and concerns of women and girls. Mexican activists on Eighteenth Street felt the energy of the Chicano movement (whether they saw themselves as part of it or not) and used the language of militancy, self-determination, social justice, and cultural pride to claim a space for themselves literally and figuratively.[14]

Mexican and Chicano/a activism had local origins. Activists drew on their history and memories of the aggressive urban renewal displacement their families had experienced; the material realities of an overcrowded, underserved, and neglected *barrio*; and their experience of racial tensions with neighbors in Pilsen. If the heterogeneous and politically progressive community of Lincoln Park enabled the Young Lords Organization to develop expansive, class-based, multiracial alliances, the highly charged and racially segregated neighborhood of Pilsen led Mexican Americans down a narrower political path. The cultural nationalism of the Chicano movement provided a response to dealing with racism, marginalization, and subordination.[15] Much as in earlier decades, as Mexican immigrants had turned inward in the face of discrimination to embrace a "Mexican" identity, in the 1960s and 1970s, second- and third-generation Mexican American youths embraced their ethnoracial identity in the context of a movement for social change.

Middle Europeans and the Making of Pilsen

Pilsen, Eighteenth Street, or the "Lower West Side" as it was officially named by University of Chicago sociologists (Community Area 31), resembled much of the rest of Chicago—layered with generations of immigrants and racially segregated. When the city was incorporated in 1837, sections of Pilsen lay within the city limits. After the expulsion of Potawatomi Indians and settlement by European Americans, the swampy region began humming with industrial activity on the South Branch of the Chicago River. German and Irish immigrants came to the region to operate small farms or build and later work on the Illinois-Michigan Shipping Canal. As railroads, quarries, lumberyards, and shipping outfits grew over the late 1800s and early 1900s, Polish and Czechoslovakian workers, soon followed by Slavs, Slovenians, and Lithuanians, replaced earlier immigrants as the workforce. The neighborhood acquired its name from its predominantly Bohemian residents. A small Italian community also settled in the southwest corner in an area that later named itself "Heart of Chicago." By 1920, the entire community area reached a very dense capacity of more than eighty-five thousand residents. Workers built or rented modest wood frame houses, often occupied by multiple families. They economized space as much as possible: lots were often doubled up, with one building in the front facing the street and another behind it housing even more tenants. Large apartment buildings served a similar function, cramming as many occupants as possible in what social reformers deemed unhealthy conditions. Pilsen became an industrial corridor, fringed by railroad tracks on the north, factories and warehouses on the east and south, and the South Branch of the Chicago River. Residents learned to tolerate the sounds, smells, and residue of industrial production that drifted through the air around them. Pilsen was a decidedly working-class community.[16]

In 1940, the neighborhood remained populated entirely by European immigrants and their descendants. Seventy-one percent of residents were "native white," and 29 percent "foreign-born white." This foreign-born population consisted of Poles (31.0 percent), Czechs (23.4 percent), Yugoslavians (12.5 percent), Lithuanians (11.8 percent), Italians (7.7 percent), and smaller ethnic groups.[17] With time, many of Pilsen's second- and third-generation European Americans had moved out to less crowded, better-quality housing in neighborhoods to the south and west. Some lived in neighboring South Lawndale, with its slightly larger homes, while the better heeled moved farther south and west to middle-class suburbs like Cicero and Berwyn.[18] By the 1960s, the population that researchers described as "middle Europeans" (eastern/central Europeans) had declined by nearly twenty thousand people compared to three decades earlier. Of the forty-eight thousand who remained, many were elderly and lacked enough capital to sell their homes and upgrade to better neighborhoods.

White residents began witnessing demographic changes in the neighborhoods around them as new groups began pressing on community boundaries. African Americans and Mexicans had lived just north of Pilsen's railroad tracks, in the Near West Side, for decades. Although a few Mexicans had come to Pilsen since the 1930s, they began moving to the eastern end of Eighteenth Street in greater numbers in the fifties. Over that decade, they grew from only 0.5 percent of the population to 14 percent.[19] (Residents restricted African Americans to a mere 1 percent of the population.) Mexicans soon established organizations such as the Manuel Perez American Legion Post 1017 and a smattering of small ethnic businesses. These settlers in the fifties were either the most socially mobile of their group (i.e., small businessmen, skilled workers) or those most capable of "passing," going relatively undetected among the predominantly Polish and Czech community. Mexicans from the more crowded and impoverished Near West Side seemed to sense class distinctions between themselves and those who had moved up to Pilsen's less crowded, more prestigious community.[20] By the early 1960s, Mexicans moved to Pilsen in growing numbers, and the eastern area became recognizable as a Mexican enclave. The 1960 census officially counted over sixty-one hundred ethnic Mexicans (both native and foreign born) and eight hundred Puerto Ricans. Together, their numbers rivaled the area's seven thousand first- and second-generation Poles. Pilsen residents continued to exclude African Americans, however, counting less than six hundred in a total population of more than forty-eight thousand people (see table 11).[21]

The most upwardly mobile Spanish-speaking families moved farther west into South Lawndale, which became affectionately known as "the

Table 11 Population changes by race, Lower West Side and South Lawndale, 1950–80

	1950	1960	1970	1980
		Lower West Side (Pilsen)		
Total population	53,991	48,448	44,498	44,951
White	53,829	47,770	41,739	20,767
% of population	99.7	98.6	93.8	46.2
Black	162	533	1,001	494
% of population	0.3	1.1	2.4	1.1
Other nonwhite races	0	145	1,691	23,689*
% of population	0.0	0.3	3.8	52.7
Spanish-speaking / Spanish-origin[†]	n/a	6,914[‡§]	24,463	34,882
Puerto Rican	n/a	800	2,211	1,557
Mexican foreign born or foreign parentage	n/a	6,114	16,123	32,178
% of population	n/a	14.0	54.9	77.6
		South Lawndale (Little Village)		
Total population	66,977	60,940	62,895	75,204
White	65,570	57,223	54,153	33,541
% of population	97.9	93.9	86.1	44.6
Black	1,340	3,595	6,478	6,468
% of population	2.0	5.9	10.3	8.6
Other nonwhite races	67	122	2,264	35,195*
% of population	0.1	0.2	3.6	46.8
Spanish-language / Spanish-origin[†]	n/a	1,116[‡]	20,044	55,726
Puerto Rican	n/a	258	1,806	2,428
Mexican foreign born or foreign stock	n/a	858	12,841	51,208
% of population	n/a	1.8	31.9	74.1

Sources: Kitagawa and Taueber, *Local Community Fact Book, 1960*; Chicago Fact Book Consortium, *Local Community Fact Book, 1970 and 1980*, 84–85, 87–88, 364.

*In 1960 and 1970, most Latinos/as were classified as white. By 1980, a larger number of "Spanish-origin" people chose to identify as "other race" or were identified as such. Nonetheless, the number identified as "of Spanish origin" in 1980 does not correspond exactly to the "other nonwhite race," as some may still have self-selected or been classified as "white" or "black." The dramatic decline in "white" population from 1970 to 1980, then, reflects not only the flight of European Americans but the shift of many Latinas/os' racial identification from "white" to "other." Some of that demographic change occurred in the previous decade (1960–70) but is not discernible because so many Latinas/os were still being identified as white.

†These terms were used in 1970 and 1980, respectively. The label "of Spanish origin" was assigned independently of race, based on the logic that Spanish-speaking people could be of any race. Most "Spanish-origin" people were counted under the "white" racial category in 1960 and 1970, though a number who self-identified as "black" are enumerated as such.

‡This is an estimate calculated by adding the total Puerto Rican and Mexican foreign born or foreign stock.

§Ruth Horowitz estimated that by the early 1970s, half of the ethnic Mexican population in the neighborhood was actually born in the United States to US-born parents, thus making them third-generation Mexican Americans. Horowitz, *Honor and the American Dream*, 241n19. If this is in fact accurate, as it may be given that the "Spanish-origin" population enumerated in 1970 is much larger than the sum of those identified as Puerto Rican or Mexican foreign born or of foreign parentage, then it stands to reason that there were many more "Spanish-language/Spanish-origin" residents in 1960 who were third-generation and not captured in that category.

Mexican suburbs." South Lawndale lay just west of Pilsen, had a similar demographic composition, and was surrounded by industry to the east, south, and west. It represented a step above Pilsen. Homes were more often brick two- or three-flats or single-family bungalows rather than the modest wood frame houses or crowded apartment buildings farther east. South Lawndale reflected the middle-class strivings of working families. But South Lawndale was witnessing population changes across its northern border as well. Like much of the city, both neighborhoods had clearly demarcated physical boundaries that enforced racial ones. Elevated railroad tracks, which ran from east to west, created the northern border for both Pilsen and South Lawndale and separated their middle European populations from growing African American neighbors to the north. As African Americans threatened the racial homogeneity of South Lawndale, and to a lesser extent Pilsen, Mexicans became critically important in the area's social dynamics.

Mexicans and Neighborhood Change

For decades, Pilsen and South Lawndale had housed a mix of foreign-born Europeans and native-born whites, "spatially integrated but socially segregated." Various European immigrants crossed paths on neighborhood streets but generally attended their own churches, cultural centers, and social clubs. Many immigrants in fact held deep-seated ethnic and national antagonisms toward one another (Poles, Slavs, Czechs, Germans, etc.), and local churches reflected these ethnic and national divisions.[22] Pilsen's East End, for example, had three Catholic parishes within several blocks of one another, attesting to the ethnic exclusivity of religious worship. Irish immigrants had founded Sacred Heart parish in the late nineteenth century; Lithuanian immigrants established Providence of God only a few blocks away in 1900; and Slovak immigrants raised St. Joseph parish and elementary school just blocks from there at the turn of the twentieth century as well.[23] Although they socialized with their own, such immigrants rarely lived in isolation from one another, unlike the stark segregation African Americans experienced. Over the course of the 1940s and 1950s, however, European ethnic differences declined in significance and European Americans more firmly gripped a shared racial identity. One researcher in the late 1960s explained that in the face of incoming Mexicans and North Lawndale African Americans whose children attended the area's public high school, "Czechs, Slovaks, Poles and Slovenians are sufficiently drawn together to overcome their historical pasts." European immigrants and their children consolidated their shared "whiteness" vis-à-vis encroaching darker people who were socially, culturally, and most significant, *racially* different.[24]

Ethnic whites in the postwar period increasingly expressed their apprehensions about and disdain for those whom they perceived to be outsiders. By 1960, Poles were the largest European ethnic group remaining in the area, but they were encountering growing numbers of Mexicans.[25] Much like the Puerto Rican / Spanish-speaking population on the North Side, the Mexican/Spanish-speaking population on the South Side witnessed more gradual racial succession than African Americans did. Whites did not abruptly abandon Pilsen en masse as they did in neighborhoods where African Americans moved in, like Chatham, North Lawndale, and East and West Garfield Park. Instead, some whites remained, for a variety of reasons, and sustained a longer period of "integration" with their new neighbors. Some viewed Mexicans as just another immigrant group, akin to the Europeans of earlier days. They saw Mexicans perhaps as less racially distant than African Americans and were willing to accommodate them as long as they were few in number and conformed to community standards. Yet many others held virulent racial contempt for Mexicans that rivaled their bigotry toward African Americans. Racially denigrated groups represented a threat to the neighborhood's status.

Mexicans encountered the kinds of territorial conflicts that were a standing feature of twentieth-century urban life: newcomers were never easily integrated, especially if they did not share the ethnoracial background of existing residents. Carlos Valencia, who moved to Pilsen in 1958 when he was a teenager, remembered very tense relations in the predominantly Polish area. As one of the first families to cross the imaginary racial boundary or "deadline" of Ashland Avenue (where Mexican families simply did not live in those years), the Valencias faced prejudice and hostility from their Polish neighbors. "We were always fighting with the Polish guys. There was lots of tension," he recalled.[26] Mexican families who were the first on the block usually faced resistance from existing residents. In the worst cases, they experienced violence meant to drive them out. In less severe cases, they underwent the usual harassment and hazing—especially among youths and children—that other groups often did.[27]

Mexicans arriving at Eighteenth Street in the late fifties and early sixties clustered in seven census tracts in the area's east end, where they ranged from at least 14 percent to 28 percent of the population. Only 15 to 30 percent of white residents in those tracts were first- or second-generation immigrants. The majority were simply "white," undifferentiated from other European ethnic groups except perhaps by residual cultural practices.

Some scholars have classified the tensions between whites and Mexicans in Pilsen as "ethnic hostility,"[28] suggesting a greater degree of equivalency or social equality than "racial hostility" might connote. Yet the experience of Mexicans reveals that such conflict often became racialized or "colored," and that it was not limited to young men or boys, as some urban historians have argued, but occurred among women and girls as well. Mexican American resident Cathy Alaniz noted the resentments that Polish neighbors vocalized toward Mexicans, explaining that "whenever the [Mexican] children go down the stairs and pass [an elderly Polish woman named Mrs. Z——] on the way, they hear her muttering, 'Mexicans!'" Mrs. Z. also referred to Alaniz's dark-skinned niece as "that black Mexican."[29] In a dualistic racial order in which African Americans presented the primary and most troubling racial threat to whites, some revealed their fears that Mexicans stood very close to African Americans, especially if they had dark skin. Mexicans who did not clearly have "white" skin were often derided with racial slurs usually applied to African Americans. Alicia Amador, a Mexican American woman who grew up in neighboring Little Village in the early 1960s, vividly recalled her experiences as a girl:

> Racism was awful over there. People cannot believe what we went through. I remember walking into a store with my brother, and we were waiting [to be attended] and people were walking ahead of us [in line]. Finally, I told the proprietor, "We've been standing here. My brother wants to buy some candy." And he said, "We don't serve niggers here."[30]

Just as Puerto Ricans on the North Side recalled memories of experiencing blatant racism as children, Mexican children heard racial epithets directed at them and adults. Education scholar Angelica Rivera interviewed various Mexican women who similarly recalled white children calling them "niggers" in the 1950s and 1960s when their families moved into "white" areas.[31] Children witnessed adults making reference to "these people" and "dirty Mexicans," which explicitly drew on historical racist stereotypes of Mexicans and characterized them as undesirable neighbors.

Encounters between Mexican children and white adults, however, were not always explicitly racialized but carried generational tensions that reflected the neighborhood's changing demographics (see table 12). Mexican families tended to be much younger than whites, which meant that elderly people in particular found themselves among growing numbers of Mexican and other Spanish-speaking children and youths. In 1950, there were 1.6 white children or youths (ages five through nineteen) for every white

Table 12 Population changes by age and selected economic data, Lower West Side and South Lawndale, 1950–80

	1950	1960	1970	1980
		Lower West Side		
Under 20 years old (%)	29.8	37.6	42.1	40.4
Median family income ($)	n/a	n/a	8,557	14,487
Below poverty level (%)	n/a	n/a	15.5	23.5
1+ person per room (%)	11.9	14.8	18.1	22.7
		South Lawndale		
Under 20 years old (%)	26.1	31.5	37.0	40.5
Median family income ($)	n/a	n/a	9,044	16,410
Below poverty level (%)	n/a	n/a	11.7	19.5
1+ person per room (%)	9.7	9.8	13.3	24.7

Sources: Kitagawa and Taueber, *Local Community Fact Book, 1960*; Chicago Fact Book Consortium, *Local Community Fact Book, 1970 and 1980*, 84–85, 87–88.

person over the age of sixty; by 1970, there were 2.5 Spanish-speaking children for every white senior citizen. (The number of white children had declined to a white youth-senior ratio of 1:1.) Mexican children quickly outnumbered white children by more than double, and thus were much more visible on neighborhood streets. By 1970, 42 percent of Pilsen's residents were under eighteen years of age. More specifically, an estimated 60 percent of Mexicans were under the age of twenty-five. In contrast, white / middle European heads of household had an average age of fifty-seven, and few had young children.[32] In South Lawndale, the numbers of Mexican/ Spanish-speaking and white children were fairly equivalent, but together they outnumbered elderly white residents more than two to one. Longstanding residents lamented "the change in the neighborhood," especially the ways newcomers brought distinct cultural practices and social norms. Jesus Garcia recalls that older residents bemoaned the fact that incoming families "[were] not following traditions of the neighborhood, having a lot of kids . . . kids running around, stepping on people's grass or riding their bikes on people's lawns, not picking up garbage, things like that."[33] This was especially troubling to white senior citizens who no longer had children at home but were encountering "other people's children," who may have behaved just as their own children had years earlier but whom they found objectionable nonetheless.[34]

By the 1970s, research studies conducted in the two neighborhoods revealed European American anxieties about the changes in the community.

[They] view the exodus [sic] of Mexicans, and to some extent the closeness of the blacks, as a threat to their very existence in every sense of the word. Informants often say that they do not object to Mexicans and blacks as such, but cannot hide a deep-seated anxiety concerning the changes they may bring in their own style of life and in the cultural and social atmosphere of the whole community.[35]

Across the tracks from Pilsen on the Near West Side, African Americans were becoming increasingly concentrated in recently built public housing projects. Farther west, North Lawndale had undergone racial succession during the 1950s. For years, North Lawndale had been home to an enclave of middle-class Russian Jews, including store owners of Maxwell Street businesses and others who had moved up and out of the Jewish slums of the Near West Side. North Lawndale's population began shrinking in the thirties as residents started moving to more fashionable neighborhoods and suburbs (e.g., Rogers Park, Skokie). The population loss was curbed, however, by a growing African American enclave on the northern edge of the neighborhood, which contributed 13 percent of the total residents in 1950. Over the next decade, North Lawndale underwent astonishing racial succession as migrating southern African Americans settled in and whites continued to move out. The population went from a mere 13,000 African Americans in 1950 to 113,000 ten years later. Inversely, whites declined from almost 87 percent of residents (87,123) to less than 9 percent (10,744).[36]

As whites moved out of the neighborhood, so too did employers. By the late 1960s, International Harvester had closed its nearby plant, taking fourteen thousand jobs. Sears, Roebuck moved its headquarters to the Loop in the early 1970s after the construction of its soaring Sears Tower, taking another ten thousand jobs. Within one decade, the area had lost 75 percent of its businesses. North Lawndale soon became a devastated urban ghetto plagued by unemployment, poverty, and crime. Compounded by city hall's neglect, the area tumbled into an abyss of disinvestment and decline.[37] When Martin Luther King Jr. came to initiate an open housing campaign in Chicago, he moved into a slum apartment in North Lawndale to draw attention to the desperately impoverished and degraded conditions that African Americans endured in the city's ghettos.[38]

Apart from population changes, the dramatic social upheaval of the era—including King's open housing campaign—also troubled many white residents. African Americans were increasingly protesting, demanding civil rights, and calling for Black Power in nearby neighborhoods; opponents responded to King's housing marches with mob violence; and the city had erupted in riots more than once only a couple of miles away on the West Side. On the North Side, police and urban renewal officials battled against Puerto Ricans. The media reported the growing number of racial minorities in the city and the seemingly simultaneous rise in gang activity and crime. Many whites feared that such crime would seep into their own neighborhoods.[39]

The physical boundary formed by the abandoned industrial zone and the Chicago, Burlington, and Quincy railroad tracks on North Lawndale's southern border became of paramount significance for South Lawndale. Whites to the south were terrified of the influx of black residents and did everything possible to prevent them from breaching that racial boundary. One group of residents established an organization called HOPE (Home Owners Preservation Enterprise), as researchers noted, "to keep the Negroes out of the area." A local white pastor explained that members of the group had approached the area Clergymen's Council for help in expelling a biracial couple who had moved onto their block. The pastor saw no reason why the African American man and white woman should be forced to leave and rejected their plea. The neighbors proceeded without him and successfully pressured the couple to move out anyway.[40]

The preoccupation with keeping distance from African Americans manifested itself not only in physical terms but discursively as well. The white South Lawndale community rather abruptly changed its name in 1964 after *Life* magazine published an article labeling [North] Lawndale "the worst ghetto in the country." The South Lawndale Community Council worried about the negative connotations of being associated with a poor black neighborhood and voted to change its name to "Little Village" instead. The romantic, parochial name would evoke the "Old World" rural and small-town origins of its early middle European immigrants and sever any associations with the "Lawndale" name. As African Americans populated the city's West Side in growing numbers, nearby white residents reinforced the physical and psychological barriers between themselves and black neighbors.[41]

Some white residents insisted that their opposition to encroaching Mexicans, African Americans, and Puerto Ricans was not racial but rather economic. One business owner, a pharmacist named "Mr. B——" who had moved to the suburb of Berwyn twenty years prior, explained in 1969 that "Europeans aren't prejudiced against Blacks or Mexicans, but they've been in business for years and people come to the neighborhood, change it, and property values deteriorate about a half."[42] The pharmacist framed white residents' decisions to leave the neighborhood in very pragmatic terms: racial minorities simply portended economic decline. The pharmacist's complaints about newcomers and their negative impact, however, belied the positive effect they had on his business: he spoke Spanish in order to attract the growing Spanish-speaking clientele that frequented his pharmacy. Mr. B. was happy to do business with Spanish-speaking customers; he just did not want them as his neighbors.

As some scholars have noted, factors other than race contributed to the exodus of whites from inner-city neighborhoods during these years. Rising tax rates, declining property values, shifting employment markets, and growing crime motivated many to give up on the city and move to the racially exclusive and more peaceful suburbs.[43] Sinking home values and the changing economy, however, were not directly caused by the influx of racial minorities; they were the result of racially biased banking practices, Democratic machine corruption, patronage that favored politically powerful neighborhoods over others, and industrial flight. Yet like African Americans, Mexican and Spanish-speaking residents embodied a social difference that became conflated with negative economic trends. Quite to the contrary, Mexicans, Puerto Ricans, and African Americans did not precipitate deindustrialization; they bore its consequences. As Mexican immigrants continued moving into the central city, it was losing jobs. One study noted that "the Mid-Chicago Industrial Development Area, which include[s] Pilsen, lost 400 companies and more than 70,000 jobs from 1955 to 1965." Moreover, Mexican immigrants and Mexican Americans faced well-documented employment discrimination. White employers and labor unions effectively kept many Spanish-speaking out of the most coveted and highly paid positions. As one industrial employer explained to researchers in the 1970s, "'Our workers used to be all European; and they were all members of the same union. Now all the European workers have moved out of the area. The same unions operate with the same restrictive hiring practices. So even if we wanted more Spanish-speaking workers . . . there's no way for them to get into the craft unions.'"[44]

Ironically, researchers believed that the increase in the Mexican population of Little Village from an estimated 10 to 50 percent between 1960 and 1970 resulted from a deliberate strategy to attract them and thereby keep African Americans out:

The great number of Latins in the area is said to be in large part due to concerted efforts of members of the important real estate and business sector of the area. Numerous informants report that many of the area's businessmen

feared that large numbers of Blacks would eventually spill over from the almost totally Black community of Lawndale to the north. . . . Rather than risk
the very likely possibility that these residential slots would be increasingly
filled by Blacks, a conscious policy of encouragement of Mexicans to settle in
26th Street, if not outright recruitment, was begun by the realtors.[45]

Indeed, other scholars have similarly suggested that Latinos/as in Chicago
have provided a residential buffer zone, to a certain extent, between whites
and African Americans. Whites seemingly tolerated Mexicans' social difference more readily than they did African Americans'. The fact that within a
matter of years, such "integrated" neighborhoods became predominantly
Mexican, however, reveal that such coexistence did not last very long.
Whites moved out of Pilsen and Little Village anyway, and few moved in
to replace them.[46]

White residents who remained often expressed resentment toward
Mexicans regardless of immigrant generation or how "Americanized" they
were.[47] The growing Latino/a population in Pilsen, and to a lesser extent
Little Village, was extremely heterogeneous—composed of US-born second-
and third-generation Mexican Americans (many of whom did not speak
Spanish), migrants from Texas, and recent arrivals from Mexico. The fact
that white residents did not differentiate among different generations of
Mexicans reveals how people of Mexican descent were persistently racialized as "Mexican." They were seen as never assimilating in the eyes of many
whites but instead appeared to be the same even after decades of living in
the city.

Mexicans' experiences with prejudice did not necessarily translate into
sympathy or affinities with African Americans, however. On the contrary,
many tried to assimilate the lessons of antiblack racism that European
immigrants had learned through the process of "Americanization" to improve their social standing. Some embraced an antiblack (and at times,
anti–Puerto Rican) stance in exchange for inclusion in white communities. Claudio Gómez, a Mexican realtor in Little Village, described as much
to a researcher in July 1969. He explained that like whites, Mexicans did
not like blacks or Puerto Ricans, and that Europeans preferred to rent to
Mexicans over these other two groups.[48] Contrary to what some historians
of Chicago have concluded, however, Mexicans' antiblack prejudice, and
even their participation in antiblack violence, does not prove that Mexicans
had successfully attained whiteness. Their claims to whiteness were highly
contested and locally dependent. Mexicans' whiteness varied by neighbor-

hood and was always tenuous.[49] While some Mexican Americans may have "passed" individually, the overwhelming majority continued to be viewed by most European Americans as "nonwhite" and "other."[50]

Socioeconomic Marginalization and the Making of a Mexican Barrio

By the late 1960s, when roughly half of Pilsen's population was Spanish-speaking (primarily Mexican), signs of a new ethnic community were everywhere. Mexicans and Puerto Ricans established businesses in the area—groceries, taverns, restaurants, barbershops, and beauty salons. Some bought homes or invested in rental properties.[51] Newcomers contributed to the economic survival of the rapidly deindustrializing and declining neighborhood. They invigorated a faltering local economy, bought up small businesses to the extent that they could, and contributed to the local tax base. The economic power of the population, however, was limited. The neighborhood became the port of entry for *recién llegados*, recently arrived immigrants. Recent arrivals, especially those who were undocumented, or "without papers," were the most economically vulnerable. Yet even second- and third-generation Mexican Americans struggled to ascend the socioeconomic ladder. Researchers and community leaders assumed a *significant* undercount in the 1970 official census count of twenty-four thousand Spanish-speaking people, due to the high numbers of illegally subdivided apartments, language barriers, and the large population of undocumented immigrants. They estimated that closer to 80 percent of the local population (thirty-six thousand people) was Mexican.[52] The median family income for the entire neighborhood measured $8,557, with 15.5 percent of all families living below the poverty line (table 12). For Spanish-speaking families, income averaged closer to $7,050, and their poverty level topped 17 percent, twice the city average. Forty-nine percent of those employed in Pilsen worked in low-wage manufacturing.[53]

Eighteenth Street showed its age, neglect, and deterioration. Housing stock was considerably older than in other parts of the city: less than 1 percent of Pilsen's housing had been constructed after 1940, while in outlying areas of Chicago, as much as 30 percent of housing stock had been built since then.[54] Doubled-up property lots created very crowded conditions. Since most buildings predated the construction of twentieth-century sewage systems, first-floor dwellings had effectively become basement apartments when the city raised street levels to install sewage lines decades earlier. Thus, the area had vaulted sidewalks, and as they eroded and fell into disrepair, their cracks and holes exposed original street levels ten to fifteen feet below. The dark abysses of crumbling sidewalks often frightened children and elderly residents, who feared falling into the gaping pits that dotted the community's walkways. Residents would place makeshift barriers—buckets, lumber, discarded furniture—to cover up the openings and prevent children, pets, or unsteady senior citizens from falling in.[55] The neighborhood's infrastructure showed decay and municipal neglect.

Because the existing white population had few remaining children and local property values had declined in these years, the school system in particular suffered from disinvestment. Few white students attended the public schools because they either had left the neighborhood or attended private parochial schools. Latino/a students thus constituted over 80 percent in most local public schools. Spanish-speaking pupils created a high demand for English language instruction, for example, but schools failed to meet that need. Officials placed a disproportionate number of such students in EMH classes, those for the "educationally and mentally handicapped."[56] As education scholar Leonard Ramirez has noted, "There was little expectation or institutionalized efforts to facilitate educational advancement or economic mobility [for Mexican children]."[57] Most school buildings were dilapidated and outdated in design and capacity. Overcrowded classrooms spilled students into libraries, gymnasiums, cafeterias, and even basement boiler rooms and coat closets. Mobile trailer units located on school playgrounds provided additional classrooms. Critics labeled them "Willis wagons," for Superintendent Benjamin Willis, who segregated racial minority students in the trailers rather than sending them to less crowded white schools.[58] Children in "Willis wagons" had to walk outdoors to reach the main building for lunch, assemblies, and tutoring sessions, or to use bathrooms. In warmer weather, this did not pose much of a problem, but during cold winters, this meant that children who often lacked warm clothing had to brave the elements several times a day. The appalling conditions of many schools, along with the indifference and sometimes outright hostility of educators and administrators, raised the ire of many parents.

Students at the nearest high school did not fare much better. Pilsen students had access only to Carter Harrison Technical High School, which lay outside neighborhood boundaries. Because it served students from a wide racially transitioning area, it was a hotbed of friction between Latinos/as, African Americans, and whites. Harrison was severely overcrowded, so Pilsen's ninth and tenth graders attended a satellite location within the neighborhood called Froebel High School. Froebel's building had been condemned and scheduled to close for years, but the board of education kept it open despite unsafe conditions. Parents vocally protested that their children were being educated in such a deplorable environment. As a result of the racially hostile climate, indifference and apathy among teachers and administrators, and dispiriting conditions, most Mexican American students left high school before completing their diplomas. Those who actually managed to graduate (reportedly only 30 percent) reaped few benefits from their education. Mexican American high school graduates faced unemployment rates of more than 26 percent, only slightly better than the 28 percent unemployment rates for nongraduates. Pilsen's Mexican American residents overwhelmingly believed that the public school system did a dismal job of educating their children and accused teachers and administrators of refusing to serve their students equitably.[59]

Chicano Nationalism in the Midwest: From Howell House to Casa Aztlán

Just as Mexican community members charged that public schools did not serve Mexican children well, local settlement houses and social service agencies did not adequately meet their needs either. The large presence of children and poor or working-class families on Eighteenth Street meant that social services were crucial to their survival. Mexican children and their families accessed institutions that maintained a European American leadership and personnel and thus lacked bilingual staff or culturally sensitive programming. Churches catered to European American parishioners, social service agencies that had long served European immigrants retained European or Anglicized names, and the directors, staff, and clergy of those organizations were largely white. Because the numbers of white families had declined dramatically by the 1960s, programming and investments in such institutions had dwindled. With the neighborhood now increasingly Mexican, activists began calling for leadership that would be more attentive to their needs and investment in the future of younger generations. They began gravitating to the language of Chicanismo and politicizing themselves to demand social service reform, resources, and cultural autonomy.

While the Southwest represented the center of Chicano nationalism, the movement—especially the struggle of farmworkers—began reaching Chicago's Mexican American youth and penetrating *barrio* streets. The Chicano movement offered a way to make sense of the community's dire socioeconomic conditions and to empower the community and gain socioeconomic equality. The movement allowed Mexican Americans to express cultural pride rather than shame over their ethnoracial origins and provided an alternative to the compulsory assimilation that Mexican Americans were expected to pursue. One sociologist in Pilsen explained, "Chicanismo symbolizes the Mexican American desire to be neither black, nor Anglo, nor 'deprived'; but to be themselves."[60] Many local residents, some of whom had been participating in various community efforts already, seized the discourse of Chicanismo to propel their activism further. The ALAS meeting in the spring of 1969, along with a Latino/a student walkout at Harrison High School the previous fall, marked a wave of increased community activism and protest. Mexican women and men of Eighteenth Street began to participate in social service agencies, form community-based initiatives, and organize meetings to address their concerns. University and community college students, armed with theories about self-determination, leftist critiques of the American government, and newfound awareness of racial oppression and class struggle, mobilized themselves and other community members into various projects. The Chicano movement provided Mexican American youth in Pilsen an alternative script that empowered them to begin visualizing a different future for themselves and their community.

Mexican American activists elaborated a capacious political identity as "Chicanos" that included *Tejanos* and recent undocumented immigrants. Their inclusiveness points to a common experience and identity they believed they shared with people of varying immigration statuses and histories in the United States. Mexicans saw themselves racialized in similar ways regardless of their citizenship status, tenure in Chicago, or how far back their immigrant roots originated. The racially tinged element of white people's discomfort with demographic changes in the neighborhood rarely distinguished between recent immigrants and second- or third-generation Mexican Americans. As one researcher explained in the midseventies, Chicanos of Eighteenth Street "are well aware that they are still not regarded as social equals to Anglos."[61]

Eighteenth Street became the physical center of the local Chicano movement.[62] Yet the local Chicano movement was multivalent, multilayered, and heterogeneous. While certainly not all Mexican Americans who participated in community efforts embraced the tenets of Chicanismo or viewed themselves as part of a movement, the movement's energy was inspirational, and it gave local activists tremendous momentum. It provided the vocabulary for a cultural orientation that many activists were beginning to espouse. It offered a language for protest politics and a basis upon which to transform local institutions.

Howell House, the main social service agency in the neighborhood, soon became a target for such change. Operated by the Presbyterian Neighborhood Service Organization (NSO), it was one of the city's many settlement houses established at the turn of the twentieth century to work with European immigrants.[63] In the late sixties, Howell House had a large hall and served as a central location for community meetings. Residents gathered there to discuss pressing neighborhood concerns, such as planning school boycotts, facilitating gang truces, staging fund-raising dances, and other events. The group ALAS used Howell as its meeting place and pushed for change within the agency as well. Noting that Howell House's board of directors was composed entirely of people who lived outside the neighborhood, ALAS urged the hiring of a Mexican American director.[64] Howell began hiring Mexican American staff members to do "street work" with young men in local gangs. Felipe "Phil" Ayala and Juan "John" Velásquez were two such young men in their early twenties who were assigned to a nearby outpost building called Bethlehem Center, whose facilities were severely deteriorated and in disrepair. In 1968, shortly after Ayala and Velásquez's work had begun, Bethlehem Center's roof collapsed under the weight of that winter's snow, forcing programs to relocate to the basement of Howell House. When a fire broke out in the building, the relocated Mexican staff in the basement were nearly forgotten in the evacuation. The dilapidated condition of their initial outpost and their neglect at Howell House hinted at the place and priority that Mexicans held in the neighborhood's social service structure.[65]

Quite a few activists identify Rodolfo "Corky" Gonzáles's Chicano Youth Liberation Conference, held in Denver, Colorado, in March of 1969, as a pivotal moment in the history of local community activism and protest. The city's *barrios* sent two busloads and many cars of young people to Denver for the Crusade for Justice meeting that spring. Altogether approximately two hundred people from Chicago attended the conference, including not only Mexican Americans but also Puerto Ricans, such as José "Cha Cha" Jiménez and a contingent of his Young Lords Organization.[66] The Chicano Youth Liberation Conference represented a turning point for many Mexican American youths. Many returned to the *barrio* inspired by the sight of so many other proud Chicano youths and infused with radical ideas and a new action-oriented approach to social change. The nationalist and largely masculinist rhetoric of "Corky" Gonzáles and the Chicano movement incited many young activists to a politics of liberation and a reassessment of Mexicans as an oppressed colonized group. A sizable delegation of street gang members from Eighteenth Street returned from the conference determined to change their community.[67]

The appeal of cultural nationalism specifically to young male members of street clubs or gangs made sense, for as historian Ramón Gutiérrez has pointed out, the Chicano movement was, among other things, about reclaiming a dignified masculinity for Chicano men. By embracing a Chicano identity, nationalism, and indigenous pride in their Aztec ancestors, "Young Chicano men, a largely powerless group, invested themselves with images of power . . . a gendered vision that rarely extend[ed] to women."[68] As young men already invested in a masculine, territorial identity, Eighteenth Street gangs embraced the promise of cultural nationalism. They began turning their energies to community empowerment, forming a chapter of the Brown Berets to that end. They began working toward uniting the neighborhood's gangs and called for an end to internecine violence. Grabbing onto the growing Community Health movement, they opened a free clinic, the Benito Juarez Health Clinic, within Howell House in the spring of 1970.[69]

The Mexican community had by then secured a new Mexican American director for Howell House, Art Vázquez, who had a background in social work and a history of social activism on the city's North Side.[70] Brown Berets soon spearheaded the effort to rename Howell House Casa Aztlán. The reclaiming of many local institutions in the name of Pilsen's Mexican residents was accompanied by a mural movement initiated by local artists and inspired by the great muralist tradition of Mexico. Marcos Raya, Ray Patlán, Aurelio Diaz, and other local artists began embellishing neighborhood walls and buildings with murals composed of symbols of the Chicano movement, Aztec imagery, and Mexican national heroes (fig. 25). Young people on Eighteenth Street had embraced a decidedly new cultural politics.[71]

Yet the terms on which Chicano activism unfolded in the city differed from those of the Southwest. Chicago's activism emerged in a city with a powerful political machine that controlled much of the federal social welfare funds that poured into the city, racially shifting neighborhoods, and coalitions with other Latin Americans—namely, Puerto Ricans.[72] Unlike in the Southwest, where Mexicans had a much longer history and greater presence, Mexicans in Chicago were not a colonized population on ancestral lands; they were immigrants like so many others in the past. Yet the ideals of the Chicano movement still resonated with many. Chicago's Chicano movement included many of the same demands for self-determination

Figure 25. Mex-Sal Hardware, at Eighteenth and May Streets, representative of
the neighborhood change by the mid-1970s. Note the Mexican-style mural on the
side of the building. ICHi-64809, Chicago History Museum.

and community autonomy as in the Southwest—protests against local
power structures, school walkouts and boycotts, demands for social services, sit-ins on college campuses, a reclaiming of Chicano masculinity,
and varying manifestations of nationalism and class consciousness, as well
as heated debates about gender oppression and the role of women in the
movement.

Cultural nationalism in the neighborhood was also tempered by an important reality—the presence of a number of liberal white academics, some
of whom lent their skills and labor to local activist efforts. Various graduate
students and social scientists who worked in the city's universities lived and
increasingly took an interest in the growing Mexican *barrio*. They had come
to study the community's social structure as ethnographers and participant
observers in local community centers and organizations. Some involved
themselves only minimally in local activism, but others demonstrated a
greater commitment, offering their grant-writing, research, and communications skills and knowledge. Their participation proved controversial for
the most ardent nationalists, who saw middle-class, white graduate students and professionals as illegitimate members of community organiza-

tions. Still others insisted on making such research relationships reciprocal: researchers could study "the natives" to advance their academic careers, but they would also have to produce results that would benefit local residents and help achieve community goals.[73]

The relationship between Chicano activists and white participants in community health initiatives offered one such model. The Eighteenth Street community benefited from expanding federal, state, and private funding for social service programs during these years that offered possibilities for community-based initiatives. Local activists soon started tapping into those resources, often with the help of liberal white professionals. In 1967, the Illinois State Psychiatric Institute (ISPI) initiated a Community Mental Health Program in Pilsen. The project was part of a growing interest in providing community health services (including mental health) to low-income urban and rural populations and was funded by a large grant from the National Institutes of Mental Health. Two years after creating the program, ISPI dispatched anthropologist Steve Schensul and several research assistants to study the neighborhood and figure out how to better attract people to mental health services. The top-down approach did not work, however, and Schensul soon discovered that the program would flourish if it emerged more organically. He concluded that he had to connect with local activists and community workers in order to truly understand residents and their needs. Schensul immediately tapped into a Howell House block club project and started working with Phil Ayala and John Velásquez. The group operated in teams in the blocks surrounding Howell House, surveying residents about their needs and concerns. This established a pattern on Eighteenth Street of cooperation between social service activists and academic researchers. For applied "action" researchers like Schensul, this model made a great deal of sense: outsiders would gain the trust, confidence, and cooperation of local residents, and they would be able to research and meet their needs most effectively, only if they worked in conjunction with grassroots initiatives and concerns.[74] Their participation was especially felt at a new community center that local activists began organizing, El Centro de la Causa.

Creating El Centro de la Causa

The wave of ethnic pride and community empowerment among Mexican Americans inspired local young people to claim the neighborhood's meager resources and European American institutions as a way of asserting their belonging in the neighborhood. They also sought to build value in their community and attract greater resources. The physical and demographic changes in the neighborhood over the past two decades made this possible. During the late 1950s, the construction of the South (later renamed the Dan Ryan) Expressway displaced hundreds of white residents on Pilsen's East End. The Catholic parish and grammar school, St. Joseph's, felt the greatest impact. St. Joe's, as it was known, had served a Slovakian immigrant population for over five decades. It lost much of its congregation to the expressway construction and out-migration to the suburbs.[75] By 1968, St. Joe's had ceased to exist as a parish. The few remaining white ethnic residents in the area no longer had school-age children, and, thus, the school closed as well.

In 1970, Howell House / Casa Aztlán youth workers John Velásquez and Phil Ayala learned of the vacant school and church buildings from Father John Harrington of the Providence of God parish two blocks away. He suggested that the buildings could possibly be reopened and used by the neighborhood.[76] The two young men decided to trespass into the locked school building and look around. The school facilities included classrooms and a large gymnasium that could be put to use by local street gangs as a recreational center and a neutral meeting place. After inspecting the facilities, Ayala and Velásquez eagerly returned to Father Harrington and announced, "Well, we're gonna move in today!" Harrington then helped them contact the Chicago Archdiocese about opening the abandoned school as a youth center. Before they had even obtained permission to lease the space, they began using the building to play basketball with neighborhood teens. They soon enlisted the support of various male community leaders through their social networks and recruited a cadre of volunteers. After a meeting with the monsignor in which they proposed their vision for the youth center, the monsignor granted them two paid staff positions.[77]

John Velásquez was the first staff person on the payroll. By the fall of 1971, when he started working at St. Joe's, he offered the second paid position, a part-time receptionist job, to a neighborhood high school student, María Ovalle. Velásquez knew Ovalle from Casa Aztlán, where she had worked the summer before her senior year. Ovalle attended the all-girls Richards Vocational School a few miles away, where she had learned some typing skills. Ovalle recalls, "I already had a part-time job, but I kinda needed the money. So I agreed to work there . . . for my senior year in high school. . . . When I started working there, I was his [John's] first employee." Others worked at the center on a volunteer basis. Ovalle worked evenings after school, when Velásquez and volunteers had begun a recreational program for neighborhood boys and young men. She filled many roles as the part-time receptionist. "[I] was the secretary, janitor, receptionist. [I] would do [lots of] things," Ovalle recalls.[78]

In November of 1971, the building officially opened as El Centro de la Causa, the Latin American Youth Center, Inc.[79] The selection of the center's name proved controversial. Phil Ayala explained that at a meeting held to choose the name, more moderate and older members of the community, such as physician Dr. Jorge Prieto and Judge David Cerda, supported the name "Latin American Youth Center." "The more radical side [of the group] . . . came up with *El Centro de la Causa,*" according to Ayala. Young men who had embraced Chicano nationalism ardently called for a name in Spanish that would reflect the politicized posture of many community youth. The tensions over naming the center represented a fracturing along both generational and political lines. Because state law at the time did not allow incorporation under a non-English name, the group compromised by adopting both names—the Spanish one to appease the younger radicals, and the English version to satisfy state incorporation laws and moderate middle-class sponsors.[80] El Centro began as a youth center, focusing on recreational and athletic programs aimed at gang violence prevention. Velásquez began hiring street workers to reach youth and draw them into the facility. This chapter's epigraph, taken from a fund-raising press release from the early 1970s, explained El Centro's founding. It aimed to empower local Mexican residents and provide opportunities for youth.

Unlike in the Southwest, where Chicanas/os were more recognizable as a racial minority, Mexican Americans in Chicago had struggled to gain visibility for decades. They had to make a case for why they qualified for federal entitlement programs aimed at remedying social inequalities. Machine-regulated War on Poverty funds that managed to trickle into local communities went primarily to African Americans, thereby earning political loyalty from the black submachine. Mexicans had no political representation within the local power structure. Without elected or appointed leaders in city hall, on the city council, or even at the ward or precinct level, they had little hope of making local officials responsive to their needs. As Mexican Americans became more visible nationally during the Lyndon B. Johnson administration, this opened up possibilities for Mexicans to demand greater attention locally. The expansion of federal and state funds provided an alternate route to resources and political power. Pilsen's activists began fighting for their share of federal and state monies to fund community-controlled service programs. They applied for grants to address drug abuse, day care, English as a Second Language instruction, and mental health.[81]

El Centro succeeded in bypassing the traditional patronage political system and establishing *community-controlled* projects to a certain extent. Staff soon began applying for funding for various projects. In the fall of 1971, Centro directors learned that ISPI's Community Mental Health Program sought to develop a program to train more bilingual, bicultural paraprofessionals. ISPI initially planned to hold classes and training at its offices, but activists insisted on hosting the program in the neighborhood at El Centro and having more control over the initiative. The center's staff and ISPI researchers wrote the grant application to the New Careers Division of the National Institutes of Mental Health (NIMH). Their proposal cited the lack of Spanish-speaking counselors, social workers, and other staff in neighborhood agencies. They named the program the "Chicano Mental Health Training Program (CMHTP)" and described its purpose as being "to train community people to become bilingual bicultural paraprofessionals in the ever broadening field of mental health."[82] CMHTP received funding in July 1972. El Centro recruited Mexican American instructors from among local university faculty and graduate students, and social service professionals. They developed a culturally sensitive curriculum on topics such as child psychology, *machismo*, marriage, and menopause, among others. CMHTP's director, Phil Ayala, negotiated to have students receive college credit through Malcolm X Community College, a branch of the City Colleges of Chicago.[83] Over two dozen neighborhood residents enrolled in the courses. Classes were conducted at El Centro, and students completed internships in local mental health or social service agencies. Within four years, the program had successfully trained forty-eight students, thirty-eight of whom received associate's degrees, and fifteen who continued on to bachelor's degrees. The program placed a total of twenty students in mental health service positions and fifteen in other human service jobs.[84]

The Central YMCA Community College, a two-year college operated by the YMCA, provided a Talent Search Program grant for one of El Centro's first programs, Project Quetzalcoatl. Funded in 1972, the program sought to encourage students to graduate from high school and pursue higher education. Program staff visited local high schools to talk to students. In less than a year, the program had fifty-six students enrolled in college and twenty-one in GED classes.[85] María Ovalle, El Centro's receptionist, represented one of the program's success stories. After graduating from high school in the spring of 1972, she worked at the center on a full-time basis and began attending the Central "Y" College. When a recruiter from the University of Illinois at Urbana-Champaign inquired at El Centro about potential students for its minority recruitment program, a staff member recommended her. Ovalle had graduated first in her class of 140 girls at Richards Vocational High School, but remarkably, no one had suggested she attend college. "You would have thought that the counselors would have encouraged me a little bit more to go to college, but they didn't," she remembers. Her involvement at El Centro opened up the opportunity to continue her education. The first in her family to go to college, Ovalle was one of very few Latinas to attend the state's flagship public university in the early 1970s.[86]

Two years after opening, El Centro won a $75,000 grant for a demonstration project it called Servicios Sociales del Barrio (Neighborhood Social Services). The program provided social services for families and youth, largely in the form of casework, and included a research component that sought to identify needs and services that were not being met in the community. Area residents came to the center with varying problems, and staff referred them to the appropriate agencies. Men often came in with legal and criminal matters, disputes with creditors, or seeking employment. Women, most of them mothers, sought emergency food, help with applications for public assistance, and legal assistance with family matters.[87] A group of men in the neighborhood also obtained funding to initiate a drug rehabilitation program they called BASTA—Brotherhood against Slavery to Addiction. They operated a methadone clinic for heroin addicts in El Centro's basement. Some nearby residents objected to the clinic, fearing the drug users it attracted, but Centro staff managed to defuse tensions and kept the program running for several years.[88]

El Centro established a community library as well. The neighborhood had long been without a public library, and while many had petitioned the city to open one in the area, activists finally saw an opportunity to develop their own community-controlled space. Their community-focused, Chicano-centric philosophy was evident in the mission statement:

> Library service in America traditionally has been aimed at the white, middle-class majority, maintaining and reflecting their ideologies, at the expense and exclusion of minority communities. El Centro de la Causa Library is an experiment in breaking with that tradition.
>
> Our library hopes to reflect the culture and language of the people in our community. [It will have] a bilingual, bicultural staff, and [provide] special materials keyed to the needs and tastes of the Latino people.

Our primary goals are to supply the community with the information it needs to survive within a hostile environment, and to improve self-concepts by raising the level of consciousness about ourselves and our culture.[89]

The library represented a concern for the epistemological and pedagogical needs of the community. El Centro not only wanted to provide social services to neighborhood people but also sought to instill a sense of history, self-knowledge, and community pride.

Research and grant writing comprised important activities at El Centro as well. White and Latino/a students and researchers from the University of Illinois Circle Campus volunteered their time and shared their skills to train other volunteers on how to conduct surveys, for example. Researchers studied everything from the efficacy of staff communications to the effectiveness of programs and community needs for services.[90] One graduate student in anthropology, Gwen Stern, was instrumental in writing a successful grant for Dar a Luz (Childbirth), a prenatal-care program for local women.

In addition to its own programs, El Centro provided office space for other community initiatives. In April 1973, the Latin American Task Force rented space within the building to work on the issue of "discrimination, prejudice, and exclusion against Spanish speaking Citizens in employment." The organization, a coalition of over fifty groups, included the Latin American Constructors, which sought to expand education and training for Mexicans in the construction trades. The task force monitored general contractors and subcontractors on their hiring of Spanish-speaking workers. It also provided training for Spanish-speaking workers and tradesmen on how to become contractors. It offered instruction on licensing requirements, the availability of jobs and bidding, and resources for obtaining construction loans and insurance.[91]

The establishment of El Centro de la Causa represented a significant achievement for Eighteenth Street's Mexican American community. It provided a physical space for programs and community meetings to supplement Casa Aztlán, which was always in demand. It also operated as a site for social functions—quinceañeras, wedding parties, fund-raising dances. Its social service programs provided sustenance for many families who were ill served by government human service agencies and who found at El Centro culturally competent and sensitive providers. In a short span of years, activists had succeeded in attracting substantial resources to serve the local population. They had made their mark on Eighteenth Street and had transformed it literally and figuratively into *"La Dieciocho."*

Figure 26. Original caption reads, "Changing Neighborhood. This corner was once the center of the old Bohemian neighborhood." J. J. Strnad Real Estate, at 1801 S. Blue Island Avenue, advertises in Spanish: "Houses for sale, one thousand dollars down payment," 1961. ICHi-51411, Chicago History Museum.

Conclusion

Eighteenth Street underwent tremendous social change within just a few years. It became home to second- and third-generation Mexican Americans, *Tejano* migrants, and recent immigrants, many of whom were undocumented. The neighborhood's diversity in large part contributed to tense social relations with white residents, who shaped their own understandings of Mexicans' "race." This identity was made and remade daily in encounters with white residents, African Americans, and one another. Over time, the accretion of such encounters instilled in Mexican Americans a stronger sense of who they were. Although this varied from one individual to the next, most Mexicans did not have the same type of "ethnic options" that European Americans historically had—the choice of assimilating into the dominant white population and choosing when and where (or whether) to accentuate one's cultural distinctiveness.[92] To a certain extent, Mexican people's experiences depended largely on their appearance and skin color, and how these were interpreted by observers—whether or not they were "black Mexicans," as some called them, or otherwise physically distinctive. Mexicans had been marked over decades as "foreign" and nonwhite regardless of their generation in the United States, and this impulse seemed to overpower the competing idea that they could in fact assimilate and become "white." Moreover, the ongoing migration of people from Mexico throughout the 1960s and 1970s ensured that Mexican Americans continued to have these racializing moments. They occurred whenever Mexican immigrants were rounded up by officials in immigration raids.[93] Recent immigrants, especially the undocumented, underscored Mexican distinctiveness and brought it into relief each time they appeared in the public eye. Their criminalized status marked Mexican people as illegitimate members of US society. Mexican Americans could certainly distance themselves from these judgments, brandishing their US citizenship, English-language skills, or US birthplace, but most were aware that they were somehow implicated in the racial ascriptions assigned to the recently arrived.[94]

Thus, most activists embraced a broader racial identity in a shared transnational formation (a "nation" that crossed borders), a "race" of indigenous people—the bronze race. The Chicano movement provided this alternative model of identity for Mexican Americans, a rejection of the pressure to assimilate. It allowed Mexican-origin people to proudly claim their heritage and ancestry, thereby challenging the expected social formation that European immigrants followed. The movement called for, as Lorrin Thomas similarly notes in the case of Puerto Ricans, "an acknowledgment of and respect for a distinctive group identity within the surrounding society." Not all people of Mexican descent embraced such a position, and conflicts over identity, assimilation, nationalism, and cultural distinctiveness played out in the neighborhood's public sphere. Still, regardless of its political scope or social content, activism became a visible feature of Chicago's Mexican community in the late 1960s and early 1970s.

The neighborhood's continuing physical deterioration, the poverty of its residents, its increasing crowdedness, and its political and economic marginalization made it in the view of most outsiders a Mexican ghetto. Yet activists made remarkable efforts to resist and reverse these conditions. Casa Aztlán and El Centro de la Causa represent but two efforts in Chicago's Eighteenth Street neighborhood that focused specifically on social service reform. Other segments of the Eighteenth Street community provided much more strident social critiques and proposed leftist political formations that more radically challenged the existing liberal democratic structure. Casa Aztlán and El Centro de la Causa became important community spaces for Mexican residents—meeting spaces for political causes, social venues for community celebrations, and providers of social services. As many residents remember, these years were truly a remarkable time in the history of the community. One woman recalled, "There were community meetings every night. *Every night* we'd be at one meeting after another. There was always something going on." People mobilized around anything and everything that concerned the Mexican population, from the need for more parks to support for the UFW grape boycott or protesting the firing of Chicana schoolteachers.[95]

The fruits of activists' labor marked Eighteenth Street as a Mexican *barrio*—*La Dieciocho*—for the next two decades. Inasmuch as centers such as Casa Aztlán and El Centro de la Causa became important spaces for cultivating a Chicano community, however, their gendered limits became increasingly visible to some. Women who had been affiliated with El Centro in particular began to identify how they might better meet the needs of Mexican American women and girls in the *barrio*. They started to argue that "the community" would never be empowered and liberated if women and girls remained oppressed. Their story is the focus of the final chapter.

SEVEN

The Limits of Nationalism: Women's Activism and the Founding of Mujeres Latinas en Acción

Given the problems that exist in the neighborhood, especially related to women, we feel that one badly needed service is simply a facility, a place where women can freely go, seek advice, have their needs served and interact [with one another].[1]

—Mujeres Latinas en Acción, *April 1974*

Mexican American youth gravitated toward the newly built community centers—Casa Aztlán and El Centro de la Causa—filled with the fervor of cultural nationalism, self-determination, and ethnic pride. They rejected their own marginalization and asserted their right and claim to their community. Yet not all participated in the newfound campaign for empowerment equally. While the activism of male participants in the Chicano movement and the nearby Young Lords Organization has secured a larger place in Chicago's historical memory, the activism of working-class Latina women has received less attention. On Eighteenth Street, Mexican women in particular participated in many community efforts.[2] Some had become involved in local church service projects. Others worked with the Pilsen Neighbors Community Council and with ALAS (Alianza Latino-Americana para el Adelanto Social). Women fought for equitable learning opportunities for their children in aging public schools, and led the campaign for bilingual education and for the creation of a new high school in the Eighteenth Street community. One group of mothers spearheaded the drive for a desperately needed day-care center in the *barrio*, and created El Hogar del Niño (The Child's Home) in 1972. Women worked in labor organizations and leftist groups that defended undocumented workers' rights. They became activists at local universities, addressing issues ranging from Latina/o recruitment in higher education to solidarity with Latin American political struggles. With few exceptions, women's roles were often limited to committee work and other auxiliary positions. Women rarely represented the community in public forums, and they certainly did not have a platform to address "women's issues." Most male activists had drawn on nationalist and race-based rhetoric to persuade Mexican American women that racial (and in some cases class) oppression was their primary concern and once racial and economic justice was achieved, all else would fall into place. Though men promoted their own gender-specific concerns—police brutality, gang violence, men's employment discrimination—as universal ones, women's concerns seemed peripheral to the greater cause. Moreover, like the Chicano movement in the Southwest, the Black Power movement, and other radical, nationalist, and leftist social movements, "the woman question" stirred controversy, with women and men holding varying opinions about the role of women within the movement.[3]

This emerged as a topic of discussion at a workshop at Howell House / Casa Aztlán in May 1970. In a community meeting, several residents and students began raising questions about women's participation in community activism. One person noted that only male speakers had made presentations at the workshop. Others suggested that the audience should be divided into smaller working groups along gender lines. Some disagreed with this idea. One unidentified male college student astutely pointed out how women were silenced in the community. He noted, "I always hear [ALAS President] Juan Morales talk at meetings but I never know what his wife has to say." He added, moreover, that "some women want to get involved but their husbands will not let them."[4] Indeed, many women attended meetings and volunteered their labor, yet their voices and interests were often missing from the agenda. Still others did not participate at all because of patriarchal restrictions on their presence in public spaces. This was the context of women's community activism on Eighteenth Street and the environment that led to the rise of Mujeres Latinas en Acción (MLEA).

Chicana writers, artists, and activists have long described their struggle against patriarchy within Mexican American communities and the sexism of nationalist/leftist radical movements both in poetry and in prose.[5] Yet we know little about such women in midwestern cities like Chicago. Mexican-origin women in the urban north empowered themselves and became agents of social change in ways that have not been well documented. As members of racialized communities and as individuals who knew the multiple dimensions of gendered inequality and the intersectionality of race and class, they mobilized around issues that were being overlooked both by the broader nationalist Chicano movement and by mainstream white feminist movements.[6]

Amid the flurry of Chicano social activism on Eighteenth Street, a small group of Mexican American women began recognizing that most community work largely excluded the needs of women and girls. They sought to redress this by creating a women's and family social service agency to address women's long-neglected concerns. Mujeres Latinas en Acción started by addressing employment training, education, reproductive health, and family relations.[7] Recognizing that racial discrimination was not the only factor that shaped Mexican women's experiences, they highlighted how gender shaped women's lives differently from those of men. Their feminist activism emerged in relation to mainstream middle-class white feminism and Chicano community activism.

MLEA traversed three potential minefields in the neighborhood—religious, generational, and cultural conventions. In a heterogeneous Mexican American community composed of US-born Mexican Americans, recent Mexican immigrants, and *Tejano/a* migrants, the Mexican American / Chicana activists involved with Mujeres encountered resistance to their work from Mexican immigrant men, Chicano nationalists, loyalist women, and religious sectors (primarily the Catholic Church). Female activists engaged in gynocentric work had to carefully negotiate the boundaries and expectations of their community.[8] Despite the assumption that ethnic or racial communities are homogeneous, and despite even some members asserting as much, the tensions and conflicts over issues that Mujeres Latinas en Acción raised revealed the "striations within" the Mexican community.[9]

The impoverished conditions of the Pilsen *barrio* that residents endured on a daily basis prompted some women to work for change. The community faced severe inequalities—"poor medical care, lack of garbage pickup, poor press, poor schools, lack of political clout, and minimal recreational facilities," in addition to dangerous housing conditions and employment discrimination, among other issues.[10] Mexican women played a critical role in the activist circles of Eighteenth Street, providing significant labor in a variety of areas. They mobilized around education, health, and social service needs, often as mothers and homemakers concerned about the well-being of their children. Women were central, for example, in the struggles against unresponsive and hostile school administrators and teachers who treated Mexican children with disdain. They marched to the board of education to fight for bilingual instruction, better teachers, and improved facilities. They fought for a much-needed high school in the community. Indeed, women have been noted as the moving force behind activism in the community. According to one magazine, "The most potent fuel in all the organizing drives [in Pilsen] . . . has been Pilsen's mothers."[11] Yet while they engaged in various community campaigns, few held leadership roles or served as spokespersons for the community.

Instead, women encountered traditional gender norms and divisions of labor within their own families that restricted their engagement outside the home. As a result, women participants in community activism often challenged generational and cultural conventions that limited first-generation immigrant women, in particular, to the household. Inez Loredo, one of Pilsen's mothers who fought for a new high school, recalled, "It was a difficult battle because the fathers would be at home angry [while] the mothers were in the street fighting for the [high school] building." She continued, "That was the most difficult thing, going outside the home. These women had never been involved with issues like these." In a traditional, patriarchal environment, many men objected to women's participation in community activism and insisted they devote themselves to their duties within the home. While some women argued that their obligations as wives and mothers required them to attend school meetings to demand bilingual education, or community gatherings to improve neighborhood sidewalks, some men (and women) maintained that women's sphere of influence should be confined *within* the household.[12]

Sexism, patriarchy, and proverbial "*machismo*" were not limited to the Mexican community, however, nor were they the reserve of Mexican men.[13] Activist women worked within and against a sexist, patriarchal, and male-dominated political structure in the city as a whole. Elected officials were predominantly male; women had few advocates in the halls of power; and working-class women in particular had not experienced the liberation that middle-class white women were beginning to achieve in their personal and professional lives. Thus, at times, Pilsen's mothers learned to carefully use sexism and patriarchy to their advantage. Lucy Gutiérrez remembers how mothers used their moral purchase when picketing board of education offices during the cold winter, often with small children in tow. She recalled, "One time I saw the alderman [during a picket] and I asked him, 'Do you think it is just that these women are out with their children in this cold, without a thing to eat?' Right then and there he gave me a check for $50 for the women."[14] At times, women manipulated patriarchal attitudes to their own advantage to gain sympathy for their plight and to further their goals.

Yet such strategies worked only when women operated within traditional roles as housewives and mothers, caregivers for others. While mothers and housewives could claim their moral authority to fight on behalf of their children and families, younger women, those who were unmarried, single mothers, or those without children, and more radical activists received criticism from conservative sectors of the community for asserting themselves publicly and especially for demanding rights. They invited particular criticism for pressing issues that related specifically to women or that would foster women's independence—women's legal rights, employment training, or reproductive control. Moreover, women rarely had the opportunity to discuss "women's" issues. For all their activism, women were not recognized as a distinct group within the *barrio* with their own specific needs. As Virginia Espino has noted about the Chicano movement, "Most male organizations viewed women's concerns in relation to their own ability to provide and protect them rather than seeing Chicanas as a viable constituency with concerns and demands of their own."[15] During the early 1970s, however, a group of progressive women claimed that ideological public space—the space in which to specifically address Chicana and Latina issues, develop women's leadership, and become visible members of their community. They also claimed material resources to improve poor women's lives.

A Woman's Place: Creating Mujeres Latinas en Acción

The significant achievement Chicano/a activists had realized in the establishment of El Centro de la Causa made an important contribution to the provision of social services and youth intervention in the Eighteenth Street neighborhood. For the first time, the Mexican community had a place that Mexicans had established themselves; the center was funded by the archdiocese and federal grants; it was a relatively autonomous social service and community center. Although, in theory, El Centro aimed to serve the community as a whole, it reflected traditional gender norms and a conservative division of labor in both its operations and its programming. The center's leadership was all male. In 1975, the agency listed Phil Ayala as director of the Chicano Mental Health Training Program (CMHTP), Humberto Pérez as director of the Right-to-Read Program, and Juan Velásquez as director of the Youth Services component.[16] Women did not hold any directorships within El Centro. Instead, they worked and volunteered in traditionally female areas—in teaching positions and as counselors, research assistants, and clerical staff. Laura Paz, for example, taught English and GED classes in the Right-to-Read Program; Elva Rios was a caseworker for Servicios Sociales; María Heinz and María (Alvarado) Capoccia were research assistants for the Chicano Mental Health Training Program; and María Ovalle served as the center's receptionist. The Education Department included other female staff, such as Isaura González, Silvia Schneirov, Pat Tarin, Cristina Vital, and Jessica Valencia.[17] Memos regarding secretarial training reflected this gendered and hierarchical division of labor. Researcher Mary Baszysz wrote to the all-male director staff in September of 1972, "At the request of several program directors, I will be conducting a secretarial training and brush-up class. . . . I hope you will allow your girl to attend each meeting regardless of how busy she may be at the time."[18] Certainly, such gender dynamics prevailed in most corporate and public sector settings at the time. But the women's movement and feminist activists had begun questioning such divisions of labor and raising awareness about women's subordination in the workplace and society more generally. Leonard Ramirez, who was himself a staff member at El Centro, observes that "Chicanas [began] criticiz[ing] *El Movimiento* for the limitations imposed on their participation. Women argued for broader inclusion, questioned expectations that they play limited roles at home, in the community and particularly in the process of social change. They urged the inclusion of gender related issues in order to broaden and strengthen the transformative agenda."[19]

Community women accessed El Centro in greater numbers as it diversified its services. Women used the Servicios Sociales program, and several participated in CMHTP, for example. The Youth Services department, however, which had an all-male staff, devoted itself almost exclusively to recreational activities for young men in local gangs. One program director acknowledged this at a board meeting, saying, "We are also neglecting the girls. They [girls] have stated to us that they have never been involved with male peers." Male staff members realized that in addition to young men, there were girls on the streets who needed services.[20] Despite such omissions and oversights, women volunteers and staff remained committed to the center and the goals of community empowerment. It became increasingly clear to some, however, that they did not have a place within the agency's vision or policy-making. One female staff member who realized this, María (Heinz) Mangual, began to sow the seeds for a women's organization, and provided much of its early leadership.

Born in El Paso, Texas, María Mangual first came to Eighteenth Street in 1971. She quickly connected with Pilsen activists and began volunteering at El Centro when it first started operating. Within months of El Centro's opening, she realized that the center's programs focused specifically on young men and on athletics. "I was looking around, and I realized that unless you were a jock, unless you were a kid involved in sports, there was nothing there for you," she explained. So she proposed an after-school program to help children with homework and to teach arts and crafts. She would volunteer her time and bring her own supplies. She met resistance from El Centro's directors at first but soon had a number of children who sought out the program daily.[21]

Mangual was a student at the University of Illinois Circle Campus, majoring in elementary education. Circle Campus was a hotbed of leftist and radical politics during these years, and Mangual encountered women's groups while a student there. She did not see the relevance of the issues and activities that they promoted, however, especially in relation to the *barrio*'s day-to-day realities. For Mangual, her experience at El Centro and in the Mexican community exposed her regularly to gripping poverty and material inequities, and these shaped her community-centered sense of activism and empowerment.[22] She recalls one of her first experiences with a feminist student organization:

> I remember going to a feminist group on campus . . . maybe it was a workshop on "Our Bodies, Our Selves," I don't know what it was. Anyway, everybody [was] laying down with their legs open, looking at themselves with a mirror. And I thought, "Oh, please! There's so much more important stuff to do than to come together to look at yourself. Can't you do this on your own time?! We need to use the time that we have together *to do things*, not to be so—I thought—self-indulgent!"[23]

After attending several women's meetings on campus, Mangual decided they were not for her. "For me, the feminist movement really was very much about *self* instead of community," she explained. This echoed Chicano men's criticisms of middle-class white feminism. As Ramón Gutiérrez notes, one of the main tenets of the Chicano movement was a rejection of Anglo bourgeois individualism. Chicana feminists repeatedly noted how the white women's movement generally focused on individual sexual politics and women's self-actualization as "modern" subjects, a privilege long reserved for white men. Working-class Chicanas, however, interpreted women's liberation as also addressing racism, classism, and other forms of oppression that middle-class white women did not always recognize. Working-class Mexican American women approached women's rights quite differently than many white feminists, as exemplified by a Chicana Farah factory striker in the 1970s: "'I don't believe in burning our bras, but I do believe in having our rights."[24]

After a short time as the after-school program coordinator, Mangual was hired as a research assistant for El Centro's new Chicano Mental Health Training Program, designed to train community residents as bilingual mental health paraprofessionals.[25] María (Alvarado) Capoccia, another staff member, worked with her. In the course of their work, she and Mangual discovered various economic obstacles that often prevented neighborhood women from attending CMHTP classes. Women sometimes lacked bus fare to get to class. Some did not have child care or food at home for their young children. Mangual and Alvarado's roles as research assistants quickly evolved into that of counselors or social workers. The women in the program started to develop relationships with one another and with the two female staff members. Through their daily interactions, they began forming a small informal network of women. Mangual quickly began seeing the urgency of advocating for women's needs.[26]

El Centro's focus on young men and their needs vexed Mangual. She remembers thinking, "This is a good place if you['re] a youth, a male youth," but women were not being well served by El Centro's agenda. Mangual came up with the idea of organizing a volleyball game as a small effort to provide recreation for neighborhood women. As with the after-school program, she encountered resistance from the male leadership. The men revealed their very traditional gendered notions of recreation and leisure when they chortled, "Chicanas don't play volleyball!" Mangual persisted: "It's exercise! It's something to do other than hang out at the bars." She eventually succeeded in convincing the men to give her the gym for one night, and to their astonishment, about thirty or forty women came out to play. The men were genuinely surprised to see so many community women express an interest in recreation. The women soon formed their own volleyball league, which met one night a week. Asking men for use of the gym once a week, however, challenged their control over community space. Mangual remembers, "It [was] a very little thing, but it really became clear for me, it just brought out the fact that this was male-oriented, male-dominated; the resources . . . were being used by the men. . . . Women [we]re not really visible in this community."[27]

The struggle to gain visibility for women entailed not only claiming a place for them but also acknowledging them as legitimate members of the community with their own needs and concerns. Often relegated to the private or domestic sphere, women and girls did not get the attention that men and boys did through their presence in the public space of the neighborhood. Mujeres noted:

> The gang related activities of adolescent males make them highly visible and a target population for streetwork, recreational programs, drug prevention and other social services. As a consequence, adolescent girls tend to be overlooked, in spite of the fact that they are often peripherally involved in gang activities themselves. There is currently no streetwork or outreach directed toward young girls or women. Recreational programs emphasize male sports team[s].[28]

The drug abuse program, BASTA—Brotherhood against Slavery to Addiction—identified itself as male centered in its name. There was clear evidence, however, that teenage girls and women in the community also suffered from drug addiction and alcoholism, but no programs targeted them, and BASTA had only one female counselor. Agencies like El Centro and Casa Aztlán, and organizations like the Brown Berets, reflected masculinist and patriarchal societal values that ignored women and girls as active members of the community. When they did open their doors to women, various obstacles made access difficult. Mangual explained, for example, that local agencies such as the Pilsen Little Village Mental Health Center were simply not sensitive to women's needs. Although the center's director explained that services were available to *anyone*, he did not take into account women's roles as primary child-care providers and their need for child care in order to access service. "If women wanted counseling at the Mental Health Center, they had to come without their kids, or have their kids wait outside," she explains.[29]

For working-class women of color, community networks have often provided the basis for organizing. Indeed, El Centro's networks with other Latino groups throughout the Midwest facilitated contact with Mexican, Chicana, and Latina women elsewhere and provided the catalyst for the creation of a Mexican women's organization on Eighteenth Street.[30] In 1972, Olga Villa, the administrative assistant of the Midwest Council of La Raza (MWCLR) in South Bend, Indiana, planned and organized a conference along with several other midwestern Latinas. MWCLR had formed in 1970 at the University of Notre Dame's Urban Studies Institute. The organization hosted its first conference, entitled "Mi Raza Primero," in January of 1972 and focused on "a promotion of self-identity and political awareness." Out of this initial meeting, women formed their own caucus and developed the idea to organize and host their own conference.[31] The organizers, who called themselves *Las Mujeres de la Raza*, invited midwestern Latinas through MWCLR's contacts with Latino and Chicano community organizations throughout ten midwestern states. El Centro de la Causa received such an invitation, and director John Velásquez asked Mangual to attend as the agency's representative. Mangual attended the conference, entitled "Adelante Mujer" (Onward Woman), in June 1972, along with more than one hundred other women from throughout the Midwest. Chicana and Latina speakers came from Texas; Washington, DC; Michigan; and Illinois. During the conference, the participants established a board consisting of women from throughout the region. These board members were tasked with organizing conferences in their own states.[32] To her surprise, Mangual returned from the gathering elected as one of two delegates to represent Illinois.

Charged with organizing a conference for Latinas in Illinois, Mangual began planning at El Centro. The agency's directors, John Velásquez and Phil Ayala, gave her a great deal of support, allowing her to use the center's copy machine, typewriters, and supplies.[33] María Ovalle, a high schooler on staff at the time, remembers providing clerical assistance for the conference as well. Women from Eighteenth Street and the Puerto Rican community on the city's North Side helped with the planning. On June 9, 1973, El Centro hosted *"La Mujer Despierta*: Latina Women's Education Awareness Conference." Local Mexican artist Marcos Raya designed the cover of the program—a drawing of an indigenous woman with a raised fist. The program reflected a biethnic collaboration, incorporating both Mexican and Puerto Rican women as speakers: Graciela Olivárez, a Chicana lawyer from Albuquerque; Gloria Fontañez, from the Puerto Rican Revolutionary Workers Union in New York City; and Rosa Ortega, a Farah striker from El Paso, Texas.[34] La Raza Unida Party provided free day care for the event.[35] Participants chose from various workshops, such as "Women and the Law," "Women and Their Bodies," "Women and Employment," "Family Health," "Women and Education," and "Community Organizing." The program outlined four main goals:

1 To bring Latino women of varied backgrounds together to interact
2 To disseminate information to Latino women on existing programs and services
3 To serve as a consciousness-raising day after which women will be able to identify problems, plan strategies and begin to implement programs to deal with these problems

4 To make women more aware of their individuality and their potential to help themselves and their communities.[36]

Mangual emphasized that the conference focused on "leadership development and political leadership . . . trying to create awareness" among Latinas.[37] Yet these goals, especially the last two, were no small task.

Nonetheless, the event proved a resounding success. Nearly two hundred Mexican and Puerto Rican women from throughout the city attended.[38] The conference provided a forum to acknowledge and publicly address the needs and concerns of *barrio* women. Moreover, it emphasized a "community-centered consciousness," symbolized by the model of *La Nueva Chicana*, a conceptualization of womanhood that many Chicana activists in the movement were promoting.[39] One woman, so moved by the day's activities, stood up at the end of the conference and proclaimed, "This has been a great day. What we need now is a women's organization!" Thus, the women were charged with developing two women's organizations in Chicago, one on the North Side to serve Latinas there, and another in Pilsen to serve the city's South Side.[40]

Mangual coordinated a first meeting in Pilsen shortly after the conference. Through her contacts with women in the Chicano Mental Health Training Program, in the building where she lived, and among friends, a small group of women began meeting regularly at El Centro. Mangual remembers their early days: "There was a lot of time spent complaining about the men in the community, becoming sort of a feminist consciousness-raising group for a lot of us."[41] The group held bimonthly meetings attended regularly by approximately twenty-five active members—largely working-class, Mexican American, and in their twenties. Some were students at local community and four-year colleges, but most (for example, the women in CMHTP) had not completed high school, much less college.[42] A few progressive white women in the neighborhood—some of whom were graduate students—also participated, although some critics objected to their participation.

The women eventually defined as their goals: "to improve the lives of women in the Latino community of Pilsen through educational programs and social services, and to effect changes in the community to allow greater participation of Latinas in decisions made that affect the community."[43] As many of the women were affiliated with El Centro, their organizing emerged largely in response to the male orientation of the center. Mujeres was guided by an overall concern to provide space and resources where women could seek solutions to their varied problems. "Given the problems that exist in the neighborhood, especially related to women, we feel that one badly needed service is simply a facility, a place where women can freely go, seek advice, have their needs served and interact [with one another]," they explained.[44] Gwen Stern reflected years later, "I don't know if people really understand what a radical idea the notion of a women's organization was at that time." In some ways, Mujeres mirrored mainstream, white, feminist community activism, promoting women's spaces and resources to help women's "self-actualization." Yet they differed in their vision that such improvements would uplift a larger community that also experienced racial discrimination and economic marginalization.

Choosing a name for the women's group proved a challenge. As Mangual recalls, it took two "marathon meeting[s]" at which the women debated and argued over the name they should adopt. The group finally selected *Mujeres Latinas en Acción*, translated as "Latin Women in Action," for state incorporation purposes (MLEA, or Mujeres for short). Although women of Mexican descent constituted the overwhelming majority in the neighborhood, the group consciously chose to use the term *Latinas*, symbolizing a desire to be inclusive of other Spanish-speaking women. The inclusion of Puerto Rican women at "La Mujer Despierta" conference similarly reflected a consciousness of the need for panethnic alliances and for a vision of women that went beyond national boundaries.[45] Such awareness was common if not always practiced among Chicago and midwestern activists. Just as Chicago's Latino young men interpreted the Chicano Youth Liberation Conference's use of *La Raza* as a more inclusive term that included not only Chicanos but other oppressed Latin American people, Las Mujeres de la Raza and the Midwest Council of La Raza conceived of the term as including other Spanish-speaking or Spanish-origin groups also. In the Midwest, where Mexicans and Mexican Americans encountered Puerto Ricans, and increasingly in the early 1970s, other Latin American immigrants, embracing a panethnic identity seemed logical, and at times politically necessary. Activists could claim greater numbers as Latinos/as rather than simply as Mexicans or Puerto Ricans. In 1973, Mexican and Puerto Rican women in Chicago began using the gendered term *Latina* to denote not only panethnic affinities but solidarity based on gender as well.[46]

Even before it had obtained a physical space, the group established committees to address various issues—day care, health care, services for teenage girls, and legal assistance for women. MLEA's first activities included various workshops for women. It used space at a local bookstore, Librería Nuestro Continente (Our Continent Bookstore), and held twelve workshops ranging from women and drug abuse to women's legal rights. The group also began working actively with the founders of El Hogar del Niño day-care center to establish another day-care facility in the neighborhood. When MLEA realized it could not find a suitable building in the area that met strict day-care licensing requirements, it turned its attention to other issues.[47]

MLEA's affiliation with El Centro soon provided a solution to finding a space for meetings and programming. The property that El Centro leased from the archdiocese included a vacant rectory. In May 1974, El Centro's all-male board of directors agreed to offer the building for the women's activities, stating that "as long as they're functioning they will have the place." The abandoned building was no prize, however, as it served as a hangout for local heroin addicts. The women thus took on the arduous task of cleaning and rehabilitating the dilapidated building for occupancy. Gwen Stern recalls how much of their early organizing involved physical work. She explained, "We spent a lot of time scrubbing floors and trying to make places look nice." The women "put pictures on the walls, and folding chairs of every different color," Alicia Amador noted. Without any funding and only their own volunteer labor, the women began projects that required little start-up money—a food cooperative, a toy cooperative, and a children's book cooperative. They started teaching classes for women: an English class, a GED class, and nutrition and health workshops.[48]

Some men in the community supported the women's initiatives, but not everyone did. The Catholic Church, for example, was particularly suspicious of the group and not supportive of its goals and philosophy or its use of church buildings. The use of the rectory was contested too by a neighborhood gang that had also approached El Centro's directors for the space. Within a few short months after the women moved in, the building mysteriously burned down. Some suspected local gang members, who quite possibly were angry about losing a prime location for dealing drugs to the area's addicts.[49] This theory was never proved, however. Some women deemed it a sort of ironic cosmic justice that church property burned down after the church had opposed the women's activism. The matter of the rectory demonstrated how the use of space in the community could be fraught with tensions. Residents did not always agree necessarily on how best to use space in the neighborhood and whose interests it should serve.

Many community people did not like the idea of women getting together to form their own organization. Among the men, two views predominated. Some men refused to take the group seriously and perhaps even felt threatened by it. They joked with the women, making sexually suggestive comments such as, "Oh, *Mujeres Latinas en Acción*? Where's the action at?" They mockingly referred to Mujeres as a dating service.[50] Other men who did tolerate or accept the group were somewhat condescending and patronizing, allowing the women to do their work but not holding very high expectations for them. The jokes and condescension belied men's growing anxiety over the way in which MLEA was challenging power relations between women and men in their personal relationships, within the community, and within the local social service structure. Yet not all women supported the gendered agenda either. Mangual recalls, "Even other women in our community who were in organizations that were considered progressive were not pleased [with us] and thought that we were not serious." Critics believed that the women's group would be short-lived. Some felt that promoting separatist gender politics diluted the power of community activism and protest. Mujeres received criticism from all sides—from traditional, religious, conservative sectors that saw them as a threat to the family and cultural norms, and from radicals and progressives who felt that women-centered activism drained resources and energy from larger community struggles. Opponents hurled insults at the women, calling them "rabble-rousers . . . lesbians . . . loose women."[51] As many Chicana feminists experienced in the Southwest, Mujeres encountered a schism between *feministas* and loyalists to "*la causa.*"[52]

Mujeres represented one of "multiple feminist insurgencies" of the second-wave women's movement.[53] Defining MLEA as feminist rests on several theoretical premises. First, MLEA members made claims "based on the rights of women as women and citizens of society."[54] MLEA did not subsume women's concerns under broader community issues or a larger ethnonational or economic struggle. Rather, it placed women's issues front and center. Second, as historian Benita Roth suggests, women took "separate roads to feminism." The women of MLEA did not simply imitate white women's feminist movement but instead practiced a women-centered politics that emanated from a particular community context.[55] This connects to a third premise—the situatedness of women's experiences and their approach to feminism. The working-class women of Mujeres located their women-centered activism in the gap between the white feminist movement and Chicano nationalist politics. They drew on feminist ideology, grounded it in the Chicano community, and reshaped its cultural contours to fit the local context. MLEA was not guided by a highly theoretical or philosophical feminism such as that which was debated by middle-class, elite, or highly educated women. Most women who participated in the group did not even call themselves feminists. Rather, they embraced what Cherríe Moraga and Gloria Anzaldúa call "a theory in the flesh," or "a politic born of necessity"[56]—a feminism of urgency based on the material needs of working-class immigrant women and their daughters. Still, MLEA's feminism operated in dialogue with white feminism, not only in conflict with it.[57]

This was especially true because some of the group's members, including progressive white women and Chicana students, were certainly influenced by white feminist ideologies. At El Centro, women involved with Mujeres may have been somewhat shielded from criticisms that they were being influenced by "Anglo women's liberation" ideas because the activist community around El Centro included white progressives, such as Tom and Mary Tully, Steve and Jeanne Schensul, Gwen Stern, and Patricia Wright. Chicano/a activists, at least those affiliated with El Centro, saw the importance of white allies. They relied on their skills to write grant proposals, for example, and to negotiate with mainstream institutions. Moreover, Chicana and Chicano activists had close friendships with some of them, even being *comadres* (godmothers) and *compadres* (godfathers) to each other's children. It was not entirely unexpected that Chicanas and white allies would influence each other's politics. While other elements of the community may have charged Mujeres with espousing white women's politics, most activists at El Centro recognized that white allies were critical to community resource development on Eighteenth Street.[58]

Despite the disapproval and intimidation from some in the community, the core group of women persevered in their work. Mangual explained that in the early days, the organization was very egalitarian and nonhierarchical in its structure. Anyone who attended meetings could speak and vote on any matters at hand. But as the group grew, the organization developed a more formal structure. Still, Mangual explained, her leadership style emphasized consensus and cooperation, a feminist practice found among Chicanas elsewhere. As *Tejana* activist Rosie Castro has remarked, "We have practiced a different kind of leadership, a leadership that empowers *others*, not a hierarchical kind of leadership."[59] This reflected MLEA's approach; it hoped to empower women, not become yet another institution, such as the schools, the Catholic Church, or the legal system, that exerted control over women's lives.

By 1974, Mujeres had a board of directors and official bylaws. The women very strategically selected their executive director, according to Mangual. While some nominated Mangual for the post of director, she declined. Instead, the women chose Luz María Prieto, the daughter of a well-known Mexican physician in Chicago, Dr. Jorge Prieto. Mangual explained,

"That was a calculated move because her dad was a very well respected physician and the name Prieto was well known and well respected. We were on such shaky grounds . . . [being called] lesbians, rabble-rousers, all kinds of bad connotations. . . . The Prieto name [wa]s going to have people think twice about what they sa[id] about [us]."[60] Luz María Prieto lent a tremendous amount of credibility to the organization.

After they lost their meeting space in the rectory to the fire, the women initiated a fund-raising campaign and searched for another space. The building had burned down in September of 1974. By December, however, the group had done fund-raising "to get rent money for a new facility. [They] held a raffle and two dances . . . and raised $1,700.00"[61] The following spring they found a storefront on the main thoroughfare in the Eighteenth Street *barrio*, where they paid two hundred dollars a month in rent. Again, the women labored hard to improve their space. "I remember how physically hard it was—how hard physically we all had to work—cleaning the place, even finding a storefront that we could rent, doing the painting ourselves, moving boxes, doing all the hard nitty gritty work," said Gwen Stern.[62] Dr. Aida Giachello, a social worker and doctoral student at the time, was one of the few Puerto Rican women involved with the organization and an early board member. She recalled, "It used to be very cold [in the Mujeres office] because we didn't have any money for heat."[63] Indeed, early financial records reveal that the organization struggled to make ends meet, scraping together funding from a variety of sources. By 1976, it was able to obtain a property at 1823 West Seventeenth Street from the Community Renewal Society. It paid one dollar for the lot and two very dilapidated buildings. In conjunction with other organizations and with some funding, MLEA secured carpentry and construction apprentices to help rehabilitate the buildings and make the space usable.[64]

MLEA was successful in attracting federal funds for some of its programming. But local foundations and grant-making agencies repeatedly turned down the organization's solicitations in the early days. "All the foundations would say, 'It's a great idea,'" recalls María Mangual, but were not willing to be the first to fund the organization. "Come back when you get some money," they would tell the women.[65] Nevertheless, the group was creative and resourceful, often holding fund-raising activities and rent parties to support its projects. Even after the organization began receiving foundation money and had obtained a permanent building that it owned outright, it still continued to fund-raise. A note in the Providence of God parish bulletin in April 1978 announced that MLEA would be having a bake sale after mass that day to benefit the organization. MLEA utilized other resources as well, such as training workshops held by the Latino Institute, an organization formed in 1975, which provided technical assistance to Latino community-based organizations, among other things. Executive Director Luz María Prieto and her staff regularly attended workshops on fund-raising, bookkeeping, proposal writing, and personnel management.[66]

The organization's programming goals continually evolved out of the problems that women faced in the community. Mexican American families became a central focus, and the group addressed the problems of women and girls within the family with a feminist approach. The family was often the locus of intergenerational conflicts, tensions over gendered expectations, and questions of morality and cultural change. Teenage girls in the neighborhood felt this in particular.[67] Mujeres offered its space at the rectory and later the storefront on Eighteenth Street as a teen drop-in center for girls to hold "rap sessions" and discuss the issues they faced at home and at school. The women soon discovered that a number of girls—usually second-generation daughters who had conflicts with their Mexican immigrant parents—were running away from home. These girls were often taken in by someone, sometimes older boyfriends or other friends, and were soon exploited and abused. Some became pregnant or, in extreme cases, addicted to drugs and engaged in prostitution. The women of the group became gravely concerned about this phenomenon and took training at the Institute for Juvenile Research to become certified as foster parents. Mangual explained, "If a young woman had run away from home, she could stay with us, we could contact the parents, and negotiate a way of going back home." Most important, Mangual continued, the women wanted to provide "some safe place to stay where [the girls were] not going to be used and abused." The women provided that place at their center, calling the program the Temporary Housing Project, and recruiting other community members to serve as foster parents as well. This represented the nontraditional type of "motherwork" that scholar Nancy Naples describes among working-class, urban African American and Latina women.[68] The program for runaway girls operated for several years.

As with many other women's groups of the era, reproductive rights soon commanded an important place on MLEA's agenda as well. Jennifer Nelson reminds us that the historical narrative of feminists' engagement with reproductive rights has privileged mainstream middle-class white women's advocacy for safe, legal abortion. Women of color, especially working-class women, however, conceived of reproductive autonomy more broadly to include "health care for the poor, child-care, and welfare rights in addition to anti-sterilization abuse efforts." Nelson continues, "For poor women and women of color, the right to bear healthy children and to raise them out of poverty was equally important."[69] For MLEA, however, this was an area where the group had to tread gingerly. In 1978, it advertised a workshop on birth control in a neighborhood newspaper with the heading "Is birth control really women's work?" The brief announcement quoted staff member Diana Avila as stating that the meeting was "not for women only." While many women and teen girls welcomed the much-needed information on birth control and reproductive health, others reacted negatively. When the group began providing referrals to Planned Parenthood (for birth control or abortions), many in the community disapproved. Gwen Stern noted that Mujeres never publicly promoted abortion, as such a position would have alienated many Catholics and other social conservatives in the community. Still, some critics, especially those affiliated with the church, charged that Mujeres advocated abortion despite the organization's careful handling of the subject.[70] MLEA chose instead to offer classes on women's health more generally and helped develop the Pilsen Mother-Infant Program, called Dar a Luz (Childbirth), to educate women on prenatal care and help them have safer pregnancies and healthier babies.

MLEA's agenda continued to develop organically, based on those issues that neighborhood women themselves raised, as Stern explained. The group soon realized, for example, that domestic violence affected many women in the *barrio* who often suffered in silence.[71] Ironically, though aggression between young men in gangs had been recognized and addressed at agencies like Casa Aztlán and El Centro (and, indeed, it was very real), the violence between men and women, which usually occurred behind closed doors or within the private sphere of the family, went unrecognized. Even if such physical conflict spilled into public places, it was considered a *personal* issue, not a community concern. Yet domestic violence—not only spousal violence but child abuse—was very common among working-class families. Mujeres thus made it the group's goal to "undomesticate" domestic violence. In 1977, the issue had barely begun to receive attention on mainstream public policy or social service agendas. María Mangual explained, "The whole infrastructure that has been developed around domestic violence in the last twenty-five, thirty years was just not there." MLEA was indeed a pioneer in the field. The group helped women recognize abuse and provided counseling and assistance to leave abusive partners when necessary.[72] In coalition with another women's organization, Southwest Women Working Together, Mujeres Latinas en Acción opened the first shelter in the city to specifically serve Spanish-speaking battered women in

1981. It was instrumental as well in testifying for HB 1618 and 1619, state legislation that addressed domestic violence.[73]

The group's intervention in family matters—especially in ways that freed women and girls from control and subjugation, promoted their autonomy and well-being, and challenged male authority—received scathing criticism. As Mangual recalls, from the beginning, Mujeres encountered a great deal of opposition and resistance, especially from the traditional, conservative, immigrant, and religious sectors of the community.

> We were viewed suspiciously; we were viewed critically. "And what were we organizing women for?" people would ask. "What kind of values would we be instilling?" And obviously, we were wrecking homes, telling women they could leave their husbands, that they didn't have to be abused! And providing safe havens for young girls who ran away from home! How disrespectful is that?![74]

Yet Mangual recalls personally observing two groups of women in dire need of services in the neighborhood. The first were immigrant women, who had recently arrived, spoke only Spanish, had small children, and were cloistered in their homes. These women had few English-language or communication skills and limited knowledge of neighborhood and city resources, and they lacked social networks. The second group was Mexican American mothers who had become pregnant at a young age, had not completed high school, lacked employment skills, and lived in poverty as well. Both groups were highly vulnerable to domestic violence and isolation, and had limited options for themselves and their children. Mangual explained, "I very clearly saw those two populations as being in tremendous need and being the groups that could make—if you changed their lives, you could make a huge impact on the quality of life of the whole community. If you could change the lives of those two groups of women . . . "[75] Mangual and Mujeres Latinas en Acción recognized that the conditions of women, girls, and mothers affected the well-being of the community as a whole. This radical notion had been absent from nationalist and masculinist critiques of society that uncritically celebrated the Chicano family and ignored its gendered dimensions and the ways in which it could be oppressive to women and girls.

Critics perceived Mujeres as attacking and disrupting the traditional Mexican/Chicano family. Yet Mujeres did not challenge the family per se (nor did it challenge heteronormativity) as much as it challenged patriarchy and male dominance within it. In the midst of the Chicano movement, Chicana women activists (including feminists) generally expressed support for the family; they did not want to do away with it. As Chicanos were articulating an identity on a national level as a racial minority, however, Chicanas had the opportunity to characterize Chicano culture, and therefore the family, according to their own visions. They tried to imagine an alternative version of this social structure, one in which women and girls could articulate their needs and desires and in which violence, abuse, and exploitation were unacceptable.[76]

Some women activists did not want to address gender dynamics within their activism, either because of their commitments to race- or class-based libratory politics or because they could not reconcile their religious beliefs with feminist ideas that challenged the very foundational patriarchal tenets of their faith. Religion, culture, and generation intertwined for many women to shape a worldview that simply could not tolerate birth control, divorce, or the violation of ideals of female chastity and virginity. Just as male chauvinism was not endemic to Mexican culture alone, however, women's resistance to feminism occurred beyond the Mexican community as well. White mainstream feminist movements encountered tremendous opposition from various corners. Conservative, traditional, and religious white women also struggled to reconcile their beliefs with feminist principles, and many never did. Mainstream American society witnessed fierce debates over women's reproductive rights (especially *Roe v. Wade*), power relations between men and women, the Equal Rights Amendment, and the way in which gender structured inequality in all aspects of daily life. That this occurred also among the Mexican community of Pilsen was not unique.

As with other Chicana and women of color feminists, the women of Mujeres did not dissociate themselves completely from the Chicano community as some white feminists did from the New Left. Their activism was not an either-or proposition. Rather, they saw themselves as an integral part of the Chicano community's struggle for social justice and continued to operate within it.[77] Their inspiration came largely from their daily experiences in the *barrio*. As María Mangual testifies, the very real needs of children, teenage girls, and young mothers prompted her to organize women to action. Mangual and her fellow activists understood that the predominantly Mexican American women of Pilsen had culturally, socially, and economically specific concerns and needs that played a role in whether they could move out of abusive relationships, return to parents' homes, or make decisions about their futures. The confluence of some or all these different factors—the Catholic Church's strong prohibition against divorce; language issues and difficulty navigating English-speaking social service bureaucracies; poverty and inequitable conditions in local neighborhoods and schools; strict and rigid norms for women's roles and gendered divisions of labor; and concern over immigration status, citizenship status, or the ability to remain legally in the United States—made Mexican women's crises all the more complex.

The founders of Mujeres also believed that women would continue to be powerless in their own lives and invisible in the community unless someone represented their interests more concretely in community forums. This advocacy strategy proved quite successful. They placed women on the boards or advisory councils of Casa Aztlán, the Pilsen Little Village Mental Health Center, the Legal Assistance Foundation, Eighteenth Street Development Corporation, and citywide boards, such as Planned Parenthood and the Mexican American Legal Defense and Education Fund (MALDEF). The networks they created through participation in such organizations later provided them with resources and contacts for fund-raising with pri-

Figure 27. María Mangual, a key founder of Mujeres Latinas en Acción, is pictured right of center holding a little girl's hand. Courtesy of Mujeres Latinas en Acción.

vate foundations.[78] Perhaps more than any other entity in the city, Mujeres Latinas en Acción nurtured and developed Mexican American women's leadership and participation in civic life.

Conclusion

Mujeres Latinas en Acción must be counted in the long tradition of women's activism and the second-wave feminist movement. It also deserves a place within the history of urban social activism of the 1970s. While it might not be characterized as a radical organization that demanded dramatic changes in societal structures, like other organizations of the civil rights era, it took a reformist approach, the most viable strategy given the political context. The organization focused on providing basic resources that would help women and girls live healthier, safer, and more fulfilling lives. MLEA worked on educating and training such women, providing them with leadership skills, and helping them recognize the resources that they possessed. Reflecting on the organization's legacy, Dr. Aida Giachello noted, "[It] was the only social service organization [for Latina women] in the Midwest for a long time. . . . For the longest time, it was the only model we had of empowering women—[a] community-based organization run by women, for women, with women."[79] Though its sphere of influence was localized, Mujeres did effect some dramatic structural changes. For battered women in the Midwest's largest Mexican *barrio*, Mujeres offered an alternative to physical, verbal, and psychological abuse and degradation. Women who had felt trapped in such conditions and saw no recourse but to endure them found other women willing to listen and help them find a way out. Mujeres gave Mexican women in general a sense of their own power, of the possibilities of their own lives. It helped many women discover their own leadership potential and instilled in them greater self-esteem. Long-time staff member Alicia Amador explained that Mujeres brought "women together in a dialogue, asking 'What do you want for yourself? What do you want as a young girl? What do you want to do as a woman? . . . What is your role in [your] home, in society?" She added, "Those were *huge* questions. They were difficult questions to answer if you're not used to being asked those kinds of [things]."[80] This was indeed radical and revolutionary for many people. While Mujeres Latinas en Acción prompted women and young girls on Eighteenth Street to reflect upon their lives, it also prompted many men in the community to take notice of women's leadership abilities and skills.

If the Mexican community was politically and economically marginalized in the city's power structure in the 1970s, women experienced this even more acutely. MLEA brought visibility to Mexican women as citizens of the city and members of society. It helped women and girls claim a space and place for themselves as members of Eighteenth Street's Mexican community. It brought women to the community's conscience. The place that MLEA secured in subsequent years within the city's social service landscape gave it legitimacy and authority in the local political environment. Over the years, Mujeres gained the respect of many people in Pilsen and beyond. Indeed, it became the most prominent Latina women's organization in Chicago. Remarkably, the organization has endured for over thirty years, expanding its social services and continuing to empower Latina women and their families. In the twenty-first century, it has continued to be an important institution not only in the Eighteenth Street neighborhood but in the city as well.

Conclusion

The growing Latin population together with a continued increase in the number
of Blacks during the 1970s may establish the two as a majority of the city's total
population. This could cause a great difference in the structure of the city, politically, commercially and ethnically.

—Gerald Ropka, *The Evolving Residential Pattern (1980)*[1]

By the end of the 1970s, Mexicans and Puerto Ricans had concentrated
in four community areas—Pilsen / Lower West Side, Little Village / South
Lawndale, West Town, and Humboldt Park.[2] Though they settled in other
parts of the city and even surrounding blue-collar suburbs, they had become the majority in these neighborhoods, which became known as quintessential *barrios* and the center of Mexican and Puerto Rican life in the city
(introduction, figs. 2–5). The population also continued to grow. Mexicans continued arriving in large numbers, both as legal immigrants and
increasingly—as a result of more restrictive immigration policies—without
authorization. Puerto Ricans continued migrating as well, but their numbers had dropped off, and return migration to the island offset population growth. New Latin American immigrants now hailed from Guatemala,
Colombia, Honduras, Ecuador, and Peru, diversifying and complicating
Latino/a interethnic dynamics.

Yet despite their continued growth in numbers, political power continued to elude them. Some local activists and policy advocates took up what
they believed to be an urgent political issue in 1980—the upcoming US
census. They spearheaded a campaign to get Spanish-speaking Chicagoans (now increasingly identifying as "Latino/a," "Hispanic," or "Spanish-
origin") to complete census surveys and be counted. They stressed the
political significance of getting their population accurately enumerated to

secure greater resources and political representation. A widespread publicity campaign sought to persuade Chicago's Latino/a residents to do their part and participate.

In early 1980, Andres de la Llata, a man who had arrived with his family from Mexico over twenty-five years earlier, appeared on the local evening news. A reporter on the streets of Pilsen was interviewing people about the upcoming census. "Yes," Mr. de la Llata replied, he would fill out the questionnaire and be counted. Local activists applauded such cooperation from ordinary working-class people. Mr. de la Llata's response and that of tens of thousands of others would help make the case for expanding public schools and bilingual education, social services and neighborhood resources, equitable access to employment (especially government jobs), and political representation at city, state, and federal levels. Indeed, the 1980 census revealed over four hundred thousand "Spanish-origin" people in the city. Some observers estimated the figure was closer to half a million. Merely documenting their dramatic numbers, however, did not automatically bring equitable political representation, resources, or employment. The Democratic political machine did not easily cede power to the new ethnic populations that swelled formerly eastern and southern European neighborhoods and had dramatically transformed the city's demographics. Forming alliances with African Americans to fight for greater resources also proved challenging. Some Latinos/as continued to insist that Mexicans were just another immigrant group like the Europeans and that Puerto Ricans were American citizens and therefore not immigrants at all. They were hoping to widen the distance between themselves and African Americans and civil rights politics. A small number of Latinos/as had gained entry into token positions with the machine, but they had not secured the greater spoils doled out to others—municipal jobs, city contracts, and patronage. The most progressive of Chicago's Latino activists, many of whom had honed their skills in Pilsen and Humboldt Park, however, rejected the machine and divisive ethnic politics, and instead expressed sympathies and affinities with progressive African Americans. They believed the interests of their communities would be best served by following a more independent and oppositional model of politics. Their grassroots efforts laid important groundwork for electoral organizing and voter registration campaigns by the early 1980s.

In 1983, the people of Chicago made history, electing the city's first black mayor, Harold Washington. This momentous occasion symbolized a triumph for many black Chicagoans, a break through the colored ceiling of local politics, and the hope that an African American as the city's titular head might help alleviate racial discrimination, social inequality, and the widespread decay that plagued many of the city's neighborhoods. Washington's election, like that of many other African American mayors throughout the country in these years, of course, fell short of those great expectations. By the time black leaders penetrated the halls of power in many urban centers, cities had suffered massive disinvestment, devastating racial strife, and nearly irreparable damage and decline in infrastructure, some of which has persisted in the twenty-first century. Chicago in the early eighties was crippled by high rates of unemployment, higher rates of poverty, and a distressed built environment in the economically depressed neighborhoods that surrounded downtown. "Racial minorities" who lived in these conditions, along with liberal and progressive whites, had catapulted Washington into office in the belief that he could potentially help solve the urban crisis and improve their lives. Included among the many who elected him were tens of thousands of Latinos/as, primarily Mexican Americans and Puerto Ricans. Only a few astute political analysts observed at the time that in addition to the massive numbers of African Americans targeted in voter registration campaigns, the city's Latino/a population provided a "crucial voting bloc" that helped Washington secure victory. Nearly 80 percent of Latino voters in that election supported Washington.[3]

Latinos/as overwhelmingly chose to join their fortunes with the city's African Americans, hoping that this strategy would finally remedy their marginalization in the local sociopolitical landscape. Washington did make great strides in opening up city government for Latinos/as, establishing a Latino Affairs Commission, and appointing leaders to key positions. Activists also built upon their growing political momentum. They brought lawsuits against the city challenging redistricting maps that had disenfranchised them and African Americans. By the mid-1980s, they started to elect Mexican and Puerto Rican representatives at the ward, aldermanic, and state level.[4]

The strategic choice Chicago's Latino/a political leaders made to identify themselves not as a white ethnic group, as European immigrants traditionally had, but as a distinct population who shared at least some common interests with African Americans reflected a clearer understanding of Latinos/as' complicated position in the social order of the urban north. In 1980, Latinos/as nationally had made an important statement on the US census about who they were. For the very first time, census respondents were able to specify if they were of "Hispanic/Spanish origin" in addition to identifying a separate "race," and their selection of a racial category would not be subject to census editors' revisions. Census enumerators would no longer take liberties in labeling Latinos/as "white" according to their racial judgments. This was the result of the efforts of Hispanic advocates in Washington, DC, to convince the federal government and Americans more broadly that Latinos/as did not fit neatly in the "racial" categories of "black" and "white," nor were they exactly a separate race. Rather, they were a collection of diverse ethnic groups who had varied racial ancestry. (And with growing numbers of Central American, South American, and Caribbean Spanish-speaking immigrants, they were becoming even more diverse.) The 1980 census thus became a watershed moment for the racial identity of Latinos/as in the United States. Nationwide, 40 percent chose to identify themselves as "other race." They rejected the long-standing practice of many in the past who had identified themselves as "white." Yet the trend in Chicago was even more marked. In the city as a whole, a striking 52 percent of Latino/a Chicagoans said they were of an "other" race; only 45 percent claimed to be "white." In the four *barrios* where Mexicans and Puerto Ricans had become concentrated, even greater numbers of people had chosen this category. Fifty-seven percent of Spanish-origin people in West Town, 62 percent of those in Little Village, 65 percent in Humboldt Park, and 66 percent in Pilsen had consciously identified themselves as some "other" race (table 13). The majority of Latinos/as in Chicago—who were still predominantly Mexican and Puerto Rican—had consciously rejected calling themselves "white." Their experiences and their self-perceptions told them otherwise.[5]

Mexicans and Puerto Ricans simply had not assimilated as European immigrants had done decades earlier but continued to have "unresolved

Table 13   Race category selected by Hispanic/Spanish-origin people in 1980 census

	Other race (%)	White (%)	African American, Asian Pacific Islander, and American Indian (%)
In the United States	40	58	2
Cook County	48	48	4
Chicago	52	45	3
West Town	57	42	1
Humboldt Park	65	34	1
Little Village	62	38	0
Pilsen	66	33	1

Source: Chicago Fact Book Consortium, *Local Community Fact Book, 1980*.

issues of integration."[6] They wrestled with the untenable and conflicting messages they had received about their place in the social order. Moreover, their class status sharply influenced the way in which their race was understood. Unlike European immigrants before the 1920s, Mexicans and Puerto Ricans had not entered vigorous industrial labor markets that offered relatively low-skilled, high-paying, manufacturing jobs, which did not demand much formal education but could provide some economic stability nonetheless. They arrived just as these industries were abandoning the urban north and heading south or overseas. Thus, they entered low-skilled and increasingly lower-paying, nonunion employment in manufacturing and the service industry. Furthermore, unlike European immigrants who experienced *ethnic* prejudice and discrimination, Mexicans and Puerto Ricans by the sixties and seventies had been racially defined by enough powerful institutions that their "nonwhite" social status was well established.[7] The children of these postwar immigrants felt the effects of racial prejudice and discrimination, which impeded their educational and socioeconomic mobility and left many of them poorly educated, economically marginalized, and socially, if not politically, disenfranchised.

Some Mexicans (fewer than those who aspired to) did fulfill the immigrant trajectory of most Europeans—social and economic success, cultural assimilation, integration in white communities—thus ostensibly challenging arguments about their racial subordination. Yet the continuous influx of Mexican immigrants over the mid- and late twentieth century complicated their path and their ability to claim whiteness. New immigrants and their continual reracialization (increasingly as "illegal") undercut claims that Mexicans were or could be white and reinforced the notion that Mexicans were some "other" race, foreign, outside the American body politic, and in fact, criminals. This characterization has indeed persisted in the twenty-first century. This does not mean that *if only Mexicans had stopped immigrating,* they would have assimilated as Europeans had and become "white," because in many ways by the 1960s American capital had conditioned Mexicans to migrate as a continuous low-wage labor source, and stopping this flow was highly unlikely.[8] Mexican workers, and increasingly others from Latin America, would keep coming in later decades in response to the economic imbalances between North and South, and to supply the low-skilled labor markets of the United States. Still, continuous migration alone does not explain the distinct ethnoracial status of Mexican Americans. Poles, Greeks, and other southern and eastern Europeans continued to immigrate to Chicago throughout the late twentieth century also, and while they might have been disparaged or denigrated for their cultural distinctiveness and unassimilated "Old World" ways, they generally experienced greater ease in integrating into white Chicago. Their racial identity as "white" rarely comes into question.

In the case of Puerto Ricans, again, some did model the immigrant success story in the mid-twentieth century—being newcomers to the mainland, working hard, and ascending the economic ladder. The persistent poverty of so many, however, despite the perceived advantages of US citizenship, maligned them (much like African Americans) as a deficient, delinquent underclass whose socioeconomic conditions are the result of collective moral failure. This characterization, of course, overlooks the social, political, and economic impact of the island's ongoing colonization by the United States.[9] While some Puerto Ricans asserted their own claims to whiteness, the experiences of many—ranging from subtle forms of prejudice to more egregious and harmful encounters with stark educational inequalities, housing and employment discrimination, and racial profiling—challenged those claims.

In the twenty-first century, Latinos/as have become much more visible in American popular culture, politics, the media, and specifically, in debates over contemporary immigration. Yet as Americans, we still struggle to fully grasp just who this population is. Some continue to see Latinos/as as recent arrivals, newcomers needing assimilation, or, at worst, illegitimate members of American society, "illegal aliens." Such characterizations are surely informed not just by ongoing immigration but also by the perplexing and seemingly incomprehensible ethnoracial identity of Latinos/as. We have not figured out how to fit this diverse population into our national racial taxonomy or how to make sense of those who are not only black or white, but perhaps "brown." Yet if we take a closer look into our past, and broaden our gaze on race in America, we may find rich new stories that offer some clues. We might make the surprising discovery that Mexicans, Puerto Ricans, and other Latinos/as have been here longer than we realize.

NOTES

ABBREVIATIONS USED IN THE NOTES

AGPR   Archivo General de Puerto Rico, San Juan, Puerto Rico

AH   Association House Collection, Chicago History Museum

BP   *Black Panther*

CA   *Chicago American*

CAP   Chicago Area Project Collection, Chicago History Museum

CD   *Chicago Defender*

CDN   *Chicago Daily News*

CMCL   Midwest Council of La Raza Collection, University Archives, University of Notre Dame

COUA   Chancellor's Office Records, University Archives, University of Illinois at Chicago

CST   *Chicago Sun Times*

CT   *Chicago Tribune*

CUNG   *Champaign-Urbana News Gazette*

ECC   El Centro de la Causa private archives

EM   *El Mundo* (San Juan, Puerto Rico)

FEPC   Fair Employment Practices Committee Records, National Archives, Great Lakes Region

FRUS   *Foreign Relations of the United States*, University of Wisconsin

FS   Florence Scala Papers, Special Collections Library, University of Illinois at Chicago

HW   Special Collections, Harold Washington Library, Chicago Public Libraries

IAF   Industrial Areas Foundation Records, Special Collections Library, University of Illinois at Chicago

LI   Latino Institute Collection, Special Collections Library, DePaul University

LMM   Luis Muñoz Marín Collection, Luis Muñoz Marín Foundation, San Juan, Puerto Rico

LP   Lincoln Park Community Collection, Special Collections Library, DePaul University

LPP   *Lincoln Park Press*

MLEA   Mujeres Latinas en Acción Records, Special Collections Library, DePaul University

MRC   Municipal Reference Collection, Harold Washington Library, Chicago Public Libraries

NWSCC   Near West Side Community Committee Records, Special Collections Library, University of Illinois at Chicago

NYT   *New York Times*

OGPRUS   Offices of the Government of Puerto Rico in the United States Collection, Center for Puerto Rican Studies, Hunter College, New York City

RRB   Railroad Retirement Board Papers, National Archives, Great Lakes Region

WC   Welfare Council of Metropolitan Chicago Collection (formerly known as Council of Social Agencies), Chicago History Museum

YL   Young Lords Collection, Special Collections Library, DePaul University

YLO   *Young Lords Organization* newspaper

INTRODUCTION

1. Chicago Commission on Human Relations, Mayor's Committee on New Residents, "Puerto Rican Americans in Chicago," 1960.

2. Marta Isabel Kollman de Curutchet, "Localization of the Mexican and Cuban Population of Chicago" (MA thesis, University of Chicago, 1967).

3. Rosa de la Llata Hernandez, interview with the author, January 21, 2009.

4. Heather Thompson, *Whose Detroit? Politics, Labor, and Race in a Modern American City* (Ithaca, NY: Cornell University Press, 2001), 8. Recent urban histories that address racial change in the city include: Amanda Seligman, *Block by Block: Neighborhoods and Public Policy on Chicago's West Side* (Chicago: University of Chicago Press, 2005); Robert O. Self, *American Babylon: Race and the Struggle for Postwar Oakland* (Princeton, NJ: Princeton University Press, 2003); and Thomas J. Sugrue, *The Origins of the Urban Crisis: Race and Inequality in Postwar Detroit* (Princeton, NJ: Princeton University Press, 1996). For the now-classic urban history of Chicago, see Arnold R. Hirsch, *Making the Second Ghetto: Race and Housing in Chicago, 1940–1960* (Cambridge: Cambridge University Press, 1983).

5. Campbell Gibson and Kay Jung, "Historical Census Statistics on Population Totals by Race, 1790 to 1990, and by Hispanic Origin, 1970 to 1990, for Large Cities and Other Urban Places in the United States," Working Paper No. 76 (Washington, DC: US Census Bureau, February 2005).

6. The community area of Chatham on Chicago's South Side, for example, epitomizes this dramatic transformation of white to black populations within a span of only a few years.

7. For social and behavioral science studies on racial succession, see, for example, Robert Huckfeldt, *Politics in Context: Assimilation and Conflict in Urban Neighborhoods* (New York: Agathon Press, 1986). For historical analyses of neighborhood change and racial strife, see Self, *American Babylon*; Seligman, *Block by Block*; Sugrue, *Origins of the Urban Crisis*; Eileen McMahon, *What Parish Are You From? A Chicago Irish Community and Race Relations* (Lexington: University of Kentucky Press, 1995); and Hirsch, *Making the Second Ghetto*. On suburbs, see, for example, Kenneth T. Jackson, *Crabgrass Frontier: The Suburbanization of the United States* (New York: Oxford University Press, 1985); and Becky Nicolaides, *My Blue Heaven: Life and Politics in the Working-Class Suburbs of Los Angeles, 1920–1965* (Chicago: University of Chicago Press, 2002).

8. Craig Wilder, *A Covenant with Color: Race and Social Power in Brooklyn* (New York: Columbia University Press, 2000), 234, 216.

9. I use the term *(im)migrant* or *(im)migration* when referring to Mexicans, Puerto Ricans, and/or Mexican Americans together, to acknowledge the fact that Mexicans have a distinct juridico-political status in the United States compared to Puerto Ricans or Mexican Americans. As foreign nationals, Mexicans are identified as "immigrants," while US-citizen Mexican Americans and Puerto Ricans are considered domestic "migrants."

10. John Walton and Luis Salces estimated much higher figures. They compared 1970 census undercount estimates for African Americans, which the Census Bureau calculated at 7.7 percent, and doubled this figure for Latinos, arguing that they had higher mobility rates, language barriers to completing the census, and greater suspicion of the census because of undocumented relatives or other members of their households. They estimated a Latina/o population closer to 496,000 by 1977. This figure did not include undocumented immigrants, whom local Immigration and Naturalization Service officials perhaps overzealously estimated to be an additional 250,000 people. INS estimates of the undocumented may have been inflated, as the perception at the time was that "illegal aliens" were ubiquitous and creating a social crisis in the country. Still, Walton and Salces used the lower INS estimates. The Chicago office in fact estimated *as many as* 500,000 illegal aliens in the city. By these calculations, in 1977 Latinos accounted for more than 20 percent of the city's population. While these estimates may seem high (some were even higher), we can safely assume that several hundred thousand Latinas/os lived in Chicago by the late 1970s. John Walton and Luis Salces, "The Political Organization of Chicago's Latino Communities" (Center for Urban Affairs, Northwestern University, 1977).

11. Roberto Suro, "For Latinos Color Has Been a Gray Area," *CT*, April 9, 1978. Thomas Guglielmo makes a distinction between race and color that provides a useful way to understand African Americans and Europeans and how they have been racialized in the United States, but again, the diversity of Latinos/as not only in their "racial" ancestry but also in their color makes such a distinction irrelevant for their case. Thomas Guglielmo, *White on Arrival: Italians, Race, Color, and Power in Chicago, 1890–1945* (Oxford: Oxford University Press, 2003).

12. Ariela Gross, "'The Caucasian Cloak': Mexican Americans and the Politics of Whiteness in the Twentieth Century Southwest," *Georgetown Law Journal* 95, no. 2 (2007): 344. Guadalupe San Miguel and Ian Haney López have both argued, as I do here, that Mexican Americans consciously chose to identify as nonwhite in the midst of the Chicano movement. This strategy departed dramatically from that used by Mexican Americans in previous decades who insisted on their whiteness. See Ian F. Haney López, *Racism on Trial: The Chicano Fight for Justice* (Cambridge, MA: Belknap Press / Harvard University Press, 2003); and Guadalupe San Miguel Jr., *Brown, Not White: School Integration and the Chicano Movement in Houston* (College Station: Texas A&M University Press, 2001). On Mexican Americans' insistence on their whiteness, see Neil Foley, "Partly Colored or Other White: Mexican Americans and Their Problem with the Color Line," in *American Dreaming, Global Realities: Rethinking U.S. Immigration History*, ed. Donna R. Gabaccia and Vicki L. Ruiz, 361–78 (Urbana: University of Illinois Press, 2006); Gross, "'Caucasian Cloak'"; and Thomas A. Guglielmo, "Fighting for Caucasian Rights: Mexicans, Mexican Americans, and the Transnational Struggle for Civil Rights in World War II Texas," *Journal of American History* 92, no. 4 (2006): 1212–37.

13. The only exception to this classification on the US census was in 1930, in the midst of the Great Depression, when Mexicans were separated out as their own distinct

racial group. In 1940, the Census Bureau returned to classifying most Mexicans as "white."

14. Gross, "'Caucasian Cloak,'" 344. See also Foley, "Partly Colored, Other White"; and Guglielmo "Caucasian Rights."

15. At first glance, the experience of Mexicans resembles that of Italians, who underwent similar types of racial subordination and exclusion upon their arrival in the United States. As Thomas Guglielmo argues, however, Italians were always "white" in their color, even if they were understood as a distinct "race" (what today we would call an ethnic group or nationality) among other Europeans. Mexicans and other Latinos/as have not been able to uniformly claim European origins, and as a result, their acceptance as "whites" has been much more uneven, and predicated often on skin color and other physical features. See Guglielmo, *White on Arrival*, 58, chaps. 1 and 2.

16. The number of "Other" race people in Chicago went from a mere 20,000 in 1970 to nearly 243,000 in 1980. The 1980 census counted a total of 422,063 people of "Hispanic origin (of any race)" in Chicago. Of these, 190,659 people, or 45 percent, chose the racial category "White" to identify themselves. One percent identified as "Asian/Pacific Islander" and "American Indian," and 2 percent identified as "Black." The self-classification of Latinos/as within Chicago differed significantly from the Cook County suburbs. In Cook County, a slightly higher number of Hispanics / Latinos/as identified as "White"—48 percent—and an equal number identified as "Other," while 3 percent identified as "Asian," "American Indian," or "Black." See Gibson and Jung, "Historical Census Statistics"; Chicago Fact Book Consortium, ed., *Local Community Fact Book Based on the 1970 and 1980 Censuses* (Chicago: Chicago Review Press, 1984), xxii–xxiii; and Clara Rodriguez, *Changing Race: Latinos, the Census, and the History of Ethnicity in the United States* (New York: New York University Press, 2000), 7.

This 1980 change in racial classification created a statistical dilemma over comparability to 1970 data that troubled statisticians tremendously. In an essay devoted to the subject, Roland Chilton and Gordon Sutton insisted that Spanish-origin people should be classified as "white" to preserve statistical validity. They completely missed the point, however, that racial identity is an extremely subjective matter. Roland Chilton and Gordon Sutton, "Classification by Race and Spanish Origin in the 1980 Census and Its Impact on White and Nonwhite Rates," *American Statistician* 40, no. 2 (1986): 197–201.

17. Gabriela Arredondo argues persuasively that Mexicans became a racial group distinct from African Americans and whites and became "Mexican" in 1920s and 1930s Chicago. She documents this process at a time when the population was relatively small (fewer than thirty thousand) and when it was localized in a handful of neighborhoods in the city. My conclusions about their racialization build upon this but expand to a much larger population (which included Puerto Ricans) that by the midcentury had spread into many more neighborhoods and encountered many more white Chicagoans. Gabriela Arredondo, *Mexican Chicago: Race, Ethnicity, and Nation, 1916–1939* (Urbana: University of Illinois Press, 2008).

18. It seems necessary to explain the distinction here between *race* and *ethnicity* as I use them in this text. *Race* generally refers to hereditary, biological characteristics that are often understood by the general public as immutable and relatively permanent features. Contemporary scholars have, of course, dismissed the significance of biological and physiological differentiation in the human population, arguing

that "race" is a socially constructed phenomenon. In other words, "race" in the late twentieth and early twenty-first century is the meaning and value we assign to the physical and geographical diversity of human beings. This, of course, is not simply abstract or ideological but has real material consequences. *Ethnicity* is often viewed as a more malleable and changing category. "Ethnicity" can refer to cultural practices, language, and other social customs that may change over time. So, for example, in late twentieth-century parlance, we understand European immigrants to the United States as consisting of various "ethnicities" or nationalities who eventually assimilated and became "American." The slippage between the concepts of "race" and "ethnicity" is quickly apparent, however, in the fact that, apart from shedding their "ethnicity," such immigrant groups also became "racially" white. That is, they were assigned a location in the racial order that provided them material privileges and benefits reserved for those who can claim that racial status.

19. On the concept of place, I draw on Noel Castree's definition as "the unique conjunction of built environment, cultures, peoples, etc." Noel Castree, "David Harvey," in *Key Thinkers on Space and Place*, ed. Phil Hubbard, Rob Kitchin, and Gill Valentine (Thousand Oaks, CA: Sage Publications, 2004), 184.

20. Laura Pulido, *Black, Brown, Yellow, and Left: Radical Activism in Los Angeles* (Berkeley: University of California Press, 2006), 4. On how white identities are inflected by class, see John Hartigan, *Racial Situations: Class Predicaments of Whiteness in Detroit* (Princeton, NJ: Princeton University Press, 1999).

21. On the ways in which the state produces difference and the consequences of this for political activism, see Clarissa R. Hayward, "The Difference States Make: Democracy, Identity, and the American City," *American Political Science Review* 97, no. 4 (2003): 501–14.

22. Adam Cohen and Elizabeth Taylor, *American Pharaoh: Mayor Richard J. Daley: His Battle for Chicago and the Nation* (Boston: Little, Brown, 2000), 347.

23. Ibid., 10.

24. The relationship between housing/neighborhood conditions and racial composition and how these determined which neighborhoods were targeted for urban renewal has been well established by a number of historians. See, for example, Guglielmo, *White on Arrival*, chap. 8; Hirsch, *Making the Second Ghetto*; and Seligman, *Block by Block*.

25. James R. Barrett and David R. Roediger, "The Irish and the 'Americanization' of the 'New Immigrants' in the Streets and in the Churches of the Urban United States, 1900–1930," *Journal of American Ethnic History* 24, no. 4 (2005): 4–33. See also Andrew Diamond, *Mean Streets: Chicago Youths and the Everyday Struggle for Empowerment in the Multiracial City, 1908–1969* (Berkeley: University of California Press, 2009), chap. 1; and Dominic A. Pacyga, "To Live amongst Others: Poles and Their Neighbors in Industrial Chicago, 1865–1930," *Journal of American Ethnic History* 16, no. 1 (1996): 55–73.

26. Gregory D. Squires, Larry Bennett, Kathleen McCourt, and Philip Nyden, *Chicago: Race, Class, and the Response to Urban Decline* (Philadelphia: Temple University Press, 1987), 111; Diamond, *Mean Streets*, 200; and John Betancur, "The Settlement Experience of Latinos in Chicago: Segregation, Speculation, and the Ecology Model," *Social Forces* 74, no. 4 (1996): 1310.

27. Adrian Burgos Jr., *Playing America's Game: Baseball, Latinos, and the Color Line* (Berkeley: University of California Press, 2007), 12.

28. Adrian Burgos contends, nonetheless, that this was "the illusion of inclusion," be-

cause Latino baseball players were not easily accepted as the social equals of whites. Gabriela Arredondo similarly comments on Mexicans in Chicago in the 1920s and 1930s that "even the plasticity of [their] racial positioning did not negate the real exclusions they experienced." *Mexican Chicago*, 3.

29. On theories of space, see, for example, Edward Soja, *Postmodern Geographies: The Reassertion of Space in Critical Social Theory* (London: Verso, 1989); David Harvey, *The Condition of Postmodernity* (Cambridge, MA: Blackwell, 1989); Noel Castree and Derek Gregory, eds., *David Harvey: A Critical Reader* (Malden, MA: Blackwell, 2006); Doreen Massey, *Space, Place, and Gender* (Minneapolis: University of Minnesota Press, 1994); and Phil Hubbard, Rob Kitchin, and Gill Valentine, eds., *Key Thinkers on Space and Place* (Thousand Oaks, CA: Sage Publications, 2004). Susan Bickford comments on the postmodern multiple meanings of space. See Susan Bickford, "Constructing Inequality: City Spaces and the Architecture of Citizenship," *Political Theory* 28, no. 3 (2000): 355–76.

30. John Betancur makes this same observation, noting that "Latinos ended up facilitating, if not financing, white flight." Betancur, "Settlement Experience of Latinos in Chicago," 1316.

31. Pierre Devise, cited in Felix Padilla, *Puerto Rican Chicago* (Notre Dame, IN: University of Notre Dame Press, 1987), 100.

32. Squires, Bennett, McCourt, and Nyden, *Chicago*, 26–27. Other jobs went to the Sun Belt region or offshore in the quest for lower wages and operational costs, less opposition from unions, and fewer regulations. Pharmaceutical, textile, and other industries began moving to places like Puerto Rico, thereby contributing to agricultural displacement and increasing unemployment. The surplus population that could not find employment in these new industries ironically left to the very cities of the Northeast and Upper Midwest that those factories were abandoning.

33. City of Chicago Department of Development and Planning, *Chicago's Spanish Speaking Population: Selected Statistics* (Chicago: City of Chicago Department of Development and Planning, 1973).

34. The Puerto Rico Department of Labor's Migration Division office in Chicago noted this as well, citing increasing difficulty in 1966 in placing migrants in jobs that paid over $1.25 an hour, were unskilled or semiskilled, and were located in the city rather than the suburbs, which required transportation. Mr. Luis Machado to Joseph Monserrat, March 25 and April 1, 1966, folder 14, box 2504, OGPRUS. For a study comparing Italian immigrants and other southern and eastern European immigrants at the beginning of the twentieth century with Mexican immigrants at the end of it, see Joel Perlmann, *Italians Then, Mexicans Now: Immigrant Origins and Second Generation Progress, 1890–2000* (New York: Russell Sage, 2005). Also useful in considering Italian immigrants' historical experiences in Chicago is Guglielmo, *White on Arrival*.

35. See George Lipsitz, *The Possessive Investment in Whiteness: How White People Profit from Identity Politics* (Philadelphia: Temple University Press, 1998), chap. 1; Jackson, *Crabgrass Frontier*; Self, *American Babylon*; and Ira Katznelson, *When Affirmative Action Was White: An Untold History of Racial Inequality in Twentieth-Century America* (New York: W. W. Norton, 2005).

36. While immigrant and second-generation youth of various European origins had sustained a long tradition of gangs and "athletic clubs," Mexican and Puerto Rican gangs incurred particular persecution from the Chicago Police Department. See Diamond, *Mean Streets*, chaps. 5 and 6.

37. Haney López and San Miguel make this claim about Mexican Americans in Houston and Los Angeles, who they argue explicitly adopted a "Chicano"/brown racial identity. Haney López, *Racism on Trial*; and San Miguel, *Brown, Not White*. Lorrin Thomas argues that Puerto Ricans in New York sought *recognition* as their strategy for political empowerment. Lorrin Thomas, *Puerto Rican Citizen: History and Political Identity in Twentieth-Century New York City* (Chicago: University of Chicago Press, 2010).

38. Only a handful of studies have focused on Latinos in the Midwest. See Dennis Nodín Valdés, *Al Norte: Agricultural Workers in the Great Lakes Region, 1917–1970* (Austin: University of Texas Press, 1991); Dionisio Nodín Valdés, *Barrios Norteños: St. Paul and Midwestern Mexican Communities in the Twentieth Century* (Austin: University of Texas Press, 2000); Zaragosa Vargas, *Proletarians of the North: A History of Mexican Industrial Workers in Detroit and the Midwest, 1917–1933* (Berkeley: University of California Press, 1993); Richard Santillán, "Rosita the Riveter: Midwest Mexican American Women during World War II, 1941–45," in *Perspectives in Mexican American Studies: Mexicans in the Midwest*, ed. Juan R. García, 115–47 (Tucson: University of Arizona Press, 1989); James B. Lane and Edward J. Escobar, eds., *Forging a Community: The Latino Experience in Northwest Indiana, 1919–1975* (Chicago: Cattails Press, 1987); Juan R. García, *Mexicans in the Midwest, 1900–1932* (Tucson: University of Arizona Press, 1996); and F. Arturo Rosales, "The Regional Origins of Mexicano Immigrants to Chicago during the 1920s," *Aztlán* 7, no. 2 (1976): 187–202.

39. On the construction of Mexicans as "illegal immigrants," see Nicholas De Genova, *Working the Boundaries: Race, Space, and "Illegality" in Mexican Chicago* (Durham, NC: Duke University Press, 2005); and Inés Valdez, "Deporting Democracy: The Politics of Immigration and Sovereignty" (PhD diss., University of North Carolina, Chapel Hill, 2011). Both De Genova and Valdez actually focus on Chicago in the late twentieth and early twenty-first centuries, respectively, though they explore the historical origins of this racialization. Leo Chavez describes the phenomenon of Latinos/as as a contemporary "threat." Leo R. Chavez, *The Latino Threat: Constructing Immigrants, Citizens, and the Nation* (Stanford, CA: Stanford University Press, 2008). Mae Ngai closely traces the historical origins of immigrant illegality (not only in relation to Mexicans) to the early twentieth century. Mae Ngai, *Impossible Subjects: Illegal Aliens and the Making of Modern America* (Princeton, NJ: Princeton University Press, 2004).

Recent exceptions to the historical neglect of urban Latino populations are Natalia Molina, *Fit to Be Citizens? Public Health and Race in Los Angeles, 1879–1939* (Berkeley: University of California Press, 2006); Arredondo, *Mexican Chicago*; and Thomas, *Puerto Rican Citizen*. This represents a new wave of scholars distinct from some of the earliest pioneers of Chicano and Puerto Rican history, who documented cities like Los Angeles, for example, from the nineteenth through the early twentieth centuries. See Richard Griswold del Castillo, *The Los Angeles Barrio, 1850–1890: A Social History* (Berkeley: University of California Press, 1979); and Ricardo Romo, *East Los Angeles: History of a Barrio* (Austin: University of Texas Press, 1983). On Santa Barbara, California, see Albert Camarillo, *Chicanos in a Changing Society: From Mexican Pueblos to American Barrios in Santa Barbara and Southern California, 1848–1930* (Cambridge, MA: Harvard University Press, 1979). Still, scholars have tended to focus on Latinos/as arriving in the 1910s and 1920s (during the Mexican Revolution and after US colonization of Puerto Rico) or in the watershed moment after the passage of the 1965 immigration law.

40. One body of ethnographic work has focused specifically on Puerto Ricans. A 2001 special issue of *Centro Journal*, the publication of El Centro de Estudios Puertorriqueños at Hunter College, features work on Puerto Ricans in Chicago by a cadre of *puertorriqueña* scholars—Marixsa Alicea, Nilda Flores-González, Irma Olmedo, Gina Pérez, Maura Toro-Morn, Ana Ramos-Zayas, and Mérida Rúa. See also Gina Pérez, *The Near Northwest Side Story: Migration, Displacement, and Puerto Rican Families* (Berkeley: University of California Press, 2004); and Ana Y. Ramos-Zayas, *National Performances: The Politics of Class, Race, and Space in Puerto Rican Chicago* (Chicago: University of Chicago Press, 2003).

Several monographs have examined Mexicans in the city from educational, ethnographic, linguistic, and historical points of inquiry. See Chris Liska Carger, *Of Borders and Dreams: A Mexican-American Experience of Urban Education* (New York: Teachers College Press, 1996); Juan C. Guerra, *Close to Home: Oral and Literate Practices in a Transnational Mexicano Community* (New York: Teachers College Press, 1998); Marcia Farr, *Rancheros in Chicagoacán: Language and Identity in a Transnational Community* (Austin: University of Texas Press, 2006); De Genova, *Working the Boundaries*; and Arredondo, *Mexican Chicago*. See also Michael Innis-Jimenez, "Persisting in the Shadow of Steel: Community Formation and Survival in Mexican South Chicago, 1919–1939" (PhD diss., University of Iowa, 2006).

Only Nicholas De Genova and Ana Ramos-Zayas's coauthored *Latino Crossings* has examined Mexicans and Puerto Ricans in relation to each other. They explore and compare the perceived differences in race and citizenship between the two groups. Nicholas De Genova and Ana Ramos-Zayas, *Latino Crossings: Mexicans, Puerto Ricans, and the Politics of Race and Citizenship* (New York: Routledge, 2003). For a comparative study of Mexican and Puerto Rican labor migration historically, see Lilia Fernandez, "Of Migrants and Immigrants: Mexican and Puerto Rican Labor Migration in Comparative Perspective, 1942–1964," *Journal of American Ethnic History* 29, no. 3 (2010): 6–39.

41. Cubans, for example, more frequently settled on the city's far north side, in middle-class white, Jewish neighborhoods. On settlement patterns and integration of Cubans in Chicago, see Kollmann de Curutchet, "Localization of the Mexican and Cuban Population"; and Gerald Ropka, *The Evolving Residential Pattern of the Mexican, Puerto Rican, and Cuban Population in the City of Chicago* (New York: Arno Press, 1980).

42. The term *brown* has also been used to describe a variety of other nonwhite people, including Filipinos and South Asians, for example.

For a study that does use a triangulation model, see Scott Kurashige, *The Shifting Grounds of Race: Black and Japanese Americans in the Making of Multiethnic Los Angeles* (Princeton, NJ: Princeton University Press, 2008). For works that have explored "others" beyond the black-white binary, see also Charlotte Brooks, "In the Twilight Zone between Black and White: Japanese American Resettlement and Community in Chicago, 1942–1945," *Journal of American History* 86, no. 4 (2000): 1655–87; Mark Wild, *Street Meeting: Multiethnic Neighborhoods in Early Twentieth-Century Los Angeles* (Berkeley: University of California Press, 2005); Tomás Almaguer, *Racial Fault Lines: The Historical Origins of White Supremacy in California* (Berkeley: University of California Press, 1994); Pulido, *Black, Brown, Yellow, and Left*; and Diamond, *Mean Streets*. Perhaps not surprisingly, these works have focused on California (more specifically, Los Angeles) and Chicago.

CHAPTER ONE

1. Committee on Minority Groups, meeting minutes, folders 4, 6, 7, and 13, box 145, and folder 4, box 147, WC.

2. Numerous scholars have discussed Operation Bootstrap at length. See, for example, Carmen Teresa Whalen, *From Puerto Rico to Philadelphia: Puerto Rican Workers and Postwar Economies* (Philadelphia: Temple University Press, 2001); J. Hernández-Alvarez, "The Movement and Settlement of Puerto Rican Migrants within the United States, 1950–1960," in *Latinos in the United States: Historical Themes and Identity*, ed. Antoinette Sedillo-López (New York: Garland Publishing, 1995); Edwin Maldonado, "Contract Labor and the Origins of Puerto Rican Communities in the United States," *International Migration Review* 13, no. 1 (1979): 103–21; and History Task Force, Centro de Estudios Puertorriqueños, *Labor Migration under Capitalism: The Puerto Rican Experience* (New York: Research Foundation of the City University of New York, 1979).

3. Although I prefer the terms *undocumented immigrant* or *undocumented worker*, I use the label *illegal alien* or *illegal immigrant* to accurately capture the legal and colloquial language used during this time period to identify Mexican immigrants who entered the United States without authorization. Nicholas De Genova calls for using the term *migrant* rather than *immigrant* to deconstruct the production of Mexican migrant "illegality" and denaturalize Mexicans' juridical position outside the US nation-state. See Nicholas De Genova, *Working the Boundaries: Race, Space, and "Illegality" in Mexican Chicago* (Durham: University of North Carolina Press, 2005).

4. For a discussion of the distinctions in citizenship between Mexican laborers and Puerto Rican migrants, see Lilia Fernández, "Of Migrants and Immigrants: Mexican and Puerto Rican Labor Migration in Comparative Perspective, 1942–1964," *Journal of American Ethnic History* 29, no. 3 (2010): 6–39.

5. These population movements disprove the idea that the period between 1924 and 1965 witnessed no significant migration, an argument that is based on the absence of widespread European immigration but completely overlooks the influx of "nonwhite," non-European migrants. See Whalen, *From Puerto Rico*, 5.

6. David G. Gutiérrez and Pierrette Hondagneu-Sotelo, "Introduction: Nation and Migration," *American Quarterly* 60, no. 3 (2008): 503. See also Ramón Grosfoguel, *Colonial Subjects: Puerto Ricans in Global Perspective* (Berkeley: University of California Press, 2003); and Matthew Guterl and Christine Skwiot, "Atlantic and Pacific Crossings: Race, Empire, and 'the Labor Problem' in the Late Nineteenth Century," *Radical History Review*, no. 91 (2005): 40–61. For a discussion of contemporary labor migrations to former colonial nation-states and settler colonies and the racist responses to such migration, see Eduardo Bonilla-Silva, "'This Is a White Country': The Racial Ideology of the Western Nations of the World-System," *Sociological Inquiry* 70, no. 2 (2000): 188–214.

7. History Task Force, *Labor Migration under Capitalism*, 15. See also Jorge Duany, *The Puerto Rican Nation on the Move: Identities on the Island and in the United States* (Durham: University of North Carolina Press, 2002), esp. chap. 4; Maldonado, "Contract Labor"; Kelvin Santiago-Valles and Gladys Jiménez-Muñoz, "Social Polarization and Colonized Labor: Puerto Ricans in the United States, 1945–2000," in *The Columbia History of Latinos in the United States since 1960*, ed. David G. Gutiérrez, 87–145 (New York: Columbia University Press, 2004); and Whalen, *From Puerto Rico*.

8. Gilbert G. González and Raul A. Fernández, *A Century of Chicano History: Empire,*

Nations, and Migration (New York: Routledge, 2003), xi; and Mae Ngai, *Impossible Subjects: Illegal Aliens and the Making of Modern America* (Princeton, NJ: Princeton University Press, 2004), 95 and chap. 4 for a detailed discussion. Ramón Grosfoguel cites Aníbal Quijano's notion of "coloniality" as "the continuity of colonial forms of domination after the end of colonial administrations produced by colonial cultures and structures in the modern/colonial/capitalist world-system" to suggest that even "independent" former colonies of the United States and Europe maintain colonial relations (and thus migration patterns) with the world's core capitalist states. Grosfoguel, *Colonial Subjects*, 4. See also De Genova, *Working the Boundaries*, on Mexican migrants. For analyses of other former colonies and their migrations to the metropole, see, for example, Dorothy Fujita-Rony, *American Workers, Colonial Power: Philippine Seattle and the Transpacific West, 1919–1941* (Berkeley: University of California Press, 2003); and Bonilla-Silva, "This Is a White Country."

9. This occurred in spite of Mexican Americans' legal classification as "white." For histories of Mexicans' incorporation in the United States, see Albert Camarillo, *Chicanos in a Changing Society: From Mexican Pueblos to American Barrios in Santa Barbara and Southern California, 1848–1930* (Cambridge, MA: Harvard University Press, 1979); Douglas Monroy, *Thrown among Strangers: The Making of Mexican Culture in Frontier California* (Berkeley: University of California Press, 1990); and David J. Weber, *Foreigners in Their Native Land: Historical Roots of Mexican Americans* (Albuquerque: University of New Mexico Press, 1973).

10. As Katherine Benton-Cohen notes, Mexicans are distinctive as migrants in that they are returning to territory that was formerly part of their own country. See Katherine Benton-Cohen, "Other Immigrants: Mexicans and the Dillingham Commission of 1907–1911," *Journal of American Ethnic History* 30, no. 2 (2011): 38.

11. See Laura Briggs, *Reproducing Empire: Race, Sex, Science, and U.S. Imperialism in Puerto Rico* (Berkeley: University of California Press, 2002); and Christina Duffy Burnett and Burke Marshall, "Between the Foreign and the Domestic: The Doctrine of Territorial Incorporation, Invented and Reinvented," in *Foreign in a Domestic Sense: Puerto Rico, American Expansion, and the Constitution* (Durham: University of North Carolina Press, 2001), 1. See also Grosfoguel, *Colonial Subjects*; and Sam Erman, "Meanings of Citizenship in the U.S. Empire: Puerto Rico, Isabel Gonzalez, and the Supreme Court, 1898–1905," *Journal of American Ethnic History* 27, no. 4 (2008): 5–33.

    From its origins, Puerto Rican legal status was fraught with limits, conditions, and qualifications. Puerto Rican citizenship was by and large qualified, restricted, and debated in the Insular Cases. For an overview of this, see David G. Gutiérrez, "Introduction," in *The Columbia History of Latinos in the United States since 1960*, ed. David G. Gutiérrez, 12–14 (New York: Columbia University Press, 2004).

12. Early scholars of Chicanos and Puerto Ricans in the United States described this condition as internal colonialism. See Mario Barrera, *Race and Class in the Southwest: A Theory of Racial Inequality* (Notre Dame, IN: University of Notre Dame Press, 1979); and Felix Padilla, *Latino Ethnic Consciousness: The Case of Mexican Americans and Puerto Ricans in Chicago* (Notre Dame, IN: University of Notre Dame Press, 1985), 4.

13. I borrow this concept of "reracialization" from Nicholas De Genova, *Working the Boundaries*. This is an important distinction between Mexicans and Puerto Ricans and European immigrants: the latter were never colonial subjects of the United States in the same way that Mexicans and Puerto Ricans were.

14. Gabriela Arredondo, *Mexican Chicago: Race, Ethnicity, and Nation, 1916–1939* (Urbana: University of Illinois Press, 2008). See also De Genova, *Working the Boundaries*, esp. chap. 6, for a historical analysis and its application to continued Mexican (im)migration in the late twentieth century. Craig Wilder cites the concept of "labor category." See Craig Wilder, *A Covenant with Color: Race and Social Power in Brooklyn* (New York: Columbia University Press, 2000), 240.

15. Briggs, *Reproducing Empire*, 3. According to Gina Pérez, their racial status was mitigated by the possibility that they *might* assimilate, and at least initially, Chicago officials and media welcomed them warmly as "model minority" (immigrants). Gina Pérez, *The Near Northwest Side Story: Migration, Displacement, and Puerto Rican Families* (Berkeley: University of California Press, 2004), 72–82.

16. Santiago-Valles and Jiménez-Muñoz, "Social Polarization," 100. On Mexican immigrants, see De Genova, *Working the Boundaries*, chap. 3.

17. Peter N. Kirstein, *Anglo over Bracero: A History of the Mexican Worker in the United States from Roosevelt to Nixon* (San Francisco: R and E Research Associates, 1977), 15; and Manuel García y Griego, "The Importation of Mexican Contract Laborers to the United States, 1942–1964," in *Between Two Worlds: Mexican Immigrants in the United States*, ed. David G. Gutiérrez, 45–85 (Wilmington, DE: Scholarly Resources, 1996). On the issue of racism in Texas and the Mexican government's negotiations, see Thomas A. Guglielmo, "Fighting for Caucasian Rights: Mexicans, Mexican Americans, and the Transnational Struggle for Civil Rights in World War II Texas," *Journal of American History* 92, no. 4 (2006): 1212–37.

18. Kirstein, *Anglo over Bracero*, 12. For a history of agricultural migrants on the East Coast in the late nineteenth and early twentieth centuries, see Cindy Hahamovitch, *The Fruits of Their Labor: Atlantic Coast Farmworkers and the Making of Migrant Poverty, 1870–1945* (Chapel Hill: University of North Carolina Press, 1997).

19. See letters from June 1942, *FRUS*, 1942, vol. 6, Mexico. *FRUS*, 1943, vol. 6, Mexico, 439. This was not the first time US growers had sought Mexican workers. They had done so during World War I as well. That experience, however, had made the Mexican government quite wary about how its workers would be treated during this new contract program. See *FRUS*, 1942, vol. 6, Mexico. See also *FRUS*, 1943, vol. 7, Mexico, 555.

 Much has been written about the Bracero Program; thus, I outline only the contours of the program and give brief details. See, for example, Richard B. Craig, *The Bracero Program: Interest Groups and Foreign Policy* (Austin: University of Texas Press, 1971); Erasmo Gamboa, *Mexican Labor and World War II: Braceros in the Pacific Northwest, 1941–1947* (Austin: University of Texas Press, 1990); Juan Ramon García, *Operation Wetback: The Mass Deportation of Mexican Undocumented Workers in 1954* (Westport, CT: Greenwood Press, 1980); and García y Griego, "Importation of Mexican Contract Laborers."

20. Kirstein, *Anglo over Bracero*, 16. Dennis Nodín Valdes, *Al Norte: Agricultural Workers in the Great Lakes Region, 1917–1970* (Austin: University of Texas Press, 1991), 93. See also *FRUS*, 1944, vol. 7, Mexico, 1321.

21. The railroads were essential to transporting defense materials, soldiers, and foodstuffs across the country, and with such high numbers of men shipping off to war, there was a great demand for maintenance of way workers. Yet the railroads began requesting foreign contract workers even before the outbreak of war, in 1941. Moreover, Peter Kirstein cites statistics from 1945 that show that most American workers who were referred for maintenance of way employment on the railroads declined

the positions because of their low wages and harsh working conditions. Kirstein, *Anglo over Bracero*, 23–40.

22. Ibid., 23, 36; and Ambassador in Mexico to Undersecretary of State, March 23, 1943, *FRUS*, 1943, vol. 6, Mexico, 540.

23. *FRUS*, 1943, 542–43; and Kirstein, *Anglo over Bracero*, 28, chap. 3.

24. García, *Operation Wetback*, 4. See also Barbara A. Driscoll, *The Tracks North: The Railroad Bracero Program of World War II* (Austin: Center for Mexican American Studies, 1999); Kirstein, *Anglo over Bracero*, 33–35; and *FRUS*, 1943, vol. 7, Mexico.

25. Kirstein, *Anglo over Bracero*, 14, 32. Peter Kirstein underscores the contradiction of the railroad Bracero Program, which the United States carried out based on the claim that its railroad system was in complete shambles. At the same time, it lent financial and technical support to Mexico's severely deteriorated railway system, "which demanded the same labor services being performed by Mexicans in the United States." Kirstein asks, "How could the United States afford to assume the major burden of rebuilding the Mexican railroad when United States government agencies and railroad companies predicted the demise of the United States railroad unless *bracero* labor was imported?" 36.

26. *FRUS*, 1943, vol. 6, Mexico, 543. On women's and children's labor in Mexico, see Ana E. Rosas, "Flexible Families. Bracero Families' Lives across Cultures, Communities, and Countries, 1942–1964" (PhD diss., University of Southern California, 2006). On how Mexico began to see the program as an opportunity for modernization of the peasant population and the nation, see Deborah Cohen, *Braceros: Migrant Citizens and Transnational Subjects in the Postwar United States and Mexico* (Chapel Hill: University of North Carolina Press, 2011).

27. See, for example, Secretary of State to Ambassador in Mexico, June 8, 1942, *FRUS*, 1942, vol. 6, Mexico, 537; Ambassador to Secretary of State, June 23, 1942, *FRUS*, 1942, vol. 6, 541; and *FRUS*, 1943, vol. 6, Mexico, throughout. On Mexico's hesitancy, see also Guglielmo, "Fighting for Caucasian Rights."

28. Kirstein, *Anglo over Bracero*, 14, 15. To be sure, Mexican Americans during this time appealed to the FEPC in cases of alleged employment discrimination. Their noncitizen Mexican brothers and sisters living in the United States, in fact, filed charges of discrimination based on citizenship as well. But for contract laborers, the FEPC could do little. See complaints from various ethnic Mexicans who cited discrimination based on race and citizenship, box 108, FEPC.

29. See *FRUS*, 1943, vol. 6, Mexico, throughout; Ambassador in Mexico to Secretary of State, February 16, 1946, *FRUS*, 1946, vol. 11, 1022–23; and Ambassador in Mexico to Secretary of State, March 18, 1946, *FRUS*, 1946, vol. 11, Mexico, 1025.

30. Kirstein, *Anglo over Bracero*, 15.

31. Ibid., 32; and Ambassador in Mexico to Secretary of State, February 17, 1944, *FRUS*, 1944, vol. 7, 1295.

32. See *FRUS*, Mexico, 1942, 1943, 1944, 1945, 1946; and Chief of Foreign Labor Section of War Manpower Commission to Chief of the Division of Mexican Affairs, *FRUS*, 1944, vol. 7, 1313.

33. See Chargé in Mexico to Secretary of State, May 2, 1945, *FRUS*, 1945, vol. 9, Mexico, 1143; Ambassador in Mexico to Secretary of State, August 23, 1945, *FRUS*, 1945, vol. 9, Mexico, 1146; Acting Secretary of State to Ambassador in Mexico, September 11, 1945, *FRUS*, vol. 9, Mexico, 1945, 1149–50; and Acting Secretary of State to Ambassador in Mexico, December 29, 1945, *FRUS*, vol. 9, Mexico, 1945, 1156–57.

34. See *FRUS, Mexico*, 1943, 1944, 1945, and 1946.

35. Ambassador in Mexico to Secretary of State, December 31, 1946, *FRUS*, 1946, vol. 9, Mexico, 1034.

36. Memorandum, January 31, 1946, *FRUS*, 1946, vol. 9, Mexico, 1019. See also Kitty Calavita, *Inside the State: The Bracero Program, Immigration, and the I.N.S.* (New York: Routledge, 1992), 28, 32, 41; and García y Griego, "Importation of Mexican Contract Laborers," 57.

37. García, *Operation Wetback*, 4.

38. Lorrin Thomas, *Puerto Rican Citizen: History and Political Identity in Twentieth-Century New York City* (Chicago: University of Chicago Press, 2010), 116.

39. Maldonado, "Contract Labor," 103–21. See also Clarence Senior, *Puerto Rican Emigration* (Rio Piedras: Social Science Center, University of Puerto Rico, 1947), 24–25. The irony, of course, was that many Mexican workers skipped out on their contracts as well.

40. The Fomento was the brainchild of Governor Rex Tugwell and Partido Popular Democrático (PPD) leader Luis Muñoz Marín. In contrast to the Nationalist Party, which in the midst of depression during the 1930s espoused a complete overthrow of American colonial powers, the PPD espoused a more moderate line—economic development (industrialization) in the hands of the island's elite. Shortly after the PPD gained control of the legislature in 1940, it created the Fomento as a type of state-run capitalist development project. When the state-supported manufacturing outfits failed to produce the expected levels of employment for the island, the Fomento administration shifted to recruiting American capital for industrial development. Felix Padilla, *Puerto Rican Chicago* (Notre Dame: University of Notre Dame Press, 1987), 45–47.

41. Monthly Progress Reports of Economic Development Administration, boxes 6, 11, 14, tarea 61–55, Fondo Departamento del Trabajo, AGPR.

    This bore a striking resemblance to the US-Mexico Border Industrialization Campaign, which was based on similar principles and in the 1950s brought industry (today's *maquilas*) to the Mexican side of the border, where tens of thousands of women do low-wage manufacturing and assembly work. Indeed, this was the economic plan in Mexico that immediately followed the end of the Bracero Program. See García y Griego, "Mexican Contract Laborers."

42. Monthly Progress Reports of Economic Development Administration, boxes 6, 11, 14, tarea 61–55, Fondo Departamento del Trabajo, AGPR.

43. Padilla, *Puerto Rican Chicago*, 49–52.

44. For more on Operation Bootstrap, see Whalen, *From Puerto Rico*; Briggs, *Reproducing Empire*; and Duany, *Puerto Rican Nation*. For critiques of "development," see, for example, Arturo Escobar, *Encountering Development: The Making and Unmaking of the Third World* (Princeton, NJ: Princeton University Press, 1995).

45. Letter to Governor Luis Muñoz Marín from women in Vega Baja, March 9, 1949, folder 741.1, box 2272, Fondo Oficina del Gobernador, AGPR. Author's translation.

46. As Carmen Whalen notes, Puerto Rican women had high labor participation rates, either in needle industries or through piecework or other forms of work at home. The feminization of Latin American and Asian labor in the late twentieth century in *maquiladoras* / assembly plants along the US-Mexico border and throughout Caribbean and Asian countries had roots in the 1940s and 1950s when US and other multinational corporations first began tapping such labor for light manufacturing

in Puerto Rico. See also Juan E. Hernández-Cruz, "A Perspective on Return Migration: The Circulation of Puerto Rican Workers" (PhD diss., New York University, 1982).

47. "Miembros de la Iglesia Evangélica Unida" to "Gobernador Luis Muñoz Marín," April 1950, folder 741.1, box 2272, Fondo del Gobernador, AGPR. Author's translation. Interestingly, this letter also reveals an initial rejection of government social welfare programs, which later became a critical form of subsistence for the island after modernization and development efforts failed. This ultimately contributed to the characterization of Puerto Ricans as a welfare-dependent population.

48. Telegrams, Manuel García to Governor Luis Muñoz Marín, March 10 and 28, 1949, folder 741.1, box 2272, Fondo Oficina del Gobernador, AGPR. Author's translation.

49. See History Task Force, *Labor Migration under Capitalism*, for a Marxist analysis of these economic changes.

50. Maura I. Toro-Morn, "Boricuas en Chicago: Gender and Class in the Migration and Settlement of Puerto Ricans," in *The Puerto Rican Diaspora: Historical Perspectives*, ed. Carmen Teresa Whalen and Victor Vazquez-Hernandez (Philadelphia: Temple University Press, 2005), 132; and History Task Force, *Labor Migration under Capitalism*. See Briggs, *Reproducing Empire*, esp. chaps. 3 and 4, for an extensive discussion of this.

51. This included the Chicago suburbs and northwest Indiana. L. Virgil Williams to Elmer W. Henderson, May 19, 1944, Latin American Problems, General Correspondence, box 108, FEPC. See also oral histories of former *braceros*, such as Andrés Héctor Quezada Lara, interviewed by Myrna Parra-Mantilla, June 16, 2003, in Bracero History Archive, item 4, http://braceroarchive.org/items/show/4 (accessed October 30, 2010); Louise Año Nuevo Kerr, "The Chicano Experience in Chicago, 1920–1970" (PhD diss., University of Illinois at Chicago, 1976), 121; and Kirstein, *Anglo over Bracero*, 23.

   Because Chicago operated as a central hub for many of the nation's railroads, it served as the headquarters for the nation's Railroad Retirement Board (RRB) and figured prominently in the railroad Bracero Program's administration. The initial meeting to discuss a labor recruitment program from Mexico took place in Chicago in October 1942.

52. Horace Cayton was a sociologist and coauthor with St. Clair Drake of *Black Metropolis: A Study of Negro Life in a Northern City* (New York: Harcourt, Brace and World, 1945), a groundbreaking and still influential study of the black community on Chicago's South Side.

53. The issue of *braceros'* ability to join unions and bargain collectively was unclear. Although theoretically Mexican contract workers could freely join unions according to the labor agreements, they were not made aware of this, and there also seemed to be some confusion among union officials about whether or not this was in fact the case. See Kirstein, *Anglo over Bracero*, 31; and *FRUS*, 1943, vol. 6, Mexico, 584.

54. "Minutes of the Meeting of the Committee on Minority Groups, Division III, Council of Social Agencies, Wed., May 10, 1945," folder 4, box 145, WC. Hillman also noted that fifteen hundred men from Barbados and Jamaica were also in the Chicago area on ninety-day contracts. Many of them were employed in "food processing industries" and were housed in the city's South Side black neighborhoods. A group of approximately one hundred men were also employed by the Republic Steel Company.

In 1944, the Railroad Retirement Board (RRB) estimated that approximately two hundred Mexicans were employed in the Chicago area in nonrail work. While the RRB did not specify the type of work, it did note that it was employment covered under the Social Security Act, and, thus, Social Security deductions had been taken from workers' paychecks. See Board Order 47–461, box 50, subseries 3, series 1, RRB.

55. "Minutes of the Meeting of the Committee on Minority Groups, Council of Social Agencies, September 26, 1945," folder 4, box 145, WC.

56. "Minutes of the Meeting of the Committee on Minority Groups, Council of Social Agencies, February 26, 1947," folder 7, box 145, WC. See chap. 2.

57. "Minutes of the Meeting to Consider Needs of Mexican Contract Laborers, Council of Social Agencies," November 19, 1945, folder 4, box 147, WC.

58. Telegram, June 15, 1945, Frank Paz to Elmer W. Henderson, Mexican Civic Committee, box 108, FEPC. Another twenty men were apparently stranded that August and housed by the MCC until they were dispatched to agricultural assignments in South Bend, Indiana. "Mexican Center Smooths Way," *CT*, August 12, 1945.

   See also "War Prisoners Fill Many Jobs, Poll Discloses," *CT*, September 19, 1943; Harry McClain, "IL Canner Using 510 Nazis in 'Grass' Fields," *CT*, May 18, 1944; and "Chicagoland Farms May Not Get Mexican Workers," *CT*, March 12, 1945.

59. See Valdés, *Al Norte*, 100–104; "Chicagoland Farms"; Calavita, *Inside the State*, 2; and García y Griego, "Mexican Contract Laborers," 69.

60. Calavita, *Inside the State*, 3.

61. See *FRUS*, 1943, vol. 7, Mexico, 584. See also Mexican Civic Committee folder, box 108, FEPC. Mexican officials, in fact, cited an instance in Chicago in which *braceros* "were being thrown in jail and kept there three or four weeks or more" for having skipped out on their contracts. *FRUS*, 1944, vol. 7, Mexico, 1324.

62. Calavita, *Inside the State*, 21, 31.

63. "Chicagoland Farms." See Valdés, *Al Norte*, 100–104; and García, *Operation Wetback*, 41–57.

64. In fact, these two areas of employment were explicitly excluded from Roosevelt's New Deal programs aimed at providing worker protections and benefits in the aftermath of the Great Depression. Not surprisingly, these fields also employed the highest number of African American and Mexican American workers compared to other occupations.

65. See, for example, Saturnino González Díaz, interview with Magdalena Mieri, August 31, 2005, in Bracero History Archive, item 173, accessed October 30, 2010, http://braceroarchive.org/items/show/173; Juan Loza, interview with Mireya Loza, August 31, 2005, in Bracero History Archive, item 175, accessed October 30, 2010, http://braceroarchive.org/items/show/175; and Pedro Pineda, interview with the author, September 1, 2005, in Bracero History Archive, item 180, accessed October 30, 2010, http://braceroarchive.org/items/show/180.

66. David G. Gutiérrez, *Walls and Mirrors: Mexican Americans, Mexican Immigrants, and the Politics of Ethnicity* (Berkeley: University of California Press, 1995), chap. 4. This occurred frequently with agricultural *braceros* as well, who reportedly skipped contracts to return to Mexico or left their jobs and then reappeared later in search of new contracts. See *FRUS*, 1943, vol. 6, Mexico, 580.

67. "6,000 Mexican Laborers to Work for U.S. Railways," *CT*, May 12, 1943; and "760 Mexicans Enter U.S. for Work on Railroads," *CT*, May 15, 1943. See Driscoll, *Tracks North*, 143–45; Felipe Nava oral history, in Miguel Ortiz, Laura Pantoja, Thomas Roman, and Ingrid Santos, "Bracero a la Aventura: Llegamos Haciendo Carril," *Telling*

Historias: Oral Histories from Chicago Based on the Curiosity of Youth and the Memories of Elders, 2002, author's personal collection; and Oscar Avila, "Mexican Workers Seek Full WW II Pay," *CT*, May 2, 2002.

68. Pineda interview. Maria de Lourdes Villar notes an undocumented immigrant's family path to Chicago by the 1980s: "The formal ending of the Bracero program in 1964 did not bring to an end what had become for [the interviewee's] family a long-term survival strategy." Maria de Lourdes Villar, "From Sojourners to Settlers: The Experience of Mexican Undocumented Migrants in Chicago" (PhD diss., University of Indiana, 1989), 46–47.

69. Jesús García, interview with the author, December 12, 2003.

70. See Marta Isabel Kollmann de Curutchet, "Localization of the Mexican and Cuban Population" (MA thesis, University of Chicago, 1967), 22. De Curutchet notes, for example, the following figures for Mexican immigrants admitted to Chicago: 1961—1,975; 1962—2,161; 1963—2,117; 1964—1,451; and 1965—2,007; for a total of 9,711 legally admitted during those five years. For other oral histories, see also the film *Bracero Stories* (directed by Patrick Mullins, Cherry Lane Productions, 2008), DVD.

71. Many scholars by now have identified this moment as the initial period of Puerto Rican migration to Chicago. See, for example, Maldonado, "Contract Labor", Elena Padilla, "Puerto Rican Immigrants in New York and Chicago: A Study in Comparative Assimilation" (MA thesis, University of Chicago, 1947); Toro-Morn, "Gender, Class, Family, and Migration"; Gina M. Pérez, "An Upbeat West Side Story: Puerto Ricans and Postwar Racial Politics in Chicago," *Centro Journal* 13, no. 2 (2001): 47–71; and Mérida Rúa, "Colao Subjectivities: Portomex and Mexirican Perspectives on Language and Identity," *Centro Journal* 13, no. 2 (2001): 117–33. For a discussion of the first domestic worker programs on the East Coast in 1946–47, see Whalen, *From Puerto Rico*, 56–63.

72. Employment contract, Puerto Rico Department of Labor, cartapacio 277, caja 15, serie 2, sección IV, LMM.

73. For more on the history of Mexican and Mexican American women as domestic workers, see Mary Romero, *Maid in the U.S.A.* (New York: Routledge, 1992).

74. Florence Wesley, untitled news clipping, *Christian Science Monitor*, November 20, 1946, folder 743, Emigración, box 2247, Fondo Oficina del Gobernador, AGPR. Japanese Americans (Nisei) who sought to leave internment camps during the war were apparently also placed as domestic servants in the homes of wealthy white Chicagoans during the 1940s. See Charlotte Brooks, "In the Twilight Zone between Black and White: Japanese American Resettlement and Community in Chicago, 1942-1945," *Journal of American History* 86, no. 4 (2000): 1664. Most Nisei, however, avoided domestic work and sought clerical jobs instead. One War Relocation Administration bulletin reported six hundred domestic job orders that had gone unfilled. Brooks, "In the Twilight Zone," 1666. This and the fact that many African Americans probably preferred not to return to domestic work after the war certainly must have contributed to the labor shortage and interest in Puerto Rican domestics.

75. "Report on Cases of Puerto Rican Laborers Brought to Chicago . . . ," 2, cartapacio 277, caja 15, serie 2, sección IV, LMM. On the supervision of working-class single women in cities, see Sarah Deutsch, *Women and the City: Gender, Space, and Power in Boston, 1870–1940* (New York: Oxford University Press, 2000); and Joanne Meyerowitz, *Women Adrift: Independent Wage Earners in Chicago, 1880–1930* (Chicago: University of Chicago Press, 1988).

76. This was a much higher wage than what Mexican *braceros* earned for maintenance of way work on American railroads. In 1943, *bracero* railroad contracts stipulated a minimum wage of forty-six cents an hour. See "6,000 Mexican Laborers to Work for U.S. Railways," *CT*, May 12, 1943.

77. "Puerto Ricans Arrive to Take Jobs in Foundry," *CT*, September 2, 1946; and Jean Van Vranken, "Géigel Presentará Enmienda a la Ley de Emigración Obrera," *EM*, January 24, 1947.

78. Manuel Pérez to Mr. Enrique Baiz Miró, October 29, 1946, cartapacio 277, caja 15, serie 2, sección IV, LMM.

79. There were no documented complaints from workers at the steel mill, and subsequent reports and letters do not mention them. A January 1947 newspaper article did make mention of those workers, citing that conditions were satisfactory. This might have been due to the fact that they earned higher wages and higher paychecks overall with more overtime pay. See Van Vranken, "Géigel Presentará Enmienda."

80. Cartapacio 251, caja 14, serie 2, sección IV, LMM.

81. "Informe Preliminar Sobre Trabajadores Puertorriqueños en Chicago," [December 1946], cartapacio 277, caja 15, serie 2, sección IV, LMM. Author's translation.

82. Ibid. Testimony of Leonard C. Lewin, December 20, 1946, cartapacio 277, caja 15, serie 2, sección IV, LMM.

83. Munita Muñoz Lee to Luis Muñoz Marín, December 9, 1946, cartapacio 277, caja 15, serie 2, sección IV, LMM. Author's translation. The irony of this, of course, was that Muñoz's father, as head of the Partido Popular Democrático, promoted the island's economic development and the ensuing migration policy that Muñoz was critiquing. Padilla, *Puerto Rican Chicago*, 44, 53.

84. Luis Muñoz Marín to Miss Munita Muñoz Lee, December 20, 1946, folder 3, box 137, Fondo Oficina del Gobernador, AGPR.

85. Manuel A. Peréz to Hon. Luis Muñoz Marín, December 18, 1946, cartapacio 251, caja 14, serie 2, sección IV, LMM.

86. Manuel A. Peréz to Miss Munita Muñoz Lee, December 17, 1946, cartapacio 251, caja 14, serie 2, sección IV, LMM.

87. Manuel A. Peréz to Sr. Director, "*El Imparcial*," December 17, 1946, cartapacio 251, caja 14, serie 2, sección IV, LMM. There may have been such letters as Pérez claimed, but I could not locate any in the archives.

88. Ibid. This argument that workers with contracts enjoyed many protections and safeguards would appear repeatedly in later years as more workers tried to travel on their own through "illegal" labor migration and officials of the Department of Labor's Migration Division publicly discouraged them from doing so.

89. Carmen Isales, "Confidential Report on Cases of Puerto Rican Laborers Brought to Chicago to Work as Domestics and Foundry Workers under Contract with Castle, Barton, and Associates, Inc.," March 22, 1947, cartapacio 277, caja 15, serie 2, sección IV, LMM.

90. Carmen Isales, "Situación de los Obreros Puertorriqueños Contratados por la Agencia de Empleos Castle, Barton and Assoc.," December 1946, cartapacio 277, caja 15, subserie 9, serie 2, sección IV, LMM; and Munita Muñoz Lee to Luis Muñoz Marín, December 9, 1946, cartapacio 277, caja 15, subserie 9, serie 2, sección IV, LMM.

91. Local private social service agencies did provide assistance to the workers. They also received assistance from the Council of Social Agencies, which formed a special committee to deal with the domestic workers' situation. The Catholic Youth Organization also became involved and subsequently established a "Puerto Rican Service"

program providing medical and dental services, language courses, and recreation. "Findings from Meeting to Promote Better Integration of the Puerto Rican Citizenry into the Community," March 26, 1953; "Meeting—February 12, 1954, Re: Puerto Ricans"; Mary A. Young to Mr. MacRae, January 28, 1954; and Mary A. Young to Joseph L. Moss, April 2, 1954—all in folder 3, box 148, WC. Pilar Díaz to Welfare Council of Metropolitan Chicago, September 21, 1953, folder 10, box 147, WC. See also meeting minutes, cartapacio 277, caja 15, serie 2, sección IV, LMM.

92. Isales, "Situación de los Obreros Puertorriqueños."

93. "Puerto Rican Senator Here to Aid Natives," *CT*, January 10, 1947; Vicente Géigel Polanco to Luis Muñoz Marín, cable/telegram, January 12, 1947, cartapacio 1, serie 8, LMM; and Van Vranken, "Géigel Presentará Enmienda."

 A year after the debacle had been resolved, a newspaper article advertised that the Puerto Rico Department of Labor would initiate a training program for domestic workers to better manage their migration. "Puerto Ricans Train for U.S. Domestic Jobs," *CT*, August 8, 1947. For more on this, see Pérez, *Near Northwest Side Story*, 62–68.

94. On Puerto Rican migration to New York, see Virginia Sánchez-Korrol, *From Colonia to Community: The History of Puerto Ricans in New York City* (Berkeley: University of California Press, 1994); and Thomas, *Puerto Rican Citizen*.

95. New York newspapers frequently ran articles that blasted Puerto Ricans for the challenges they presented to local institutions (such as schools) and the social burdens they imposed upon welfare agencies, housing, and so forth. See clippings in cartapacio 1, caja 15, serie 9, LMM.

96. See Duany, *Puerto Rican Nation*; Maldonado, "Contract Labor"; Pérez, *Near Northwest Side Story*; and Thomas, *Puerto Rican Citizen*, chap. 5.

97. "Puerto Rico Opens Employment Bureau to Serve Midwest," *CT*, January 24, 1949; and Anthony Vega, untitled report, July 22, 1953, folder 10, box 147, WC.

98. "Operations—Reports," box 26, tarea 61-55, Fondo Departamento del Trabajo, AGPR.

99. Untitled newspaper clipping, n.d., box 14, tarea 61-55, Fondo Departamento del Trabajo, AGPR.

100. Progress Report of Mexican Civic Committee, 4, MCC flyer, box 108, FEPC.

101. Año Nuevo Kerr, "Chicano Experience in Chicago," 70, 78–79.

102. "Report on the Conference on the Mexican Americans in Chicago"; and Frank Paz, "Status of the Mexican American in Chicago," speech, 7, folder 4, box 147, WC.

103. See chap. 2 for more on this. On the struggle for "recognition" among Puerto Ricans in New York, see Thomas, *Puerto Rican Citizen*.

104. See Angelica Rivera, "Re-inserting Mexican-American Women's Voices into 1950s Chicago Educational History" (PhD diss., University of Illinois at Urbana-Champaign, 2008), 40, 112, 122. *Braceros* themselves have testified to the hostility and animosity they felt from *Tejano* migrant farmworkers, for example, who resented *braceros* for being cheaper labor and driving down wages. See, for example, Pineda interview.

105. Richard Santillán, "Rosita the Riveter: Midwest Mexican American Women during World War II, 1941-45," in *Perspectives in Mexican American Studies: Mexicans in the Midwest*, ed. Juan R. García, 115–47 (Tucson: University of Arizona Press, 1989); and Rosa de la Llata Hernandez, interview with the author, January 21, 2009.

106. "4 Rail Workers, Lost in Smoke, Killed by Train," *CT*, March 3, 1944. A middle-aged

woman, Antonia Vásquez, was also injured during the incident and hospitalized, although she was not identified as a worker.

107. Mexican American Council newsletter, February 1953, 5, folder 10, box 147, WC. The issue of illegal alien Mexicans first appeared in the local press in September 1947. "Mexican Aliens Jailed," *CT*, September 4, 1947.

108. For a comprehensive view of intraethnic relations between Mexican Americans and Mexican immigrants, see Gutiérrez, *Walls and Mirrors*. See also García, *Operation Wetback*; and Matt García, *A World of Its Own: Race, Labor, and Citrus in the Making of Greater Los Angeles, 1900–1970* (Chapel Hill: University of North Carolina Press, 2001), chap. 5.

109. Dora Tannenbaum, Sara McCaulley, and H. Daniel Carpenter, Hudson Guild Neighborhood House, Colony House, and the Grand Street Settlement, *The Puerto Rican Migration . . . A Report*, 1955, box 1207, tarea 96–20, Fondo Oficina del Gobernador, AGPR.

110. See García, *Operation Wetback*; Ngai, *Impossible Subjects*, chap. 4; and García y Griego, "Importation of Mexican Contract Laborers." Matt García cites a 1958 thesis on the Bracero Program in Southern California that noted, "Many farmers preferred 'wetbacks' to locals or *braceros* mainly because the wetbacks worked twice as hard for half the pay." García, *World of Its Own*, 186. See also *FRUS*, 1950, vol. 2, Mexico, 955.

Interestingly, as early as 1947, Mexico argued that the American government should begin to study "the possibility of punishing the employers of illegal crossers." *FRUS*, 1947, vol. 8, Mexico, 826.

111. García, *Operation Wetback*, 97; Ernesto Galarza, *Merchants of Labor: The Mexican Bracero Story: An Account of the Managed Migration of Mexican Farm Workers in California, 1942–1960* (Charlotte, CA: McNally and Loftin, 1964); and Ngai, *Impossible Subjects*, chap. 4.

112. García, *Operation Wetback*, 224; and "Illegal Alien Here since 1921 Wants to Leave," *CT*, September 22, 1954.

113. Roberto Medina oral history, quoted in Mervin Méndez, "Recollections: The 1966 Division Street Riots," *Diálogo: Center for Latino Research DePaul University*, no. 2 (1997): 31.

114. *FRUS*, 1944, vol. 7, Mexico, 1324, 1327.

115. See, for example, de Curutchet, "Localization of the Mexican and Cuban Population," 72; and Rivera, "Re-inserting Mexican-American Women's Voices," 57, 126.

116. Cohen and Taylor, *American Pharaoh*.

117. The Border Industrialization Program, for example, which began immediately after the Bracero Program ended, signaled one form of "offshore" flight of American industry to lower-wage foreign labor markets. On the Border Industrialization Program, see Jefferson Cowie, *Capital Moves: RCA's Seventy-Year Quest for Cheap Labor* (Ithaca, NY: Cornell University Press, 1999), chaps. 4 and 6.

CHAPTER TWO

1. Marta Isabel Kollman de Curutchet, "Localization of the Mexican and Cuban Population of Chicago" (MA thesis, University of Chicago, 1967), 26.

2. Cordi Marian Settlement report, n.d. [ca. 1957], folder 373, IAF.

3. Rosa de la Llata, interview with the author, January 21, 2009.

4. In this chapter, I use the term *Spanish-speaking* to refer to Mexicans and Puerto Ricans collectively—rather than the contemporary label *Latina/o*—to accurately capture the

parlance of the time. Although certainly second-generation children of immigrants and Mexican American migrants from Texas may not necessarily have spoken Spanish, the phrase connoted what Mexicans and Puerto Ricans believed they had most in common—a shared linguistic and colonial heritage from Spain.

5. Louise Hutchinson, "Quiet 'Revolt' Making City Happier Place for Mexicans," *CT*, March 29, 1953; and Evelyn Kitagawa and Karl E. Taeuber, *Local Community Fact Book: Chicago's Metropolitan Area, 1960* (Chicago: Chicago Community Inventory, University of Chicago, 1963), 70. See also Humbert S. Nelli, "The Myth of Urban Renewal: Chicago's Near West Side Italian Community in the 1960s," *Italian American Identity* (April 1977): 51–54.

6. The neighborhood's diversity was not unique to Chicago; Mexican and Puerto Rican (im)migrants historically made their homes in diverse (im)migrant communities in cities like Los Angeles and New York. See, for example, George Sanchez's discussion of Boyle Heights in Los Angeles and Virginia Sánchez-Korrol's and Lorrin Thomas's discussions of Puerto Rican *colonias* in New York City. George J. Sanchez, *Becoming Mexican American: Ethnicity, Culture, and Identity in Chicano Los Angeles, 1900–1945* (New York: Oxford University Press, 1993); Virginia Sánchez-Korrol, *From Colonia to Community: The History of Puerto Ricans in New York City* (Berkeley: University of California Press, 1994); and Lorrin Thomas, *Puerto Rican Citizen: History and Political Identity in Twentieth-Century New York City* (Chicago: University of Chicago Press, 2010).

7. I use the term *ethnoracial* to capture distinctions in identity and social position based on *both* ethnicity and race. European immigrants and their descendants, for example, could claim both an ethnic identity (Italian, Polish, Irish, etc.) and a racial identity (white). Mexicans and Puerto Ricans, I suggest, could also hold both an ethnic (national) identity and a racial one simultaneously or at different moments, but these were not always consistent and could shift depending on the context. Their claim to a white racial identity, for example, was very tenuous, highly contested, and unstable and contingent upon outside observers. For more on white ethnic identity and race, see, for example, Mary Waters, *Ethnic Options: Choosing Identities in America* (Berkeley: University of California Press, 1990); and Matthew Frye Jacobson, *Whiteness of a Different Color: European Immigrants and the Alchemy of Race* (Cambridge, MA: Harvard University Press, 1998).

8. Clara E. Rodríguez, *Changing Race: Latinos, the Census, and the History of Ethnicity in the United States* (New York: NYU Press, 2000), x, 6.

9. In their community studies, University of Chicago researchers divided up the city into seventy-five "community areas," as they called them, giving them names, such as the Near West Side. Such designations did not usually match the names that community residents themselves gave to their neighborhoods. Moreover, these community areas often encapsulated multiple smaller neighborhoods, known to their inhabitants by street names—such as Halsted-Roosevelt, Taylor Street, Maxwell Street—or by other nicknames, such as "Black Bottom."

10. According to the legend, Mrs. O'Leary's cow tipped over a lantern and set the neighborhood, and soon the city, ablaze. The story seemed plausible, as the densely populated area often housed people and their livestock in close quarters, and most homes were essentially wooden shacks. That newspapers would blame an Irish immigrant family for the fire reflected the nativism and anti-immigrant prejudice of the time. See Dennis Grammenos, "Space and Representation in Chicago's Near West Side: A Discourse Analysis" (PhD diss., University of Illinois, 2000), 58–64.

11. For a description of the Near West Side before the twentieth century, see Thomas L. Philpott, *The Slum and the Ghetto: Neighborhood Deterioration and Middle-Class Reform, Chicago, 1880–1930* (New York: Oxford University Press, 1978). See also the works of social workers and reformers, such as Jane Addams, *Forty Years at Hull-House* (New York: Macmillan, 1935); and Edith Abbott, *The Tenements of Chicago, 1908–1935* (Chicago: University of Chicago Press, 1936). See also Judith Ann Trolander, *Professionalism and Social Change: From the Settlement House Movement to Neighborhood Centers, 1886 to the Present* (New York: Columbia University Press, 1987).

12. Irving Cutler, *The Jews of Chicago: From Shtetl to Suburb* (Urbana: University of Illinois Press, 1996), 58–72. From Ira Berkow, *Maxwell Street* (New York: Doubleday, 1977), cited in Carolyn Eastwood, *Near West Side Stories: Struggles for Community in Chicago's Maxwell Street Neighborhood* (Chicago: Lake Claremont Press, 2002), 23. Cutler notes that in the 1920s, the entire area (including the businesses on Halsted Street and the wholesale shops on Twelfth Street) ranked third highest in sales in the entire city, 70.

13. Like most other parts of the city that housed ethnically diverse populations, immigrants clustered in their own "colonies" or "districts" within a given community. Moreover, they were often associated spatially with a specific street, which served as a metonym for the larger ethnic settlement. Thus, although Italians lived on other intersecting and nearby streets, "Taylor Street" stood in for *their* neighborhood.

14. See Gerald D. Suttles, *The Social Order of the Slum: Ethnicity and Territory in the Inner City* (Chicago: University of Chicago Press, 1968), 18; Thomas Guglielmo, *White on Arrival: Italians, Race, Color, and Power in Chicago, 1890–1945* (Oxford: Oxford University Press, 2003); and Humbert S. Nelli, *Italians in Chicago, 1880–1930: A Study in Ethnic Mobility* (New York: Oxford University Press, 1979).

15. Andrew T. Kopan, "Greek Survival in Chicago: The Role of Ethnic Education, 1890–1980," in *Ethnic Chicago*, ed. Melvin G. Holli and Peter d'A. Jones, 138–45, 160–64 (Grand Rapids, MI: William B. Eerdmans, 1984).

16. Kopan, "Greek Survival in Chicago," 117; and Suttles, *Social Order of the Slum*, 27. In 1920 the foreign-born made up 30 percent of the city's population. Louise Año Nuevo Kerr, "The Chicano Experience in Chicago, 1920–1970" (PhD diss., University of Illinois, 1976), 21.

17. For a history of the Great Migration, see James R. Grossman, *Land of Hope: Chicago, Black Southerners, and the Great Migration* (Chicago: University of Chicago Press, 1989). For a history of white racial violence against African Americans, see, for example, William M. Tuttle Jr., *Race Riot: Chicago in the Red Summer of 1919* (New York: Atheneum, 1970); Arnold R. Hirsch, *Making the Second Ghetto: Race and Housing in Chicago, 1940–1960* (Cambridge: Cambridge University Press, 1983); Horace Cayton and St. Clair Drake, *Black Metropolis: A Study of Negro Life in a Northern City* (New York: Harcourt, Brace and World, 1945); and Otis Dudley Duncan and Beverly Duncan, *The Negro Population of Chicago: A Study of Residential Succession* (Chicago: University of Chicago Press, 1957). See also Philpott, *Slum and the Ghetto*, esp. chap. 7.

18. According to sociologist Louis Wirth, Jews on the Near West Side were less resistant to incoming blacks than whites in other areas and allowed them to settle nearby. Eastwood, *Near West Side Stories*, 204. Thomas Philpott disputes this, however, claiming that Jews objected to blacks just as much as other whites did. See Philpott, *Slum and the Ghetto*, chap. 7.

19. Guglielmo, *White on Arrival*, 49. Thomas Philpott notes that referring to a neighborhood as an Italian "colony" did not mean it was only Italian. Rather, European ethnics might occupy certain buildings, or cluster along parts of street blocks, but they were fairly intermixed, never segregated the way blacks were. *Colony* or *settlement* referred more to a social world or network of coethnics, not necessarily a highly segregated ghetto. An area called "Little Ireland," for example, was only one-third Irish, and only 3 percent of the city's Irish-stock population lived there. Philpott, *Slum and the Ghetto*, 143. Dominic Pacyga calls this the "myth of ethnic segregation." Dominic A. Pacyga, "To Live amongst Others: Poles and Their Neighbors in Industrial Chicago, 1865–1930," *Journal of American Ethnic History* 16, no. 1 (1996): 55–73.

20. William Ayers, *A Kind and Just Parent: The Children of Juvenile Court* (Boston: Beacon Press, 1997), 24–27.

21. The first estimate comes from City of Chicago, Department of Development and Planning, *The People of Chicago: Who We Are and Who We Have Been* (Chicago: City of Chicago, Department of Development and Planning, 1976). When economist Paul Taylor did research in the Chicago area in the late 1920s, he estimated closer to thirty thousand Mexican immigrants and their US-born children. His estimate, however, included small colonies outside of Chicago proper, in northwest Indiana, and the south suburbs of Chicago. Paul S. Taylor, *Mexican Labor in the United States*, vol. 2 (New York: Arno Press, 1932, repr. 1970). Chicago had a small population of other Latin American immigrants also, but Mexicans constituted the largest nationality by far.

22. On Mexican immigrants in Chicago prior to World War II, see Año Nuevo Kerr, "Chicano Experience"; Gabriela Arredondo, *Mexican Chicago: Race, Ethnicity and Nation, 1916–1939* (Urbana: University of Illinois Press, 2008); Michael Innis-Jimenez, "Persisting in the Shadow of Steel: Community Formation and Survival in Mexican South Chicago, 1919–1939" (PhD diss., University of Iowa, 2006); F. Arturo Rosales, "Mexicans, Interethnic Violence, and Crime in the Chicago Area during the 1920s and 1930s: The Struggle to Achieve Ethnic Consciousness," in *Perspectives in Mexican American Studies: Mexicans in the Midwest*, ed. Juan R. García, 59–97 (Tucson: University of Arizona Press, 1989); F. Arturo Rosales, "The Regional Origins of Mexicano Immigrants to Chicago during the 1920s," *Aztlán* 7, no. 2 (1976): 187–202; Taylor, *Mexican Labor in the United States*, vol. 2; and David Stafford Weber, "Anglo Views of Mexican Immigrants: Popular Perceptions and Neighborhood Realities in Chicago, 1900–1940" (PhD diss., Ohio State University, 1982).

　　On Mexican immigrants in the Midwest more generally, see Juan R. García, *Mexicans in the Midwest, 1900–1932* (Tucson: University of Arizona Press, 1996); Francisco A. Rosales and Daniel T. Simon, "Chicano Steel Workers and Unionism in the Midwest, 1919–1945," *Aztlán* 6, no. 2 (1975): 267–75; Richard Santillán, "Rosita the Riveter: Midwest Mexican American Women during World War II, 1941–45," in *Perspectives in Mexican American Studies: Mexicans in the Midwest*, ed. Juan R. García, 115–47 (Tucson: University of Arizona Press, 1989); Dennis Nodín Valdés, *Al Norte: Agricultural Workers in the Great Lakes Region, 1917–1970* (Austin: University of Texas Press, 1991); Dionisio Nodín Valdés, *Barrios Norteños: St. Paul and Midwestern Mexican Communities in the Twentieth Century* (Austin: University of Texas Press, 2000); and Zaragosa Vargas, *Proletarians of the North: A History of Mexican Industrial Workers in Detroit and the Midwest, 1917–1933* (Berkeley: University of California Press, 1993).

23. Such Americanization programs served primarily European immigrants, however, such as Italians, Poles, Greeks, and Russian Jews. For Mexican immigrants' participation in Hull House's pottery programs, see Cheryl R. Ganz and Margaret Strobel, eds., *Pots of Promise: Mexicans and Pottery at Hull-House, 1920–40* (Urbana: University of Illinois Press, 2004); "Life Sings on thru Poverty in Booth House," *CT*, November 16, 1947; and Año Nuevo Kerr, "Chicano Experience," 52–53.

24. St. Francis had been established by German immigrants and was completed in 1875. It became Italian as Germans moved away. In the early 1920s, only one Spanish-language parish existed in the entire city, Our Lady of Guadalupe in South Chicago. See Eastwood, *Near West Side Stories*, 272–73. See also Phil Ayala, interview with the author, December 4, 2003. St. Francis of Assisi, Eighth Grade Graduation Program, box 89, folder 3, CAP.

25. Ayala interview; Adrian Canales, Mikale Haepp, Josue Olivas, and Amanda Rojas, "Movement and Settlement: A Lower West Side Story," based on oral history with Jovita Duran, in *Telling Historias: Oral Histories from Chicago Based on the Curiosity of Youth and the Memories of Elders*, 2002, author's personal collection; and "Mexican Settlement to Give Annual Exhibit," *CT*, August 11, 1946. The Cristero Rebellion, which was a reaction to the persecution of the Catholic Church in Mexico in the mid- to late 1920s, played a significant role in converting many Mexicans to Protestant sects. The Near West Side included, for example, Mexican Methodist, Pentecostal, and Mennonite churches. See Arredondo, *Mexican Chicago*; Suttles, *Social Order of the Slum*, 44; and Año Nuevo Kerr, "Chicano Experience," 54–57.

26. For more on the Mexican community during the 1920s and 1930s, see Año Nuevo Kerr, "Chicano Experience"; and Arredondo, *Mexican Chicago*.

27. See Arredondo, *Mexican Chicago*. See also Michael McCoyer, "Darkness of a Different Color: Mexicans and Racial Formation in Greater Chicago, 1916–1960" (PhD diss., Northwestern University, 2007).

28. This event has been well documented by multiple scholars. See, for example, Tuttle, *Race Riot*; and Guglielmo, *White on Arrival*. For the experience of Mexicans in the riots, see Arredondo, *Mexican Chicago*, chap. 2; and McCoyer, "Darkness of a Different Color."

29. On Mexican Americans and whiteness, see Gross, "'Caucasian Cloak'"; Foley, "Partly Colored / Other White"; and Guglielmo, "Fighting for Caucasian Rights."

30. Louis Wirth and Eleanor H. Bernert, eds., *Local Community Fact Book of Chicago* (Chicago: University of Chicago Press, 1949). The 0.3 percent nonwhite and nonblack population would have included Chinese, Filipinos, Japanese, and others. See, for example, Brooks, "In the Twilight Zone"; and Barbara M. Posadas, "Crossed Boundaries in Interracial Chicago: Pilipino American Families since 1925," in *Unequal Sisters: A Multicultural Reader in U.S. Women's History*, ed. Vicki Ruiz and Ellen Carol DuBois, 362–75 (New York: Routledge, 2000).

31. Chicago Community Inventory, "Nonwhite Population Change for the City of Chicago, 1940–1950," press release, folder 4, box 73, CAP; and Año Nuevo Kerr, "Chicano Experience," 2–3.

32. Rodríguez, *Changing Race*, x, 6. See also Ian F. Haney López, *White by Law: The Legal Construction of Race* (New York: New York University Press, 1996). Other groups, such as Japanese Americans, shared similar struggles. Although officially they were identified as nonwhites by the Census Bureau, socially they occupied a space between black and white in the urban landscape. See Brooks, "In the Twilight Zone."

33. "Minutes of the Meeting of the Committee on Minority Groups," October 3 and December 5, 1947, folder 7, box 145; Frank X. Paz, "Mexican-Americans in Chicago: A General Survey," January 1948, folder 4, box 147; meeting minutes, May 5, 1948, and February 23, 1949, folder 4, box 147—all in WC; "Call Conference Here on Status of 35,000 Mexican Americans," CT, May 16, 1949; "Report on the Conference on the Mexican Americans in Chicago," n.d., folder 4, box 147, WC; and Año Nuevo Kerr, "Chicano Experience," 150.

34. "Report on the Conference on the Mexican Americans in Chicago"; Frank Paz, "Status of the Mexican American in Chicago," speech given at conference, 1949, 7, folder 4, box 147, WC.

35. Paz, "Status of the Mexican American in Chicago."

36. Ibid. For a discussion on the racialization of Mexican Americas in relation to crime, see Edward Escobar, *Race, Police, and the Making of an Identity: Mexican Americans and the Los Angeles Police Department, 1900–1945* (Berkeley: University of California Press, 1999).

37. "Report on the Conference on the Mexican Americans in Chicago"; "A Brief History of the Committee on Minority Group Relations, Division of Education and Recreation, Welfare Council of Metropolitan Chicago," October 1950, folder 13, box 145, WC; and untitled document, Mexican American Council, April 1953, 1, folder 10, box 88, CAP.

38. Untitled document, Mexican American Council, April 1953, 3, folder 10, box 88, CAP.

39. American Council of Spanish Speaking People (ACSSP) newsletter, March 1, 1953, 4, folder 10, box 88, CAP.

40. Ibid. As other Chicano historians have pointed out, contrary to popular belief, the 1940s and 1950s represented a period of significant civil rights organizing, which preceded the better-known 1960s and 1970s radical era. MAC, like many such organizations of its generation in the Southwest, aspired to respectability and "Americanness" but also defended its members against prejudiced assaults and violations of their rights.

41. Bernice Stevens Decker, "Mexican-Americans Win Help in Chicago," reprinted from *Christian Science Monitor*, date unknown, 1950, folder 10, box 88, CAP.

42. See, for example, Raquel Márquez, "The Mexican American Council of Chicago," *Vida Latina*, May 1956, 30.

43. Mexican American Council, untitled document, April 1953; Mexican American Council newsletter, February 1953; and Porfirio Miranda, report on Mexican immigrants and history in Chicago, n.d. [ca. 1953]—all in folder 10, box 88, CAP. The Catholic Church seemed to oppose community participation in any non-Catholic organizations, especially in Protestant settlement houses.

44. See Angelica Rivera, "Re-inserting Mexican American Women's Voices into 1950s Chicago Educational History" (PhD diss., University of Illinois at Urbana-Champaign, 2008), 64; Cordi Marian Settlement report, ca. 1956, folder 373, IAF; Hutchinson, "Quiet 'Revolt'"; and Márquez, "Mexican American Council."

45. On Puerto Ricans, see "Boricuas Piden Ayuda en Chicago," EM, February 3, 1954, 1. See also Luis Sanchez Cappa, "Funcionario Chicago Llega Hoy a Discutir Situación de Boricuas," EM, February 4, 1954, 5; and Luis Sanchez Cappa, "Vino a Discutir Su Plan de Repatriar Obreros," EM, February 5, 1954, 1.

46. Not all of these workers necessarily lived in Chicago, as many worked on agricul-

tural contracts outside the city. Walter E. Parker to John Gandy, September 22, 1953, folder 10, box 147, WC.

47. See, for example, the oral histories of former Young Lords whose parents settled in Chicago after working agricultural circuits. Eugenia Rodriguez, interview with José "Cha Cha" Jiménez, December 6, 1993, and Carlos Flores, interview with Mervin Méndez, September 11, 1995—both located in box 2, YL. Also José Jiménez and Modesto Rivera, interview with the author, June 19, 2004.

48. See, for example, Migration Division, New York Office press release, "Job Opportunities in Chicago and Ohio," October 10, 1955, folder 23, and "Job Opportunities in Areas of Chicago," May 23, 1956, folder 24—both in box 308, Identification and Documentation Program, OGPRUS. See also "Boletín de Información," box 25, División Técnica, 1953–54, P-R, Fondo Departamento del Trabajo, AGPR.

49. "Establecen en Chicago Oficina Mediano Oeste," *EM*, October 30, 1953, 23; "Findings from Meeting to Promote Better Integration of the Puerto Rican Citizenry into the Community," March 26, 1953, folder 3, box 148, WC; Commonwealth of Puerto Rico, Department of Labor, Migration Division, *Un Amigo en Chicago*, 1956, OGPRUS; and Gina Pérez, *The Near Northwest Side Story: Migration, Displacement, and Puerto Rican Families* (Berkeley: University of California Press, 2004). The film's title perhaps had a dual meaning. "A friend in Chicago" could refer to the impetus for a potential migrant's move to the city (he or she had "a friend in Chicago" who encouraged him or her to come), but it was also meant to connote that the Migration Division office would be "a friend" for migrants in need. Migration Division, *Annual Report, 1956–57*, 133, folder 4, box 1, OGPRUS.

50. Migration Division, *Annual Report, 1956–57*, 132–34, folder 4, box 1, OGPRUS. See also Pérez, *Near Northwest Side Story*, 68–71.

51. Commonwealth of Puerto Rico, Department of Labor, Bureau of Employment and Migration, Migration Division report, July 22, 1953, folder 10, box 147, WC.

52. Kitagawa and Taueber, *Local Community Fact Book*, 248, 272. The poverty level in 1960 reflected incomes below three thousand dollars, though it is not clear for how large a household this measured poverty.

53. "Dispersión de Migrantes," *EM*, May 11, 1953, 6. See also "Estudio Revela Migrantes Isla Se Extienden por Toda la Nación," *EM*, June 6, 1953, 1; City of Chicago, *Chicago's Spanish Speaking Population*, 7; and Kitagawa and Taeuber, *Local Community Fact Book*, 71. Felix Padilla underestimates the significance of the Near West Side as one of Puerto Ricans' first settlements, focusing instead on North Side neighborhoods. His own statistics reveal, however, that the area had one of the largest concentrations of Puerto Ricans by 1960. Felix Padilla, *Puerto Rican Chicago* (Notre Dame, IN: University of Notre Dame Press, 1987), 79.

54. Waitstill H. Sharp to Miss Hazel Holm, January 23, 1951, folder 3, box 148, WC. Sharp was the director of the Chicago Council against Racial and Religious Discrimination, and his comments to Miss Holm hint at a possible concern over Chicagoans developing prejudice against Puerto Ricans if they became too visible as a distinct group in the city's neighborhoods. Thus, the Migration Division's putative warning against settling in *barrios* may have had twin purposes: (1) to encourage assimilation and (2) to reduce potential discrimination against Puerto Ricans. This admonition may have emerged from Elena Padilla's master's thesis, which argued that migrants who dispersed throughout the city assimilated at much higher rates than those who congregated in ethnic enclaves. The origins of antipathy toward Mexicans may lie

in the experience of the first wave of migrants in 1946–47. Puerto Rican officials expressed concern, for example, over their women's socializing and intermarrying with Mexican men. See Elena Padilla, "Puerto Rican Immigrants in New York and Chicago: A Study in Comparative Assimilation" (MA thesis, University of Chicago, 1947), 57, 99.

55. See Manuel Martinez, *Chicago: Historia de Nuestra Comunidad Puertorriqueña* (Chicago: Reyes and Sons, 1989); and Padilla, *Puerto Rican Chicago*, 78–84.

56. José "Cha Cha" Jiménez, interview with the author; José "Cha Cha" Jiménez, untitled manuscript, n.d., YL; and Aida Sanchez-Romano, interview with the author, September 15, 2004. From the moment Puerto Ricans arrived as contract laborers in 1946–47, Mexicans provided social support, welcoming them to the MCC, helping them find housing, and offering social opportunities. The fact that another Spanish-speaking group lived in the city helped them with their transition. Padilla, "Puerto Rican Immigrants," 87. Puerto Ricans also created enclaves farther north, in the city's Near North Side neighborhood. See chap. 4.

57. Knights of St. John, *El Mensajero*, April 1958, folder 152, IAF.

58. See Pérez, *Near Northwest Side Story*; Marixsa Alicea, "Cuando Nosotros Vivíamos . . . Stories of Displacement and Settlement in Puerto Rican Chicago," *Centro Journal* 13, no. 2 (2001): 167–95; and Padilla, "Puerto Rican Immigrants," 63, 72, 79–81.

   Puerto Ricans had a history of settling near or among African Americans in New York and other cities as well. See Juan Flores, "'Que Assimilated, Brother, Yo Soy Asimilao': The Structuring of Puerto Rican Identity in the U.S.," *Journal of Ethnic Studies* 13, no. 3 (1985): 1–16.

59. Nick Von Hoffman, research notes, n.d. [mid-1950s], folder 259, IAF; Padilla, *Puerto Rican Chicago*, 91, 126–37; and Martinez, *Chicago*, 122–26.

60. Memo from Helen McLane, Community Fund of Chicago, to Robert H. MacRae, Mary A. Young, Hollis Vick, and Alice K. Ray, Welfare Council, February 15, 1955, folder 3, box 148, WC.

61. Near West Side Community Council, *Near West Side Chronicle*, monthly newsletter, January 1959, folder 2, box 92, CAP. For a more detailed discussion of the knights and the Catholic Church's role in the Puerto Rican community, see Martinez, *Chicago*, 100–101, 120–26. On the predominance of Irish clergy in the Catholic Church, see James R. Barrett, and David R. Roediger, "The Irish and the 'Americanization' of the 'New Immigrants' in the Streets and in the Churches of the Urban United States, 1900–1930," *Journal of American Ethnic History* 24, no. 4 (2005): 4–33.

62. The archdiocese had traditionally established national parishes for each nationality—Lithuanians, Poles, Czechs, French, Germans, and so on. By the 1920s, however, Cardinal George Mundelein had moved away from a national parish model to a "territorial" or neighborhood parish, which, for all intents and purposes, essentially still mimicked ethnic boundaries. David Badillo, *Latinos and the New Immigrant Church* (Baltimore: Johns Hopkins University Press, 2006), 84. The territorial parish, however, may have assisted in the assimilation of white ethnics who were less segregated in their own churches and rapidly becoming "American" Catholics. See also Eileen McMahon, *What Parish Are You From? A Chicago Irish Community and Race Relations* (Lexington: University of Kentucky Press, 1995).

63. Padilla, *Puerto Rican Chicago*, 129. See also John J. Lennon, "A Comparative Study of the Patterns of Acculturation of Selected Puerto Rican Protestant and Roman Catholic Families in an Urban Metropolitan Area" (San Francisco: R and E Research Associates, 1976), 36–37.

64. Felix Padilla stresses the ethnic solidarity that the Caballeros nurtured and minimizes the religious content of the organization. David Badillo, in contrast, argues that evangelizing those men who did not regularly attend mass or take the sacraments constituted an important part of the group's mission. This was shrouded, however, in the ethnic solidarity and social and cultural activities that the Caballeros promoted. Both authors agree, nonetheless, that the group and its leadership served as the most visible political representative of the Puerto Rican population until the mid-1960s. Padilla, *Puerto Rican Chicago*, 126–37; and Badillo, *Latinos and the New Immigrant Church*, 87–88.

65. *Las Iglesias Catolicas de Habla Hispana Les Dan la Bienvenida a Chicago*, pamphlet, n.d., folder 151, IAF.

    The Catholic diocese did not maintain a monopoly on Spanish-Speaking churchgoers, as several Protestant denominations, such as the Latin American Mennonite Church, also provided services to Spanish-speaking residents. Casa Central, for example, has served for decades as a Protestant social service agency for Puerto Ricans. Originally established on the Near West Side, it later relocated to its present location in Humboldt Park. Martinez, *Chicago*, 101; and Near West Side Community Council, *Where to Find It . . . 1957–59 Directory of Community Resources*, folder 36, box 20, supplement 2, West [Near West] Side Community Collection, HW.

66. David Badillo argues that the committee primarily served Puerto Ricans and left the ministry of Mexican Catholics to the Claretian fathers. Yet the committee's first location also provided a home for the Federation of Mexican Americans. Later, the committee served Cubans who were fleeing the early stages of the island's Communist revolution. Near West Side Community Council, *Where to Find It*; and Badillo, *Latinos and the New Immigrant Church*, 86. The Claretian fathers served Mexicans in three parishes: Our Lady of Guadalupe in South Chicago, Immaculate Heart of Mary in Back of the Yards, and St. Francis of Assisi on the Near West Side. See also Near West Side Community Council, *Chronicle*, January 1959, October 1959, folder 2, box 92, CAP.

67. Alicea, "Cuando Nosotros Vivíamos," 174. Lennon mentions racial/ethnic prejudice that white ethnics in national parishes expressed. Lennon, "Comparative Study," 117. This was a common experience among Italian immigrants as well, who were excluded from Catholic churches by Irish Americans decades earlier. See Barrett and Roediger, "Irish and the 'Americanization' of the 'New Immigrants,'" 22.

68. On racial violence, see Hirsch, *Making the Second Ghetto*. Don Mitchell, *The Right to the City: Social Justice and the Fight for Public Space* (New York: Guilford Press, 2003), 18; and Tina Vicini, "How Communities Fight Social Plague," *Chicago Herald American*, October 21, 1952, 1, folder 36, box 20, supplement 2, West [Near West] Side Community Collection, HW.

69. Barrett and Roediger, "Irish and the 'Americanization' of the 'New Immigrants.'" Chicago also had sizable Japanese, Chinese, and Filipino populations in central city neighborhoods during these years. Brooks, "In the Twilight Zone." See also Suttles, *Social Order of the Slum*; and Andrew Diamond, *Mean Streets: Chicago Youths and the Everyday Struggle for Empowerment in the Multiracial City, 1908–1969* (Berkeley: University of California Press, 2009).

70. Suttles, *Social Order of the Slum*, 27, 44.

71. Ibid., 20; Padilla, *Puerto Rican Chicago*, 84; and Guglielmo, *White on Arrival*, 47–48. See also Nelli, *Italians in Chicago* and "Myth of Urban Renewal"; and Scala interview with Studs Terkel, cited in George Rosen, *Decision-Making Chicago-Style: The Genesis of a University of Illinois Campus* (Urbana: University of Illinois Press, 1980), 99.

72. Suttles, *Social Order of the Slum*, 31–32.

73. Phil Ayala, interview with the author; Suttles, *Social Order of the Slum*, 49; and Guglielmo, *White on Arrival*, 47–48. Mexicans experienced a sort of "in-betweenness," much as Charlotte Brooks describes about Japanese Americans resettled after internment. Because of their much larger numbers and other factors, however, anti-Mexican prejudice seemed much more prevalent than that against Japanese Americans. Brooks, "In the Twilight Zone," 1657, 1669.

74. Philpott, *Slum and the Ghetto*, 285; Guglielmo, *White on Arrival*, 47–48; and Año Nuevo Kerr, "Chicano Experience," 29.

    Comparable to the early East Los Angeles communities of Boyle Heights and Lincoln Heights, or the Puerto Rican *colonias* in New York City, the Near West Side was home to a diverse working-class immigrant and second-generation population. See Sanchez, *Becoming Mexican American*, and Sánchez-Korrol, *From Colonia to Community*. For a more general history of diverse immigrant communities in early twentieth-century Los Angeles, see Mark Wild, *Street Meeting: Multiethnic Neighborhoods in Early Twentieth-Century Los Angeles* (Berkeley: University of California Press, 2005).

75. Frank X. Paz, "Mexican-Americans in Chicago: A General Survey," Committee on Mexican Interests, Council of Social Agencies, Chicago, January 1948, 8, folder 4, box 147, WC.

76. On Chicago's housing shortages in the 1940s, see Guglielmo, *White on Arrival*, 146–71; Hirsch, *Making the Second Ghetto*, 17–28; and Laura McEnaney, "Nightmares on Elm Street: Demobilizing in Chicago, 1945–1953," *Journal of American History* 92, no. 4 (2006): 1265–91. On the housing shortage and Japanese Americans, see Brooks, "In the Twilight Zone," 1674.

77. Padilla, *Puerto Rican Chicago*, 118.

78. Mérida Rúa, "Claims to 'the City': Puerto Rican Latinidad amid Labors of Identity, Community, and Belonging in Chicago" (PhD diss., University of Michigan, 2004), 40. On housing discrimination in Philadelphia for Puerto Ricans, see Whalen, *From Puerto Rico*, 191–93.

79. Suttles, *Social Order of the Slum*, chap. 12; Padilla, *Puerto Rican Chicago*, 61; Mary A. Young to Hollis Vick, September 16, 1954, Memorandum re: Meeting of Mr. Ballard and Mr. Fernando Sierra, folder 3, box 148, WC; Migration Division, *Annual Report, 1954–55*, 78, folder 2, box 1, OGPRUS; and Migration Division, *Annual Report, 1958–59*, 147, OGPRUS. On gang violence in Philadelphia, see Whalen, *From Puerto Rico*, chap. 6.

80. Diamond notes in *Mean Streets*, "That the attempt of a single African American to inhabit an apartment in an area some forty or fifty blocks away would mobilize a young man to join the cause of racial hatred and end up in police custody suggests that communal or territorial concepts fail to explain the dynamics behind this white collective action against housing integration" (167).

81. Rúa, "Claims to 'the City,'" 40. Even Puerto Rican and Mexican boys had tension with each other, as Mexican youths sometimes tried to exclude them from their social groups. Hull House report, April 28, 1958, folder 1, box 111, CAP. Again, similarly to Japanese Americans, Puerto Ricans also experienced a kind of "in-betweenness" in Chicago. Brooks, "In the Twilight Zone," 1657, 1669.

82. Elena Padilla asserted that "color visibility" made Puerto Ricans more conspicuous and deterred their assimilation among whites. "Puerto Rican Immigrants," 34, 50, 72. Felix Padilla argues that Puerto Ricans did not encounter racial/ethnic tensions

with whites because of economic conflicts (e.g., competition in the workplace), since Puerto Ricans migrated to fill entry-level, low-wage, low-skilled jobs in the vanishing industrial manufacturing sector, the lowest rungs of which many whites had already abandoned. *Puerto Rican Chicago*, 11.

83. Rúa, "Claims to 'the City,'" 40, 41. Puerto Ricans also expressed prejudice against blacks, even if they were as dark as or darker than they were. Padilla, "Puerto Rican Immigrants," 76, 77, 81, 91.

84. On summer camps, see, for example, "W. Side Scouts Will Have Own Camp Periods," *CT*, July 29, 1945; "200 Youth Ask to Vacation at Mexican Camp," *CT*, July 28, 1946; and "Neighbor Group Will Mark 10th Year of Service," *CT*, August 9, 1947. The Near West Side Community Council, a group dedicated to interracial cooperation, sponsored such camps as well.

   Committee on Minority Groups, "Meeting on Inter-racial Situation," June 25, 1943, folder 4, box 145, WC. See also West Side Community Committee, folder 12, box 110, CAP; "Hard to Reach Youth Project," Summary Report, August 27, 1957, folder 13, box 110, CAP; and the copious street workers' reports in the Chicago Area Project Collection. See as well Guglielmo, *White on Arrival*, 49; and Diamond, *Mean Streets*.

85. Ana Castillo, "Dirty Mexican," in *My Father Was a Toltec and Selected Poems* (New York: Norton, 1995), 8. The title of Castillo's poetry collection makes reference to a local street gang in the neighborhood, the Toltecs, to which her father purportedly belonged. See also Suttles, *Social Order of the Slum*. Diamond cites this as well, *Mean Streets*, 233–34.

86. Paz, "Mexican Americans in Chicago"; Phil Ayala, interview with the author, March 25, 2004; Suttles, *Social Order of the Slum*, 61; and Joe Escamilla, interview with the author, August 31, 2004. See also Guglielmo, *White on Arrival*, 54.

87. Suttles, *Social Order of the Slum*, 144; Hirsch, *Making the Second Ghetto*; and Guglielmo, *White on Arrival*. For more on how Italian Americans in Chicago consolidated their white identity, especially vis-à-vis African Americans by the 1940s, see Guglielmo, *White on Arrival*, 47–48, 57n54.

88. See "Relatan Vida de Migrantes PR en Chicago," *EM*, March 19, 1953, 10; "Hacen Elogio de Boricuas en Chicago," *EM*, March 25, 1953, 1; and "Puertorriqueños en Chicago," *EM*, March 26, 1953, 6.

89. "Puerto Ricans—Study 1953," folder 10, box 147, WC; and Memo re: meeting held in Mr. MacRae's office, September 10, 1953, folder 10 box 147, WC.

   Social scientists who embraced recent theories of cultural relativism began to see the process of (im)migration itself, rather than migrants' innate cultural traits, as the cause of social disintegration. The act of moving to a different cultural environment (and not migrants themselves) caused their difficulties in adjusting to a new language, customs, and community standards. Franz Boas, Ruth Benedict, Margaret Mead, and other anthropologists asserted that distinct cultural groups were not necessarily inferior but simply different. Progressive social reformers thus believed that the breakdown of immigrant families and rise in delinquency was the result of shame and low self-esteem that many in the second generation felt over their parents' immigrant origins. Diana Selig, *Americans All: The Cultural Gifts Movement* (Cambridge, MA: Harvard University Press, 2008), 183–86.

90. The study was eventually completed, and a report finally materialized several years later. See Chicago Commission on Human Relations, *Puerto Rican Americans in Chicago* (Chicago: Mayor's Committee on New Residents, 1960).

91. This episode contradicts Gina Pérez's contention that the Puerto Rican community in Chicago gradually shifted from model minority status in local public opinion in the 1950s to a slum-dwelling "underclass" by the mid-1960s. Perez correctly notes that the Migration Division office's "principal focus was to promote a positive image of migrants and maintain a favorable working relationship with civic groups and government agencies." But Migration Division officials struggled with negative stereotypes, prejudice, and discrimination as early as 1953, not only after the 1966 Division Street riots. Gina M. Pérez, "An Upbeat West Side Story: Puerto Ricans and Postwar Racial Politics in Chicago," *Centro Journal* 13, no. 2 (2001): 50. This characterization of Puerto Ricans as welfare dependent also predates the academic discourse that emerged with the publication of Oscar Lewis's *La Vida: A Puerto Rican Family in the Culture of Poverty—San Juan and New York* (New York: Random House, 1966); and Nathan Glazer and Daniel Patrick Moynihan, *Beyond the Melting Pot: The Negroes, Puerto Ricans, Jews, Italians, and Irish of New York City* (Cambridge, MA: MIT Press, 1963).

92. "Puerto Ricans Pour into City and Ask Dole," *CT*, February 2, 1954; "Puerto Rican Influx Brings New Inquiry," *CT*, February 3, 1954; "Agree to Stem Puerto Rican Immigration," *CT*, February 8, 1954; and "Boricuas Piden Ayuda en Chicago," *EM*, February 3, 1954, 1. See also Cappa, "Funcionario Chicago" and "Vino a Discutir Su Plan de Repatriar Obreros." An editorial in the same paper opined that Puerto Rican migrants in Chicago should not be treated with prejudice and discrimination in their search for public aid, as they are citizens and are free to move about the country as they wish. "Puertorriqueños en Chicago," *EM*, February 4, 1954, 6. On the "Puerto Rican problem" in New York City, see, for example, Lorrin Thomas, *Puerto Rican Citizen*, esp. chaps. 4 and 5.

93. Alvin Rose, speech, January 9, 1954; and Mary A. Young to Mr. MacRae, January 29, 1954—both in folder 3, box 148, WC.

94. "Rexford Tugwell Señala Boricuas Tienen Derecho a Ir a Chicago," *EM*, February 6, 1954, 1. Tugwell had been part of Franklin D. Roosevelt's progressive "brain trust" during his presidency.

95. "Boletin de Información: Puertorriqueños Van a Trabajar No en Busca de Ayuda," Departamento del Trabajo, Estado Libre Asociado de Puerto Rico, March 26, 1954, Fondo Departamento del Trabajo, Tarea 61–55, box 25, AGPR. For a discussion of this episode, see also Rúa, "Claims to 'the City.'"

96. For more on the recession, see Harold G. Vatter, *The U.S. Economy in the 1950s: An Economic History* (New York: Norton, 1963), 63–97. National unemployment had actually reached a dramatic low of 1.8 percent in October 1953 but then climbed precipitously to over 6 percent by mid-1954. Much like what Mexicans experienced during the Great Depression, Puerto Ricans were often the "last hired, first fired."

97. See Migration Division, *Annual Report, 1953–54*, and *Annual Report, 1954–55*, folders 1–2, boxes 1 and 2, OGPRUS; and "Puerto Rican Migration to U.S. Is Slowed," *CT*, April 25, 1954, 13.

98. See "News Summary," *CT*, February 2, 1954, referring to "Puerto Ricans Pour into City and Ask Dole" and "Mexican Horde Repulsed by Border Patrol."

99. Año Nuevo Kerr, "Chicano Experience," 144, 146. See also Ngai, *Impossible Subjects*, chap. 2.

100. "Set Up Patrol to Seize Mexican Aliens Here," *CT*, February 1, 1952; "135 Mexicans Begin Trip Home," *CT*, February 7, 1952; "Move to Speed Deporting of Aliens in Jail," *CT*, March 5, 1952, B9; "100 'Wetbacks' Sent South on Way to Mexico," *CT*,

September 3, 1953, A4; "Midwest Drive on Wetbacks to Open Friday," *CT*, September 15, 1952, A2; "Drive on Aliens by U.S. Brings 320 Detentions," *CT*, September 28, 1954, 23; and "¿Está Usted Viviendo Ilegalmente en Este País?" *Vida Latina*, October 1954, 18, 20.

101. Perhaps because of the Welfare Council's prompting in these meetings, the 1960 *Local Community Fact Book* did begin to enumerate Puerto Ricans separately in its statistical summaries. The use of the term *Spanish-speaking* may have come from Puerto Rican leaders (like the Migration Division), who may have preferred to emphasize their linguistic difference or Spanish heritage rather than conjure up images of racial difference with the label *Puerto Rican*. This may have been the case with the Cardinal's Committee on the Spanish Speaking as well.

102. Martin Ortíz to Miss Hollis Vick, March 19, 1953, folder 10, box 147, WC.

103. Ibid.; and "Findings from Meeting to Promote Better Integration of the Puerto Rican Citizenry into the Community," March 26, 1953, folder 3, box 148, WC. See also Rúa, "Claims to 'the City.'"

104. "Five Congressmen Shot Down," *CT*, March 2, 1954, 1; "Five Congressmen Shot in House by 3 Puerto Rican Nationalists," *NYT*, March 2, 1954, 1; and "Woman, 3 Men Captured after Firing at Filled Floor," *Washington Post*, March 2, 1954, 1. Only the *CT* reported the quote of "Viva Mexico!" raising doubts as to whether this was indeed uttered. See also Rúa, "Claims to 'the City.'"

105. "Police Squads Round Up Five Puerto Ricans," *CT*, March 5, 1954, 7.

106. "Protest 'Mass Arrests' of Puerto Ricans," *CT*, March 10, 1954, 3; "FBI Seizes 11 Puerto Ricans, Six in Chicago," *CT*, May 27, 1954, C12; and "Five Chicagoans Deny Puerto Rico Party Conspiracy Charge," *CT*, June 9, 1954, 26. In the end, thirteen Puerto Ricans, including the original four and other conspirators from New York and Puerto Rico, were tried and convicted of seditious conspiracy. See "Puerto Rican Trial Begins, Four Plead Guilty," *CT*, September 8, 1954, 21; "Puerto Rican Tells Court of Purchase of Guns in Chicago," *CT*, September 21, 1954, B12; and "Convict 13 Puerto Ricans of U.S. Plot," *CT*, October 13, 1954, 1.

107. "Mexican Group Decries Attack by Terror Gang," *CT*, March 8, 1954, 2; Jose E. Chapa letter to unnamed recipient, March 10, 1954, and Martin Ortíz to Clinton White, March 10, 1954—both in folder 10, box 88, CAP.

108. Near West Side Community Council, *Chronicle*, November 1955, folder 547, NWSCC; and Luis Leal, interview with the author, February 2, 2009.

109. Migration Division, *Annual Report, 1953–54*, 46, and *Annual Report, 1955–56*, 86–87, folders 1 and 2, box 1, OGPRUS.

CHAPTER THREE

1. Near West Side Community Council, *Chronicle*, October 1958, folder 549, NWSCC.

2. Carolyn Eastwood, *Near West Side Stories: Struggles for Community in Chicago's Maxwell Street Neighborhood* (Chicago: Lake Claremont Press, 2002), 4.

3. Evelyn Kitagawa and Karl E. Taeuber, eds., *Local Community Fact Book: Chicago's Metropolitan Area, 1960* (Chicago: Chicago Community Inventory, University of Chicago, 1963), 70. As a result of the Depression, through the 1930s, only 15,500 homes were built throughout the entire city. None of these, however, were built in poor neighborhoods. Arnold R. Hirsch, *Making the Second Ghetto: Race and Housing in Chicago, 1940–1960* (Cambridge: Cambridge University Press, 1983), 18.

4. Adam Cohen and Elizabeth Taylor, *American Pharaoh: Mayor Richard J. Daley: His Battle for Chicago and the Nation* (Boston: Little, Brown, 2000), 10. For a theory on

how inequality is constructed in cities, see Susan Bickford, "Constructing Inequality: City Spaces and the Architecture of Citizenship," *Political Theory* 28, no. 3 (2000): 355–76.

5. Samuel Zipp, "The Battle of Lincoln Square: Neighbourhood Culture and the Rise of Resistance to Urban Renewal," *Planning Perspectives* 24, no. 4 (2009): 409–33.

Chavez Ravine is where Mexican Americans experienced similar displacement by the construction of a baseball stadium in the fifties. Eric Avila, *Popular Culture in the Age of White Flight: Fear and Fantasy in Suburban Los Angeles* (Berkeley: University of California Press, 2006), chap. 5; Herbert Gans, *The Urban Villagers* (New York: Free Press, 1962); Donald Craig Parson, *Making a Better World: Public Housing, the Red Scare, and the Direction of Modern Los Angeles* (Minneapolis: University of Minnesota Press, 2005), chap. 6; and Dana Cuff, *The Provisional City: Los Angeles Stories of Architecture and Urbanism* (Cambridge, MA: MIT Press, 2000), chap. 7.

6. Chicago Plan Commission, *Master Plan of Residential Land Use of Chicago* (Chicago: Chicago Plan Commission, 1943), 122. The CPC included downtown department store magnates such as Marshall Field; railroad, shipping, and manufacturing men; and other prominent businessmen. It essentially functioned as the city's planning department until 1959. (After that, it continued to serve in an advisory capacity to the newly established Department of City Planning.) Amanda Seligman, *Block by Block: Neighborhoods and Public Policy on Chicago's West Side* (Chicago: University of Chicago Press, 2005), 74. The CPC planned as early as 1951 to reduce the density of the city's "west central" area, which included the Near West Side, at least in half, from 172,000 people to a range of 67,000 to 95,000. Chicago Plan Commission, *A Plan for the West Central Area of Chicago* (Chicago: Chicago Plan Commission, 1951), vii.

7. Gregory D. Squires, Larry Bennett, Kathleen McCourt, and Philip Nyden, *Chicago: Race, Class, and the Response to Urban Decline* (Philadelphia: Temple University Press, 1987), 159.

8. Census data come from Kitagawa and Taueber, *Local Community Fact Book*. Other nonwhites included Asian Americans (Japanese, Filipinos, Chinese), and Mexicans with "visible" Indian ancestry.

9. See Chicago Plan Commission, *Facing the Future with the Chicago Plan Commission* (Chicago: Chicago Plan Commission, December 1941). See other Chicago Plan Commission publications, such as *Rebuilding Old Chicago*, 1941; *Forty-Four Cities in the City of Chicago*, April 1941; *Population Facts for Planning Chicago*, 1942; *Building New Neighborhoods: Subdivision Design and Standards*, June 1943; *Chicago Looks Ahead*, 1945; *Housing Goals for Chicago*, 1946; and annual reports from 1940 to 1950. Squires, Bennett, McCourt, and Nyden, *Chicago*, 154.

10. Cited in Thomas Guglielmo, *White on Arrival: Italians, Race, Color, and Power in Chicago, 1890–1945* (Oxford: Oxford University Press, 2003), 149. For more on the HOLC, see Kenneth T. Jackson, *Crabgrass Frontier: The Suburbanization of the United States* (New York: Oxford University Press, 1985), 195–203.

11. *Ten Square Miles of Chicago*, a report to the Land Clearance Commission, June 1948, 2. Kitagawa and Taueber, *Local Community Fact Book*, 248. *What About Our Schools?* pamphlet, 1952, folder 2, box 7, West [Near West] Side Community Collection, HW.

12. Kitagawa and Taueber, *Local Community Fact Book*, 70.

13. Chicago Daily News, *The Road Back: A Dramatic Expose of Slum Housing in Chicago*

(Chicago: Metropolitan Housing and Planning Council, 1954), 31–32. The city of Chicago, in fact, did not have a uniform building code until 1956. See "Facts on the Metropolitan Housing and Planning Council of Chicago," n.d. [ca. 1962], MRC. On housing shortages and struggles between tenants and landlords in postwar Chicago, see Laura McEnaney, "Nightmares on Elm Street: Demobilizing in Chicago, 1945–1953," *Journal of American History* 92, no. 4 (2006): 1265–91.

The living conditions of Mexican immigrants were not very different from those of earlier European immigrants. As Humbert Nelli notes, "In the early years of the century Italian immigrants . . . typically occupied overcrowded tenements with as many as 20 or 30 people, including boarders who slept in shifts on kitchen floors and anywhere else they could find room, occupying three and four room apartments." Over time, however, those conditions had improved. "By 1960 . . . four room apartments which a half century before had accommodated 15 to 30 people typically housed three or four, and sometimes only one or two." Humbert S. Nelli, "The Myth of Urban Renewal: Chicago's Near West Side Italian Community in the 1960s," *Italian American Identity* (April 1977): 53.

14. "Chicago's Public Housing Today," [ca. 1955], folder 38, box 20, supplement 2, West [Near West] Side Community Collection, HW.

15. Hirsch, *Making the Second Ghetto*, 124. Hirsch reaches very different conclusions about public housing in Chicago than Don Parson does about Los Angeles. Parson argues that public housing from the 1930s to the 1950s in Los Angeles was driven by the left-liberal popular front's vision for "community modernism." This ideal was stymied, however, by the 1950s by the political tactics of the Red Scare, which silenced the Left and shaped an urban-planning agenda that resulted in "corporate modernism." Parson, *Making a Better World*.

16. Cohen and Taylor, *American Pharaoh*, 68.

17. That same year, the United States Congress passed the Wagner-Steagall Act, a federal housing law that affirmed future support for public housing. On the PWA and public housing, see Jackson, *Crabgrass Frontier*, 221–24. In Chicago, with its tradition of settlement houses, labor unions, and radical leftist politics, there was considerable support for public developments, in contrast to cities like Los Angeles, where by the 1950s some business leaders disparaged them as communist and socialist experiments.

18. Cohen and Taylor, *American Pharaoh*, 72–73; Guglielmo, *White on Arrival*, 151–52, 231n24, 153, 230n15; Hirsch, *Making the Second Ghetto*, 14; and Bradford Hunt, *Blueprint for Disaster: The Unraveling of Chicago Public Housing* (Chicago: University of Chicago Press, 2009), 54. The Addams Homes were the only housing project in Chicago that housed both black and white residents in the pre–World War II period.

19. The first one was the Ida B. Wells project, built immediately after the JAH and intentionally located in the Black Belt region. See Hirsch's discussion of the creation of the Ida B. Wells housing project in Hirsch, *Making the Second Ghetto*, chap. 1.

20. Guglielmo, *White on Arrival*, 153, 231n24. For a more detailed history of the CHA's segregated housing policy, see Hirsch, *Making the Second Ghetto*.

21. Guglielmo, *White on Arrival*, 230n15.

22. Squires, Bennett, McCourt, and Nyden, *Chicago*, 104; Jackson, *Crabgrass Frontier*; and Roger Biles, "Public Housing and the Postwar Urban Renaissance, 1949–1973," in *From Tenements to the Taylor Homes: In Search of an Urban Housing Policy in Twentieth-*

Century America, ed. John Bauman, Roger Biles, and Kristin Szylvian, 143–62 (University Park: Pennsylvania State University Press, 2000). See also McEnaney, "Nightmares on Elm Street."

23. Chicago Urban League, "Chicago's Negro Residential Areas as Related to Urban Renewal" (Chicago, February 1957). See also Ruth Moore, "Urban League Deplores Segregation in Chicago Area Renewal Projects," *CST*, July 4, 1958.

24. Biles, "Public Housing," 146. Local columnist Jack Mabley echoed this in a scathing critique of the growing black slum in the West Side's Garfield Park community. See Jack Mabley, "Erasing Slums? Renewal Just Moving Them!" *CA*, May 29, 1962.

25. Byrne, cited in Squires, Bennett, McCourt, and Nyden, *Chicago*, 152; and Bauer, cited in Biles, "Public Housing," 147.

26. Amanda Seligman argues that describing the exodus of Chicago West Side whites with the term *white flight* "narrow[s] the breadth of their struggles to preserve their neighborhoods." *Block by Block*, 4. Robert Self makes a similar claim in *American Babylon*, 2.

27. Kitagawa and Taeuber, *Local Community Fact Book*, 70. The Near West Side actually started to lose population beginning in 1920. This resembles the Lower East Side of Manhattan, also a historic immigrant port of entry, which experienced a similar population decline in earlier decades, from 1910 to 1940. Jackson, *Crabgrass Frontier*, 185.

28. Wolf Von Eckardt, *Bulldozers and Bureaucrats: Cities and Urban Renewal* (Washington, DC: New Republic, 1963), 48.

29. See Hirsch's critical analysis of Chicago's public housing policy: Hirsch, *Making the Second Ghetto*. For a critique of Hirsch, see the 2003 special issue of the *Journal of Urban History* 29, no. 3.

30. Kitagawa and Taeuber, *Local Community Fact Book*, 70; and *Report to the Housing Committee of the City Council of Chicago*, in Chicago Plan Commission, *City-Planning Reports on 15 Suggested Public Housing Sites*, 1950, MRC.

31. Kitagawa and Taeuber, *Local Community Fact Book*, 70.

32. This did not include an additional high-rise development specifically for low-income senior citizens named after local black leader William Jones. The Henry Horner Homes provided the backdrop for a scathing exposé of living conditions in Chicago's public housing: Alex Kotlowitz, *There Are No Children Here: The Story of Two Boys Growing Up in the Other America* (New York: Doubleday, 1991).

    In 1950, African Americans occupied only 58 units in JAH, but by 1960, they lived in over half of them, 720. By the 1970s, they occupied the Addams Homes in their entirety and were completely concentrated in that housing project rather than being dispersed, as they previously were, throughout other nearby census tracts. The black population, in other words, had been effectively corralled into the Addams Homes. George Rosen, *Chicago-Style: The Genesis of a University of Illinois Campus* (Urbana: University of Illinois Press, 1980), 131–32.

33. See Chicago Plan Commission, *Master Plan of Residential Land Use of Chicago*; Chicago Plan Commission, *Chicago Looks Ahead*, 1945; and Chicago Plan Commission, *Ten Square Miles*—all in MRC. Proposed low-income public housing sites (as opposed to senior citizen housing, for example) throughout the 1950s and 1960s were located either in the Near North, South, or West Sides, or on the far South Side. See Chicago Plan Commission, *City-Planning Reports on 15 Suggested Public Housing Sites*.

    Amanda Seligman makes an important distinction between the public housing second ghetto and the one that extended to the far West Side community of Austin. She writes, "The West Side ghetto born after World War II was the product of the neighborhood's exclusion from postwar urban redevelopment, the political power-lessness of preceding white residents, and their racism." Seligman, *Block by Block*, 9.

34. The acronym *NIMBY* refers to the expression "not in my backyard," used to describe local opposition to growth and development, particularly of institutions such as prisons, public housing, mental health facilities, landfills, and other projects that homeowners find objectionable. The term connotes a self-centeredness among citizens who have little interest in where such projects get located, as long as they are not in their own communities.

35. Squires, Bennett, McCourt, and Nyden, *Chicago*, 102. See also Hirsch, *Second Ghetto*.

36. Cohen and Taylor, *American Pharaoh*, 184, 185. The central city neighborhoods contrasted sharply with the city's "Bungalow Belt," the newer lower-middle-class neighborhoods farther away from the city center, characterized by single-family brick bungalows. While not enjoying as high a status as the suburbs, the Bungalow Belt stood as a testament to European immigrants' success—a symbol of working-class families' achievement of economic stability and social respectability. The racial geography of such areas also testified to the obstinate exclusion of African Americans and, until the 1980s, Latinos/as. See Cohen and Taylor, *American Pharaoh*, 150.

37. Rúa, "Claims to 'the City,'" 38.

38. Migration Division, *Annual Report, 1956–57*, 138, folder 4, box 1, OGPRUS.

39. This was the case in public schools as well, where African Americans and Latinos/as (both Puerto Ricans and Mexicans) would be counted as integrated because they shared classrooms with each other. As early as 1958, for example, the NAACP "found that 91% of Chicago's elementary schools were segregated . . . being either 90% black and Puerto Rican or 90% white." Cohen and Taylor, *American Pharaoh*, 283. Education scholars have found in the decades since that segregation of Latina/o students in urban areas has increased dramatically, so that the overwhelming majority of Latina/o students in the 1980s, 1990s, and into the 2000s attend schools that are majority "minority"/nonwhite.

40. Gamaliel Ramirez, interview with the author, June 4, 2004; "Knights Blast Public Housing," June 17, 1958, folder 151, IAF; and Phil Ayala, interview with the author, December 4, 2003. See also chap. 4 for an account of the Lucas family. In some cases, while Mexicans and Puerto Ricans escaped black violence in public housing, they entered other communities only to encounter white violence against them instead. See chaps. 4 and 6.

41. Biles, "Public Housing," 151–52. Lawrence Vale writes, "Once public housing became reconceptualized as a publicly funded resource for coping with the needs of the most desperate city-dwellers, public neighborhoods inevitably became treated as storage facilities rather than as communities." Lawrence J. Vale, *Reclaiming Public Housing: A Half Century of Struggle in Three Public Neighborhoods* (Cambridge, MA: Harvard University Press, 2002), 8. See also Hunt, *Blueprint for Disaster*. On the drug trade, crime, and public housing, see Sudhir Venkatesh, *American Project: The Rise and Fall of a Modern Ghetto* (Cambridge, MA: Harvard University Press, 2000); and Susan J. Popkin et al., *The Hidden War: Crime and the Tragedy of Public Housing in Chicago* (New Brunswick, NJ: Rutgers University Press, 2000).

42. Cited in Cohen and Taylor, *American Pharaoh*, 111.

43. Guglielmo, *White on Arrival*, 231n24; and Gerald D. Suttles, *The Social Order of the Slum: Ethnicity and Territory in the Inner City* (Chicago: University of Chicago Press,

1968), 120–21. Suttles argues that if blacks had not been restricted only to public housing, they would have been better integrated socially with other ethnic groups in the area, 9.

44. Near West Side Community Council pamphlet, n.d., folder 7, box 91, CAP; NWSCC, *Chronicle*, December 1959, folder 550, NWSCC; and NWSCC letter to "Dear Friends," March 24, 1950, folder 6, box 91, CAP.

45. Seligman, *Block by Block*, 5.

46. Georgie Anne Geyer, "The Heritage of Jane Addams: Florence Scala Fills the Void," *Chicago Scene*, n.d., 22–27, in folder 7, FS. Rosen, *Decision-Making*, 100–103; and Near West Side Community Council, *Near West Side Chronicle*, January 1957, folder 1, box 92, CAP. See also Near West Side Planning Board, pamphlet, n.d., "Near West Side Community Council" folder, box 92, CAP.

47. Rosen, *Decision-Making*, 104; *Near West Side Chronicle*, January 1957, folder 1, box 92, CAP; "West Side Unit Seeks to Build Planning Group," *CT*, October 17, 1948, W7; Ruth Logan, "New Era May Dawn in Plan for West Side," *CT*, June 12, 1949, W1; "Near West Side Area Girds for Future," *CT*, July 17, 1949, W1; and Carolyn Eastwood, interview with Florence Scala, in *Near West Side Stories*, 159. For an example of Scala's involvement in the NWSPB, see her remarks in "Proceedings of the Fifth Anniversary Meeting of the Near West Side Planning Board," October 27, 1953, folder 5, box 92, CAP. Georgie Anne Geyer, "Woman at War: Leads Neighbors Fighting UI Site," *CDN*, March 23, 1961.

48. Near West Side Planning Board, flyer, March 1952, folder 11, box 88, CAP; and Fred W. Beuttle, Melvin G. Holli, and Robert V. Remini, *The University of Illinois at Chicago: A Pictorial History* (Charleston, SC: Arcadia Publishing, 2000), 79.

49. Housing and Home Finance Agency, *Approaches to Urban Renewal in Several Cities* (Washington, DC: Urban Renewal Administration, 1954). Models of neighborhood development throughout the nation did not become widely known until later decades. See, for example, Daniel V. Folkman, ed., *Urban Community Development: Case Studies in Neighborhood Survival* (Milwaukee: Regents of the University of Wisconsin, 1978).

50. Chicago Land Clearance Commission, report, 1950, folder 204, NWSCC.

51. Seligman, *Block by Block*; and Housing and Home Finance Agency, *Approaches to Urban Renewal*. Because state politics were dominated by powerful Chicago politicians, they were usually rather successful in promoting or negotiating with other state legislators for the passage of laws that furthered the city's agenda.

52. Thomas Buck, "West Side Area Maps Own Way to Clear Slums," *CT*, January 20, 1950, A14. Immediately, the Metropolitan Housing and Planning Council objected, however, stating that such a reclassification would impede the redevelopment of the city by preventing the slum clearance that many areas needed. "Defends Giving Slums Chance of Remodeling," *CT*, January 26, 1950.

53. Ironically, the city was contributing to its own population loss by participating in the construction and becoming part of the network of federal highways that made suburban commutes to downtown jobs less taxing. This was the case, for example, in places like Los Angeles, where the Pasadena Freeway, designed to attract people to shop in downtown Los Angeles, inadvertently led to rapid suburbanization. Jackson, *Crabgrass Frontier*, 167. See also Raymond A. Mohl, "Planned Destruction: The Interstates and Central City Housing," in *From Tenements to the Taylor Homes: In Search of an Urban Housing Policy in Twentieth-Century America*, ed. John Bauman, Roger Biles, and Kristin Szylvian, 226–45 (University Park: Pennsylvania State University Press, 2000).

54. The Congress continued to open sections until its completion in 1960. Chicago Plan Commission, *Plans and Progress* (December 1953), 1.

55. From Dennis McClendon, "Expressways," Encyclopedia of Chicago, accessed February 9, 2008, http://www.encyclopedia.chicagohistory.org/pages/440.html. Chicago Plan Commission, *Plans and Progress*, 2.

56. Near West Side Planning Board, flyer, March 1952, folder 11, box 88, CAP; William Jones, Near West Side Planning Board, to Dear Friend, May 19, 1955, and attached sheet mapping out neighborhood into quadrants, Supplement 2, folder 36, box 20, West [Near West] Side Community Collection, HW; and Near West Side Community Council, *Near West Side Chronicle*, May 1956, folder 548, NWSCC.

57. Downs's boosterish speech belied the harmful role he would play in the neighborhood's future. As one of Daley's most trusted advisers, he worked with him closely on housing and redevelopment policy. James C. Downs remarks in "Proceedings of the Fifth Anniversary Meeting of the Near West Side Planning Board," October 27, 1953, folder 5, box 92, CAP. Cohen and Taylor, *American Pharaoh*, 223.

58. The NWSPB was unique in that it preempted urban redevelopment plans for the neighborhood. This is in contrast to other communities, such as the residents of Bunker Hill in Los Angeles, who developed an "Alternative Redevelopment Plan" in response to the city's redevelopment plans, which would displace them. Parson, *Making a Better World*, 156.

59. See Near West Side Community Council, *Near West Side Chronicle*, October 1958, 7, folder 549, NWSCC.

60. Chicago Urban Renewal Summary, December 31, 1956, folder 420, IAF; and Community Conservation Board, "Near West Side Conservation Survey," 1957.

61. Suttles, *Social Order of the Slum*, 21. Florence Scala, interview with Robert H. Young, ca. 1965, 15, folder 10, box 1, FS. This affirms Amanda Seligman's argument that some white residents in Chicago actually sought to stay in their neighborhoods rather than leave for the suburbs. Seligman, *Block by Block*. For a quote from Scala, see Guglielmo, *White on Arrival*, 171.

62. "Proceedings of the Fifth Anniversary Meeting of the Near West Side Planning Board."

63. The passing of William Jones in late 1959 slowed the momentum of interracial cooperation. Near West Side Community Council, *Chronicle*, December 1959, folder 550, NWSCC.

64. Near West Side Planning Board pamphlet, n.d.; Mr. James C. Downs to Mr. Clayton C. Meyers, July 21, 1955; "Proceedings of the Fifth Anniversary Meeting of the Near West Side Planning Board"—all in box 92, CAP. Scala, interview with Young.

65. Robert Whiting to Mr. D. E. Mackelman, "Housing and Population in the Near West Side Area Lying South of Congress Expressway," 1958; and CLCC letter to area residents, April 17, 1958—both in folder 206, NWSCC. Georgie Ann Geyer, "New UI Site Challenge—Is Deal Legal?" *CDN*, July 14, 1961, folder 90, box 8, COUA; and Rosen, *Decision-Making*, 111.

66. Scala, interview with Young; Rosen, *Decision-Making*, 110, chap. 5.

67. According to David Levine, higher education expanded dramatically between the world wars and became much more accessible to middle-class and immigrant students rather than just the white Protestant elite. See David O. Levine, *The American College and the Culture of Aspiration, 1915–1940* (Ithaca, NY: Cornell University Press, 1986).

68. Rosen, *Decision-Making*; "House Passes Bill on 4-Year Branch for UI," June 25, 1951,

paper unknown, folder 41, box 4, COUA, 125; and "U. of I. May Set Up 4-Year Branch Here," *CST*, October 16, 1952. See also Dean C. C. Caveny to Administrators and Faculty, February 13, 1957, folder 40, box 6, COUA; and Seligman, *Block by Block*, 99.

69. Rosen, *Decision-Making*, 17–39. Universities in the decades after the war experienced expansion, especially of enrollments as a result of the baby boom generation coming of college age. See Hugh Davis Graham and Nancy Diamond, *The Rise of American Research Universities: Elites and Challengers in the Postwar Era* (Baltimore: Johns Hopkins University Press, 1997), esp. chap. 1. Graham and Diamond write: "The growth in the postwar United States of a mass market in higher education was not only compatible with the rise to world dominance of the American research university, it was essential to the efficient functioning of the American academic marketplace. During the postwar era three new forces drove American higher education to unprecedented levels of growth and achievement: the rising tide of economic prosperity, the baby boom, and the revolution in federal science policy" (11). For more specifically on changes in higher education during the 1960s, see Clark Kerr, *The Great Transformation in Higher Education, 1960–1980* (Albany: SUNY Press, 1991).

70. John Drieske, "Sees Big U. of I. Unit Opening Here in 6 Years," *CST*, March 3, 1953, and Caveny to Administrators and Faculty, February 13, 1957, folder 40, box 6, COUA.

71. Rosen, *Decision-Making*, 45–48, 58, 62–63. Daley would continue to support business elites' interests, as his legacy of urban renewal projects attests. Squires, Bennett, McCourt, and Nyden, *Chicago*, 70.

72. In 1960, whites were already outnumbered by African Americans, 25,409 and 41,097, respectively. Somewhere within these two categories, however, and perhaps in the 365 "other race" enumeration, lay 3,676 Puerto Ricans as well. Kitagawa and Taeuber, *Local Community Fact Book*, 69. For more on West Garfield Park and its battle to keep African Americans out of its neighborhood, see Seligman, *Block by Block*.

73. Cohen and Taylor, *American Pharaoh*, 218, 293.

74. Holman D. Pettibone to Dr. David Henry, May 1, 1957; and Hughston M. McBain press release, May 2, 1957—both in folder 49, box 7, COUA. Chicago Department of Planning, *Plans and Progress*, February 1961, 3; and Rosen, *Decision-Making*, chap. 4. Apparently, the legal obstacles to various suburban locations and even the Garfield Park location were orchestrated behind the scenes by city officials and prominent downtown business magnates who flexed their political power to ensure that the site would be located in the central city area. See Seligman, *Block by Block*, chap. 4.

75. Rosen, *Decision-Making*, 73.

76. Seligman provides the most detailed history of Garfield Park's efforts to attract the university to its neighborhood. See *Block by Block*, chap. 4. See also Rosen, *Decision-Making*, 66–68, 77–78.

77. Rosen, *Decision Making*, 77–79; and "Charge Daley Breaks Word with Church," *CUNG*, February 12, 1961, folder 89, box 8, COUA.

78. Rosen, *Decision-Making*, 79.

79. Ruth Moore, "Odds Favor U. of I. Site on W. Side," *CST*, July 6, 1960, folder 89, box 8, COUA; Rosen, *Decision-Making*, 81, 83, 84; and "U. of I. Panel to Urge Harrison-Halsted Site," *CST*, February 10, 1961, folder 89, box 8, COUA. At this time, 180

of the 310 buildings scheduled for demolition had already been cleared. Seligman, *Block by Block*, 115.

80. A bond issue had been passed by the state legislature and put on the ballot in 1958, but Illinois voters failed to pass it. The second attempt was successful because the proposal was rewritten to fund six state universities with $195 million. Fifty million dollars of this would go to the University of Illinois's Chicago campus. Rosen, *Decision-Making*, 59; Fred Mohn, press release, September 14, 1961, folder 40, box 6, COUA; and "Near West Project Gets Green Light," *Urban Renewal Review* 2, no. 2 (May–June 1963), folder 92, box 8, COUA.

81. Department of City Planning, *Plans and Progress*, February 1961; Helen Fleming, "Board Unanimous on Halsted UI Site," *CDN*, February 10, 1961; and Fran Myers, "UI Harrison-Halsted Site Is Unanimously Approved," *CUNG*, February 15, 1961— all in folder 93, box 9, COUA.

    After the announcement, the university immediately petitioned the Chicago Land Clearance Commission to approve an area just south of the cleared land (from Arthington to Roosevelt and the South Expressway to Blue Island) as well as an adjacent section to the west (from Harrison to Congress and Morgan to Racine). Eventually, it also sought an additional thirty-four acres just west of that from Racine to Ashland. It hoped to clear this area for residential construction by private developers. Thomas Buck, "Plan to Seek More Land for U. of I. Branch," *CT*, February 20, 1961, folder 9, box 94, COUA.

82. Seligman, *Block by Block*, 116.

83. Karl Treen to Dean Caveny, February 12, 1961, folder 56, box 8, COUA. The author's estimate of the number of "Spanish-speaking" people was clearly exaggerated.

84. Rosen, *Decision-Making*, 87–88.

85. See Seligman, *Block by Block*, 116.

86. "500 Residents Protest U. of I. Site," *CST*, February 21, 1961, folder 94, box 9, COUA; Rosen, *Decision-Making*, 115; and Robert Gruenberg, "'Slum' Study—and Footnotes," *CDN*, April 10, 1961, folder 95, box 9, COUA. Elderly residents' responses resembled those of people to be displaced in other urban renewal areas throughout the country. On Los Angeles's Bunker Hill neighborhood, for example, see Parson, *Making a Better World*, 147–62. On Lincoln Square in Manhattan, see Zipp, "Battle of Lincoln Square."

87. Elise McCormick, "West Side's Uprooted Find a Saint Joan," *CST*, October 1, 1961, folder 98, box 9, COUA. Her brother Ernest Giovangelo suggested that the participants at the meeting urged her to take the lead. Rosen, *Decision-Making*, 115.

88. "Proceedings of the Fifth Anniversary Meeting of the Near West Side Planning Board"; and Near West Side Community Council, *Near West Side Chronicle*, January 1959, folder 2, box 92, CAP.

89. Scala interview, in Eastwood, *Near West Side Stories*, 166.

90. Some newspaper articles exclusively featured Italian American business owners and homeowners as the would-be victims of the displacement and completely ignored Mexican families. "More Than Buildings to Be Destroyed in Harrison-Halsted Neighborhood," newspaper unknown, February 22, 1961, folder 94, box 9, COUA. Scala, interview with Young, 6–7.

91. "Campus Site Residents to Protest Today," *CT*, February 14, 1961, folder 93, box 9, COUA; "Charge Daley Breaks Word with Church"; and "UI Site Protest Fails at City Hall," *CDN*, February 14, 1961, folder 93, box 9, COUA.

92. "Granata Vows Fight on U. of I. Chicago Site," *CT*, February 22, 1961, folder 94, box 9; "Warn City Long Fight Looms on U. of I. Site," *CDN*, April 13, 1961, folder 96, box 9; Edward Schreiber, "Two Legislators Assail West Side U. of I. Site," *CT*, April 14, 1961, folder 96, box 9; and "U. of I. Site Foes Boo Daley," *CDN*, March 30, 1961, folder 95, box 9—all in COUA.

93. "Plead for UI to Stay Out of West Side," *CUNG*, April 15, 1961, folder 96, box 9, COUA.

94. Fran Myers, "UI Harrison-Halsted Site Is Unanimously Approved," *CUNG*, February 15, 1961, folder 93, box 9, COUA; and Ruth Dunbar, "U. of I. Board OK's Harrison-Halsted Site," *CST*, February 16, 1961, folder 93, box 9, COUA. In later years, Velasquez actually became a member of the university's board of trustees.

95. Rosen, *Decision-Making*, 131; and "U.I. Site Choice Grave Injustice," letter from Frances Sarafin, *Austin News*, March 15, 1961, folder 94, box 9, COUA. She noted, "The Spanish speaking people are also discussing ways to save their homes, schools, and churches. An article to this effect has been sent to President Kennedy, the *Tribune*, and *Garfieldian*."

96. Eastwood, *Near West Side Stories*, 269; Rosen, *Decision-Making*; Beuttle, Holli, and Remini, *University of Illinois at Chicago*, 80–81; "U of I Site Residents Go on a Protest March," *CST*, March 20, 1961; "Protest Rally Today against U. of I. Campus," *CT*, March 20, 1961, folder 94, box 9, COUA; and "Area Parade Protests U. of I. Site Choice," *CST*, March 21, 1961.

97. Malcolm Wise, "Daley Reasserts Backing of U. of I. Halsted Site," *CST*, March 21, 1961; and H. Martine Landwehr, "Persistent Harrison-Halsted Women Pickets May Stir Up Storm over U.I. Site," *Northwest Journal*, March 22, 1961—both in folder 95, box 9, COUA.

98. "U. of I. Site Foes Boo Daley," *CDN*, March 30, 1961; "Hecklers Boo U. of I. Site Bills," *CA*, March 30, 1961; Ralph Walters, "150 Boo Daley in Council as He Offers U. of I. Plan," *CST*, March 31, 1961; "Illini Site Clearers Face Blocked Path," *CA*, April 7, 1961; and Ruth Moore, "Near West Side U. of IL. Site Approved by City Plan Unit," *CST*, April 7, 1961—all in folder 95, box 9, COUA.

99. Edward Schreiber, "Two Legislators Assail West Side U. of I. Site," *CT*, April 14, 1961; Malcolm Wise, "Tears, Threats at Illini Site Hearing," *CST*, April 14, 1961; and "Gag Is Ruled Out," *CST*, April 15, 1961—all in folder 96, box 9, COUA.

100. "State: Kerner Submits His Budget," *CST*, April 23, 1961, folder 90, box 8; photos, *CDN*, April 19, 1961, folder 96, box 9; and Malcolm Wise, "OK Illini Site; Mayor Besieged," *CST*, April 19, 1961, folder 96, box 9—all in COUA. "Fear Sitdown Strike: Daley OK's Parley with U. of I. Foes," *CA*, April 19, 1961, folder 96, box 9, COUA. See photos in that issue as well.

101. Paul Gapp, "Future Uncertain for Bank at UI Site," *CDN*, March 17, 1961, folder 94, box 9, COUA.

102. Scala, interview with Studs Terkel, cited in Rosen, *Decision-Making*, 99.

103. "Douglas Urges Retaining All of Hull House," *CT*, July 25, 1961, folder 90, box 8; "Hull House to Continue Work, Says New Chief," *CDN*, September 12, 1961, folder 91, box 8; and Jack Mabley, "Mabley's Report: City 'Renewal'—Harrison Halsted Style," *CA*, March 21, 1962, folder 93, box 9—all in COUA.

104. Ruth Moore, "Near West Side U. of IL. Site Approved by City Plan Unit," *CST*, April 7, 1961, folder 95, box 9; and "Residents, Illini Students Clash," *CA*, April 19, 1961, folder 96, box 9—both in COUA.

105. Rosen, *Decision-Making*, 83. On social settlement houses and their leadership, see Judith Ann Trolander, *Professionalism and Social Change: From the Settlement House Movement to Neighborhood Centers, 1886 to the Present* (New York: Columbia University Press, 1987).

106. Rosen, *Decision-Making*, 112–13; and "Charge Daley Breaks Word with Church."

107. Near West Side Community Council, *Chronicle*, Summer 1959, 7, folder 550, NWSCC; and "Plan to Raze Hull House Is Hit by Board," *CT*, February 11, 1961, folder 89, box 8, COUA.

108. Scala, interview in Eastwood, *Near West Side Stories*. On Daley's power as machine boss, see Cohen and Taylor, *American Pharaoh*.

109. Phil Ayala, interview with the author, December 4, 2003. Georgie Ann Geyer, "Women Plan Food Sale to Finance Court Battle," *CDN*, July 28, 1961; and "Street Carnival Welcomes Mableys," *CA*, July 30, 1961—both in folder 90, box 8, COUA.

110. Eastwood, *Near West Side Stories*, 172.

111. Rosen, *Decision-Making*, 119; and Geyer, "Heritage of Jane Addams," 22.

112. Rosen, *Decision-Making*, 118–19. More than 10 percent of the area's employed population worked for the government. Kitagawa and Taueber, *Local Community Fact Book*, 265. The Harrison-Halsted struggle purportedly sparked a number of women-led community initiatives throughout the city in the following years. See, for example, Studs Terkel, "Ya Gotta Fight City Hall," *Chicago Guide*, September 1973, 145–47; Squires, Bennett, McCourt, and Nyden, *Chicago*; and Von Hoffman.

113. "Council OK's Illini Campus Site 41 to 3," *CT*, May 11, 1961; "AFL Council Here Backs U. of I. Site," *CDN*, April 5, 1961; and "CFL Supports Halsted Site for the U of I," *CT*, April 5, 1961, folder 95, box 9, COUA. Rosen suggests that trade unions supported the construction of the campus not only for the jobs it would create but also because they saw it as an opportunity for working-class youth to obtain a college education. *Decision-Making*, 63.

114. "Residents, Illini Students Clash," *CA*, April 19, 1961, folder 96, box 9, COUA. "Campus Foes Picket Daley's Home, Meet Counter Pickets," *CST*, May 8, 1961; and "Picket Daley's Home in Protest of U. of I. Site," *CT*, May 8, 1961—both in folder 90, box 8, COUA.

115. Georgie Ann Geyer, "New UI Site Challenge—Is Deal Legal?" *CDN*, July 14, 1961. This was certainly a result of President Kennedy's close relationship with Daley and his political debt to the mayor who had handed him a victory in Illinois in 1960.

116. "West Side Foes of U. of I. Site Regroup Forces," *CA*, July 22, 1961; "Begin Setting Stage for Suit on U. of I. Site," *CT*, July 22, 1961, folder 90, box 8; Dale Morrison, "It's War, Say U. of I. Site Foes," *CDN*, August 11, 1961, folder 91, box 8; "U. of I. Site Gets Final State OK," *CST*, August 9, 1961, folder 91, box 8; and "Court OKs U. of I. Site Acquisitions," *CST*, July 25, 1962, folder 92, box 8—all in COUA.

117. Sherwood Ross, "5 Go to Court Here to Fight U. of I. Condemnation Suits," *CDN*, June 6, 1962; and "Judge Assails Both Sides in U. of I. Campus Dispute," *CT*, June 9, 1962—both in folder 100, box 9, COUA.

118. Mabley, "Mabley's Report: City 'Renewal'—Harrison Halsted Style"; Tom Littlewood, "State Top Court OKs Chicago U. of I. Site," *CST*, February 27, 1963, folder 92, box 8, COUA; Rosen, *Decision-Making*, 117–18; and "Near West Project Gets Green Light," *Urban Renewal Review* 2, no. 2 (May–June 1963), folder 92, box 8, COUA.

119. "Price O.K. Expected on U. of I. Site," *CA*, April 18, 1962; and "$4.6 Mil Price Set on Illini Campus," *CDN*, April 18, 1962—both in folder 92, box 8, COUA. The

University of Illinois would join Fordham University and Saint Louis University in benefitting from federal largesse for the sake of college campuses. Biles, "Public Housing," 153.

120. "Near West Project Gets Green Light"; and Terkel, "Ya Gotta Fight City Hall."

121. Kitagawa and Taueber, *Local Community Fact Book,* 71. For personal accounts of Mexican families' displacement, see Alicia Amador, interview with the author, March 26, 2004; Phil Ayala, interview with the author, December 4, 2003; María Ovalle, interview with the author, June 6, 2004; and Sylvia Puente, interview with the author, March 22, 2004.

122. Rosen, *Decision-Making;* and Jim Yuenger, "'Why I Got to Move?'" *CT,* April 26, 1964, folder 92, box 8, COUA.

123. Yuenger, "'Why I Got to Move?'"

124. Near West Side Community Committee, annual reports, 1964 and 1965, folder 1, box 92, CAP; and Suttles, *Social Order,* 145.

125. "Little Mexico Rising from Ashes of Row," *CDN,* April 29, 1961, folder 97, box 9, COUA; and annual report for West Side Community Committee, 1962, 6, folder 1, box 92, CAP.

126. Felix Padilla, *Puerto Rican Chicago* (Notre Dame, IN: University of Notre Dame Press, 1987), 83. Very few Mexican or Puerto Rican families managed to remain in the Taylor Street vicinity. Victor and Esther Santiago, who had bought a home on Fillmore Street in 1955, were among the few able to avoid the bulldozers and stay in the neighborhood. See Ana Mendieta, "Urban Renewal Takes Toll on Ethnic Neighborhood," *CST,* June 18, 2001.

127. Kitagawa and Taeuber, *Local Community Fact Book,* 71; and Harry Golden Jr., "City's Latino Population Rises 125%," *CST,* December 9, 1973, 56.

128. Annual report for West Side Community Committee, 1962, 6.

129. Suttles, *Social Order,* 22, 120–21.

130. Scala, interview with Robert Young, 23–24.

131. On the campus design, see Stefan Muthesius, *The Postwar University: Utopianist Campus and College* (New Haven, CT: Yale University Press, 2000), 201.

132. Geyer, "Heritage of Jane Addams"; Terkel, "Ya Gotta Fight City Hall"; and Scala, interview with Young, 23.

133. "$66,000,000 in Six Bond Issues Defeated," *CST,* April 11, 1962, folder 418, IAF; and Robert Rose, "Revolt on Taxes Wasn't Only Reason Urban Renewal Bonds Were Defeated," *CDN,* April 14, 1962.

134. Herbert Gans, *The Urban Villagers* (New York: Free Press, 1962); Zipp, "Battle of Lincoln Square"; Avila, *Popular Culture,* chap. 5; Parson, *Making a Better World,* chap. 6; and Dana Cuff, *The Provisional City: Los Angeles Stories of Architecture and Urbanism* (Cambridge, MA: MIT Press, 2000), chap. 7.

135. John Friedman, "Life Space and Economic Space: Contradictions in Regional Development," cited in Barry Bluestone and Bennett Harrison, *The Deindustrialization of America: Plant Closings, Community Abandonment, and the Dismantling of Basic Industry* (New York: Basic Books, 1982), 20.

136. Hull House joined with other settlements on the North Side of the city and formed a conglomerate, Jane Addams / Hull House Association. A historic mural, the first ever painted by a Mexican in Chicago, Adrian Lozano, was torn down during the demolition of Hull House. See David A. Badillo, "Incorporating Reform and Religion: Mexican Immigrants, Hull-House, and the Church," in *Pots of Promise: Mexicans and*

Pottery at Hull-House, 1920–40, ed. Cheryl R. Ganz and Margaret Strobel, 50–51 (Urbana: University of Illinois Press, 2004).

137. John R. Logan and Harvey L. Molotch, *Urban Fortunes: The Political Economy of Place* (Berkeley: University of California Press, 1987). See also Bickford, "Constructing Inequality."

138. Squires, Bennett, McCourt, and Nyden, *Chicago*, 133, 135.

139. Ibid., 105, 135.

140. St. Francis of Assisi elementary school, which had served hundreds of Mexican children over the years, closed its doors in 1965 because the building was sold and the land taken over by the university. Eastwood, *Near West Side Stories*, 273. Rosa de la Llata, interview with the author, January 21, 2009.

141. Ovalle, interview with the author, June 6, 2004.

CHAPTER FOUR

1. Gregory D. Squires, Larry Bennett, Kathleen McCourt, and Philip Nyden, *Chicago: Race, Class, and the Response to Urban Decline* (Philadelphia: Temple University Press, 1987), 93–94.

2. Chicago Commission on Human Relations, *Puerto Rican Americans in Chicago* (Chicago: Mayor's Committee on New Residents, 1960).

3. Felix Padilla, *Puerto Rican Chicago* (Notre Dame, IN: University of Notre Dame Press, 1987), 148.

4. Mérida Rúa, "Claims to 'the City': Puerto Rican Latinidad amid Labors of Identity, Community, and Belonging in Chicago" (PhD diss., University of Michigan, 2004), 30; and Felix Padilla, *Latino Ethnic Consciousness: The Case of Mexican Americans and Puerto Ricans in Chicago* (Notre Dame, IN: University of Notre Dame Press), 43.

5. See Ana Mendieta, "Urban Renewal Takes Toll on Ethnic Neighborhood," *CST*, June 18, 2001, for the stories of several families. See also José "Cha Cha" Jiménez, untitled and undated manuscript, box 1, YL; Eugenia Rodríguez, interview with José "Cha Cha" Jiménez, box 2, YL; and José "Cha Cha" Jiménez and Rivera interview with the author, June 19, 2004.

6. The term *ethnic whites* is used to distinguish European immigrants who were classified as white but retained a distinct ethnic identity. See James R. Barrett and David R. Roediger, "The Irish and the 'Americanization' of the 'New Immigrants' in the Streets and in the Churches of the Urban United States, 1900–1930," *Journal of American Ethnic History* 24, no. 4 (2005): 4–33.

7. Some scholars argue that ethnic whites had not firmly established their whiteness, pointing to the fact that they continued to have tensions with other ethnic groups. Regardless of such residual conflicts, however, they were not undergoing the more intense racial judgments and scrutiny that more recent (im)migrants such as Mexicans and Puerto Ricans did. See Andrew Diamond, *Mean Streets: Chicago Youths and the Everyday Struggle for Empowerment in the Multiracial City, 1908–1969* (Berkeley: University of California Press, 2009); and Dominic A. Pacyga, "To Live amongst Others: Poles and Their Neighbors in Industrial Chicago, 1865–1930," *Journal of American Ethnic History* 16, no. 1 (1996): 55–73.

8. On the construction of white racial identities vis-à-vis African Americans, see Noel Ignatiev, *How the Irish Became White* (New York: Routledge, 1995); David Roediger, *Wages of Whiteness: Race and the Making of the American Working Class* (New York: Verso, 1991); and Pacyga, "To Live amongst Others."

9. Elena Padilla also referred to Puerto Ricans as "immigrants" in her 1947 master's thesis, suggesting she initially drew on a model of social assimilation and integration applied to European immigrants. Elena Padilla, "Puerto Rican Immigrants in New York and Chicago: A Study in Comparative Assimilation" (MA thesis, University of Chicago, 1947).

10. Floreal Forni, *The Situation of the Puerto Rican Population in Chicago and Its Viewpoints about Racial Relations* (Chicago: Community and Family Study Center, University of Chicago, 1971), 2. Among white residents of one Philadelphia neighborhood surveyed in 1953, only 7 percent of them believed that Puerto Ricans were racially "white." Less than half realized that they were citizens. Carmen Teresa Whalen, *From Puerto Rico to Philadelphia: Puerto Rican Workers and Postwar Economies* (Philadelphia: Temple University Press, 2001), 188.

11. On Puerto Ricans and the informal economy, see Kelvin Santiago-Valles and Gladys Jiménez-Muñoz, "Social Polarization and Colonized Labor: Puerto Ricans in the United States, 1945–2000," in *The Columbia History of Latinos in the United States since 1960*, ed. David G. Gutiérrez (New York: Columbia University Press, 2004), 98.

    Grosfoguel, Negrón-Muntaner, and Georas contend that "regardless of phenotype, all Puerto Ricans are considered a racial group in the social imaginary of most Americans, accompanied by racial stereotypes such as laziness, violence, stupidity, and dirtiness." Ramon Grosfoguel, Frances Negrón-Muntaner, and Chloe Georas, "Introduction: Beyond Nationalistic and Colonialist Discourses: The *Jaiba* Politics of the Puerto Rican Ethno-nation," in *Puerto Rican Jam: Essays on Culture and Politics*, ed. Frances Negrón-Muntaner and Ramon Grosfoguel (Minneapolis: University of Minnesota Press, 1997), 21.

12. Gina Pérez suggests that the riots marked a discursive shift in the way whites and the city power structure viewed Puerto Ricans. Their hopes for being understood as "model minorities" who would assimilate like Europeans had turned sour as they came to be associated with urban African Americans who were increasingly expressing their political discontent through public uprisings throughout the country. Gina Pérez, *The Near Northwest Side Story: Migration, Displacement, and Puerto Rican Families* (Berkeley: University of California Press, 2004).

13. For an early study of the area, see, Harvey Warren Zorbaugh, *The Gold Coast and the Slum: A Sociological Study of Chicago's Near North Side* (Chicago: University of Chicago Press, 1929). Joanne Meyerowitz discusses some of this area in her study of single working women in the late nineteenth and early twentieth centuries who lived in SROs, boarding houses, and kitchenettes. Joanne Meyerowitz, *Women Adrift: Independent Wage Earners in Chicago, 1880–1930* (Chicago: University of Chicago Press, 1988).

14. Nearly 48 percent of all units were occupied by only one person. Evelyn Kitagawa and Karl E. Taeuber, *Local Community Fact Book: Chicago's Metropolitan Area, 1960* (Chicago: Chicago Community Inventory, University of Chicago, 1963), 30, 273.

15. Eugenia Rodríguez interview. Myrna Rodriguez, interview with the author, October 11, 2004. Puerto Ricans encountered some housing discrimination and widespread shortages but to a lesser degree than what African Americans faced in the 1940s. On African American housing discrimination, see Arnold R. Hirsch, *Making the Second Ghetto: Race and Housing in Chicago, 1940–1960* (Cambridge: Cambridge University Press, 1983); and Horace Cayton and St. Clair Drake, *Black Metropolis: A Study of Negro Life in a Northern City* (New York: Harcourt, Brace and World, 1945).

16. Kitagawa and Taueber, *Local Community Fact Book*, 30, 31, 246. Nicholas Von Hoff-

man reports, 1956, folder 260, IAF. The area also had a high number of elderly residents, many of whom lived in local apartment hotels. Nicholas Von Hoffman to Monsignor Edward M. Burke, July 23, 1956, folder 260, IAF.

17. Native born, yet newcomers to the city, white Appalachians presented another type of whiteness, one punctuated by class, culture, and region in ways different from those of European immigrants and their children. Appalachians were estimated at about fifty thousand in these years and settled primarily on the Near North Side and in Lakeview/Uptown. For oral histories with southern whites, see Studs Terkel, *Division Street: America* (New York: Pantheon Books, 1967), 57, 98, 103.

18. James B. LaGrand, *Indian Metropolis: Native Americans in Chicago, 1945–1975* (Urbana: University of Illinois Press, 2002), 113, 119.

19. Jack Lait and Lee Mortimer, *Chicago Confidential* (New York: Crown Publishers, 1950); and Nicholas Von Hoffman notes on "Harper Richard, Dearborn Association," n.d., folder 259, IAF.

20. Citywide, the median family income for all Chicagoans was $6,738. Puerto Ricans in other areas had income as high as $5,825. Kitagawa and Taueber, *Local Community Fact Book*, 3, 272.

21. Jiménez and Rivera interview; Alfredo Matias, interview 2 with Miguel Morales, October 4, 1995, box 2, YL; and Carlos Flores interview, box 2, YL.

22. Kitagawa and Taueber, *Local Community Fact Book*, 31, 285. Many buildings in the area had extensive fire hazards and building code violations and were in fact targeted for slum clearance in the North-LaSalle project. See "City Suit Asks Receiver for 21 Slum Buildings," *CT*, December 31, 1959; and "Offers 19 Old Buildings to Renewal Unit," *CT*, March 20, 1960.

23. Adam Cohen and Elizabeth Taylor, *American Pharaoh: Mayor Richard J. Daley: His Battle for Chicago and the Nation* (Boston: Little, Brown & Co., 2000), 373.

24. Housing and Home Finance Agency, *Approaches to Urban Renewal in Several Cities* (Washington, DC: Urban Renewal Administration, 1954), 8. The Near North Side bears a remarkable resemblance to the Bunker Hill neighborhood of Los Angeles, a rooming house / tenement area also targeted for private urban redevelopment in the late 1940s / early 1950s. See Donald Craig Parson, *Making a Better World: Public Housing, the Red Scare, and the Direction of Public Housing* (Minneapolis: University of Minnesota Press, 2005), 147–62.

25. Parson, *Making a Better World*, esp. chaps. 5 and 6.

26. Chicago Plan Commission, *Plans and Progress* monthly report, August 1954, 2, MRC; and Nicholas Von Hoffman to Monsignor Edward M. Burke, July 23, 1956, folder 260, IAF. On the use of high-rise architecture in public housing, see Bradford Hunt, *Blueprint for Disaster: The Unraveling of Chicago Public Housing* (Chicago: University of Chicago Press, 2009), 121–40.

Of course, tenants differed dramatically in income; education; employment rates; social, cultural, and human capital; and greater political power. Sandburg Village residents possessed immeasurable advantages over public housing tenants; most were likely to be single professionals or childless couples with less need for public services than the residents of public housing.

27. Department of City Planning, *Plans and Progress* monthly report, April 1960, MRC; Chicago Urban Renewal Summary, December 31, 1956, folder 420, IAF; and Robert Young, "Chicago First with Urban Renewal Plan," *CT*, March 1, 1958. For an account of similar residential development on the city's South Side, see Hirsch, *Making the Second Ghetto*, chap. 4.

28. Department of City Planning, *Plans and Progress* monthly report, April 1960, MRC; "75,000 Dwellings Razed in Ten Years," *CDN*, April 6, 1962; and Chicago Plan Commission, *Stated Policies of the Chicago Plan Commission*, April 16, 1957, MRC.

29. See Squires, Bennett, McCourt, and Nyden, *Chicago.*

30. Housing and Home Finance Agency, *Approaches to Urban Renewal*, 5.

31. Squires, Bennett, McCourt, and Nyden, *Chicago*, 94; and Ed Marciniak, *Reclaiming the Inner City: Chicago's Near North Revitalization Confronts Cabrini-Green* (Washington, DC: National Center for Urban Ethnic Affairs, 1986), 32–36.

32. Chicago is laid out in a grid pattern so that many of its streets run continuously from north to south or east to west and span the entire city. In this chapter, I make mention of streets such as Division Street and North Avenue, which run east and west and traverse the various neighborhoods of the Near North Side, West Town, and Humboldt Park.

33. While most other families were forced to move from Armitage by the early 1970s, the Flores family managed to keep their home for two decades. Mendieta, "Urban Renewal Takes Toll." Flores interview; and Omar López, interview 1 with Miguel Morales, February 10, 1995—both in box 2, YL. Myrna Rodriguez interview; Jiménez and Rivera interview; and Reverend Walter L. Coleman, interview with the author, June 23, 2004.

34. Thomas Guglielmo, *White on Arrival: Italians, Race, Color, and Power in Chicago, 1890–1945* (Oxford: Oxford University Press, 2003), 155–57, and, more generally, chap. 8; and Hunt, *Blueprint for Disaster*, 56–57.

35. Hirsch, *Making the Second Ghetto*; and Chicago Plan Commission, *City Planning Report on 15 Suggested Public Housing Sites*, Site One, 1950, MRC. See also Marciniak, *Reclaiming the Inner City*, 29; and Hunt, *Blueprint for Disaster*. Hirsch provides a compelling analysis of how public housing served the interests of private development. Hunt challenges Hirsch's "second ghetto" thesis, arguing that it was not race but progressives' commitment to slum clearance that led to the erection of high-rise projects. In tracing the policy history of such projects, however, the racial motivations behind the political objections to public housing in some wards cannot be underestimated. Moreover, the cost argument for favoring high-rise buildings—because they were cheaper than smaller buildings—ignores the widespread corruption and fraud in local construction unions as well as the rampant patronage and "featherbedding" that existed in the CHA. See Cohen and Taylor, *American Pharaoh*, 187, 188, 200.

36. Barbara Hayes, interview with Terkel, *Division Street*, 171–78. On the decline of Chicago's public housing, see Hunt, *Blueprint for Disaster*.

37. Alexander Von Hoffman, *House by House, Block by Block: The Rebirth of America's Urban Neighborhoods* (New York: Oxford University Press, 2003), 139–40. See also Cohen and Taylor, *American Pharaoh*, 185, 187, 200.

38. Roger Biles, "Public Housing and the Postwar Urban Renaissance, 1949–1973," in *From Tenements to the Taylor Homes: In Search of an Urban Housing Policy in Twentieth-Century America*, ed. John Bauman, Roger Biles, and Kristin Szylvian, 143–62 (University Park: Pennsylvania State University Press, 2000), 147; and Hunt, *Blueprint for Disaster*. On Cabrini-Green specifically, see Marciniak, *Reclaiming the Inner City*.

39. Albert G. Rosenberg, Chicago Housing Authority, to Hollis Vick, September 22, 1953, folder 10, box 147, WC; John Kearney, migration specialist, to Eulalio Torres, February 1960, folder 756, box 2938, OGPRUS; and Monse Lucas-Figueroa, interview with the author, June 21, 2004.

40. Lucas-Figueroa interview. In *Blueprint for Disaster*, Hunt persuasively demonstrates that public housing had youth-adult ratios that were significantly higher than other neighborhoods and the city more generally. On youth violence in Chicago, particularly among young men, see Diamond, *Mean Streets*.

41. Lucas-Figueroa interview. While this specific policy cannot be confirmed *within* Cabrini-Green, other scholars have documented evidence of such racial segregation. See Hunt, *Blueprint for Disaster*, 55–56; and Guglielmo, *White on Arrival*, 152–53. See chap. 3 for a discussion of the Jane Addams Homes. See also Cohen and Taylor, *American Pharaoh*, 333–34.

42. José Muñiz, Community Project reports, January, March, and July 1960, folder 16, box 108, and folder 12, box 93, CAP. See also Puerto Rico Department of Labor, Migration Division, untitled document, July 22, 1953, folder 10, box 147, WC. For more on the Puerto Rico Migration Division, see chap. 1. "Knights of St. John Hit CHA, Cite Rent Policies," *CST*, June 16, 1958, folder 152, IAF; and "Knights Blast Public Housing," June 17, 1958, folder 151, IAF.

43. Migration Division, annual report, 1959–60, 160, box 1, folder 7, OGPRUS. The project's image as a dangerous place was sealed in 1970, when two white police officers were shot and killed at the projects. By then very few Spanish-speaking people remained in public housing. Gerald Ropka, *The Evolving Residential Pattern of the Mexican, Puerto Rican, and Cuban Population in the City of Chicago* (New York: Arno Press, 1980), 126.

44. Lawrence J. Vale, *Reclaiming Public Housing: A Half Century of Struggle in Three Public Neighborhoods* (Cambridge, MA: Harvard University Press, 2002), 9. Vale's study of the demise of public housing in Boston contrasts dramatically with the Chicago experience, however, as Boston was 91 percent white in 1960 and the majority of public housing was intentionally built in predominantly white areas for white residents (22–26). See also Gerald Suttles, *The Man-Made City: The Land-Use Confidence Game in Chicago* (Chicago: University of Chicago Press, 1990), 60–66. For more on Cabrini-Green, see Marciniak, *Reclaiming the Inner City*.

45. Gabriela Arredondo describes these dynamics in relation to Mexican immigrants in Chicago in the 1920s and 1930s. See Gabriela Arredondo, "Navigating Ethno-Racial Currents: Mexicans in Chicago, 1919–1939," *Journal of Urban History* 30, no. 3 (2004): 399–427.

46. José Muñiz, *Community Project Report*, January 1960, folder 12, box 93, CAP. See also Migration Division, annual report, 1959–60, 160, box 1, folder 7, OGPRUS. For a study of how a white working-class neighborhood excluded Hispanics and maintained its racial composition, see Judith DeSena, *Protecting One's Turf: Social Strategies for Maintaining Urban Neighborhoods* (Lanham, MD: University Press of America, 1990).

47. Lucas-Figueroa interview. She also noted that landlords discriminated against large families, in some cases refusing to accept families with many children.

48. Cited in Padilla, *Puerto Rican Chicago*, 60. This was a common experience for Puerto Rican migrants in their search for housing. On this dynamic in Philadelphia, see Whalen, *From Puerto Rico*, 191.

49. José Muñiz, *Community Project Report*, January 1960, folder 12, box 93, CAP. See also Chicago Commission on Human Relations, *Puerto Rican Americans in Chicago* (Chicago: Mayor's Committee on New Residents, 1960); and Whalen, *From Puerto Rico*, 188.

50. Pacyga, "To Live amongst Others," 56. Eileen McMahon discusses the ethnic diver-

sity among European immigrants in what were purportedly "Irish" neighborhoods. Eileen McMahon, *What Parish Are You From? A Chicago Irish Community and Race Relations* (Lexington: University of Kentucky Press, 1995).

51. See, for example, Georgie Anne Geyer, "Chicago's Proud Puerto Ricans: An Upbeat 'West Side Story,'" *CDN*, June 5, 1965, 22. Pérez cites this article along with others that celebrated the Puerto Ricans' assimilation and social mobility in *Near Northwest Side Story*.

52. In Philadelphia, for example, Puerto Ricans recall receiving negative attention and anticipating police harassment after the attack on President Truman. Whalen, *From Puerto Rico*, 193.

53. This was not an uncommon experience for immigrants. Italians and other ethnic groups were often relegated to basements by Irish-dominated Catholic churches. Barrett and Roediger in fact contend that the American Catholic Church was essentially controlled and dominated by Irish Americans for much of the early twentieth century. Barrett and Roediger, "Irish and the 'Americanization' of the 'New Immigrants,'" 17–22.

54. Three other councils existed at the same time: one in the predominantly black South Side Woodlawn neighborhood, one on the Near West Side, and one in West Town. Martínez maintains that Catholic priests were the first leaders of the Puerto Rican community, suggesting the paternalistic role priests played among migrants. Reverend Leo Mahon, "The Knights of St. John," folder 151, IAF; Manuel Martínez, *Chicago: Historia de Nuestra Comunidad Puertorriqueña* (Chicago: Reyes and Sons, 1989), 123; and Marixsa Alicea, "Cuando Nosotros Vivíamos . . . Stories of Displacement and Settlement in Puerto Rican Chicago," *Centro Journal* 13, no. 2 (2001): 174.

55. Padilla, *Puerto Rican Chicago*, 83. See Alfredo Matias, interview 2. Noted also in Robert Cross, "Proud Old, Stubborn Old Wicker Park," *Chicago Tribune Magazine*, November 7, 1971, 26, folder 6, box 17, AH. Even there, however, Puerto Ricans often moved from apartment to apartment, plagued by poor housing conditions, racial conflict, high rents, and other problems. See Forni, *Situation of the Puerto Rican Population*, 62–66.

56. Report, 1959, West Town Mobilization for Youth, folder 9, box 16, AH; Kitagawa and Taueber, *Local Community Fact Book*, 62–63; and Cross, "Proud Old, Stubborn Old Wicker Park," 27.

57. "$66,000,000 in Six Bond Issues Defeated," *CST*, April 11, 1962; Robert Rose, "Revolt on Taxes Wasn't Only Reason Urban Renewal Bonds Were Defeated," *CDN*, April 14, 1962; and Jack Mabley, "Erasing Slums? Renewal Just Moving Them!" *CA*, May 29, 1962.

58. Migration Division, annual report, 1953–54, 44, box 1, folder 1, OGPRUS; and Kitagawa and Taueber, *Local Community Fact Book*, 247.

59. Kitagawa and Taeuber, *Local Community Fact Book*, 63. Chicago Fact Book Consortium, ed., *Local Community Fact Book Based on the 1970 and 1980 Censuses* (Chicago: Chicago Review Press, 1984), 452. The 1950 census did not identify Puerto Ricans in a separate category, but their numbers certainly would have been very low (fewer than two thousand persons). The 1960 census did distinguish Puerto Ricans, but in 1970 it used the panethnic term *Spanish language* instead, thus capturing other Latino groups as well. In Humboldt Park, this included a sizable number of Mexicans, possibly Cubans, and South Americans, but the largest group was Puerto Rican.

60. Mexicans soon outpaced Puerto Ricans in Humboldt Park, but the characterization of the community remained Puerto Rican.

61. Barrett and Roediger, "Irish and the 'Americanization' of the 'New Immigrants,'" 7. For examples of white resistance to nonwhite neighbors, see George Lipsitz, *The Possessive Investment in Whiteness: How White People Profit from Identity Politics* (Philadelphia: Temple University Press, 1998); McMahon, *What Parish Are You From?*; Guglielmo, *White on Arrival*; and Hirsch, *Making the Second Ghetto*. On white working-class communities and identity, see, for example, Becky Nicolaides, *My Blue Heaven: Life and Politics in the Working-Class Suburbs of Los Angeles, 1920–1965* (Chicago: University of Chicago Press, 2002). On Poles in Chicago and their relations with other Europeans, see Pacyga, "To Live amongst Others."

62. John Bartlow Martin, "Crime without Reason," *Saturday Evening Post*, November 5, 1960, folder 12, box 93, CAP. See also Omar López, interview 1; and Alicea, "Cuando Nosotros Vivíamos," 172.

63. Squires, Bennett, McCourt, and Nyden, *Chicago*, 111; and John J. Betancur, "The Settlement Experience of Latinos in Chicago: Segregation, Speculation, and the Ecology Model," *Social Forces* 74, no. 4 (1996): 1310.

64. Appalachian migrants brought their own cultural peculiarities and regional idiosyncrasies, which differed from those of Russian, Polish, German, and Italian Americans. Hartigan and numerous other scholars have examined the diversity of whiteness and how it is inflected by class, ethnicity, and geography in distinct ways. Moreover, Barrett and Roediger, among others, note that whiteness was not the same for all European immigrants. Irish immigrants, for example, who had a much longer history in the United States compared to Italians or Poles, embodied a more highly valued whiteness than southern or eastern European immigrants. Indeed, many aspired to the socioeconomic and political dominance that the Irish enjoyed as assimilated "Americans." See John Hartigan, *Racial Situations: Class Predicaments of Whiteness in Detroit* (Princeton, NJ: Princeton University Press, 1999); and Barrett and Roediger, "Irish and the 'Americanization' of the 'New Immigrants.'"

65. Social and behavioral scientists have tried to explain these interethnic, cross-cultural dynamics. Researchers have established that people form their own identities and make choices (both "personal" and "political") based on their social context and in relation to those around them (insiders versus outsiders). Theories of "symbolic interactionism," the concept of "social affinity," or axioms that maintain that any given social group naturally tries to keep unfamiliar people out have offered explanations for these dynamics. This ostensibly accounts for why some whites reacted with prejudice against racially different neighbors.

   On "social affinity," see Jeff Greenberg and Thomas Pyszczynski, "The Effect of an Overheard Ethnic Slur on Evaluations of the Target: How to Spread a Social Disease," *Journal of Experimental Social Psychology* 21 (1985): 61–72; and John Darley and Paget Gross, "A Hypothesis-Confirming Bias in Labeling Effects," *Journal of Personality and Social Psychology*, 44 (1983): 20–33. See also Robert Huckfeldt, *Politics in Context: Assimilation and Conflict in Urban Neighborhoods* (New York: Agathon Press, 1986); and Herbert Blumer, "Symbolic Interactionism," in *Four Sociological Traditions*, edited by Randall Collins (New York: Oxford University Press, 1994). On "defended neighborhoods," see Suttles, *Social Order of the Slum*; and DeSena, *Protecting One's Turf*.

66. I calculated the number of white (non–Puerto Rican) adults by taking the total of all white adults in that age range and subtracting the small number who were Puerto Rican (a mere 220 people) in census tracts 283–320. Social Explorer—Census 1960 Tracts Only Set, http://www.socialexplorer.com.

67. Alicea, "Cuando Nosotros Vivíamos," 173. Indeed, this was the experience that

many Mexican children had in the Pilsen and Little Village neighborhoods also (see chap. 6). See Hunt, *Blueprint for Disaster*, for a useful analysis of the demographics of Chicago's high-rise public housing projects, where children often outnumbered adults four to one.

68. Don Porteus, "Summer Program, Triangle Satellite Report, 1967," folder 4, box 16, AH. The higher numbers in elementary grades reflected the relative youth of most migrant families, but also revealed a high dropout rate among Puerto Rican high school students. In 1973, Isidro Lucas estimated a dropout rate of 71 percent for Puerto Rican students in Chicago. Cited in Gilbert Cardenas and Ricardo Parra, *La Raza in the Midwest and Great Lakes Region* (Notre Dame, IN: Centro de Estudios Chicanos, Institute for Urban Studies, University of Notre Dame, January 1973), 29.

69. See *Local Community Fact Books*, 1960, 1970, and 1980.

70. Porteus, "Summer Program, Triangle Satellite Report, 1967." Interestingly, this example demonstrates that policing neighborhood racial boundaries did not fall only to men and boys; women also asserted the racial boundaries of their blocks against interlopers.

71. Cited in Padilla, *Puerto Rican Chicago*, 59.

72. Native white Americans also deployed such racial slurs against Irish and Italian immigrants, as well as Mexicans (see chap. 6).

73. White male youths aged ten to nineteen totaled 10,278 in West Town, while Puerto Rican boys of the same age numbered only 579. Calculated from data in Social Explorer, Census 1960 Tracts Only Set for census tracts 283–320. On white male youths as the enforcers of neighborhood boundaries, see Diamond, *Mean Streets*.

74. Art Vázquez, "Neglect, Mistreatment, Police Misunderstanding Produce: A Puerto Rican Protest," *Renewal*, August 1966. On racial violence among youths more generally, see Diamond, *Mean Streets*, esp. chaps. 1 and 5.

In the early sixties, Benny Bearskin, a Winnebago man, recalled that when his family moved into an Italian American West Side neighborhood, they had their windows broken because neighbors mistakenly believed they were Mexican. Terkel, *Division Street*, 108. The story cited by Diamond might be the same family. Diamond, *Mean Streets*, 199.

75. Obed López interview. On white gangs policing neighborhood racial boundaries, see Barrett and Roediger, "Irish and the 'Americanization' of the 'New Immigrants'"; and Diamond, *Mean Streets*, 220. Puerto Rican youth confronted white gangs in other cities like Philadelphia and New York. On Philadelphia, see Whalen, *From Puerto Rico*, chap. 6.

76. Martin, "Crime without Reason."

77. Interestingly, West Town's black population tended to have slightly higher incomes than Puerto Ricans. A survey conducted in 1967 found that nearly 43 percent of Puerto Ricans earned less than $4,499, while this was true for less than 29 percent of blacks and 13 percent of whites. This suggests that the area's African Americans had a higher economic status and more economic stability than African Americans in other parts of the city. Forni, *Situation of the Puerto Rican Population*, 34.

78. Stefaniak became involved in community affairs after urban renewal threatened his home and became president of the Northwest Community Organization, an Alinsky-style group. Cross, "Proud Old, Stubborn Old Wicker Park," 22; and Sam King, "Puerto Ricans Are Eager to Work, Want No Handouts," *CDN*, August 11, 1959. Puerto Ricans in West Town ranged from the extremely poor (dependent on public assistance) to the lower-middle-class (property owners, skilled workers, small busi-

ness owners). Individuals' identities were inflected by their social standing in the community, and class differences gained greater significance, especially for the merchant class, who sought to distinguish themselves from those "on welfare," gang members, and hoodlums.

79. Quoted in Cross, "Proud Old, Stubborn Old Wicker Park," 24.

80. Squires, Bennett, McCourt, and Nyden, *Chicago*, 139. Squires et al. note that in the 1970s, one group, the Citizens Action Program, did understand these interrelated factors and fought aggressively against the city and its progrowth, antineighborhood policies.

81. Cited in Cohen and Taylor, *American Pharaoh*, 203.

82. "Pal of Police Tells How Alliance Began," *CT*, January 20, 1960, 1; "Daley Stalls on the Future of O'Connor," *CT*, January 20, 1960, 3; "Handling of $24,000 Burglary Attacked," *CT*, January 23, 1960, 1; "Kohn Reveals 28 Ways Cops Can Make Fast Buck," *CT*, February 16, 1960, 1; "Now See Who's Investigating Police Graft," *CT*, February 18, 1960, 3; Wayne Thomas, "Cops Turned Burglars! City Horrified," *CT*, February 23, 1960, 12; "Morris Feared by Shady Cops and Hoodlums," *CT*, March 15, 1960, 2; and "Guilty Policy Cop Accused as Bootlegger," *CT*, October 28, 1965, 14.

83. "Now See Who's Investigating Police Graft"; Thomas, "Cops Turned Burglars!"; and "Bandit Says Cop Took His Showup Spot," *CT*, February 27, 1960, 1.

   Such revelations of corruption, political influence, and the questionable character of some officers went much further back. See "Chicago Indictment Stirs Call for Thorough Screening of Police," *Christian Science Monitor*, October 13, 1951, 3.

84. Mayor Richard J. Daley's response to the revelation of police corruption was to oust the police superintendent, Timothy J. O'Connor, and replace him with Orlando Wilson. Such scandals hardly tempered police venality. By 1972, twenty-five policemen were indicted for wrongdoing, followed by fifty-seven officers brought before the grand jury by the following year. In 1981, the "Marquette 10" policemen were charged as part of a drug ring, and in the following year another thirteen officers were indicted by the courts. All told, police were arrested en masse five times between 1972 and 1982. Suttles, *Man-Made City*, 191–92.

85. Susan Bickford, "Constructing Inequality: City Spaces and the Architecture of Citizenship," *Political Theory* 28, no. 3 (2000): 363.

86. "Chicago Indictment Stirs Call"; and Diamond, *Mean Streets*, 253. On police abuse of African Americans in Philadelphia in the postwar period, see Karl E. Johnson, "Police-Black Community Relations in Postwar Philadelphia: Race and Criminalization in Urban Social Spaces, 1945–1960," *Journal of African American History* 89 (2004): 118–34.

87. Kitagawa and Taueber, *Local Community Fact Book, 1960*; and Social Explorer Tables (SE), Census 1960 Tracts Only Set, http://www.socialexplorer.com.

88. Obed and Carol Lee López, interview 1 with Mervin Méndez, October 17, 1995, box 2, YL. This occurred among Mexicans as well, dating as far back as the 1920s and 1930s. See Gabriela Arredondo, "Navigating Ethno-Racial Currents: Mexicans in Chicago, 1919–1939," *Journal of Urban History* 30, no. 3 (2004): 399–427. On the Irish-dominated police and conflicts with southern and eastern Europeans, see Barrett and Roediger, "Irish and 'Americanization' of the 'New Immigrants,'" 9. On African Americans and police relations, see Johnson, "Police-Black Community Relations."

89. José F. Muñiz, *Community Project Report*, March 1960, folder 16, box 108, and July

1960, folder 12, box 93, CAP; "Police Forced Confession: 'Crazy Tony,'" *CT*, May 16, 1962; and Chicago Commission on Human Relations, "Puerto Rican Americans in Chicago," 1960, 52, 56–57.

90. See Migration Division, annual reports, 1958–59, box 1, OGPRUS; and José F. Muñiz, *Community Project Report*, March 1960, folder 16, box 108, and July 1960, folder 12, box 93, CAP.

91. Terkel, *Division Street*, 88–92; and King, "Puerto Ricans Are Eager to Work." See also Padilla, *Puerto Rican Chicago*, 147–48; and Graciano López, interview with Mervin Mendez, January 19, 1996, box 2, YL.

92. Chicago Commission on Human Relations, *Puerto Rican Americans in Chicago*, 1960, 52.

93. Diamond, *Mean Streets*, 253. Diamond's study examines the long history of gangs in Chicago, demonstrating that they were not a new problem introduced by Puerto Rican youths but that immigrant and second-generation youths of all nationalities had participated in street life and gangs throughout the twentieth century. On Latino and black male youth and police abuse in other contexts, see, for example, Edward Escobar, *Race, Police, and the Making of an Identity: Mexican Americans and the Los Angeles Police Department, 1900–1945* (Berkeley: University of California Press, 1999); and Craig Wilder, *A Covenant with Color: Race and Social Power in Brooklyn* (New York: Columbia University Press, 2000), chap. 9. On youth of color and their struggle for dignity, see Luis Alvarez, *The Power of the Zoot: Youth Culture and Resistance during World War II* (Berkeley: University of California Press, 2008).

94. Cited in "Revisiting the 1966 Division Street Riot," special issue, *Diálogo: Center for Latino Research, DePaul University*, no. 2 (1997): 10.

95. Daley may have been motivated by political interest in finally recognizing the Puerto Rican community with a parade. Community leaders had mobilized Puerto Ricans to come out and vote six years earlier during the Kennedy campaign. As US citizens, Puerto Ricans could register to vote rather easily, and thus had the potential to become an important voting bloc. Still, Puerto Ricans hardly held the political power that other ethnic groups in the city did.

96. Obed and Carol Lee López, interview 1. See also Mervin Méndez, "Recollections: The 1966 Division Street Riots," *Diálogo: Center for Latino Research, DePaul University*, no. 2 (1997): 29–35; "16 Injured in Night-Long Street Fighting," *CA*, June 13, 1966; and "Burn Cops' Cars; 35 Held," *CT*, June 13, 1966, 1.

   Puerto Ricans had conflicts with law enforcement even as far away as Elgin, Illinois, where the Migration Division allegedly helped avert a confrontation between the community and local police the following month. Ironically, the division framed the police as victims of Puerto Rican hostility, referring to "tensions among the Puerto Ricans against the Police Department." Nonetheless, the local police chief issued an apology to the community, though the circumstances are not clear. Luis Machado to Joseph Monserrat, August 19, 1966, folder 14, box 2504, OGPRUS.

   Contrary to what some have claimed, this was not the first Puerto Rican riot on the mainland. Padilla, *Puerto Rican Chicago*, 144–55. On riots and conflict with police in other cities, see Whalen, *From Puerto Rico*, 183–94; "Two Housing Problems," *NYT*, July 8, 1961, 8; John Sibley, "West Side Forces Mobilized by City," *NYT*, July 12, 1961, 20; Milton Honig, "4 More Held in Newark Riot," *NYT*, September 29, 1961, 22; and "Racial Clash Denied in Riot at Newark," *NYT*, September 30, 1961, 12.

97. Stories on the beatings of July 1965 appeared in *El Puertorriqueño* and the *Chicago*

Daily News. Cited in Padilla, *Puerto Rican Chicago,* 124. As is common in many poor inner-city neighborhoods, fire hydrants often provide children and teens relief from summer heat, especially in communities that lack swimming pool facilities. Opening hydrants, however, has historically been illegal, and thus, law officers regularly close any that they find open.

98. From *El Puertorriqueño,* August 11, 1965, cited in Padilla, *Puerto Rican Chicago,* 124. See also "Cops Brutal in Arrest: Latin Group," *CDN,* August 2, 1965, 13.

   Such incidents prompted a huge investigation of nearly two hundred victims who came forward and a lawsuit brought by fifty African American men, who alleged that police from one South Side district beat and tortured them with cattle prods, pistols, and other weapons throughout the 1970s. See the extensive reporting of John Conroy during the 1990s in the *Chicago Reader.*

99. "7 Shot in New Disorder," *CT,* June 14, 1966, 1; and "Revisiting the 1966 Division Street Riot," *Diálogo: Center for Latino Research, DePaul University,* 11.

100. "500 Police Keep Watch on N.W. Side," *CT,* June 15, 1966, 1; Padilla, *Puerto Rican Chicago,* 149–50; Vázquez, "Puerto Rican Protest," 14–15; Méndez, "Recollections," 32; Cohen and Taylor, *American Pharaoh,* chaps. 9 and 10; Alan B. Anderson and George W. Pickering, *Confronting the Color Line: The Broken Promise of the Civil Rights Movement in Chicago* (Athens: University of Georgia Press, 1986); and Obed López interview. One observer noted that a recently formed gang, the Latin Kings (today one of the most powerful gangs in the city), actually coordinated much of the violence of the riots. Latin Kings members descended upon the streets and retreated, according to their leader's orders. Omar López interview 1.

101. "500 Police Keep Watch on N.W. Side."

102. Donald Headley, quoted in Méndez, "Recollections," 32; Padilla, *Puerto Rican Chicago,* chap. 4; "Two Police Cars Burned in N.W. Side Disturbance," *CST,* June 14, 1966; YMCA, "The West Town Streets Unit's Role in the Division Street Puerto Rican Incidents," n.d., folder 12, box 93, CAP; and Vázquez, "Puerto Rican Protest," 13. Vázquez noted that the most extensive coverage of the Puerto Rican parade down State Street, in the June 12 issue of the *Chicago Sun-Times,* did not even feature Puerto Ricans. Rather, the paper printed a large photo of the police department band, showcasing its performance in the parade. See also articles in *Chicago Defender, Chicago Sun-Times, Chicago American,* and *Chicago Tribune,* June 12–15, 1966.

103. Padilla, *Puerto Rican Chicago,* 145–55. In various cities in the Northeast, Puerto Ricans increasingly found themselves in violent conflicts with African Americans *and* local white law enforcement. In the aftermath, the specific racial contours of such riots were difficult to identify. See, for example, "Two Housing Problems"; Sibley, "West Side Forces Mobilized by City"; Honig, "4 More Held in Newark Riot"; and "Racial Clash Denied in Riot at Newark."

104. "Controlling Mobs," *CT,* June 14, 1966, 20; and "The Cause of Riots," *CT,* June 15, 1966, 20.

105. Peter Johnsen, "Puerto Ricans," *CT,* June 18, 1966.

106. "Why Different Today?," *CT,* July 8, 1966, 10.

107. Luis Machado to Joseph Monserrat, June 17, July 8, and July 22, 1966, folder 14, box 2504; and Migration Division annual report, 1966, box 1—both in OGPRUS.

108. Obed and Carol Lee López, interview 1. See also Pérez, *Near Northwest Side Story.*

109. The West Side rose up in protest for a third time following Dr. Martin Luther King Jr.'s assassination on April 4, 1968. Jon Rice, "The World of the Illinois Panthers,"

in *Freedom North: Black Freedom Struggles outside the South, 1940–1980*, ed. Jeanne F. Theoharis and Komozi Woodard, 41–64 (New York: Palgrave Macmillan, 2003); and Squires, Bennett, McCourt, and Nyden, *Chicago*, 84.

110. "Puerto Rican Riot Hearing Set Friday," *CDN*, July 13, 1966; "Puerto Rican Grievances Heard by City," *CT*, July 16, 1966; "Puerto Rican Urges Control on Creditors," *CDN*, July 16, 1966; and "Key City Changes Asked by Heads of Puerto Ricans," *CST*, July 16, 1966.

111. Vázquez, "Puerto Rican Protest," 12–13; Luis Machado to Joseph Monserrat, September 16, 1966, folder 14, box 2504, OGPRUS; "1,500 Gather as Cops Kill Berserk Man," *CT*, August 2, 1966; editorial and "Grand Jury Absolves Police in Laboy Killing," *EP*, September 30–October 6, 1966, issue; "Cops Fatally Shoot Boy, 14, in Stolen Car," *CT*, September 9, 1966; and "Youth Shot to Death by Cop," *CDN*, September 9, 1966.

112. "Warns the Jail May Ruin Police-PR Harmony," *CST*, December 7, 1967.

Puerto Ricans were experiencing police brutality and tense relations with law enforcement in cities like New York as well. See Barbara Wyden, "Kids and Cops," *NYT*, February 23, 1964; Gertrude Samuels, "'I Don't Think the Cop Is My Friend,'" *NYT*, March 29, 1964; Jack Roth, "Police Cleared in Slaying of 2," *NYT*, April 9, 1964, 20; "Police Establish Puerto Rican Aids," *NYT*, March 29, 1965, 35; "Police Quell Riot of 500 in Brooklyn Area," *CT*, July 9, 1966, 7; and "New Jersey Riots Erupt for 2d Night," *CT*, August 2, 1966.

113. Forni, *Situation of the Puerto Rican Population*, 69, 57.

114. Ibid., 58–59. On police relations with Puerto Ricans in Philadelphia, see Whalen, *From Puerto Rico*, 192–93.

115. "Report on June Riot Tells Cause, Remedy," newspaper unknown, December 16, 1966, box 16, AH. See also "Summer Riot Aftermath: City, County Are Sued," *CST*, December 20, 1966, box 16, AH; and Padilla, *Puerto Rican Chicago*, 148–55. This was a rather outdated response to the problems of the Puerto Rican community. Over a decade earlier, New York and Philadelphia officials had identified "the Puerto Rican problem" rather than structural discrimination and prejudice as the cause of difficulties among the migrants. See Whalen, *From Puerto Rico*, chap. 6.

116. Cohen and Taylor, *American Pharaoh*, 456–57.

117. Omar López, interview with Miguel Morales, February 10, 1995, box 1, YL.

118. Norm Wells, "Demographic Sketch: Association House Service Area," June 1969, 4, folder 5, box 20, AH.

119. Chicago Fact Book Consortium, *Local Community Fact Book Based on 1970 and 1980 Censuses*.

120. The figures for Humboldt Park were as follows: 1950—1.0 percent, 1960—3.7 percent, 1970—5.8 percent, and 1980—9.9 percent. For West Town, they were 1950—1.8 percent, 1960—6.4 percent, 1970—9.1 percent, and 1980—12.7 percent. From *Local Community Fact Book*, 1970 and 1980, 60, 63.

121. Cross, "Proud Old, Stubborn Old Wicker Park," 24, 27; and *Local Community Fact Book, 1970 and 1980*, 61.

The phenomenon of building conflagrations was prevalent throughout Chicago's inner-city poor neighborhoods. On one night, two buildings just blocks away from each other caught fire in the spring of 1955, which killed and injured a number of Spanish-speaking tenants, among others. See "2 Fire Probes Open Today," *CT*, April 29, 1955. The black West Side also witnessed dozens of neighborhood buildings burned to the ground. In Humboldt Park, some tenants reported being warned that they should vacate their apartments when buildings were scheduled to be burned down. See Cross, "Proud Old, Stubborn Old Wicker Park"; Alicea, "Cuando Nosotros Vivíamos"; Pérez, *Near Northwest Side,* 87–88; and Myrna Rodriguez interview.

Leven et al. offer an economic analysis of the real estate market in inner-city neighborhoods: "In simple economic terms, the housing markets of most of our nation's central cities display a curious anomaly—chronic excess supply of low- to moderate-income housing. Clearly, by the 1960s, if not earlier, we had all we needed, as witnessed by soaring vacancy rates [except in New York City], while by the mid- or late 1960s investors attested to the excess by withholding maintenance to the point where abandonment became the only economically viable alternative for very large numbers of units." While they do not mention arson, their suggestion that abandonment provided an expedient solution to disposing of dilapidated real estate points to why some owners might have resorted illegally to arson and insurance fraud. Charles Leven, James Little, Hugh Nourse, and R. B. Read, *Neighborhood Change: Lessons in the Dynamics of Urban Decay* (New York: Praeger Publishers, 1976).

CHAPTER FIVE

1. Interview notes, n.d. [1971], folder 20, box 51, Stanley Steiner Collection, Special Collections, Stanford University Library.

2. Felix Padilla, *Puerto Rican Chicago* (Notre Dame, IN: University of Notre Dame Press, 1987), 121.

3. Michael Flamm argues that the excesses of African American violence and crime led to the growing "law and order" platform of conservative politicians in the 1960s. See Michael W. Flamm, *Law and Order: Street Crime, Civil Unrest, and the Crisis of Liberalism in the 1960s* (New York: Columbia University Press, 2005). For a more nuanced analysis of the era's politics, see also Thomas J. Sugrue, *The Origins of the Urban Crisis: Race and Inequality in Postwar Detroit* (Princeton, NJ: Princeton University Press, 1996); Heather Ann Thompson, *Whose Detroit? Politics, Labor, and Race in a Modern American City* (Ithaca, NY: Cornell University Press, 2001); and Becky Nicolaides, *My Blue Heaven: Life and Politics in the Working-Class Suburbs of Los Angeles, 1920–1965* (Chicago: University of Chicago Press, 2002).

4. John Kearney, migration specialist, to Eulalio Torres, February 1960, folder 756, box 2938, OGPRUS. See also Migration Division, annual report, 1959–60, box 1, folder 7, OGPRUS.

5. A surge of literature has documented the Young Lords in New York, thus creating the misperception that the group originated there. The New York Young Lords *Party* lasted somewhat longer than the Chicago group and, because of its location in New York, gained much more public attention and visibility. For firsthand accounts, see Pablo Guzmán, "La Vida Pura: A Lord of the Barrio," and Iris Morales, "Palante, Siempre Palante! The Young Lords," in *The Puerto Rican Movement: Voices from the Diaspora,* ed. Andres Torres and Jose E. Velasquez (Philadelphia: Temple University Press, 1998); and Miguel Melendez, *We Took the Streets: Fighting for Latino Rights with the Young Lords* (New York: St. Martin's Press, 2003). For historical and cultural analyses of the New York group, see Johanna Fernandez, "Between Social Service Reform and Revolutionary Politics: The Young Lords, Late Sixties Radicalism, and Community Organizing in New York City," in *Freedom North: Black Freedom Struggles Outside the South, 1940–1980,* ed. Jeanne F. Theoharis and Komozi Woodard, 255–85 (New

York: Palgrave Macmillan, 2003); Cynthia Young, *Soul Power: Culture, Radicalism, and the Making of the U.S. Third World Left* (Durham, NC: Duke University Press, 2006), 122–35; and Jeffrey O. G. Ogbar, "Brown Power to Brown People: Radical Ethnic Nationalism, the Black Panthers, and Latino Radicalism, 1967–1973," in *In Search of the Black Panther Party: New Perspectives on a Revolutionary Movement*, ed. Jama Lazerow and Yohuru Williams, 252–86 (Durham, NC: Duke University Press, 2006). See also Lorrin Thomas, *Puerto Rican Citizen: History and Political Identity in Twentieth Century New York* (Chicago: University of Chicago Press, 2010), chap. 6, for an excellent analysis of the Young Lords politics that connects it to the leftist activism of Puerto Ricans in 1930s New York.

6. This characterization has begun to change, however, as former Lords in New York, for example, have elaborated on its panethnic and multiracial origins.

7. Floreal Forni, *The Situation of the Puerto Rican Population in Chicago and Its Viewpoints about Racial Relations* (Chicago: Community and Family Study Center, University of Chicago, 1971), 111.

8. Elena Padilla, "Puerto Rican Immigrants in New York and Chicago: A Study in Comparative Assimilation" (MA thesis, University of Chicago, 1947); Manuel Martínez, *Chicago: Historia de Nuestra Comunidad Puertorriqueña* (Chicago: Reyes and Sons, 1989); and "Death Toll In Factory Blaze Rises to 27," *CT*, April 18, 1953, 1.

9. Evelyn Kitagawa and Karl E. Taeuber, *Local Community Fact Book: Chicago's Metropolitan Area, 1960* (Chicago: Chicago Community Inventory, University of Chicago, 1963), 246.

10. Myrna Rodriguez, interview with the author, October 11, 2004.

11. Robert Cross, "Big Noise from Lincoln Park," *CT Magazine*, November 2, 1969, 126.

12. Kitagawa and Taeuber, *Local Community Fact Book*, 28.

13. Chicago Fact Book Consortium, ed., *Local Community Fact Book Based on the 1970 and 1980 Censuses* (Chicago: Chicago Review Press, 1984), 20.

14. *CDN*, March 17, 1962, 25.

15. Chicago Plan Commission, *Report of Activities* (Chicago: Chicago Plan Commission, 1955); Chicago Plan Commission, *Plans and Progress*, monthly report, May 1957; and Department of City Planning, *Plans and Progress*, monthly report, January 1962, 3, and July 1962—all in MRC.

16. Cross, "Big Noise from Lincoln Park."

17. Frank Browning, "From Rumble to Revolution: The Young Lords," *Ramparts*, October 1970, box 5A, YL. *Ramparts* was a leftist magazine published in Berkeley, California.

18. "The Puerto Rican Project in Chicago," 1, folder 4, box 100, CAP. Puerto Rican youth joined gangs and had conflicts with rival groups since their initial period of settlement. See Chicago Commission on Human Relations, *Puerto Rican Americans in Chicago* (Chicago: Mayor's Committee on New Residents, 1960), 54.

19. On street gangs and youth violence in Chicago, see Andrew Diamond, *Mean Streets: Chicago Youths and the Everyday Struggle for Empowerment in the Multiracial City, 1908–1969* (Berkeley: University of California Press, 2009). For an account of the birth of the Vice Lords, a black street gang, see David Dawley, *A Nation of Lords: The Autobiography of the Vice Lords* (1973; repr., Prospect Heights, IL: Waveland Press, 1992).

20. Diamond, *Mean Streets*, chaps. 1, 5. See also Adam Cohen and Elizabeth Taylor, *American Pharaoh: Mayor Richard J. Daley: His Battle for Chicago and the Nation* (Boston: Little, Brown & Co., 2000), 29.

21. Many ethnic gangs in Chicago in earlier decades often shifted into politics, becoming key participants in the local machine. See Diamond, *Mean Streets*.

22. Figures taken from 1960 census data and calculated by averaging the number of boys aged ten to nineteen in census tracts 106, 107, 108, 112, 115, 116, 117, and 118. Original Tables (ORG), Census 1960 Tracts Only Set, US Census Bureau, accessed October 14, 2010, http://www.socialexplorer.com.

23. Hilda Vasquez Ignatin, "Young Lords Protect and Serve," *YLO* 2, no. 2 (March 1969): 6, http://www.lib.depaul.edu/speccoll/guides/lpnc_lords.htm.

24. See Hilda Vasquez Ignatin, "Young Lords Serve and Protect," *Movement*, May 1969, 4, box 5A, YL.

25. See Omar López interview, February 17, 1995, box 3, YL; Ignatin, "Young Lords Serve and Protect"; Young Lords Organization, *Que Viva el Pueblo: A Biographical History of José Cha-Cha Jiménez, General Secretary of the Young Lords Organization* (Chicago: Young Lords Organization, 1973), 15; *Pitirre YLO*, October 1971, box 5A, YL; and Browning, "From Rumble to Revolution."

26. Ignatin, "Young Lords Protect and Serve."

27. See Dawley, *Nation of Lords*; Diamond, *Mean Streets*, 253–81. One Mexican American gang in Chicago had similarly transformed itself into the Brown Berets (see chap. 6). The predominantly Puerto Rican Latin Kings gang tried to make the shift as well but was less successful in leaving behind the criminalized activities of the streets.

28. See David Farber, *Chicago '68* (Chicago: University of Chicago Press, 1988); Flamm, *Law and Order*, 157; and "Four Days of Rage: The Power Play That Failed," *CT*, November 23, 1969, 142.

29. See "Urban Renewal Case," *Pitirre* 2, no. 7 (Summer 1970), box 5A, YL; and Young Lords Organization, *Que Viva el Pueblo*, 16.

30. Black Panther Party and Platform, printed in *YLO*, vol. 1, no. 1, March 19, 1969, box 5A, YL. For a more detailed discussion of the formation of the Illinois chapter of the Black Panther Party, see Jon Rice, "The World of the Illinois Panthers," in *Freedom North: Black Freedom Struggles outside the South, 1940–1980*, ed. Jeanne F. Theoharis and Komozi Woodard, 41–64 (New York: Palgrave Macmillan, 2003). Jiménez's relationship with Hampton and the BPP was certainly crucial to the YLO's politicization, but Jeffrey Ogbar attributes the credit for politicizing Jiménez directly to Hampton, suggesting that he specifically wanted to train and groom Jiménez. See Ogbar, "Brown Power to Brown People," 265.

31. It is unclear what other groups were in attendance, but we can surmise that organizations such as LADO (Latin American Defense Organization), the Spanish Action Committee of Chicago, and the Brown Berets might have been present. Although they had encountered some Mexican Americans in their neighborhood, exposure to "Chicanos" in Pilsen and South Chicago raised their awareness of a larger pan-Latino presence and activist base in the city. Some Mexican American young people—namely, students—in the Eighteenth Street / Pilsen neighborhood had begun embracing the Chicano movement at the very same time and were thus using this term rather than *Mexican American*. See chap. 6.

32. Ignatin, "Young Lords Serve and Protect," 6.

33. Omar López interview, February 10, 1995. Unlike other Latino enclaves, Lincoln Park had a number of progressive religious institutions, DePaul University, and local white activists.

34. Omar López interview, February 10, 1995.

35. R.V., "Class War in Lincoln Park," *LPP*, March 1969, box 4, YL.

36. Ignatin, "Young Lords Serve and Protect."

37. "LPCA: Poor Folk Need Not Apply," *DePaul University News*, February 21, 1969. Some DePaul students also supported the area's working class and poor in their struggle against urban renewal.

38. *YLO* 2, no. 7 (Summer 1970); Carlos Flores, interview with Mervin Mendez, September 11, 1995, box 2, folder 9, YL; Monse Lucas-Figueroa, interview with the author, June 21, 2004; and Eugenia Rodríguez, interview with José "Cha Cha" Jiménez, December 6, 1993, box 2, YL.

39. Lucas-Figueroa interview.

40. "Youths Damage Center," *CT*, January 23, 1969; "YLO Visits Urban Renewal," *YLO* 1, no. 1 (March 1969); and "Letters: Latin Resigns from C.C.C.," *LPP* 2, no. 2 (March 1969). See also Ignatin, "Young Lords Serve and Protect."

41. Carolyn Shojai, "Threats, Shouts at Lincoln Park Council Meeting," *CT*, May 25, 1969, N5. The YLO and Comancheros disrupted another meeting the following month, with violence breaking out between them and some audience members. Carolyn Shojai, "Gangs Disrupt Lincoln Park Unit's Meeting," *CT*, July 30, 1969, B12.

42. See Ridgely Hunt, "The People vs. the Police," *CT*, September 7, 1969.

43. Jiménez was arrested almost weekly. On one occasion, he was charged with inciting felonious mob action months after disrupting and causing property damage at the Lincoln Park Conservation Community Council in late January. "Jury Indicts 8 Members of Youth Gangs," *CT*, June 15, 1969, N9. He was also accused of kidnapping his own daughter. "Cha Cha Jimenez Accused of Kidnapping Own Child," *BP*, See also Angie (Navedo) Adorno, interviews with Mary Martinez, January 27, 1995, and February 8, 1995, box 2, YL.

44. Ignatin, "Young Lords Serve and Protect," 6–7.

45. "500 March for Welfare Justice," *YLO* 1, no. 2 (May 1969): 5; "Jury Indicts 8 Members of Youth Gangs," *CT*, June 14, 1969, N9; Joseph Boyce and William Jones, "Street Gangs Are Becoming a Power Block," *CT*, June 16, 1969, 1; William Jones and Joseph Boyce, "Nearly 200 Street Gangs Roam Every City Area," *CT*, June 22, 1969, 4; "Second-March Blues," *Kaleidoscope*, April 25–May 6, 1969, 3; and "Interview with Cha Cha Jimenez: Chairman—Young Lords Organization," *BP*, June 7, 1969, 17.

46. Hunt, "People vs. the Police"; and "Uptown Confronts Pigs," *YLO* 1, no. 1 (March 1969): 2. Angie Navedo noted, "If you were going to a meeting, if you would meet someplace to go to a meeting, the Red Squad would be right behind you." Navedo interview, February 8, 1995. On Red Squads, see also Edward Escobar, *Race, Police, and the Making of an Identity: Mexican Americans and the Los Angeles Police Department, 1900–1945* (Berkeley: University of California Press, 1999); and Frank Donner, *Protectors of Privilege: Red Squads and Police Repression in Urban America* (Berkeley: University of California Press, 1990).

47. *YLO* 1, no. 1 (March 1969): 1, 4, 11, 12. Indeed, a number of black gangs, such as the Blackstone Rangers, had transitioned into community work and were becoming rather successful at attracting public and private funding sources to their activities. See, for example, "Jury Indicts 8 Members of Youth Gangs"; Boyce and Jones, "Street Gangs Are Becoming a Power Block"; and Jones and Boyce, "Nearly 200 Street Gangs Roam Every City Area."

48. Hunt, "People vs. the Police"; and Gerald Suttles, *The Man-Made City: The Land-Use Confidence Game in Chicago* (Chicago: University of Chicago Press, 1990), 189.

49. Ignatin, "Young Lords Serve and Protect," 6.

50. "Cops and Robbers: Who Is Which?," *YLO* 1, no. 1 (March 1969): 5; Ignatin, "Young Lords Serve and Protect," 7; and "Pigs Murder Black Youth in Jail Cell," *YLO* 1, no. 2 (May 1969): 13.

51. Navedo interview, January 27, 1995, 19, 20; and Young Lords Party, "13 Point Program and Platform," n.d. [ca. 1971], box 1, YL. For one account of the origins of the Black Panther Party in Oakland, California, see Robert O. Self, *American Babylon: Race and the Struggle for Postwar Oakland* (Princeton, NJ: Princeton University Press, 2003), chap. 6. See also Jama Lazerow and Yohuru Williams, eds., *In Search of the Black Panther Party: New Perspectives on a Revolutionary Movement* (Durham, NC: Duke University Press, 2006).

52. Untitled article, *YLO* 1, no. 2 (May 1969): 3; Navedo interview, January 27, 1995; and Janet Jones, "You Can't Stop Us," *Movement*, June 1969. See also "Protest Police Killing," *CT*, May 6, 1969, C5; "Inquest Finds Policeman Lamb Justified in Killing Ramos," *CT*, May 30, 1969, 5; and "Young Lord Murdered by Off Duty Pig," *BP*, May 19, 1969, 14.

53. Jones, "You Can't Stop Us."

54. Ibid.; Eugenia Rodríguez interview; and untitled article, *YLO* 1, no. 2 (May 1969): 3, 8.

55. Browning, "From Rumble to Revolution," 20; and Omar López interview, February 10, 1995.

56. See "Serve the People or Get Out," *Kaleidoscope*, May 31–June 13, 1969, 5. The Young Patriots were a group of Appalachian white youths from the Uptown neighborhood of Chicago. Like the Young Lords and the Black Panthers, they had adopted radical politics and fought for the rights of poor people. Rising Up Angry was similarly a group of white youths from the Logan Square community who had also fought for community empowerment.

57. Robert Cross, "Mike Gray: In a Hurricane, the Eye," *CT*, July 12, 1970, L16. See also Alfredo Matias interview, September 29, 1995; Navedo interview, January 27, 1995, 17; Omar López interview, February 10, 1995; *Brief Notes: The Young Lords*, n.d., courtesy of José "Cha Cha" Jiménez; and Jones, "You Can't Stop Us," 4. Jon Rice credits Fred Hampton with coining the *Rainbow Coalition* term. Young Lords members proudly insist that their coalition was the first to use the term, long before the Reverend Jesse Jackson popularized it more widely in his organization, Operation P.U.S.H. For a discussion of the interracial coalition that Hampton and the Panthers cultivated, see Rice, "World of the Illinois Panthers," 54–59; and Ogbar, "Brown Power to Brown People."

58. See James Tracey, "The (Original) Rainbow Coalition," AREA Chicago, http://www.areachicago.org/p/issues/solidarities/original-rainbow-coalition/; and Mike Gray (filmmaker), http://mike-gray.org/multimedia/american.htm; http://nationalyounglords.com/—both accessed September 13, 2009. Cross, "Mike Gray," 19; and Omar López interview, February 10, 1995.

59. Jones, "You Can't Stop Us"; Ronald Koziol, "S.D.S. Leader, 4 Aides Released on Bond," *CT*, May 13, 1969, 11; "Group Stages Protest over Police Action," *CT*, May 14, 1969, 5; and Ronald Koziol and Joseph Boyce, "Top Red Linked to Protest at Police Station," *CT*, May 15, 1969.

60. "McCormick Take-over," *YLO* 1, no. 2 (May 1969); Omar López interview, February 10, 1995; and Browning, "From Rumble to Revolution," 20. DePaul University also received criticism for supporting urban renewal plans. Some students at the university vocally opposed the plans and supported the Poor People's Coalition.

61. Jones, "You Can't Stop Us," 4; and Ronald Koziol, "Parley Fails; Gang Holds Seminary Unit," *CT*, May 16, 1969.

62. James Bowman, "Rebels Move In, Seminary Closes," *CDN*, May 15, 1969; and "Seminary to Ask Court to End Sit-in," *CT*, May 18, 1969. Interestingly, the coalition that occupied the seminary, in addition to protesting the murder of Manuel Ramos by a white police officer, also noted the harassment and beating of Jesse Maldonado, a young man who had been facilitating gang truces in the Pilsen / Eighteenth Street neighborhood. This further reveals the alliances that activists on the North Side had with Mexican American activists on the city's South Side.

63. Navedo interview, January 27, 1995, 14; Bowman, "Rebels Move In"; "New Threats Made in Seminary Seizure," *Chicago Today*, May 15, 1969; untitled, *LPP*, May 19, 1969; "McCormick Take-over"; "We're Fighting For" interview with Cha Cha Jiménez, *Movement*, July 1969, 12; and Omar López interview, February 10, 1995. See also "Seminary to Ask Court to End Sit-in"; and "Five-Day Sit-in at McCormick Seminary Ends," *CT*, May 19, 1969.

64. Browning, "From Rumble to Revolution," 21. The seminary agreed to pay his fee.

65. Ibid.; Thomas Buck, "7 Hit Lincoln Park Renewal Plan," *CT*, February 10, 1970; Thomas Buck, "Assail Lincoln Park Decision," *CT*, February 12, 1970; and "'Reconsider Our Plan,' Poor Coalition Pleads," *CT*, June 14, 1970, N9. The matter became a public controversy in the local press. The city's Department of Development and Planning commissioner, Lewis Hill, in fact addressed the topic at a speech he gave before the City Club in spring 1970. See Department of Development and Planning, *Plans and Progress*, monthly report, May 1970, 4–6, MRC.

66. They protested to the Methodist leadership and eventually relocated their congregation elsewhere. Omar López interview, February 10, 1995. On vanguard politics and "serve-the-people" programs, see Laura Pulido, *Black, Brown, Yellow, and Left: Radical Activism in Los Angeles* (Berkeley: University of California Press, 2006), chap. 4.

67. See "Gang Members Begin Sit-in at N. Side Church," *CT*, June 12, 1969, B22; "Young Lords Still Holding N. Side Church," *CT*, June 14, 1969; Young Lords Organization, "Proposal for the Development of a Leadership Training Program," n.d.; "Health Care Is a Human Right," box 81, Manuscript Collection, Special Collections, DePaul University Library; Navedo interviews, January 27, 1995, and February 8, 1995, 7—both in box 2, YL; *Brief Notes: Young Lords*; and Lucas-Figueroa interview.

68. "Free Health Care," n.d., Lincoln Park Conservation Association, DePaul University Library, Special Collections, Lincoln Park Community Collection; and "Near North Gets Health Centers," *CT*, March 26, 1970.

   Community health clinics had become popular throughout the country during this time. In the War on Poverty era, when the federal government experimented with more democratic forms of governance among poor communities, such clinics were appearing in many urban areas. In Chicago, however, Mayor Daley held a tight grip on most local institutions and would not tolerate autonomous, independent institutions that were not under his control. Indeed, the Democratic machine steered the federal Community Action Program, Model Cities, and all other federally funded programs meant to provide the urban poor an opportunity for greater participation in civic society. See Cohen and Taylor, *American Pharaoh*, 317–20, 342–46.

69. Omar López interview, February 10, 1995. See issues of the *YLO* newspaper. On Maoist theory and its role in the Third World left, see Pulido, *Black, Brown, Yellow, and Left*, 95, 134–38.

70. Omar López interview, February 17, 1995; and Navedo interview, January 27, 1995.

71. Navedo interview, January 27, 1995, 21; and Omar López, interview February 17, 1995. For a brief summary of the successive displacement of Puerto Ricans in the city and the Chicago 21 Plan, see Young Lords, R.T.A. Flyer [1973?], box 1, YL.

72. See issues of the *YLO* newspaper. See also Navedo interview, February 8, 1995.

73. As other scholars have noted, the slogan was grammatically incorrect, missing the preposition *a* after the word *tengo*, something that Edna Acosta-Belén and Carlos E. Santiago explain "was in itself indicative of the differences between Puerto Ricans on the island and the diaspora in their command of the Spanish language." Acosta-Belén and Santiago, *Puerto Ricans in the United States: A Contemporary Portrait* (Boulder, CO: Lynne Rienner Publishers, 2006), 167n4.

74. Advertisement for "At Random," *CT*, June 14, 1969, N6. Jiménez indeed seemed to struggle with personal issues during these years, including conflicts with the mother of his children and alleged drug addiction.

75. Untitled article, *YLO* 1, no. 5 (January 1970). Chicana writers commented on this dynamic in the Chicano movement.

76. Untitled article, *YLO* 1, no. 5 (January 1970).

77. These gender dynamics differed across YLO chapters, however. As the Young Lords expanded across the country and in Puerto Rico, women took more prominent leadership roles in some of those branches, such as in New York and Philadelphia. See, for example, Carmen Teresa Whalen, "Bridging Homeland and Barrio Politics: The Young Lords in Philadelphia," in *The Puerto Rican Movement: Voices from the Diaspora*, ed. Andres Torres and Jose E. Velasquez, 107–23 (Philadelphia: Temple University Press, 1998); and Morales, "Palante, Siempre Palante!"

78. Navedo interview, February 8, 1995; Lucas-Figueroa interview; and Omar López interview, February 10, 1995. The referral system with Grant Hospital broke down, however. After a while, the hospital began billing patients and initiating collection procedures. Browning, "From Rumble to Revolution," 22. See also "Nonprofit Group Seeks to Simplify Health Care," *CT*, September 17, 1970, N10.

79. The clinic also established an agreement with a local pharmacy that honored all prescriptions written by doctors from the health clinic. Lucas-Figueroa interview.

80. Ibid.; Browning, "From Rumble to Revolution," 22; and letter from Anselma Benitez, *YLO* 2, no. 6 (February–March 1970).

81. Browning, "From Rumble to Revolution," 22; Benitez letter, *YLO* 2, no. 6 (February–March 1970); "City Council to Consider Health Bill," *CT*, December 13, 1970, S9; and "Council's Hearing on Clinics Erupts in Disorder; 3 Ejected," *CT*, June 2, 1971, 5. It is unclear how long the health clinic stayed in operation, but the Board of Health inspections began in the summer of 1970.

82. Browning, "From Rumble to Revolution," 22; Lucas-Figueroa interview; "City Attacks Our Health Center," *YLO* 2, no. 7 (Summer 1970): 4; Sheila Wolfe, "City Is Harassing Clinics, Group Says," *CT*, November 17, 1970; and Frank Zahour, "City Council to Study Free Clinic Ordinance," *CT*, December 6, 1970, NW8. Ultimately, the Board of Health opened its own clinics instead of allowing autonomous community organizations to operate their own. See Robert Cross, "Chicago's Dissident Doctors," *CT*, June 4, 1972, G18.

83. "Give Alcatraz Back to the Indians," *YLO* 1, no. 5 (January 1970); *Brief Notes: Young Lords*; "Chicano Youth Conference," *Young Lords Organization* 1, no. 2 (May 1969); and "We're Fighting for Freedom Together. There's No Other Way," *BP*, August 2, 1969, 9.

Not all Chicano activists/radicals of the era espoused a strict cultural nationalist platform. Many identified as part of the US Third World Left and embraced an internationalist, multiracial, and anticapitalist vision. Just as the Black Panthers had conflict with black nationalist, procapitalist groups, however, Latinas/os similarly encountered sectarian divisions among themselves.

84. Omar López interview, February 10, 1995; Navedo interview, February 8, 1995; and Jiménez, cited in Ogbar, "Brown Power to Brown People," 272.

85. Ogbar, "Brown Power to Brown People," 271. Latino police, such as Officer Jesse Acosta, punished protestors and Lords sympathizers with as much brutality as white officers. "Spring Training," *Kaleidoscope*, March 14–27, 1969, 3.

86. *Brief Notes: Young Lords*, 8. A number of Mexican families, including de Rivero's, lived in the area, hence the participation of some Mexican American youths in the YLO. Carlos Flores, presentation, Lincoln Park Camp, August 7, 2004. The group also included a Cuban and reportedly two Colombians.

87. Ignatin, "Young Lords Serve and Protect."

88. Morales, "Palante, Siempre Palante!," 212; *Brief Notes: Young Lords*; and Guzmán, "Vida Pura," 156–57. Much has been written about the Young Lords Party in New York. See also Michael Abramson, *Palante: The Young Lords Party* (New York: McGraw-Hill, 1971); Melendez, *We Took the Streets*; Fernandez, "Between Social Service Reform"; Ogbar, "Brown Power to Brown People"; and Iris Morales, director, *Palante, Siempre Palante! The Young Lords* (New York: Third World Newsreel, 1996). On the Philadelphia chapter of the Young Lords Party, see Whalen, "Bridging Homeland and Barrio Politics."

89. Young Lords Organization, *Que Viva el Pueblo*, 27; Navedo interview, February 8, 1995; and Browning, "From Rumble to Revolution," 22.

90. Philip Caputo, "5,000 Mourners Walk Past Coffin of Hampton in Suburb," *CT*, December 10, 1969; Rice, "World of the Illinois Panthers"; Paul Kleppner, *Chicago Divided: The Making of a Black Mayor* (DeKalb: Northern Illinois University, 1985), 76; and James Coates, "Documents Bare FBI's Role in Fatal Panther Raid," *CT*, November 22, 1977, 6.

91. John O'Brien, "Couple Found Stabbed in Their Home," *CT*, September 30, 1969; Omar López interview, February 10, 1995; and Alfredo Matias interview, September 29, 1995.

92. Matias interview, October 4, 1995, 3; Navedo interview, February 8, 1995, 10–13; and "Young Lords' Jiménez Surrenders," *CST*, December 4, 1972.

93. Navedo interview, February 8, 1995. East Lakeview / Wrigleyville was also home to a small gay community, called "Boys Town." Middle-class, white gay and lesbian couples in Boys Town contributed to the area's gentrification. They were the pioneers, living among poor whites, African Americans, Native Americans, and Puerto Ricans in the area, buying property and renovating it, establishing fashionable small businesses (restaurants, boutiques), and opening the way for heterosexual urban professionals. Indeed, by the 1980s, Wrigleyville had become a more affordable version of Lincoln Park, offering a short commute to downtown for white-collar workers.

94. Navedo interview, February 8, 1995. Press release, "Jose Cha-Cha Jimenez Files Petitions for 46th Ward Aldermanic Race"; and "The Dawning of a New Day," flyer, June 20, 1974—Jiménez aldermanic campaign press releases, speeches, and announcements, box 1, YL.

95. Guzmán, "Vida Pura," 157; and Whalen, "Bridging Homeland and Barrio Politics."

96. Omar López interview, February 17, 1995; and Browning, "From Rumble to Revolution," 21.

97. "Panther Rally," *YLO* 1, no. 2 (May 1969): 13.

98. Hasan Jeffries refers to the "opening of political space" that makes particular struggles possible. Hasan Kwame Jeffries, *Bloody Lowndes: Civil Rights and Black Power in Alabama's Black Belt* (New York: NYU Press, 2009).

99. Lorrin Thomas demonstrates how the Young Lords Party in New York actually carried into the 1970s the legacy of Puerto Rican leftists of the 1930s. Thomas, *Puerto Rican Citizen*, chap. 6.

100. See Pulido, *Black, Brown, Yellow, and Left*, 89, 60. See also Ogbar, "Brown Power to Brown People." See *BP*, especially 1969 issues, for stories on Los Siete de la Raza, Reies Tijerina, and the YLO. For an analysis of the nuanced YLO politics of the New York branch, as documented in the Newsreel film *El Pueblo Se Levanta*, see Young, *Soul Power*, 122–35.

101. Fernandez, "Between Social Service Reform."

CHAPTER SIX

1. "El Centro de la Causa / Latin American Youth Center, Inc.," press release, n.d., ECC.

2. I refer to the neighborhood interchangeably as Pilsen and Eighteenth Street, as these are the two names most commonly used to identify the community. In the city's decennial *Community Fact Book*, the neighborhood is officially termed the "Lower West Side," Community Area 31. Many Mexican people in the city refer to the neighborhood as "Eighteenth Street," or "*La Dieciocho*," after the main commercial strip that cuts through the area. Similarly, Little Village, or *La Villita*, which I discuss later, is sometimes referred to as "Twenty-Sixth Street," after its main commercial avenue. In many Chicago neighborhoods, a principal street name becomes the metonym for the larger community. See, for example, Karen Mary Davalos, "Ethnic Identity among Mexican and Mexican American Women in Chicago, 1920–1991" (PhD diss., Yale University, 1993), 188.

3. *Middle European* was the term used by local researchers during these years to refer to people from central Europe—Poland, Czechoslovakia, Lithuania, Yugoslavia—who made up the majority of the white population in the neighborhood.

4. As explained in previous chapters, *Spanish-speaking* was the official census term used to describe people of diverse Latin American origins collectively. It was used regardless of actual language fluency (i.e., second-, third-, or fourth-generation Mexican Americans might be identified as "Spanish-speaking" ethnically even if they did not speak Spanish). I use the term to clarify that while Pilsen was known as a *Mexican barrio*, it also had small numbers of other Latinos/as (Puerto Ricans, Central Americans, etc.).

5. This is not to be confused with Hull House, Jane Addams's settlement in the Near West Side neighborhood from which many Mexican Americans were displaced by the University of Illinois Circle Campus construction. Hull House closed down in the early 1960s. See chap. 3.

6. This walkout occurred seven months after the Chicana/o student walkouts in East Los Angeles in 1968.

7. The United Farm Workers maintained an office in Chicago at 1300 South Wabash in the city's South Loop, affiliated with the Catholic archdiocese's Latin American Committee.

8. "ALAS Acts," press release, April 26, 1969, ECC.

9. I intentionally use the term *Mexican* to refer to *both* US-born or -raised Mexican-

origin people *and* Mexican immigrants, as this has been the most common ethnic identifier used among people of Mexican origin in Chicago, regardless of generation. Second- or third-generation people who identified with their heritage generally identified simply as "Mexican" during this time, as they continue to do in the twenty-first century. This is in part a reflection of their interactions with European American residents who continued to identify them as "Mexican" regardless of generation in the United States. The term *Mexican American* was used less frequently among the population and represented a more assimilationist term more frequently invoked when dealing with whites, the city, government agencies, or social institutions. Moreover, the use of the term *Mexican* reflected the mixed nativity and origins of most families, who might have Mexican-born grandparents, Mexican-born but US-raised children, and US-born and -raised grandchildren.

The term *Chicano* gained currency among the politically conscious, but it did not receive as widespread usage as it did in the Southwest. Throughout this chapter, I use the terminology as it appears in archival documents or in oral history interviews in order to be historically accurate. Still, in general, I use the term *Mexican* to denote any person of Mexican descent regardless of nativity but use the term *Mexican American* when I wish to specify only those born or raised in the United States and *Mexican immigrant* to refer to those who arrived as adults. Even into the 1990s, anthropologist Karen Mary Davalos found that Mexican women continued to identify most frequently as *Mexican* over other ethnic terms. Davalos, "Ethnic Identity," 58. For more on ethnic identity in Pilsen, see also Leonard Ramirez, "Women of 18th Street: Narratives of Education and Struggle" (PhD diss., University of Illinois at Chicago, 2004).

10. A significant portion of that area, however, is occupied by industry and manufacturing plants, thereby reducing the amount of livable residential space even further. Chicago Fact Book Consortium, *Local Community Fact Book Chicago Metropolitan Area: Based on the 1970 and 1980 Censuses* (Chicago: Chicago Review Press, 1984), 84–85, 87–88. See also Nicholas De Genova, *Working the Boundaries: Race, Space, and "Illegality" in Mexican Chicago* (Durham, NC: Duke University Press, 2005), 118–19. On Puerto Ricans in Pilsen, see Evelyn Kitagawa and Karl E. Taeuber, *Local Community Fact Book: Chicago's Metropolitan Area, 1960* (Chicago: Chicago Community Inventory, University of Chicago, 1963), 77; and Marixsa Alicea, "Cuando Nosotros Vivíamos . . . Stories of Displacement and Settlement in Puerto Rican Chicago," *Centro Journal* 13, no. 2 (2001): 167–95.

11. Ramirez, "Women of 18th Street," 107.

12. Carlos Muñoz Jr., *Youth, Identity, Power: The Chicano Movement* (London: Verso, 1989), 8. For an excellent discussion of the diversity of the Chicano movement and its limits, see Ramirez, "Women of 18th Street."

13. Jesus Garcia, interview with the author, December 12, 2003; María Mangual, interview with the author, March 16, 2004; Laura Paz, interview with the author, April 30, 2004; Leonard Ramirez, interview with the author, July 2, 2004; and Patricia Wright, interview with the author, April 6, 2004.

14. See, for example, Gwen Stern, "Ethnic Identity and Community Action in El Barrio" (PhD diss., Northwestern University, 1976); Ruth Horowitz, *Honor and the American Dream: Culture and Identity in a Chicano Community* (New Brunswick, NJ: Rutgers University Press, 1983); Stephen L. Schensul, "Anthropological Fieldwork and Sociopolitical Change," *Social Problems* 27, no. 3 (1980): 309–19; and Ramirez, "Women of 18th Street."

South Chicago represented another important center of Chicano protest and activism in the city but is beyond the scope of this chapter.

15. For life histories of Chicanas who participated in the Chicano movement in Pilsen, see Ramirez, "Women of 18th Street." On the Chicano movement in Milwaukee, Wisconsin, and its connections with Crystal City, Texas, see Marc Rodriguez, "Obreros Unidos: Migration, Migrant Farm Worker Activism, and the Chicano Movement in Wisconsin and Texas, 1950–1980" (PhD diss., Northwestern University, 2000).

16. Chicago Fact Book Consortium, Local Community Fact Book Chicago Metropolitan Area, 86. By 1960, however, 23 percent of housing units were owner occupied. Kitagawa and Taeuber, Local Community Fact Book, 76–77. See also Mary Bakszysz and Kay Guzder, "Description of the 18th and 26th Street Communities," n.d.; and "Pilsen," n.d.—both in ECC.

17. See, among others, Bakszysz and Guzder, "Description of the 18th and 26th Street Communities." See also Louis Wirth and Eleanor H. Bernert, eds., Local Community Fact Book of Chicago (Chicago: University of Chicago Press, 1949).

18. A white pastor at the Millard Congregational Church in Little Village, Pastor Anderson, explained to two researchers in 1969 that he was leaving the neighborhood because the congregation could not support him anymore. Only 130 members remained in his church, and 50 percent of them had moved to Cicero or Berwyn but still returned only on Sundays for services. These Bohemian families, Anderson claimed, moved out after their children graduated from eighth grade because they did not want to send their children to Farragut High School, where they would mix with black students. Sister María del Rey and Mary Bakszysz, "Operation of the Millard Congregational Church," September 9, 1969, ECC.

19. Joanne Belenchia, cited in De Genova, Working the Boundaries, 118. See also Stern, "Ethnic Identity," 52.

20. Near West Side Community Council, "Where to Find It . . . 1957–59 Directory of Community Resources," folder 36, box 20, supplement 2, West [Near West] Side Community Collection, HW; and Gerald D. Suttles, The Social Order of the Slum: Ethnicity and Territory in the Inner City (Chicago: University of Chicago Press, 1968), 145.

21. Suttles, Social Order of the Slum, 14, 30–31; and Kitagawa and Taueber, Local Community Fact Book, 248.

22. Dominic A. Pacyga, "To Live amongst Others: Poles and Their Neighbors in Industrial Chicago, 1865–1930," Journal of American Ethnic History 16, no. 1 (1996): 55–73. On the Irish American Catholic Church and other European immigrant groups, see James R. Barrett and David R. Roediger, "The Irish and the 'Americanization' of the 'New Immigrants' in the Streets and in the Churches of the Urban United States, 1900–1930," Journal of American Ethnic History 24, no. 4 (2005): 4–33.

23. Less than one mile west of this area stood the Czechoslovakian parish of St. Procopius, the Polish St. Adalbert's, and St. Pius V, which originally served Irish immigrants.

24. "The Middle European Community of South Lawndale," n.d. [ca. 1970], 7, ECC; and Stern, "Ethnic Identity," 63.

Numerous scholars have documented this dynamic of "investing" in whiteness. See, for example, George Lipsitz, The Possessive Investment in Whiteness: How White People Profit from Identity Politics (Philadelphia: Temple University Press, 1998); David Roediger, Wages of Whiteness: Race and the Making of the American Working Class (New York: Verso, 1991); and Thomas J. Sugrue, The Origins of the Urban Crisis: Race *and Inequality in Postwar Detroit* (Princeton, NJ: Princeton University Press, 1996). Arnold Hirsch traces how European American "ethnics" became white through their opposition to blackness. Arnold Hirsch, *Making the Second Ghetto: Race and Housing in Chicago, 1940–1960* (Cambridge: Cambridge University Press, 1983), chap. 6. Thomas Guglielmo also notes that although Italians were always "white" in their skin color, they consciously claimed their whiteness beginning in the 1940s in relation to African Americans and housing. Thomas Guglielmo, *White on Arrival: Italians, Race, Color, and Power in Chicago, 1890–1945* (Oxford: Oxford University Press, 2003).

25. Poles and Mexicans had a long-standing history of conflict that dated back to the 1920s and 1930s on the Near West Side, in Back of the Yards, and in South Chicago. See Gabriela F. Arredondo, *Mexican Chicago: Race, Ethnicity and Nation, 1916–1939* (Urbana: University of Illinois Press, 2008).

26. Carlos Valencia, personal communication with the author, June 20, 2004. See also Stern, "Ethnic Identity," 53, 84. On the history of Polish-Mexican conflict, see Arredondo, *Mexican Chicago*; Paul S. Taylor, *Mexican Labor in the United States*, vol. 2 (Berkeley: University of California Press, 1932; repr., New York: Arno Press, 1970); and Thomas L. Philpott, *The Slum and the Ghetto: Neighborhood Deterioration and Middle-Class Reform, Chicago, 1880–1930* (New York: Oxford University Press, 1978), chap. 12.

27. Angelica Rivera, "Re-inserting Mexican-American Women's Voices into 1950s Chicago Educational History" (PhD diss., University of Illinois at Urbana-Champaign, 2008), 130; Diamond, *Mean Streets*; and Barrett and Roediger, "Irish and 'Americanization' of 'New Immigrants.'"

28. Stern, Horowitz, and other social scientists who studied the neighborhood drew on "ethnic" explanations for the tension and hostility between whites and Latinos/as. Still, some researchers in Pilsen / Little Village documented dynamics that were unmistakably "racial." Of course, during this period, the idea that Mexican Americans were a *racial* minority was still debatable. The Chicano movement, in fact, played a critical role in asserting that Chicanos constituted a *racial* rather than an ethnic group and were a colonized nation within the United States.

29. Cathy Alaniz, interview with Emile Schepers, September 15, 1970, ECC. I have replaced this person's last name with just the initial so as to conceal her identity.

30. Alicia Amador, interview with the author, March 26, 2004.

31. Rivera, "Re-inserting Mexican-American Women," 124, 125.

32. Chicago Fact Book Consortium, *Local Community Fact Book Chicago Metropolitan Area*, 364, 453; Stern, "Ethnic Identity," 21, 24; and Horowitz, *Honor and the American Dream*, 43.

33. Jesus Garcia, interview with the author, June 22, 2004.

34. I borrow this term from education scholar Lisa Delpit, who writes about white teachers and their relationship to students of color. Lisa Delpit, *Other People's Children: Cultural Conflict in the Classroom* (New York: New Press, 1995).

35. "Middle-European Community of South Lawndale," 6. In "Description of the 18th and 26th Street Communities," Bakszysz and Guzder described the "continuous movement of populations into, within, and out of the area."

36. Chicago Fact Book Consortium, *Local Community Fact Book Chicago Metropolitan Area*, 82. See also Hirsch, *Making the Second Ghetto*, chap. 1; and Amanda Seligman, *Block by Block: Neighborhoods and Public Policy on Chicago's West Side* (Chicago: University of Chicago Press, 2005), 19–22, 34.

37. Adam Cohen and Elizabeth Taylor, *American Pharaoh: Mayor Richard J. Daley: His Battle for Chicago and the Nation* (Boston: Little, Brown, 2000), 222. The Chicago Tribune Company published a salacious account of North Lawndale's grinding poverty and degradation in the mid-1980s. Chicago Tribune, *The American Millstone: An Examination of the Nation's Permanent Underclass* (Chicago: Contemporary Books, 1986).

38. Cohen and Taylor, *American Pharaoh*, 360–62. On King and the civil rights campaign in Chicago, see Alan B. Anderson and George W. Pickering, *Confronting the Color Line: The Broken Promise of the Civil Rights Movement in Chicago* (Athens: University of Georgia Press, 1986).

39. On working-class white communities on Chicago's West Side, see Seligman, *Block by Block*. On working-class white suburbs in Southern California, see Becky Nicolaides, *My Blue Heaven: Life and Politics in the Working-Class Suburbs of Los Angeles, 1920–1965* (Chicago: University of Chicago Press, 2002).

40. The researchers conducted their work in 1969, but HOPE had been established years earlier. Del Rey and Bakszysz, "Operation of the Millard Congregational Church."

41. "Middle European Community of South Lawndale," 1. See also Seligman, *Block by Block*. Like other inner-city poor black neighborhoods throughout the country, during the 1960s, North Lawndale lost many buildings and businesses as a result of riots, fires, absentee property ownership, and white flight and disinvestment.

42. Mr. and Mrs. [B.], interview with Elisabeth Houston, July 21, 1969, ECC. I have replaced the last name with just the initial so as not to reveal these people's identities.

   Property values in Pilsen were already low in the 1960s prior to the in-migration of Latinas/os. By the early 1970s, however, when the neighborhood had become predominantly Latina/o, banks and mortgage lenders redlined the area. Land was severely undervalued, and it was extremely difficult to get mortgages or home improvement loans. Redlining thus contributed to the continued decline and deterioration of the community. Patricia Wright, presentation at Juan Velásquez Symposium, November 19, 2003, El Centro de la Causa, Chicago.

43. Seligman, *Block by Block*; Robert O. Self, *American Babylon: Race and the Struggle for Postwar Oakland* (Princeton, NJ: Princeton University Press, 2003); Sugrue, *Origins of the Urban Crisis*; and Heather Thompson, *Whose Detroit? Politics, Labor, and Race in a Modern American City* (Ithaca, NY: Cornell University Press, 2001).

44. Robert Mier, Robert Giloth, and David Less, *Industrial Employment Opportunities and the Hispanic Community: The Case of Pilsen* (Chicago: UIC Center for Urban Economic Development, School of Urban Planning and Policy, 1979), 6, 32. See also Maria de Lourdes Villar, "From Sojourners to Settlers: The Experience of Mexican Undocumented Migrants in Chicago" (PhD diss., University of Indiana, 1989).

   Spanish-speaking workers were sometimes favored in many workplaces over African Americans, whom some employers refused to hire. But when Mexican immigrants and other Spanish-speaking workers were hired, they generally received much lower wages than white workers had in the past. Thus, much as in housing, Latinos/as were a compromise for white employers: they tolerated them but paid them far less.

45. Bakszysz and Guzder, "Description of the 18th and 26th Street Communities," 13; and Stern, "Ethnic Identity," 29.

46. See Gregory D. Squires, Larry Bennett, Kathleen McCourt, and Philip Nyden, *Chicago: Race, Class, and the Response to Urban Decline* (Philadelphia: Temple University

Press, 1987), 111. Bradburn et al. make an important distinction in a diachronous and synchronous definition of racial integration. They note that a neighborhood may appear to be in an integrated "state" at a given moment, but researchers must also examine whether there is a "process" of continuous integration wherein both whites and the racial minority group are moving into the neighborhood. Norman M. Bradburn, Seymour Sudman, and Galen L. Gockel, *Side by Side: Integrated Neighborhoods in America* (Chicago: Quadrangle Books, 1971), 4–7.

47. Amador interview. See also Mrs. and Mrs. [B.], interview with Houston; del Rey and Bakszysz, "Operation of Millard Congregational Church"; and Alaniz, interview with Schepers—all in ECC.

48. Claudio Gómez, interview with Elisabeth Houston, July 23, 1969, ECC. On Mexicans and whiteness, see Neil Foley, "Becoming Hispanic: Mexican Americans and the Faustian Pact with Whiteness," in *Reflexiones 1997: New Directions in Mexican American Studies*, ed. Neil Foley, 53–70 (Austin: Center for Mexican American Studies, 1997); Ariela Gross, "'The Caucasian Cloak': Mexican Americans and the Politics of Whiteness in the Twentieth Century Southwest," *Georgetown Law Journal* 95, no. 2 (2007): 337–92; and Thomas A. Guglielmo, "Fighting for Caucasian Rights: Mexicans, Mexican Americans, and the Transnational Struggle for Civil Rights in World War II Texas," *Journal of American History* 92, no. 4 (2006): 1212–37.

49. Scholars have documented the fluidity of racial categories and Mexicans' place in Chicago's racial hierarchy earlier in the century. See, for example, Taylor, *Mexican Labor*. Gabriela Arredondo argues that although Mexicans did not fit into the black-white paradigm of race relations in the city in the 1920s and 1930s, they nonetheless became racialized as nonwhite and foreign. Arredondo, *Mexican Chicago*. On Mexicans and their racial identity in the 1960s, see Ian F. Haney López, *Racism on Trial: The Chicano Fight for Justice* (Cambridge, MA: Belknap Press / Harvard University Press, 2003); and Guadalupe San Miguel Jr., *Brown, Not White: School Integration and the Chicano Movement in Houston* (College Station: Texas A&M University Press, 2001).

50. Puerto Ricans occupied a much more liminal racial position, which might explain why some Mexicans avoided them as well. Puerto Ricans sometimes had a higher status than African Americans too. Still, over thirty-six hundred of them lived in North Lawndale, suggesting either a conscious choice to live among African Americans or the reality of housing discrimination that kept them out of other neighborhoods. Kitagawa and Taueber, *Local Community Fact Book*, 272.

51. Stern, "Ethnic Identity," 31; and Stephen L. Schensul, "Action Research: The Applied Anthropologist in a Community Mental Health Program," in *Anthropology Beyond the University*, ed. Alden Redfield, 106–19 (Atlanta: University of Georgia Press, 1973).

52. Chicago Fact Book Consortium, *Local Community Fact Book Chicago Metropolitan Area*, 364; Stern, "Ethnic Identity," 21, 29; and Horowitz, *Honor and the American Dream*, 33, 239n3. The issue of an accurate census count of Latinas/os in the Chicago metro area would become a cause that some Latina/o leaders in the city took up in the mid-1970s. Arguing that members of the Latina/o community would not receive the resources they needed if they were not accounted for more accurately, they championed the cause of a fair census count for Latinas/os in 1980.

53. Chicago Fact Book Consortium, *Local Community Fact Book Chicago Metropolitan Area*, 364, 453; Stern, "Ethnic Identity," 21, 24; and Horowitz, *Honor and the American Dream*, 43.

54. Chicago Association of Commerce and Industry, *Community Area Data Book for the City of Chicago: 1975 Census Data by 75 Community Areas* (Chicago: Chicago Association of Commerce and Industry, 1976), vi.

55. Chicago Fact Book Consortium, *Local Community Fact Book Chicago Metropolitan Area*, 86; and Leonard Ramirez, interview with the author, July 2, 2004. Even two decades later (in the 1990s), gaping sidewalk holes continued to be a neighborhood problem. See Davalos, "Ethnic Identity," 198.

56. Horowitz, *Honor and the American Dream*, 45.

57. Ramirez, "Women of 18th Street," 106–7.

58. Horowitz, 45, chap. 7; and Stern, "Ethnic Identity," 27–28. Not until the groundbreaking *Lau v. Nichols* case, decided by the US Supreme Court in 1973, did public schools have a legal mandate to provide equitable instruction for students who needed English language instruction. As a result, prior to this, many children languished in classrooms with limited comprehension or interaction with teachers. On the public schools' racial segregation and the use of "Willis wagons," see John L. Rury, "Race, Space, and the Politics of Chicago's Public Schools: Benjamin Willis and the Tragedy of Urban Education," *History of Education Quarterly* 39, no. 2 (1999): 117–42.

59. See Horowitz, *Honor and the American Dream*, 31, 44, chap. 7; and Stern, "Ethnic Identity," 27–28.

60. Horowitz, *Honor and the American Dream*, 219.

61. Ibid., 48.

62. South Chicago was an important center of Chicano activism as well (the neighborhood had its own Brown Berets chapter, for example). But perhaps due to geography and demographics, Eighteenth Street became better known and the hub of activity among Chicana/o activists.

63. For the work of Jane Addams's famous Hull House with Mexican immigrants, see Cheryl R. Ganz and Margaret Strobel, eds., *Pots of Promise: Mexicans and Pottery at Hull-House, 1920–40* (Urbana: University of Illinois Press, 2004).

64. Mary Bakszysz, "ALAS Meeting," July 24, 1969, ALAS folder, ECC.

65. Valencia, personal communication with the author; Joel González, personal communication with the author, December 26, 2004; and Phil Ayala, interview with the author, March 25, 2004.

66. González, personal communication with the author; and José "Cha Cha" Jiménez, personal communication with the author. Also, Hector and María Gamboa, interview with the author, December 18, 2004; Ayala interview, March 25, 2004; Laura Paz interview; and group interview with the author, July 24, 2004. Documents reveal that some of the neighborhood's street gang members may have maintained a working relationship with Corky González. An ALAS report noted that some young men traveled to Denver again in 1970.

67. This was similar to the Young Lords Organization and African American gangs whose members tried to transform themselves from criminalized street gangs to radicals and revolutionaries.

68. "ALAS Information," April 25, 1970, ECC; and Ramón A. Gutiérrez, "Community, Patriarchy, and Individualism: The Politics of Chicano History and the Dream of Equality," *American Quarterly* 45, no. 1 (1993): 45–46.

69. For more on the Brown Berets in Los Angeles, see Ernesto Chávez, "'Birth of a New Symbol': The Brown Berets' Gendered Chicano National Imaginary," in *Generations*

of Youth: Youth Cultures and History in Twentieth-Century America, ed. Joe Austin and Michael Willard, 205–22 (New York: New York University Press, 1998). See also Haney López, *Racism on Trial,* chaps. 7 and 8.

Mexican American men also formed a chapter of the Brown Berets in South Chicago. Group interview with the author, July 24, 2004. See also "Howell House Workshop—May 1970," 3, ECC. The use of Benito Juarez (the first indigenous president of Mexico) as a Chicano national hero would also extend to visual imagery in murals and artwork, and to the naming of the local high school.

70. See "Block Clubs," "Howell House," and "Casa Aztlán" folders, ECC.

71. Cultural nationalism and the Chicano movement appealed largely to younger generations. Older activists in the community did not necessarily embrace such ideologies or the leftist politics of radical groups, for that matter. Rather, they operated on a more traditional model of community empowerment, one put forth to a great extent in Chicago by Saul Alinsky and the Industrial Areas Foundation. Many of Pilsen's mothers who fought for better education in the community worked with the local Alinsky group, the Pilsen Neighbors Community Council.

72. Mayor Daley controlled much of the city through patronage, but his power was also waning. The Democratic National Convention of 1972, which marked a moment when national politics shifted dramatically toward including more women and racial minorities, also marked Daley's slow political descent. He would remain in office only four more years before he passed away, but many observers saw his power and stature fading. Cohen and Taylor, *American Pharaoh.*

73. Researchers such as anthropologist Sol Tax practiced "action anthropology" with Native Americans in Chicago as well. See James La Grand, *Indian Metropolis: Native Americans in Chicago, 1945–1975* (Urbana: University of Illinois Press, 2002), 169.

Two graduate students who lived in the neighborhood and studied the community were Gwen Stern and Ruth Horowitz. Stern describes much more intimate involvement in local organizations and community efforts. Her name also appeared on a number of federal grant applications, for example, and she helped establish the Dar a Luz (Childbirth) Mother-Infant Program at El Centro de la Causa. She also had closer personal relationships with Mexican American activists such as María Mangual, among others.

74. Other researchers and students, including self-identified Chicano/a students from the University of Illinois Circle Campus and the University of Chicago's School of Social Service Administration, contributed to the community centers as well. Students and researchers participated in block club organizing, the Pilsen Little Village Community Mental Health Center, Latino Youth Alternative High School, El Hogar del Niño (The Child's Home) day-care center, and to a lesser extent, Mujeres Latinas en Acción. The research they conducted provided both an essential tool for the development of social service programs in the community and many of the archival documents for this chapter. On the work of Steve Schensul, see Schensul, "Action Research" and "Anthropological Fieldwork and Sociopolitical Change."

75. On expressway construction in inner cities, see Raymond A. Mohl, "Planned Destruction: The Interstates and Central City Housing," in *From Tenements to the Taylor Homes: In Search of an Urban Housing Policy in Twentieth-Century America,* ed. John Bauman, Roger Biles, and Kristin Szylvian, 226–45 (University Park: Pennsylvania State University Press, 2000).

76. Reverend John M. Harrington, "A Ministry of Social Justice: A Parochial Model in a Mexican American Community" (DMin diss., St. Mary of the Lake Seminary, 1981),

10. Also, John Harrington, personal communication with the author, December 10, 2004.

77. Ayala interview, March 25, 2004; and Harrington, personal communication with the author.

78. María Ovalle, interview with the author, June 6, 2004.

79. Archdiocese of Chicago, *A History of the Institutions of the Archdiocese of Chicago,* vol. 2 (Chicago: Archdiocese of Chicago, 1981), 857; and Ramirez, "Women of 18th Street," 13.

80. The debate over naming the center reflected the disagreements within the community over the utility and appropriateness of nationalist Chicano ideology and rhetoric. As in the Southwest, some older-generation Mexicans / Mexican Americans took much more reformist, or moderate, approaches to social change and community empowerment. Ayala interview, March 25, 2004. El Centro eventually became a Catholic Charities agency.

81. Albert Vázquez, "The Effects of a Change in the Cultural Orientation of a Community Mental Health Clinic," n.d.; "Press Conference, January 20, 1969"; and Mary Bakszysz, "ALAS Meeting," July 24, 1969—all in ECC. Horowitz, *Honor and the American Dream,* 49–50.

The Daley administration in Chicago was notorious for controlling federal funds that were meant to empower community residents. Daley reportedly kept a tight grip on federal dollars, which his loyalists parceled out as patronage in exchange for votes at election time.

82. Chicano Mental Health Training Program funding application to the Department of Health, Education, and Welfare, September 30, 1972; "Chicano Mental Health Training Program," n.d.; syllabi, Chicano Mental Health Training Program; "The Chicano Mental Health Training Program—Abstract," August 1973, 1—all in ECC.

83. The college, formerly known as Crane Junior College, adopted the name *Malcolm X* when the city tore down the old building and built a new facility. Residents and activists in the all-black neighborhood where the school was located successfully petitioned to name the newly constructed campus. Phil Ayala explained, however, that in the nationalist climate of the times, getting the college's administrators to incorporate Mexicans into Malcolm X proved difficult. Administrators seemed to view Mexicans as just another white ethnic group. Ayala recalled, "He [the dean] considered us whites, so he didn't want to deal with us. . . . [I told him] if you don't reconsider this, I'm gonna have four hundred Mexicans here picketing that the blacks are doing reverse discrimination [*sic*]." Ayala interview, March 25, 2004.

84. Phil Ayala to Dr. Bertrand Brown, director of Department of Health, Education, and Welfare, National Institutes of Mental Health, May 12, 1976, ECC; and Ayala interview, March 25, 2004.

85. Minutes, El Centro board meeting, March 15, 1973, ECC. The center also offered GED and English classes with Right to Read federal funding. "Right to Read" program sheet, May 28, 1974; and "Abstract-Objective: Project Venceremos," n.d.—both in ECC.

86. Ovalle interview.

87. El Centro Board of Directors, meeting minutes, March 22, 1973, ECC. See also Servicios Sociales case files, ECC.

88. Humberto Martinez, "BASTA: A Chicano Addict Rehabilitation Program," n.d., ECC. Documents reveal that white residents had more negative opinions overall toward El Centro. A survey done in September 1973 in a two-block radius of the center

revealed that some whites had not heard of the center and many of those who had held very negative views of its activities. This seems to have been a result of both racial attitudes toward Mexicans and fears about drug users and street gangs that frequented the center. "Research Results of Community Survey," n.d., ECC.

89. "El Centro de la Causa Library," n.d., ECC.

90. See "Research and Evaluation at El Centro de la Causa," n.d., ECC.

91. El Centro Board of Directors, meeting minutes, April 5, 1973; El Centro de la Causa press release, n.d.—both in ECC.

92. Mary Waters, *Ethnic Options: Choosing Identities in America* (Berkeley: University of California Press, 1990).

93. On intraethnic Mexican–Mexican American relations, see David Gutiérrez, *Walls and Mirrors: Mexican Americans, Mexican Immigrants, and the Politics of Ethnicity* (Berkeley: University of California Press, 1995).

94. Yet remarkably, most, especially those living in Pilsen and Little Village, continued even decades later to use the term *Mexican* to describe their ethnoracial identity. Karen Mary Davalos's ethnographic research in Pilsen in the 1990s attests to this ongoing use of the ethnoracial signifier of *Mexican* among women of Mexican descent. Davalos, "Ethnic Identity," 58.

95. Paz, interview with the author (emphasis in the original), Patricia Wright interview, Leonard Ramirez, interview with the author, June 25, 2004, and July 2, 2004; and Hector and María Gamboa, interview with the author, December 18, 2004.

CHAPTER SEVEN

1. Untitled document on Mujeres Latinas en Acción, April 24, 1974, ECC.

2. Leonard Ramirez's recently published book provides a good corrective to this lacuna. See *Chicanas of 18th Street* (Urbana: University of Illinois Press, 2011).

   The focus in this chapter is primarily Mexican American women, since they were the largest Latina ethnic group in the neighborhood. Puerto Rican women participated in significantly fewer numbers, and their community involvement occurred primarily on the city's North Side neighborhoods (West Town, Humboldt Park, Lincoln Park). See chap. 5.

3. Chicanas' marginalization within the Chicano movement has been well documented. See, for example, Marisela R. Chavez, "'We Lived and Breathed and Worked the Movement': The Contradictions and Rewards of Chicana/Mexicana Activism in El Centro de Acción Social Autónomo–Hermandad General de Trabajadores, Los Angeles, 1975–1978," in *Las Obreras*, ed. Vicki L. Ruiz, 83–105 (Los Angeles: UCLA Chicano Studies Research Center, 2000); Alma M. García, ed., *Chicana Feminist Thought: The Basic Historical Writings* (New York: Routledge, 1997); Ramón A. Gutiérrez, "Community, Patriarchy, and Individualism: The Politics of Chicano History and the Dream of Equality," *American Quarterly* 45, no. 1 (1993): 44–72; and Mary Ann Villareal, "The Synapses of Struggle: Martha Cotera and Tejana Activism," in *Las Obreras*, ed. Vicki L. Ruiz, 273–95 (Los Angeles: UCLA Chicano Studies Research Center, 2000). For a study of Puerto Rican women's political development as feminists in the mainland United States, see Teresa I. Nazario-Crespo, "Social Support Networks of Migrant Puerto Rican Women" (EdD diss., Boston University, 1986).

4. "Howell House Workshop—May 1970," no author, ECC. Indeed, as Yolanda Tarango has noted, the church has been one of the only spaces in which Latina women have been able to "legitimately, if indirectly, engage in developing themselves." Cited in

Vicki L. Ruiz, "Claiming Public Space at Work, Church, and Neighborhood," in *Las Obreras*, ed. Vicki L. Ruiz, 13–39 (Los Angeles: UCLA Chicano Studies Research Center, 2000), 24.

5. See, for example, Gloria Anzaldúa, *Borderlands / La Frontera: The New Mestiza* (San Francisco: Spinsters / Aunt Lute, 1987); García, *Chicana Feminist Thought*; and Cherríe Moraga and Gloria Anzaldúa, eds., *This Bridge Called My Back: Writings by Radical Women of Color* (New York: Kitchen Table Press, 1983).

6. For an example of Mexican American women activists in East Los Angeles, see Mary S. Pardo, *Mexican American Women Activists: Identity and Resistance in Two Los Angeles Communities* (Philadelphia: Temple University Press, 1998).

7. MLEA was similar to the Chicana Service Action Center in Los Angeles.

8. Traditionalists in the community certainly charged that the Mexican American women involved with Mujeres were adopting Anglo sensibilities and social norms. This was a critique throughout the Southwest as well, aimed at Chicana feminists in a variety of contexts. Chicano nationalists often referred to Chicana feminists as "*vendidas,*" or sellouts. More than a genuine concern over preserving cultural authenticity, however, such criticisms represented an attempt to reassert patriarchal power and to discipline women for challenging patriarchy and traditional gender norms.

9. Karen Mary Davalos, "Ethnic Identity among Mexican and Mexican American Women in Chicago, 1920–1991" (PhD diss., Yale University, 1993), 103. Gabriela Arredondo uses the term *striations within* to discuss the diversity of Chicago's Mexican immigrant community in the 1920s and 1930s. Gabriela Arredondo, *Mexican Chicago: Race, Ethnicity and Nation, 1916–1939* (Urbana: University of Illinois Press, 2008).

10. Ruth Horowitz, *Honor and the American Dream: Culture and Identity in a Chicano Community* (New Brunswick, NJ: Rutgers University Press, 1983), 34. Horowitz conducted an in-depth ethnographic study of Pilsen (she called it "32nd Street") in the early 1970s. See also Gwen Stern, "Ethnic Identity and Community Action in El Barrio" (PhD diss., Northwestern University, 1976); and Stephen L. Schensul, "Anthropological Fieldwork and Sociopolitical Change," *Social Problems* 27, no. 3 (1980): 309–19.

11. Alfredo S. Lanier, "Doing It Their Way: Why Pilsen Is So . . . Stubborn," *Chicago Enterprise*, October 1988, 16–20.

12. Inez Loredo, oral history interview, cited in Janette Cisneros, María Galarza, and Flor Cortés, "Las Amas de Casa Abren las Puertas" (Housewives Open Doors), in *Telling Historias: Oral Histories from Chicago Based on the Curiosity of Youth and the Memories of Elders*, 2002, author's personal collection. Author's translation.

Horowitz probably overstates the cultural rigidity and traditionalism of the community. She cites the cultural norms, mores, and expectations of traditional Mexican society, especially in rural areas and small villages, but she does not emphasize enough that these were in flux in Chicago. *Honor and the American Dream*, chap. 4, 52–76. Second-generation Mexican American couples especially had to negotiate their own expectations of each other as they developed their romantic partnerships.

13. See Mirta Vidal, in García, *Chicana Feminist Thought*, 22. See also Benita Roth's documentation of white women on the New Left, *Separate Roads to Feminism: Black, Chicana, and White Feminist Movements in America's Second Wave* (Cambridge: Cambridge University Press, 2004), chap. 2.

14. Lucy Gutiérrez, oral history interview, cited in Elia Cuenca, Bertha Soto, and Janet

Tapia, "La Lucha de las Mujeres a Nuestra Salud" (Women's Struggle for Our Health), *Telling Historias*. Author's translation.

15. Virginia Espino, "'Woman Sterilized as Gives Birth': Forced Sterilization and Chicana Resistance in the 1970s," in *Las Obreras*, 2000, 71.

16. El Centro to Mrs. Helen Corona, Catholic Charities, April 7, 1975, ECC.

17. See "New Approaches to Development in Bilingual, Bicultural Communities," report from conference held August 29–30, 1973, ECC.

18. Mary Baszysz, research assistant, Community Research Unit of the Community Mental Health Program, to Philip Ayala, Ramíro Borja, Humberto Martínez, José Ovalle, and Juan Velásquez, September 25, 1972, ECC.

    Chicana feminists noted this dynamic in the Chicano movement in the Southwest as well. See Gutiérrez, "Community, Patriarchy, and Individualism." See also Angie Chabram-Dernersesian, "I Throw Punches for My Race, but I Don't Want to Be a Man: Writing Us—Chica-Nos (Girl, Us) / Chicanas—into the Movement Script," in *Cultural Studies*, ed. Lawrence Grossberg, Cary Nelson, and Paula Treichler (New York: Routledge, 1992).

19. Ramirez, *Chicanas of 18th Street*, 23.

20. El Centro Board of Directors, meeting minutes, April 12, 1973, and May 3, 1974, ECC.

    As Ramón Gutiérrez has noted about the Chicano movement, "Although [it] persistently had advocated the self-actualization of all Chicanos, Chicanos still actually meant only males." Gutiérrez, "Community, Patriarchy, and Individualism," 47.

21. María Mangual, interview with the author, December 8, 2003.

22. Ibid.; and Gutiérrez, "Community, Patriarchy, and Individualism." The quintessential Chicana critique of elitist white feminism is the now-classic text Moraga and Anzaldúa, *This Bridge Called My Back*.

23. Mangual interview, March 16, 2004. Chicanas in the Southwest had similar reactions to some white feminist activism. See, for example, Ana Nieto-Gomez's description of white feminism in Roth, *Separate Roads*, 44.

24. Cited in Ruiz, "Claiming Public Space," 14. This was Mangual's interpretation of white feminism. Certainly, some white feminist activism included community-focused projects such as community clinics, reproductive health, and community day care. Chicana feminists certainly identified themselves much more than white feminists as specifically working-class. See, for example, the mission statement of Mujeres Activas en Letras y Cambio Social (MALCS; Women Active in Letters and Social Change), whose 1983 declaration reads, "We are the daughters of Chicano working class families involved in higher education. We were raised in labor camps and barrios, where sharing our resources was the basis of survival. Our values, our strength derive from where we came. Our history is the story of the working class people—their struggles, commitments, strengths, and the Chicano/Mexicano experience in the United States." Mujeres Activas en Letras y Cambio Social, accessed December 14, 2011, http://www.malcs.org/.

25. The program was truly remarkable in the amount of federal funding it attracted from the National Institutes for Mental Health. See Horowitz, *Honor and the American Dream*, 242n23.

26. Mangual interviews, December 8, 2003, and March 16, 2004. Some feminist scholars have noted the role that emotion, empathy, and compassion have played in so-

cial movements and organizing. See, for example, Belinda Robnett, *How Long? How Long? African-American Women in the Struggle for Civil Rights* (New York: Oxford University Press, 1997), esp. chap. 3.

Gretchen Lemke-Santangelo notes that for working-class African American women, their networks and community work have historically occurred informally. She writes, "Unlike those of middle-class 'club' women, [black working-class women's] activities frequently occurred outside of formal organizations or political institutions." Gretchen Lemke-Santangelo, *Abiding Courage: African American Migrant Women and the East Bay Community* (Chapel Hill: University of North Carolina Press, 1996), 153.

27. Mangual interview, December 8, 2003. See Gutiérrez, "Community, Patriarchy, and Individualism." Throughout the Southwest as well, as Chicanas increasingly spoke out against the patriarchal oppression, sexism, and misogyny they experienced within the Chicano movement, they brought into relief the stratified, exclusionary, and oppressive elements of the Chicano "community" or "family." See Chabram-Dernersesian, "I Throw Punches," for a discussion of how Chicanas were discursively excluded from the Chicano movement's script. See also readings in García, *Chicana Feminist Thought.*

I disagree with Benita Roth that women of color necessarily organized based on inequalities among women. While this was true to a certain extent, the more salient point of reference for Mujeres was the men in their community. Roth, *Separate Roads*, 25, 31.

28. Untitled document on Mujeres Latinas en Acción, April 24, 1974, ECC; and Gwen Stern, interview with the author, April 2, 2004.

29. Mangual interview, March 16, 2004. This struggle for visibility can be understood within the context of similar Chicana activism in the Southwest, activism that largely sought to claim public space for women, to make their needs and concerns public and put them on the community agenda. For examples of work on Mexican American women activists, see Espino, "'Woman Sterilized as Gives Birth'"; and Pardo, *Mexican American Women Activists*. Vicki Ruiz also describes how Mexican women involved in labor movements and community activism "claimed public space" in Ruiz, *From out of the Shadows: Mexican Women in Twentieth-Century America* (New York: Oxford University Press, 1998), chaps. 4–6.

30. As Benita Roth notes, feminist activism, especially that of women of color, often originated in the racial or ethnic community activism of such women. Thus, Chicano movement social networks often provided the basis for women's networks. We must recognize that gender-based movements among white leftists, Chicanas, and African American women were born on the Left or in race-based movements. Roth, *Separate Roads*, 4–5.

31. The first-ever national Chicana conference had occurred only one year earlier, in 1971 in Houston, entitled "La Conferencia de Mujeres por la Raza." See Ruiz, *From out of the Shadows*, 108; and Marta Cotera and Francisca Flores, in García, *Chicana Feminist Thought*, 155–61. Chicana women's feminist organizing followed closely on the heels of the white women's movement. The first white radical women's liberation conference took place only three years earlier, in November 1968. The radical women's movement separated itself institutionally from the New Left in 1971. Roth, *Separate Roads*, 70–71.

32. Ricardo Parra, "Midwest Chicano Organizations: Past, Present, and Possibilities,"

1974, folder 10, box 13, CMCL. See also *Midwest Council of La Raza Progress and Activities Report*, November 1, 1972, to November 30, 1972, 4, folder 21, box 1, CMCL.

In some ways, Chicana women's efforts to organize themselves separately were a radical move; it was about demanding the right to organize as women and advocate for women's concerns. White women encountered similar opposition for doing this as well. Roth, *Separate Roads*, 51.

33. Roth explains that "women's energy was a much-fought-over resource" in social movements and community activism. Roth, *Separate Roads*, 22.

34. The program listed Olivárez as coming from Albuquerque, although it seems she was actually from Tucson.

This historical moment represented a particularly gendered, woman-centered example of the formation of *Latinidad* in the early years of contemporary Latina/o coalitional politics. For a study of contemporary coalition building among pan-Latina women, see Milagros Ricourt and Ruby Danta, *Hispanas de Queens: Latino Panethnicity in a New York City Neighborhood* (New York: Cornell University Press, 2002).

35. Mangual interview, March 16, 2004. María Ovalle, interview with the author, June 6, 2004. María Mangual, guest speaker, "Juan Velázquez Symposium," November 19, 2003, El Centro de la Causa, Chicago.

36. Conference program, "*La Mujer Despierta*," June 9, 1973, author's personal collection. I am indebted to María Ovalle for sharing a copy of the original program with me.

37. Untitled document on Mujeres Latinas en Acción, April 24, 1974, ECC; and Mangual interview, December 8, 2003.

38. This included women from Little Village, Back of the Yards, and South Chicago, one of the city's earliest neighborhoods where Mexican and Puerto Rican steelworkers and their families settled.

39. The notion of "*La Nueva Chicana*" among Raza women embodied a community-centered consciousness. See García, *Chicana Feminist Thought*, pt. 1.

40. The North Side center never materialized, owing perhaps to different community and gender politics among the predominantly Puerto Rican population there. Various Puerto Rican women did occupy prominent roles in community organizing, educational activism, and nationalist groups, but none of them specifically organized a women's group. Some did establish a chapter of a national Puerto Rican women's group, the National Puerto Rican Women's Forum, in the 1970s.

41. Mangual interviews, December 8, 2003, and March 16, 2004.

42. As Mangual stated, "Some of [the women in CMHTP] had their GED; some of them had to get their GED real quick to come into the [program]." Mangual interview, March 16, 2004. For a discussion of Martha Cotera's feminist work in this regard with women in Texas, see Villareal, "Synapses of Struggle."

43. "Work Statement—Mujeres Latinas en Acción," n.d., in "Reports, Organization Development Folder, 1977," box 16, LI.

44. Untitled document on Mujeres Latinas en Acción, April 24, 1974, ECC; Mangual interview, December 8, 2003; and Stern interview.

45. Puerto Rican women were involved in the initial conference; however, since there were fewer of them, they did not participate subsequently in great numbers. Puerto Rican women on the North Side were actually charged with organizing their own group, according to Mangual, but their efforts never materialized, for reasons that are unclear.

46. Panethnic identification had emerged as early as the 1920s and 1930s in Chicago, in local newspapers read by both working-class Mexican immigrants and middle-class professionals from various Latin American countries. By the 1950s and 1960s, the terms *Latino, Latin American,* and *Spanish-speaking* (or simply *Spanish*) had gained currency among grassroots groups such as LADO (the Latin American Defense Organization), the Spanish Civic Committee, and the Young Lords Organization, which specifically called for the liberation of all Latinos. The feminine term *Latina* appeared in the early 1950s in a locally published magazine called *Vida Latina,* which targeted a pan-Latino audience, but it had not yet been used to denote women as a panethnic group. For an ethnographic study of community-based Latina panethnicity in New York City in the 1980s and 1990s, see Ricourt and Danta, *Hispanas de Queens.*

47. "Mujeres Latinas en Acción Historical Synopsis," n.d. and "Proposal for Funding for Mujeres Latinas en Acción," January 1974—both in MLEA.

48. Minutes, El Centro board of directors meeting, May 7, 1974, ECC; Mangual interview, December 8, 2003; Stern interview; Phil Ayala, interview with the author, March 25, 2004; and Alicia Amador, interview with the author, March 26, 2004. See also "20 Years Later, MLEA Founders Look Back," in *Mujeres Latinas en Acción Annual Report, 1992–93,* author's collection.

49. Amador interview; Mangual interview, December 8, 2003; and Stern interview. Gwen Stern, a doctoral student at the time doing research in Pilsen, postulated that perhaps the local gang members thought that the women "were just getting out of hand." Stern interview; and "20 Years Later." Other Chicanas in the Southwest encountered violence, vandalism, and threats as well, such as Irene Blea, a Chicana student activist at the University of Colorado, Boulder. Roth, *Separate Roads,* 158.

50. Amador interview. See also Judy Langford Carter and Carol Botwin, "Where the Action Is," *Redbook Magazine,* May 1978, 34, Alicia Amador private collection. This resembled some of the negative reactions and sexual taunting that Chicanas in the Southwest received as well. See Leticia Hernández interview, cited in Roth, *Separate Roads,* 140. White women as well encountered such hostility from men on the Left. White men initially responded with hostility to white feminists, did not take them seriously, and continued to expect them to provide sexual and domestic service. Roth, *Separate Roads,* 62–67, 137.

51. Mangual interview, December 8, 2003. Alicia Amador, whose sister María (Maruca) Martinez was one of the early staff members, explained that even she was reluctant to get involved when her sister approached her. Amador did not think the organization would last very long. Amador interview.

52. The controversial statement issued from the Chicano Youth Liberation Conference in Denver, Colorado, in March of 1969 epitomized this. The women's caucus at the conference reportedly declared that "Chicanas did not want to be liberated" in the way that white women were advocating their own liberation. Alma García provocatively asks, "Who [then] was to be freed and liberated? Only men?" García, *Chicana Feminist Thought,* 17.

53. Maylei Blackwell, "Geographies of Difference: Mapping Multiple Feminist Insurgencies and Transnational Public Cultures in the Americas" (PhD diss., University of California, Santa Cruz, 2000). Because of the insistence of Latina, black, Asian, and Native American feminists, white feminist scholars today have become increasingly conscious about acknowledging the centrality of women of color's feminism and activism within the larger second-wave movement rather than simply consigning

that history to a separate chapter or a footnote. See, for example, Jennifer Nelson, *Women of Color and the Reproductive Rights Movement* (New York: New York University Press, 2003); and Roth, *Separate Roads*.

54. Guida West and Rhoda Lois Blumberg, eds., *Women and Social Protest* (New York: Oxford University Press, 1990), cited in Roth, *Separate Roads*, 9.

55. Roth, *Separate Roads*, 4. Roth explicitly challenges the whitewashing of the second-wave feminist movement.

56. Moraga and Anzaldúa, *This Bridge Called My Back*, 23.

57. Roth, *Separate Roads*, 8.

58. Compare this to Chicana feminist activism in the Southwest, where there was much more vocal resistance to Anglo feminism and more pointed criticisms of Chicanas' being *"vendidas"* (sellouts) for gravitating to women's issues. See Roth, *Separate Roads*, chap. 3.

59. Ruiz, *From out of the Shadows*, 100.

60. Mangual interview, March 16, 2004.

61. "Mujeres Latinas en Acción Historical Synopsis," n.d., MLEA private collection.

62. "20 Years Later."

63. Dr. Aida Giachello, interview with the author, January 12, 2004, Chicago. The organization received technical assistance in 1973 from the newly formed Latino Institute. In an accounting analysis that the institute conducted for the organization, its records showed no payments to the local gas company, although there were checks to the local phone company and the electric company. See "Mujeres Latinas en Acción, 1975–76" folder, box 86, LI.

64. The MLEA continued to occupy these buildings as its main service offices until 2006. *Mujeres Latinas en Acción, Annual Report*, 2008 fiscal year, accessed March 2, 2009, http://www.mujereslatinasenaccion.org/#.

65. Mangual interview, December 8, 2003.

66. Untitled, undated news clipping, Alicia Amador private collection. See also boxes 20 and 21, LI.

67. Horowitz describes in detail the tensions and conflicts over young women's virginity as a matter of family honor in the community. Families policed girls' and women's sexuality carefully, though they ignored men's promiscuity.

68. Mangual interview, December 8, 2003; Emmett George, "It's Action for Women of Pilsen," *CT*, February 26, 1976; Mujeres Latinas en Acción, "What Is Latin Women in Action?" September 1977, Alicia Amador private collection; and Nancy Naples, *Community Activism and Feminist Politics: Organizing across Race, Class, and Gender* (New York: Routledge, 1998), 3.

69. Nelson, *Women of Color*, 2. While abortion was a critical issue in the pre–*Roe v. Wade* years, white feminists began to see that reproductive control encompassed other concerns as well, especially as articulated by working-class women of color. White feminists became especially sensitive to people of color's interpretations of reproductive control as eugenicist "population control," especially given the widespread forced sterilization of poor women of color.

70. Mangual interview, December 8, 2003; and Stern interview. One article in a local Spanish-language newspaper declared, *"Las Mujeres Latinas Apoyan el Aborto"* (Mujeres Latinas Support Abortion). "Las Mujeres Latinas Apoyan el Aborto," *El Mañana*, date unknown, Amador private collection. When the organization began placing women on local boards of community and nonprofit agencies, for example, it strategically placed Gwen Stern, a white woman in the organization, on the board

of Planned Parenthood rather than placing a Mexican American woman from the community.

71. For a compelling psychological study of Latinas and domestic violence (i.e., physical abuse, sexual abuse, incest), see Yvette Flores-Ortíz, "Re/Membering the Body: Latina Testimonies of Social and Family Violence," in Arturo J. Aldama, ed., *Violence and the Body: Race, Gender, and the State*, 347–59 (Bloomington: Indiana University Press, 2003).

72. Stern interview; and Mangual interview, December 8, 2003. "Latinas Contra el Abuso Tendra Conferencia Sobre Atropellos en el Hogar," news clipping, source unknown, May 5, 1977, folder 20, box 11, CMCL. A 1977 newspaper article was perhaps one of the first public calls for attention to the issue of domestic abuse. "Battered Women Called Nation's 'Silent Crisis,'" *CT*, June 27, 1977, 5, folder 21, box 11, CMCL. The Chicana Service Action Center in Los Angeles developed a battered women's shelter and provided related services by 1978 as well. Anna Nieto-Gomez, "Chicana Service Action Center," in García, *Chicana Feminist Thought*, 148–49.

   Mujeres eventually broadened the term *domestic violence* to include violence against children as well, whether perpetrated by men, women, or other family members. In 2008, combating domestic violence in its myriad forms continued to be one of the agency's central programs.

73. Even in 1981, MLEA noted, "There is still only one shelter facility in Chicago, specifically for battered women. It is located on the north side and typically turns away five individuals each day who need shelter." Moreover, the group noted that from June to December 1980, fifteen of its clients were turned away from other shelters for lack of English-language skills. Proposal to Chicago Community Trust, [1981], MLEA.

74. Mangual interview, December 8, 2003.

75. Mangual interview, March 16, 2004. Sunita Peacock identifies similar dynamics with South Asian immigrant women. See Sunita Peacock, "Sita's War and the Body Politic: Violence and Abuse in the Lives of South Asian Women," in Aldama, *Violence and the Body*, 360–74.

76. Roth, *Separate Roads*, 138, 139. Feminist analyses of the family varied between white women who viewed it as oppressive (even the middle-class family) and black feminists who often saw family as a refuge from a racist society. Motherhood also held different meanings for these women. Roth, *Separate Roads*, 102. See Peacock's discussion of Swayam, a women's organization in Calcutta, India, that similarly seeks to "help the abused woman change the *established norms and values* within Indian and other South Asian societies that *deem violence acceptable*." Peacock, "Sita's War," 371.

77. The experience of racial minority women contrasted sharply with that of white women. Black and Chicana women, for example, were much more likely to continue their activism within their racialized communities and to see themselves ideologically as part of that struggle. White women, on the other hand, were more likely to completely sever their institutional ties to leftist organizations. Roth, *Separate Roads*, 74.

78. Mangual interview, December 8, 2003; and Stern interview. Historian Susan Hartmann argues that women and men in nonfeminist, mainstream organizations successfully promoted women's issues and advocated for feminist policies, calling them "the other feminists." Susan M. Hartmann, *The Other Feminists: Activists in the Liberal Establishment* (New Haven, CT: Yale University Press, 1998).

79.   Giachello interview.

80.   Amador interview.

CONCLUSION

1.   Gerald Ropka, *The Evolving Residential Pattern of the Mexican, Puerto Rican, and Cuban Population in the City of Chicago* (New York: Arno Press, 1980), 191.

2.   The Latino/a population began expanding to outer neighborhoods and to some surrounding suburbs, but just as I have described in the previous pages, their movement did not go uncontested by existing residents.

3.   Wilfredo Cruz, *City of Dreams: Latino Immigration to Chicago* (Lanham, MD: University Press of America, 2007), 58.

4.   Ibid., 57–58. In 1991, Chicago elected the first Latino/a congressional representative from the Midwest, Luis V. Gutierrez. Congressman Gutierrez had participated in many of the community struggles of the seventies and became a vocal advocate for immigration reform, naturalization of immigrants, and the expulsion of the US Navy from the Puerto Rican island of Vieques.

5.   Clara Rodriguez, *Changing Race: Latinos, the Census, and the History of Ethnicity in the United States* (New York: NYU Press, 2000), 7; and Chicago Fact Book Consortium, ed., *Local Community Fact Book Based on the 1970 and 1980 Censuses* (Chicago: Chicago Review Press, 1984). The degree to which the choice of "other" reflected people who considered themselves as "mixed," or of more than one race, is not clear. Less than 1 percent of all other Americans in 1980 chose this category.

6.   Leonard Ramirez, "Women of 18th Street: Narratives of Education and Struggle" (PhD diss., University of Illinois at Chicago, 2004), 57.

7.   Mexican immigrants had gone through this process in the 1920s and 1930s and, as Gabriela Arredondo notes, emerged as nonwhite in the eyes of their European immigrant neighbors. After an immigration hiatus during the thirties and early forties when the second generation did their best to assimilate and become Americans, however, a new wave of contract laborers and undocumented immigrants reopened the question of Mexicans' racial status. See Gabriela Arredondo, *Mexican Chicago: Race, Ethnicity and Nation, 1916–1939* (Urbana: University of Illinois Press, 2008); and Louise Año Nuevo Kerr, "The Chicano Experience in Chicago: 1920–1970" (PhD diss., University of Illinois, 1976).

8.   See, for example, Nicholas De Genova, *Working the Boundaries: Race, Space, and "Illegality" in Mexican Chicago* (Durham, NC: Duke University Press, 2005).

9.   For structural analyses of Puerto Rican migration and poverty, see, for example, Jorge Duany, *The Puerto Rican Nation on the Move: Identities on the Island and in the United States* (Durham: University of North Carolina Press, 2002); History Task Force, Centro de Estudios Puertorriqueños, *Labor Migration under Capitalism: The Puerto Rican Experience* (New York: Research Foundation of the City University of New York, 1979); Kelvin Santiago-Valles and Gladys Jiménez-Muñoz, "Social Polarization and Colonized Labor: Puerto Ricans in the United States, 1945–2000," in *The Columbia History of Latinos in the United States since 1960*, ed. David G. Gutiérrez (New York: Columbia University Press, 2004); and Carmen Teresa Whalen, *From Puerto Rico to Philadelphia: Puerto Rican Workers and Postwar Economies* (Philadelphia: Temple University Press, 2001).

The letter f *following a page number denotes a figure. The letter* t *following a page number denotes a table.*

Chicagoland: City and Suburbs in the Railroad Age
by Ann Durkin Keating

The Elusive Ideal: Equal Educational Opportunity and the Federal Role in Boston's Public Schools, 1950–1985
by Adam R. Nelson

Block by Block: Neighborhoods and Public Policy on Chicago's West Side
by Amanda I. Seligman

Downtown America: A History of the Place and the People Who Made It
by Alison Isenberg

Places of Their Own: African American Suburbanization in the Twentieth Century
by Andrew Wiese

Building the South Side: Urban Space and Civic Culture in Chicago, 1890–1919
by Robin F. Bachin

In the Shadow of Slavery: African Americans in New York City, 1626–1863
by Leslie M. Harris

My Blue Heaven: Life and Politics in the Working-Class Suburbs of Los Angeles, 1920–1965
by Becky M. Nicolaides

Brownsville, Brooklyn: Blacks, Jews, and the Changing Face of the Ghetto
by Wendell Pritchett

The Creative Destruction of Manhattan, 1900–1940
by Max Page

Streets, Railroads, and the Great Strike of 1877
by David O. Stowell

Faces along the Bar: Lore and Order in the Workingman's Saloon, 1870–1920
by Madelon Powers

Making the Second Ghetto: Race and Housing in Chicago, 1940–1960
by Arnold R. Hirsch

Smoldering City: Chicagoans and the Great Fire, 1871–1874
by Karen Sawislak

Modern Housing for America: Policy Struggles in the New Deal Era
by Gail Radford

Parish Boundaries: The Catholic Encounter with Race in the Twentieth-Century Urban North
by John T. McGreevy